MW00903843

RVers BEST PUBLIC CAMPGROUNDS

State and County Campgrounds, Corps of Engineers, National Forest, National Park, National Monument, Bureau of Land Management Parks, all within 30 minutes of an Interstate Highway, for fees typically $19 or less

By Lee Zaborowski

RVers BEST PUBLIC CAMPGROUNDS, copyright © 2010 by Lee Zaborowski. All rights reserved. No part of this publication may be reproduced, stored in a retrieval system or transmitted in any form or by any means, electronic, mechanical, recording or otherwise without the prior written permission of the author.

While every effort has been made to insure the accuracy of this publication, the author and publisher shall have neither liability nor responsibility to any person or entitiy with respect to any loss or damage caused, or alleged to be caused, directly or indirectly by the information contained in this publication.

ISBN is 1453612130
EAN-13 is 9781453612132

3

Contents

Contents 3

Quick Start Guide, About the
Author and Book 4

Alabama (AL) 6

Arizona (AZ) 14

Arkansas (AR) 22

California (CA) 30

Colorado (CO) 38

Connecticut (CT)
and Rhode Island (RI) 45

Delaware (DE),
Maryland (MD), and
District Columbia (DC) 48

Florida (FL) 53

Georgia (GA) 66

Idaho (ID) 74

Illinois (IL) 78

Indiana (IN) 87

Iowa (IA) 94

Kansas (KS) 102

Kentucky (KY) 108

Louisiana (LA) 114

Maine (ME) 119

Maryland (MD) 48

Massachusetts (MA) 123

Michigan (MI) 128

Minnesota (MN) 137

Mississippi (MS) 144

Missouri (MO) 151

Montana (MT) 158

Nebraska (NE) 164

Nevada (NV) 169

New Hampshire (NH) 173

New Jersey (NJ) 177

New Mexico (NM) 180

New York (NY) 186

North Carolina (NC) 195

North Dakota (ND) 202

Ohio (OH) 206

Oklahoma OK) 215

Oregon (OR) 221

Pennsylvania (PA) 227

Rhode Island (RI) 45

South Carolina (SC) 235

South Dakota (SD) 242

Tennessee (TN) 247

Texas (TX) 253

Utah (UT) 266

Vermont (VT) 271

Virginia (VA) 275

Washington (WA) 281

West Virginia (WV) 287

Wisconsin (WI) 291

Wyoming (WY) 297

State Chapter Introductions. Each state presents a unique blend of public park and campground providers, services, fees, and reservation options. You should become familiar with a state's introduction content before looking at individual campgrounds.

Camp Map Numbers. The numbering of campgrounds in a state is lowest to highest Interstate number, and lowest to highest Exit number on each Interstate.

Finding a Park/Campground. Use whatever combination you prefer - Interstate and Exit number; nearby town and Directions; or GPS coordinates. Any mix of these should lead you quickly to the Park/Campground location.

Abbreviations. There are some abbreviations, most should be familiar:

BLM - Bureau of Land Management
Bus - Interstate Business Route
Blvd - Boulevard
COE - Corps of Engineers
Cty -   County
FM -   Farm to Market (road designation)
FS -   Forest Service
Fwy - Freeway
Hwy - Highway
NF -   National Forest
NM -   National Monument
NP -   National Park
NPS - National Park Service
Rd -   Road
St -   Street
TVA - Tennessee Valley Authority

Fees. The one true statement about fees is that they constantly change. Fees in this book were compiled during the Winter – Spring months of 2009-10. The fee range given with each camp is from basic to best set-up for that camp. If there is a notable discount, that is also given. State park systems are noted for add-on additional fees beyond the site fee. Possible additional fees include some combination of - vehicles being towed or towing, park entrance fees, and assorted use surcharges.

Phone Numbers. Numbers given are, with few exceptions, for the destination park or camp, not a remote location.

Websites. Listed websites are typically for the destination park or camp. Neverthe-less, some States have chosen to send people directly to a reservation system for basic information and site reservations.

Directions. Distance segments should be correct within a few tenths of a mile. At turns, compass information is usually given (east, etc.) unless curvy roads confuse orientation. It is always wise to confirm directions against onboard maps, GPS, etc. A good habit is to call the park about recent changes or possible road construction issues.

America the Beautiful Senior Pass. This is a lifetime Pass available to U.S. Citizens and permanent residents who are 62 years and older, which provides access to recreation areas managed by five Federal agencies. It also provides the pass owner a discount on some Expanded Amenity Fees such as camping. The cost of the Senior Pass is $10, and it is valid for the lifetime of the pass owner. Golden Age Passports continue to be valid for a lifetime and are equivalent to the new Senior Pass. Federal regulations and discount fees were under review at the time this book was published. For current information go to -

http://store.usgs.gov/pass/senior.html

Types of Camp Sites. Sites are categorized and named differently, as defined by the state. Most common labels are basic or primitive (dry), electric, electric/water (standard), full hook up (water/electric/sewer), premium (waterfront).

Camp Accommodations. The number of sites given is usually the number of RV sites. It is not uncommon to see a lower than official number as group and tent sites are not counted. The length number (i.e. 40 feet) is the maximum length RV the campground normally will accommodate. The majority of states will not allow you to bring firewood into a park. The best advice is not to carry firewood. Many camps will sell you wood, which is a good pest control option, and sales help park budgets.

Security. A majority of the campgrounds listed have one or more forms of the following types of on-site security - ranger, host, patrol, gate. That information is not consistently known, so if this is a concern for you, call the camp to inquire.

Online Registration. The majority of states and the Federal Government use Reserve America (RA) as their registration system service provider. The states using RA generally charge an online registration service fee, as well as assorted fees to cancel or change a reservation. Some states have created their own online and/or telephone statewide reservation system, some states do it on a park-by-park basis. Generally, calling the Park directly in advance of your arrival to gauge demand and the actual necessity of getting a reservation is a good idea. For some selected parks, a year ahead is not too soon.

Pets. As a rule, and almost without exception, public campgrounds will allow pets (3 or more dogs can be a problem) out in the camp if on a leash. Leash length varies by state between 4-10 feet. The exceptions most often found are no pets on beaches, in buildings, or certain parks (this is rare).

Points of Interest. Every park and campground stop is a unique experience. The space in Chapters for each campground region could never do any community or area justice. Two or three highlights are noted to get you thinking about possible visitor destinations.

Corrections and Cautions. The Author is not responsible for any mishaps you may experience. Readers should plan ahead and proceed cautiously, especially with respect to routing information. If you should find an error, enhancement or update please let us know. We're also open to suggestions to improve this book. Send your information or comments to -

drleerv@gmail.com

Thanks

About the Author. Lee Zaborowski is a retired educator, both as a teacher and administrator in Adult and Continuing Education programs. Lee has authored before, this is his fourth book. He has three children and four grandchildren.

Lee fell in love with the outdoors, as a youth during the 40s and 50s, during the then annual summer trip to a resort in northern Wisconsin. Since those days he's lugged canvas tents around Idaho to fly fish, and progressed to long bicycle touring/camping trips all over the United States, carrying clothes, camping gear, tools, etc. in panniers on the bike.

Today, Lee and his wife, Jeanne, and the two family cats tour the States in their RV. Both Lee and Jeanne enjoy photography. All the photographs in the book were take by one or the other of them.

About the Book. As they RVed the country, Lee & Jeanne became enamored with the wonderful network of public campgrounds across the country - there are over 9,000 in all! They enjoyed the sylvan environment of public camps, the relative quiet, lower fees, and sense of duty and responsibility shown by the vast majority of state, federal & county hosts and rangers.

The individual campgrounds will accommodate most RVs and were selected for amenities, convenience and proximity to an Interstate road. Occasionally you will encounter a challenging route or road getting to one of the campgrounds. We tried to keep those situations to a minimum.

Given the many thousands of turn and mileage directions, there is probably the inevitable error or two in the book. Lee especially apologies in advance if you experience one. Email the address on this page if you have something to report.

"May the road rise up to meet you.
May the wind be always at your back.
May the warm rays of sun fall upon your home.
And may the hand of a friend always be near."

Irish prayer/blessing

ALABAMA

Alabama has roughly the same number of state campground parks as you will find federal campgrounds. There are relatively few local government campgrounds.

Based on location and access for RVs, a majority of the campgrounds selected are state parks. The RV traveler should find variety and much to enjoy in each of these parks. The parks listed here vary in site size from 13 to 496 with 105 being the average number of sites for the locations selected. You can learn more about the State Parks at -

http://www.alapark.com/

The Alabama State Parks offer diverse options in addition to the usual campground amenities including restaurants, expansive fishing facilities with equipped harbors, as well as lodges. Many park campgrounds offer senior discounts, allow pets, have onsite picnic tables and grills and ample parking for visitors. **Advance reservations are recommended**.

There is no statewide, centralized campground information and registration system for the Alabama State Parks. Each park has a detailed website. Campsites fees were typically in the $20-$30 range. The websites and telephone numbers for each park are listed in the book.

[1] **Meaher State Park**
N30 40.224 W87 55.857

[2] **Blakeley State Park**
N30 42.824 W87 54.099

[3] **Gulf State Park**
N30 16.068 W87 39.021

[4] **Florala State Park**
N30 59.888 W86 19.066

[5] **Jennings Ferry Camp**
N32 48.617 W87 48.406

[6] **Lake Lurleen State Park**
N33 17.752 W87 40.612

[7] **Cheaha State Park**
N33 28.629 W85 48.492

[8] **DeSoto State Park**
N34 30.059 W85 37.088

[9] **Chickasabogue Park**
N30 46.710 W88 06.469

[10] **Gunter Hill Campground**
N32 21.602 W86 28.908

[11] **Oak Mountain State Park**
N33 21.164 W86 43.083

[12] **Rickwood Caverns State Park**
N33 52.580 W86 51.900

[13] **Monte Sano State Park**
N34 44.633 W86 30.731

[14] **Joe Wheeler State Park**
N34 47.581 W87 22.796

[15] **Chewacla State Park**
N32 33.240 W85 28.829

NOTES:

Alabama

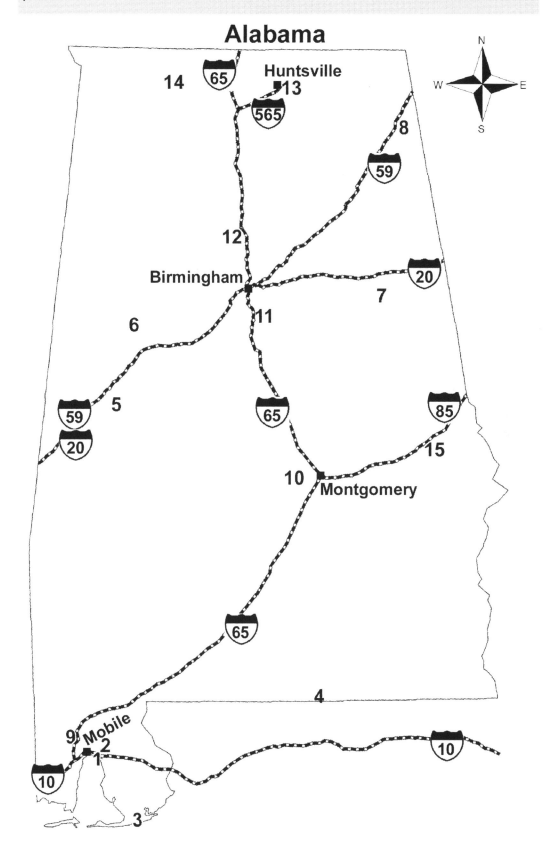

Exit 35
Meaher State Park [1]
Near Mobile
State Rate: $30
(251) 626-5529
http://www.alapark.com/Meaher/

Directions
2 miles from I-10. From Exit 35 take Battleship Pkwy. (Hwy 90/98) north and west to the park entrance.

Camp Accommodations
Roads & parking aprons are paved, 56 shaded sites, full utilities, some waterfront. Amenities include nature trails, boating and the boardwalk. The park has a large pier and excellent freshwater and saltwater fishing access plus a modern bathhouse with laundry facilities.

Points of Interest -
Experience the rich history of Mobile at the Museum of Mobile, the Conde-Charlott Museum House, the Bellington Gardens or the Carnival Museum. Be sure to visit the Southern Market. Coastal activities include Delta Excursions and lots of fresh seafood.

Exit 35
Blakeley State Park [2]
Near Mobile
State Rate: $30
(251) 626-5581
www.BlakeleyPark.com

Directions
7 miles from I-10. From Exit 35 go north on US Highway 98 to US Highway 31 and take a right. Turn left on Highway 225 and go 4 1/2 miles. Park is on left.

Camp Accommodations
The Apalachee Campground is a newer camp with secluded wilderness sites. The 26 sites are tight for RVs over 40 feet. Roads and parking aprons are gravel but all have full utilities. All sites are pull through with shade trees.
NO restrooms or bath facilities.

Points of Interest -
Blakeley State Park hosts year around events including Bluegrass Festival events, boat tours of the Mobile-Tensaw Delta (one of Alabama's Ten Natural Wonders), and significant area Civil War locations. Be sure to visit Blakeley, one of the oldest towns in the State of Alabama.

Exit 44
Gulf State Park [3]
Near the Gulf of Mexico
State Rate: $25 base less the
Senior Discount of 15%
(251) 948-6353; (800) 252-7275
http://www.alapark.com/GulfState/

Directions
30 miles from I-10. From Exit 44 go due south on US 59 to the City of Gulf Shores. At Hwy 180 turn left (east) to State Park Road.

Camp Accommodations
Gulf State Park is a 496 site improved campground with modern bathhouses. RV sites are paved with larger lots and pullouts. The park has full utilities, handicap accessible showers, is pet friendly, includes free wireless Internet access and is approximately 1.5 mi. from Gulf beaches.

Points of Interest -
Located on the coast of Alabama in the City of Gulf Shores, you will find two mi. of white sand beaches. You can enjoy nature programs and events, hiking trails, and geocaching. Visit the Ft. Morgan National Historic Landmark. There is tennis, golf and a large lake for fishing and swimming.

Exit 56 or 85 of I-10 (both in Florida)
Florala State Park [4]
In Florala on the AL state line
State Rate: $22-$25

(334) 858-6425

http://www.alapark.com/Florala/

Camp Accommodations
Roads are paved and parking aprons are gravel. There are 28 campsites with full utilities and shade trees. Sites are a bit narrow, but with a great view. This 40-acre park also offers swimming, paddleboat rentals, and fishing.

Directions
27 miles from I-10. From the west take Florida Exit 56, go north on US 85, turn right on US 54 to the Park. From the east take Florida Exit 85 on Hwy 331 north, turn left at US 54 to the Park.

Points of Interest -
The Park stretches along the shores of Lake Jackson. Within walking, the City of Florala has many antique shops, Victorian mansions, & art galleries. The oldest Masonic Celebration is also there. The Worlds Domino Tournament and the Rattle Snake Rodeo are big attractions.

Exit 40 of I-20/59
Jennings Ferry Camp [5]
Southwest of Tuscaloosa
COE Rate: $18
America/Beautiful Rate: $9

(205) 372-1217

http://www.recreation.gov/

Camp Accommodations
52 paved, electric/water sites, 10 pull through, up to 167 feet. Some sites are waterfront with decks & built-in seating. Services include ADA restrooms, showers, flush toilets, dump station, fire rings, fishing, grills, hiking, lantern post, laundry, picnic tables, potable water, pet friendly.

Directions
10 miles from I-20/59. From Exit 40 take Hwy 14 towards and through Eutaw. Look for signs to turn right off Hwy 14 at Jennings Ferry Rd.

Points of Interest -
The camp is on the Black Warrior River. Who can forget that Tuscaloosa is the Home of Forrest Gump. Be sure to visit the University of Alabama campus, for football fans the Paul W. Bryant Museum is not to be missed. Historic homes are located on the Black Warrior River.

Exit 68 of I-20/59
Lake Lurleen State Park [6]
North of Tuscaloosa
State Rate: $21 less
Senior Discount of 15%

(205) 339-1558

http://www.alapark.com/lakelurleen/

Camp Accommodations

91 shaded sites, some pull throughs, water/electricity, dump station, 35 with sewer. Some sites are narrow. Named for Alabama's only female Governor, Lurleen Wallace, the park is along the banks of the lake. Facilities include a camp store, hiking, biking, beach, fishing, & is pet friendly.

Directions

12 miles from I-20/59. From Exit 68 take Black Warrior Pkwy north for 7 miles. Turn left on McFarland (Hwy 6/82) then immediate right on Mt. Olive (Cty 23), 5 miles to Park.

Points of Interest -

Who can forget that Tuscaloosa is the Home of Forrest Gump. Be sure to visit the University of Alabama campus, and if you're a football fan the Paul W. Bryant Museum is not to be missed. Many historic homes are located on the Black Warrior River.

Exit 191 of I-20
Cheaha State Park [7]
East of Birmingham
State Rate: $21 less
Senior Discount of 15%

(256) 488-5111

www.alapark.com/CheahaResort/

Camp Accommodations

Cheaha State Park, set in Talladega National Forest, is considered the pinnacle of Alabama's natural beauty. Two campgrounds provide 73 full hook-up, shaded sites (many pull through) with accessible full service bath houses. Amenities include restaurant, country store, and pet friendly.

Directions

12 miles from I-20. From Exit 191 take Hwy 1/431 south for 4 miles to the Skyway Mountainway (Hwy 281). Turn right and go 8 miles to the campground.

Points of Interest -

In Birmingham, for vehicle & aviation buffs, the Barber Vintage Motorsports Museum (the largest collection of motorcycles in the world) and the Southern Museum of Flight hold unique collections of artifacts. Other possibilities include the Ruffiner Mountain Nature Center and the Botanical Gardens.

Exit 231 of I-59
DeSoto State Park [8]
Near GA State Line
State Rate: $23 less
Senior Discount of 15%

(256) 845-5075

www.alapark.com/DeSotoResort/

Camp Accommodations

In the rustic tradition of the Civilian Conservation Corps, there are 96 sites on paved roads, graveled sites, full hook-ups, up to 60 feet deep with good space for slide-outs. Amenities include picnic tables, cable TV, grills, and comfort stations with coin-operated laundry.

Directions

14 miles from I-59. From Exit 231 follow Hwy 117 for 7 miles to County Roads 630 and then 106 (Wester Rd) for 7 miles to the Park

Points of Interest -

Visit Fort Payne, home of the country music group "Alabama." Fort Payne is within 30 miles of substantial water recreational areas notably Guntersville Lake and Lake Weiss and Mentone, a popular mountain resort. Fort Payne Depot Museum is a good place to discover local history.

Exit 13 of I-65
Chickasabogue Park [9]
Near Chickasaw
Mobile County
County Rate: $18

(251) 574-2267

www.mobilecountyal.gov/

Camp Accommodations

Can accommodate any size motor home - 38 RV gravel sites, 14 are pull-thru with many shaded sites and full utilities. Restrooms and showers, security, public phone, laundry, firewood, handicap access, daily paper available, self-service RV wash.

Directions

4 miles from I-65. From Exit 13, on west side of exit take Hwy 213 (N. Shelton Beach Rd.), go south 2.2 mi to Whistler then east (left) 0.7 mi to Aldock Rd and north (left) 1 mi. follow signs.

Points of Interest -

Near the Park office is the oldest Methodist/Episcopal church in Alabama. It is now a museum with exhibits from various periods of foreign, Indian, and local occupation. Also visit Bellingrath Gardens and the USS Alabama Battleship.

Exit 167 of I-65
Gunter Hill Campground [10]
West of Montgomery
COE Rate: $18
America/Beautiful Rate: $9

(334) 872-9554

http://www.us-parks.com/camping/al/
gunter-hill-campground.html

Camp Accommodations

146 gravel camp sites, electric/water, 10 ADA, up to 65 feet, overlooking the Alabama River. Amenities include accessible restrooms, dump station, flush toilets, laundry, potable water, showers, convenience store, telephone, pet friendly.

Directions

15 miles from I-65. From Exit 167 go west on US 80 for 9 miles. Turn right on County Road 7 for 5 miles to Old Selma Road. Turn left for 1 mile, follow signs.

Points of Interest -

Close to Montgomery and Selma where both cities have a wide variety of Civil Rights and Civil War locations worth visiting. The Montgomery Motor Speedway is nearby for race buffs - but some weekends may be a bit noisy for others for a few hours.

Exit 246
Oak Mountain State Park [11]
South of Birmingham
State Rate: $23 less
Senior Discount of 15%

(205) 620-2527

www.alapark.com/OakMountain/Camping/

Camp Accommodations

Alabama's largest State Park. 85 improved, wooded sites with full hook-ups, pet friendly. Nestled in a large cul-de-sac, which borders Beaver Lake and is surrounded by rolling hills topped with majestic Longleaf Pines, this campground is a favorite spot. RV storage available.

Directions

3 miles from I-65. From Exit 246, on west side of exit take Oak Mountain Park Rd. south to John Findley Dr. (State Park Rd), follow the signs.

Points of Interest -

In Birmingham, vehicle & aviation buffs will enjoy the Barber Vintage Motorsports Museum or the Southern Museum of Flight. Other possibilities include the Ruffiner Mountain Nature Center and the Botanical Gardens. Also see and tour the Russell Cave National Monument near Bridgeport.

Exit 289
Rickwood Caverns State Park [12]
North of Birmingham
State Rate: $18 less
Senior Discount of 15%

(205) 647-9692

http://www.alapark.com/
RickwoodCaverns/

Camp Accommodations

13 developed campsites, 9 of which are landscaped but are tight and all back in. Campsites are shaded and patrolled 24 hours. Comfort facilities include restrooms, seasonal showers, and dump station.

No site utilities.

Directions

3 miles from I-65. From Exit 289, on west side of exit take Rickwood Caverns Rd. west and turn south to Rickwood Park Rd.

Points of Interest -

Offering more than a mile of underground wonder in Rickwood Cave, this park offers unique opportunities to examine an underground pool and 260 million-year-old formations. Cave tours are $10 (adults). For your safety & convenience, access to the cave is available only with a tour guide.

Exit 340
Monte Sano State Park [13]
East of Huntsville
State Rate: $18-$24

(256) 534-6589

www.alapark.com/MonteSano/
Camping/

Camp Accommodations

84 campsites, some pull throughs, 21 with full utilities, 63 have water and electric only. Sites are roomy, separated & mostly shaded. The camp roads are paved, camp sites are gravel. Scenic views. The Von Braun Astronomical Society's Planetarium is located inside the park.

Directions

28 miles from I-65. From Exit 340 go 17 miles east on I-565 to Exit 17. Follow Governors Drive east (becomes US 431) for 7 miles. Turn left on Monte Sano Blvd. Go 2.5 miles and turn right on Nolen Ave for 1 mile to the park.

Points of Interest -

The vistas of Monte Sano (Spanish for "Mountain of Health") are 1,600 feet above sea level. Monte Sano has attracted visitors since the 1820's. There are ample hiking trails and wildlife. The planetarium is open on weekends. Huntsville, home of the 'Space & Rocket Center' is close by.

Exit 351 of I-65
Joe Wheeler State Park [14]
West of Athens
State Rate: $21
Senior Discount of 15%

(256) 247-1184

http://www.alapark.com/JoeWheeler/

Camp Accommodations

The campground features large sites among towering pines. Roads and camp-sites are paved and fairly level. 16 camp sites, 110 with full hook-ups, includes water, electric and sewage. The camp includes a restaurant, modern bathhouse with hot showers and is pet friendly.

Directions

30 miles from I-65. From Exit 351 go west for 26 miles on Hwy 2/72 to Hwy 101 (Wheeler Dam Hwy). Go south 4 miles to Park.

Points of Interest -

Decatur, known as "the River City" or "Chicago of the South" combines with Huntsville for a unique feel of the south. The area hosts air balloon festivals, horse racing and a variety of festivals throughout the year for visitors. Decatur is the home of Mellow Mix Cat Food.

Exit 51 of I-85
Chewacla State Park [15]
South of Auburn
State Rate: $25
Senior Discount available

(334) 887-5621

http://www.alapark.com/Chewacla/

Camp Accommodations

A smaller park with 36 sites with full utilities. The quiet park environment includes a swimming area, playground, hiking trails, picnic areas with tables, grills and shelters. Could be full on weekends of Auburn University home football games.

Directions

One mile from I-85. From I-85 Exit 51 go south on Hwy 15/29 but turn immediately left on Shell Toomer Pkwy for a mile to the Park entrance.

Points of Interest -

Area attractions include historic downtown Opelika, the Tuskegee Airman National Historic Site, the Julie Collins Smith Museum of Fine Art, Auburn University, and plenty of retail and restaurant options.

ARIZONA

There are close to 250 public camp-grounds in Arizona (most are remote and/or not RV accessible). Almost 75% are located on Federal Lands, the balance split between State and Local Government agencies. The parks listed here vary in site size from 11 to over 400 with 85 being the average number of sites for the locations selected.

A majority of the parks listed are part of the Arizona State Park System. They have an excellent webpage at:

<http://azstateparks.com/index.html>

You will find a wealth of useful information, such as park closings or special events. For example, in the fall some parks close or are on a 5 day a week schedule.

There is no statewide registration system for the Arizona State Parks and a number of parks do not allow advanced registration. Campsites fees were typically in the $14-$22 range. The websites and telephone numbers for each park listed in the book are noted in the campground entry.

It is worth noting that The Maricopa County Parks and Recreation system in Maricopa County, home of Phoenix, Arizona has an excellent set of parks.

[1] **Dome Rock Mountain**
N33 38.869 W114 16.982

[2] **Lost Dutchman State Park**
N33 27.812 W111 28.877

[3] **Picacho Peak State Park**
N32 38.781 W111 23.886

[4] **Catalina State Park**
N32 24.950 W110 56.270

[5] **Kartchner Caverns State Park**
N31 49.028 W110 20.848

[6] **Roper Lake State Park**
N32 45.524 W109 42.571

[7] **Virgin River Canyon**
N36 57.058 W113 47.613

[8] **Lake Pleasant County Park**
N33 51.839 W112 19.121

[9] **Cave Creek Regional Park**
N33 49.424 W112 00.916

[10] **Dead Horse Ranch State Park**
N34 45.256 W112 01.112

[11] **Patagonia Lake State Park**
N31 29.392 W110 51.218

[12] **Kaibab Lake Campground**
N35 16.871 W112 09.424

[13] **Dogtown Lake Camp**
N35 12.779 W112 07.565

[14] **Bonito Campground**
N35 22.332 W111 33.372

[15] **Homolovi Ruins State Park**
N35 01.437 W110 37.806

[16] **Cholla Lake County Park**
N34 56.359 W110 17.304

NOTES:

Arizona

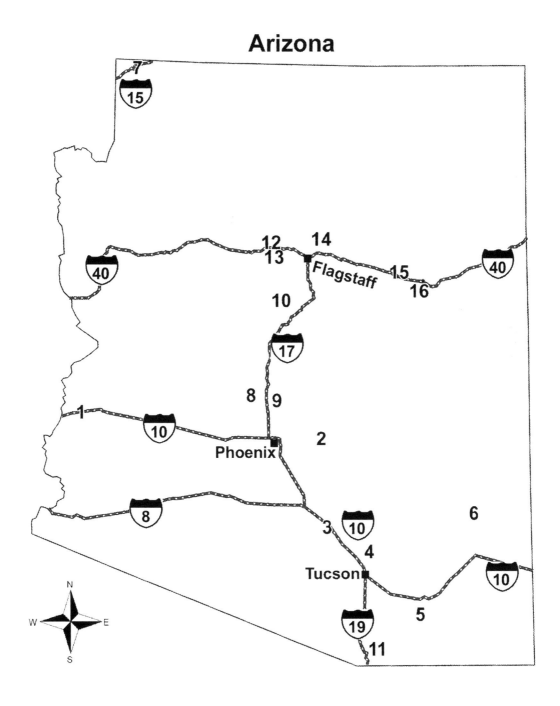

Exit 19
Dome Rock Mountain [1]
(aka Quartzsite)
Near Town of Quartzsite
BLM Rate: $1

(928) 317-3200

http://www.blm.gov/az/st/en/fo/
yuma_field_office.html

Camp Accommodations

A dry camping facility, roads and parking sites are varied. There are hundreds of pull through locations to park your RV and it is pet friendly. Do your own thing, as long as you park in designated BLM areas.

Directions

2 miles from I-10. From Exit 19 in the town of Quartzsite go west on Kuehn Rd. Stay west on Dome Rock Road for about 1 mile and you will see camp areas.

Points of Interest -

Many RVers go to Quartzsite during the winter months. Folks often form groups based on RV brand or extended relationships. The flea markets are memorable! If you know how to manage your electricity/water for a few days or a week this place is worth experiencing.

Exit 154
Lost Dutchman State Park [2]
Near Phoenix
State Rate: $15

(480) 982-4485

http://azstateparks.com/parks/lodu/
facilities.html

Camp Accommodations

70 gravel sites, paved roads, no size restrictions on RVs. Amenities include dump station, ADA restroom, drinking fountains and showers, water, picnic table, barbeque grill, and is pet friendly. Books & souvenirs are available in the Visitor Center. NO utilities, no reservations.

Directions

33 miles from I-10. From Exit 154 take US 60 (divided highway) east 25 miles to Exit 196. Go left on S. Idaho Rd for 2.5 miles & bear right on N. Apache Trail (Hwy 88) for 5 miles to park.

Points of Interest -

Lost Dutchman State Park (named after the fabled gold mine) offers a variety of hiking trails and nature trails, such as the Superstition Mountains (a source of mystery and legend since early times). Park trails offer good opportunities for bird watching & wildlife viewing.

Exit 219
Picacho Peak State Park [3]
South of Casa Grande
State Rate: $10-$15

(520) 466-3183

http://azstateparks.com/Parks/PIPE/
facilities.html

Camp Accommodations

85 sites, some ADA, no RV size limit, some pull throughs, and the option for electricity. Access to all sites is paved. Amenities include a dump station, picnic table and barbeque/fire ring. Potable water is available at the dump station. There are modern, ADA restrooms & showers.

Directions

The park is within sight of Exit 219 of I-10.

Points of Interest -

As you approach the park you will see 1,500-foot Picacho Peak, located in the Park. You can enjoy the view along the peak as you hike the trails that wind up to the top. The park and surrounding area encompass unique geological characteristics, which includes varied desert growth.

Exit 240
Catalina State Park [4]
North Side of Tucson
State Rate: $15-$20

(520) 628-5798

http://azstateparks.com/parks/CATA/
index.html

Camp Accommodations

120 spacious sites, no RV length restriction, pull throughs, 95 with electric and water hookups and 25 without hookups. Roads & parking slips are paved and there is a dump station. Amenities include a picnic table and BBQ grill, shade trees, pet friendly, modern restrooms, & showers.

Directions

15 miles from I-10. From Exit 240 go east on Tangerine Road for 14 miles, then right on N. Oracle for a mile to the park entrance.

Points of Interest -

Visit the Sonora Desert Museum & the Old Tucson Studio (a movie studio & theme park), which holds various festivals, fairs, & with museums will provide visitors many opportunities to experience the uniqueness of the area. Tucson is the home of the University of Arizona.

Exit 302
Kartchner Caverns State Park [5]
South of Bensen
State Rate: $22

(520) 586-4100

http://azstateparks.com/Parks/KACA/
facilities.html

Camp Accommodations

62 sites, electric/water, 35-60 feet, 12 pull through. Amenities include a dump station, table, showers, restrooms, hiking, and pet friendly. There are 3 ADA sites (1 pull through), which have paved access to the site & adjacent restroom, a paved pad and ADA accessible table. NO reservations.

Directions

9 miles from I-10. From Exit 302 go south on Hwy 90. Park is on the right.

Points of Interest -

Enjoy the Visitor Center, deli and exhibits. The main attraction is Kartchner Caverns. The Caverns is home to one of the world's longest soda straw stalactites (over 21 feet) & other unusual formations such as shields, totems, helictites, & rimstone dams.

Exits 352/355
Roper Lake State Park [6]
South of Safford
State Rate: $12-$19

(928) 428-6760

http://azstateparks.com/Parks/ROLA/
facilities.html

Camp Accommodations

45 shaded sites, 45+ feet, many reservable, with water/electric hookups, some pull throughs. Amenities include a dump station, is pet friendly, and has bathrooms with hot showers, fire ring, BBQ grills, picnic tables and a small shade Ramada.

Directions

29 miles from I-10. From either Exit 352 or 355 go north on Hwy 191 to W. Roper Lake Rd. Park is on the right.

Points of Interest -

The stone hot springs are inviting. The Dos Arroyos Trail leads to a re-created Indian village containing replicas of dwellings, grinding stones, roasting pits, & other tools and artifacts. There is a Visitor Center, hiking, fishing, swimming, & watchable wildlife viewing.

Exit 18 of I-15
Virgin River Canyon [7]
Between Mesquite & St. George
BLM Rate: $8
America/Beautiful Rate: $4

(435) 688-3200

http://www.blm.gov/az/st/en/prog/
recreation/camping/dev_camps/vrg.html

Camp Accommodations

75 developed gravel sites on paved roads, up to 50 feet long (30 are pull-through), some shaded. Amenities include dump station, cooking grills, picnic tables, pets allowed, flush toilets, two handicapped-accessible sites. NO reservations.

Directions

The park is within sight of Exit 18, on the south side of I-15.

Points of Interest -

Located in the Virgin River Gorge, the campground is surrounded by colorful cliffs and rocky canyons. Enjoy river access, wildlife viewing, hiking, and scenic views. Notable area destinations and sights include Zion National Park, Snow Canyon, and Quail Creek.

Exit 223 of I-17
Lake Pleasant County Park [8]
North of Phoenix
Maricopa County Rate: $10-$18

(928) 501-1710

http://www.maricopa.gov/parks/
lake_pleasant/Camping.aspx

Camp Accommodations

148 lake view, paved sites, some pull throughs. 'Developed Sites' have water/electricity and dump station. There are no utilities at 'Semi-developed Sites.' Amenities include a Ramada, table, grill, fire ring, restrooms & showers, and is pet friendly. NO reservations.

Directions

17 miles from I-17. From Exit 223 take Hwy 74 (Carefree Hwy) west. Go 15 miles to Castle Hot Spring Road. Turn right (north) 2 miles to park entrance.

Points of Interest -

Lake Pleasant provides ample campsite views of the water and a variety of water sports - half the sites are close to water's edge, the other are on a bluff overlooking the water. Shopping opportunities abound on I-17. Phoenix is close by with many sights and Baseball Spring Training.

Exit 223 of I-17
Cave Creek Regional Park [9]
North of Phoenix
Maricopa County Rate: $15-$20

(623) 465-0431

http://www.maricopa.gov/parks/
cave_creek/Camping.aspx

Camp Accommodations

The campground has 38 sites, all paved, with a few pull throughs. All sites are 'Developed Sites' and have water, electricity and dump station. Amenities include a Ramada, picnic table, barbecue grill and fire ring, restrooms, showers and is pet friendly. NO reservations.

Directions

8 miles from I-17. From Exit 223 take Hwy 74 (Carefree Hwy) east 7 miles to 32nd St. Turn left (north) one mile to the Park entrance.

Points of Interest -

Hohokam Indians resided here around 800-1400 A.D. Stone huts, pit houses, terraced field & irrigation ditches remain, as well as petroglyphs. The County sponsors a star gazing program. Shopping opportunities are on I-17. Phoenix is close with sights & Baseball Spring Training.

Exit 287 of I-17
(or from Sedona via Hwy 89)
Dead Horse Ranch State Park [10]
Southwest of Sedona
State Rate: $12-$19

(928) 634-5283

http://azstateparks.com/Parks/DEHO/
index.html

Camp Accommodations

100+ paved RV sites, some pull throughs, up to 65 feet. Sites have water/electric service (campsites may be used as non-electric sites). Amenities include advance registrations, modern ADA restroom/showers, Visitors Center, and gift shop.

Directions

13 miles from I-17. From Exit 287 go west on Hwy 260 11 miles to Main St. Cottonwood (Hwy 89A), turn left. Go 2 miles to N 10th Street. You'll see a brown Park sign before the 10th Street turn.

Points of Interest -

Dead Horse Ranch State Park adjoins Verde River Greenway State Natural Area. Use the Park as base camp to enjoy the natural surroundings of the Greenway. There are hiking trails, fishing, swimming, and watchable wildlife viewing opportunities. Be sure to visit Sedona and Jerome.

Exit 1 of I-19
Patagonia Lake State Park   [11]
North of Mexico Border
State Rate: $15-$22

(520) 287-6965

http://azstateparks.com/Parks/PALA/
index.html

Camp Accommodations

34 paved RV sites, some shoreline, water, electric, picnic table and a fire ring. Most will accommodate any size RV but some are narrow or close to adjoining sites. Amenities include a dump station, Ramada, ADA restrooms, showers, and is pet friendly. NO reservations.

Directions

15 miles from I-19. From Exit 1 go 2 miles north on I-19 BUS. Turn left at AZ-82 E/W Patagonia Hwy. Go 11 miles then turn left. Go 2 miles on Patagonia Lake Rd. to the Park.

Points of Interest -

Railroad buffs will note that the tracks of the New Mexico/Arizona railroad lie beneath the lake! Fishermen catch bass, crappie, bluegill, catfish, and rainbow trout. Birdwatchers see the canyon towhee, Inca dove, vermilion flycatcher, black vulture, and hummingbird species.

Exit 165
Kaibab Lake Campground [12]
West of Flagstaff
Kaibab NF Rate: $18
America/Beautiful Rate: $9

(928) 635-5600

http://www.fs.fed.us/r3/kai/recreation/
campgrounds/kaibab.shtml

Camp Accommodations

72 sites, dry camping, 36 pull-throughs, some ADA sites. Amenities include a dump station, shade trees, pets allowed, family friendly, flush toilets (ADA), pet friendly, firewood available. NO reservations.

Directions

2 miles from I-40. From Exit 165 turn north on Hwy 64 for 1 mile to campground sign. Turn left 1 mile to campground.

Points of Interest -

Sites are spacious and some overlook the lake. The campground is convenient to Williams, where you can take the Grand Canyon Railway train to the south rim of the Grand Canyon National Park. Spend a day in Old Town Flagstaff with quaint shops and restaurants.

Exit 167
Dogtown Lake Camp [13]
West of Flagstaff
Kaibab NF Rate: $18
America/Beautiful Rate: $9

(928) 635-5600

http://www.fs.fed.us/r3/kai/recreation/
campgrounds/kaibab.shtml

Camp Accommodations

51 gravel sites, some overlook the lake, paved roads, dry camping, 36 pull throughs, ADA friendly sites, dump station, shade trees, pets allowed, family friendly, ADA flush toilets, pet friendly, firewood. NO reservations.

Directions

6 miles from I-40. From Exit 167 go south on Garland Prairie Road for about six miles.

Points of Interest -

The area was a 'prairie dog town' before the lake was formed. Go to Williams, where you can take the Grand Canyon Railway train to the south rim of the Grand Canyon National Park. Spend a day in Old Town Flagstaff with quaint shops and restaurants.

Exit 201
Bonito Campground [14]
North of Flagstaff
Coconino NF Rate: $18
America/Beautiful Rate: $9

(928) 526-0866

www.forestcamping.com/dow/southwst/
cococmp.htm#bonito

Camp Accommodations

43 paved sites, dry camping, 15 pull through, some ADA friendly sites. Amenities include shade trees, pets allowed, family friendly, flush toilets (wheelchair friendly), pet friendly, ice and firewood available.

Directions

14 miles from I-40. From Exit 201 take US Rt. 89 north 12.5 miles to Sunset Crater/Wupaiki signs. Turn right at sign and go 1.9 miles to campground sign, turn left into camp.

Points of Interest -

In Sunset Crater Volcano National Monument see volcano cinder cones, expanses of lava and ash, still black in color. Wupatki National Monument contains pueblos with a distinctive deep red color. Spend a day in Old Town Flagstaff with quaint shops and restaurants.

Exit 257
Homolovi Ruins State Park [15]
Borders Winslow
State Rate: $12-$19

(928) 289-4106

http://azstateparks.com/Parks/HORU/
facilities.html

Camp Accommodations

52 RV sites, up to 83 feet, some pull-throughs, all with electric hookups. Water is available at the dump station and, from April-mid October, water is available at the sites. Amenities include a dump station, ADA restrooms, showers, Visitors Center, and is pet friendly. NO reservations.

Directions

1 mile from I-40. From Exit 257 go 1 mile north on Hwy 87 to the Park entrance.

Points of Interest -

Hopi consider Homolovi part of their homeland & still make pilgrimages here. To protect this site, the Hopi supported the idea of Homolovi Ruins State Park. Visit the La Posada Hotel, the "last great railroad hotel" and 'Stand on a Corner' with The Eagles. Meteor Crater is close by.

Exit 277
Cholla Lake County Park [16]
East of Joseph City
County Rate: $12-$19

(928) 288-3717

http://www.rvtoads.com/rvparks/
cholla-lake-county-park.html

Camp Accommodations

11 gravel RV sites up to 50 feet, of which 12 are pull-throughs. There is room for slide outs, some are shaded. Amenities include a dump station, restrooms, showers and is pet friendly. NO reservations.

Directions

1 mile from I-40. From Exit 277 turn south to the Frontage Rd (Old Route 66) and go 1 mile east to the Park.

Points of Interest -

Enjoy a drive to the Painted Desert in Petrified Forest National Park. Visit Winslow and the famous La Posada Hotel, the "last great railroad hotel." Go "Standin' on a Corner in Winslow, AZ" with The Eagles. Meteor Crater is close by.

ARKANSAS

Campgrounds managed by the Corps of Engineers and the State of Arkansas tended to be the most accessible and best suited for Rvers. Sixty percent of the camps listed here are in State Parks, the rest are on COE lands. The typical campground cited in the book has close to 70 sites and the fee will be around $15.

The State Parks of Arkansas have a comprehensive website. You can book a campsite online, by phone, or at the park. Go to -

http://www.arkansasstateparks.com/park-finder/

Arkansas State Parks generally are located on or near water. Most of the park campsites have water and electric hookups, dump stations, picnic tables, grills and lantern hangers. You need to call the individual campground to get information related to paved sites. All parks are pet friendly.

RV camping rates for all the state parks are:
- Class AAA (50 amp/water/sewer)-$27
- Class AA (electricity/water/sewer)-$24
- Class A (50 amp/water)-$21
- Class B (electricity/water)-$17
- Class C (electricity or water)-$13
- Class D (no hookups)-$10

Discounts for all the state parks are:
- Arkansas citizens over age 62 is 50%/ Su-Th; 25%/Fr-Sa & holidays.
- Out-of-State citizens over age 62 is 25%/ Su-Th.
- 100% Disabled U.S. citizen is 50% anytime with written proof.

(**See State website for details**)

[1] **Millwood State Park** N33 40.870 W94 00.001	[10] **Willow Beach Camp** N34 42.052 W92 08.289
[2] **Crater of Diamonds State Park** N34 02.489 W93 40.573	[11] **Village Creek State Park** N35 10.284 W90 43.647
[3] **White Oak State Park** N33 41.323 W93 07.042	[12] **Lake Poinsett State Park** N35 32.022 W90 41.272
[4] **DeGray Lake State Park** N34 15.355 W93 07.729	[13] **Tar Camp** N34 27.741 W92 06.820
[5] **Lake Catherine State Park** N34 26.223 W92 55.141	[14] **Rising Star** N34 09.925 W91 44.210
[6] **Brady Mountain Camp** N34 34.814 W93 15.779	[15] **Lake Fort Smith State Park** N35 38.961 W94 09.559
[7] **Aux Arc Campground** N35 28.059 W93 49.329	[16] **Devils Den State Park** N35 46.941 W94 14.974
[8] **Lake Dardanelle State Park** N35 14.939 W93 12.784	[17] **Horseshoe Bend Camp** N36 17.193 W94 01.448
[9] **Toad Suck Ferry Camp** N35 04.663 W92 32.652	

NOTES:

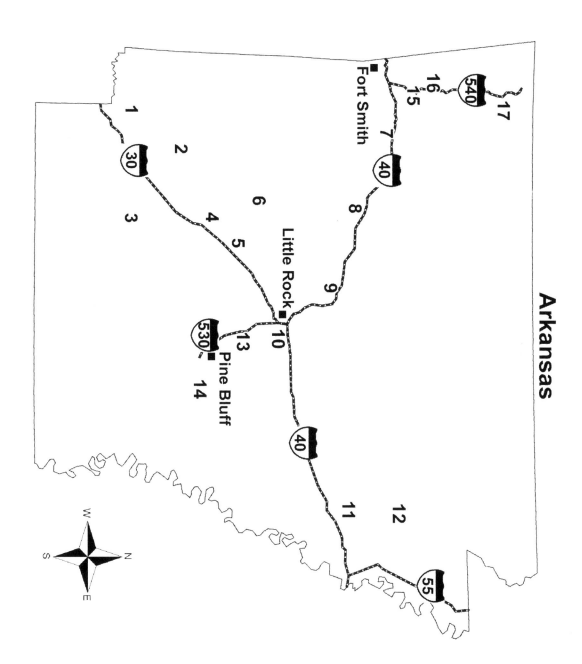

Arkansas

Exit 223 in Texas (In Texarkana on the AR/TX state line)
Millwood State Park [1]
North of Texarkana
Rates and Discounts - See Pg. 18

(870) 898-2800

www.arkansasstateparks.com/park-finder/parks.aspx?id=26

Camp Accommodations

112 RV sites (2 AA, 110 B) up to 62 feet long, some ADA, dump station. Amenities include showers, flush toilets, nature and bicycle trails, & Interpretive Programs. The Visitors Center/Marina has gifts, groceries, fishing supplies, & boats for rent.

Directions

25 miles from I-30. From Exit 223 drive 16 miles north on Hwy 71 to Ashdown, then 9 miles east on Hwy 32 to the park entrance.

Points of Interest -

In Texarkana visit the Ace of Clubs house built in the shape of a playing card. Tour Historic Washington State Park. Music buff's will seek the mural of favorite son Scott Joplin. Check out the Perot Theater (an Italian Renaissance Theater built in 1924), & find Photographer's Island.

Exit 30
Crater of Diamonds State Park [2]
Northeast of Nashville AR
Rates and Discounts - See Pg. 18

(870) 285-3113

http:// www.craterofdiamondsstatepark.com/

Camp Accommodations

59 RV wooded campsites (all B), some ADA accessible. The campground underwent a total renovation during 2009-10. Amenities include a dump station, showers and flush toilets, nature and bicycle trails, Visitors Center, restaurant, Interpretive Programs, & museum.

Directions

43 miles from I-30. From Exit 30 go north on Hwy 278 for 27 miles to Nashville. Take Hwy 27 north and go 13 miles to Murfreesboro, then Hwy 301 southeast 3 miles to the park.

Points of Interest -

This camp is farther off the Interstate for parks selected for the book but the unique appeal of the Crater of Diamonds made it a must addition. This is the only site in the world where the public can search for diamonds and "finder's keepers!" About 800 gems are found each year!

Exit 44
White Oak State Park [3]
South of Arkadelphia
Rates and Discounts - See Pg. 18

(870) 685-2748

www.arkansasstateparks.com/park-finder/parks.aspx?id=16

Camp Accommodations

41 newly paved RV campsites on the shore of White Oak Lake (all B) up to 55 feet long, some ADA accessible. Amenities include a dump station, showers, flush toilets, Interpretive Programs, nature and bicycle trails. The Visitors Center/Marina has groceries, fishing supplies, & boats.

Directions

22 miles from I-30. From Exit 44 drive 20 miles east on Hwy 24. At Bluff City go 100 yards south on Hwy 299, then 2 miles southeast on Hwy 387 to Park entrance.

Points of Interest -

The camp recently underwent significant renovations, to better accommodate large RVs. In Prescott, with it's historic downtown, visit the Depot Museum. For the history buff, Civil War history abounds in the area. Visit President Clinton's Home Museum in Hope, just 15 miles away.

Exit 78
DeGray Lake State Park [4]
North of Arkadelphia
Rates and Discounts - See Pg. 18

(501) 865-2801

http://www.degray.com/camping/

Camp Accommodations

112 campsites (all B), some pull through, with water and electric hookups. Some sites are situated on the lakeshore, others in shaded woodlands. Special ADA sites are also available. Amenities include a dump station, showers and flush toilets, restaurant, Interpretive Programs, nature and bicycle trails.

Directions

6 miles from I-30. From Exit 78 drive 6 miles north on Scenic 7 Byway to the park.

Points of Interest -

Enjoy park guided lake cruises, kayak tours, Elderhostel, arts/crafts workshops, safaris, snorkeling, owl prowls, & square dances. Visit Garvan Woodland Gardens (University of Arkansas' Botanical Garden) or Hot Springs, AR, 'America's First Resort' & have a thermal springs spa.

Exit 97
Lake Catherine State Park [5]
Near Hot Springs
Rates and Discounts - See Pg. 18

(501) 844-4176

www.arkansasstateparks.com/
lakecatherine/

Camp Accommodations

68 paved campsites (42 AAA sites with 60 foot pads, 26 B), water/electric hookups, some are pull throughs. Sites are lakeshore or water view (most are ADA). Amenities include a dump station, showers, flush toilets, Visitor's Center, Interpretive Programs, nature and bicycle trails.

Directions

12 miles from I-30. From Exit 97 near Malvern go 12 miles northwest on Hwy 171 to the park.

Points of Interest -

The Park features rustic style facilities using native stone & wood, constructed by the Civilian Conservation Corps in the 1930s. Near by, Diamondhead, a private resort community offers golf, snack bar, restaurant & Olympic-size swimming pool that park visitors are welcome to enjoy.

Exit 98
Brady Mountain Camp [6]
Northwest of Hot Springs
COE Rate: $14-$16
America/Beautiful Rate: $7-$8

(501) 767-2108 x3050

http://www.recreation.gov

Camp Accommodations

Located on Lake Ouachita, with 74 paved sites, 57 with electric hookups. Amenities include a dump station, ADA restroom, flush toilet, Interpretive Trail, potable water, marina, swimming, fish cleaning station, and hot showers.

Directions

33 miles from I-30. From Exit 98 drive 17 miles northwest on Hwy 270 to Hot Springs, then west 10 miles to Brady Mountain Access Road. Turn right and follow access road 6 miles north to the park.

Points of Interest -

Visit Hot Springs, 'America's First Resort.' Enjoy a thermal springs spa. Wander downtown Hot Springs, with its classic hotels, Victorian architecture, art studios and renowned Bathhouse Row. Enjoy antique, crystal and rock shops, boutiques, specialty malls & a variety of restaurants.

Exit 35
Aux Arc Campground [7]
South of Ozark
COE Rate: $18
America/Beautiful Rate: $9

(479) 667-1100

http://www.recreation.gov

Camp Accommodations

The camp, located on Ozark Lake along the Arkansas River, offers 60 sites (accommodates RVs up to 70 feet) on paved roads with electric and water hook ups. Amenities include a dump station, ADA restroom, flush toilet, potable water, hot showers and is pet friendly.

Directions

4 miles from I-40. From Exit 35 drive 2 miles on Hwy 23 to Ozark, continue 2 mi. to Hwy 309. Turn left and follow signs to the park.

Points of Interest -

The City of Ozark has that wonderful small town feel. The square is filled with antique and gift shops. Come evening the beautiful lights of an arching bridge reflects off the river. Venture into nearby Arkansas Wine Country, among the largest and oldest wine producing areas in the South.

Exit 81
Lake Dardanelle State Park [8]
South of Russellville
Rates and Discounts - See Pg. 18

(479) 967-5516

http://www.arkansasstateparks.com/park-finder/parks.aspx?id=6

Camp Accommodations

74 campsites on gravel (16 AAA, 14 AA, 44 B), with water and electric hookups. Sites are mostly waterfront. Amenities include a dump station, showers and flush toilets, Visitor's Center, Interpretive Programs, nature and hiking trails.

Directions

11 miles from I-40. From Exit 81 at Russellville, take Hwy 7 south for 7 miles to the town of Dardanelle, turn right on Hwy 22 and travel 4 miles to the main park.

Points of Interest -

Located between the Ozark & Ouachita Mountains, the Park features a large Visitor Center overlooking the Lake. As a major bass fishing tournament site, the fishing tournament weigh-in pavilion is the first of its kind in the nation. Visit the main streets of Dardanelle and Russellville.

Exit 129
Toad Suck Ferry Camp [9]
West of Conway
COE Rate: $18-$20
America/Beautiful Rate: $9-$10

(501)759-2005

http://www.recreation.gov

Camp Accommodations

48 sites for RVs up to 75 feet, with electric and water hookups. Amenities include a dump station, restroom, flush toilet, potable water, and hot showers. The Toad Suck Ferry name was bestowed on the river ferry, a riverside tavern, a settlement, and a huge modern dam.

Directions

7 miles from I-40. From Exit 129 drive west for 7 miles on Hwy 60, follow signs into the campground.

Points of Interest -

The river provides the perfect atmosphere to relax & watch riverboats & barges. Visit Conway, the second fastest growing city in Arkansas and home to 3 colleges, earning it the nickname "The City of Colleges." Enjoy the Conway Symphony, Community Arts, & Arkansas Shakespeare Theatre.

Exit 159 of I-40
Willow Beach Camp [10]
East of Little Rock
COE Rate: $18-$20
America/Beautiful Rate: $9-$10

(501) 534-0451

http://www.recreation.gov/

Camp Accommodations

21 sites for RVs up to 80 feet, with electric and water hookups. Amenities include a dump station, ADA restroom, flush toilet, potable water, hot showers, and accessible fishing.

Directions

10 miles from I-40. From Exit 159 drive 3 miles south on I-440 to Hwy 165, then east for 3 miles. Go south 3 miles on Colonel Maynard Road & west 1 mile on Blue Heron to the campground.

Points of Interest -

On the east side of Little Rock. Discover the city by 'Little Rocks Tour' bus. Little Rock is the place to be with the bustling River Market District featuring restaurants, shops, bars, & museums. The Clinton Presidential Center is a significant addition to Little Rock.

Exit 242 of I-40
Village Creek State Park [11]
North of Forrest City
Rates and Discounts - See Pg. 18

(870) 238-9406

http://www.arkansasstateparks.com/park-finder/parks.aspx?id=21

Camp Accommodations
96 campsites (24 AAA, 5 A, 67 B), on concrete pads, many with full utilities and some pull throughs. Sites are mostly along Lake Dunn. Amenities include showers and flush toilets, Visitor's Center, Interpretive Programs, concerts, special events, nature and hiking trails.

Directions
13 miles from I-40. From Exit 242 at Forrest City drive 13 miles north on Hwy 284 to the park entrance

Points of Interest -

Find the trail path crossing the 'Trail of Tears,' the relocation of Native Americans from their homelands to Indian Territory (present day Oklahoma). Forrest City, on Crowley's Ridge, the rugged & beautiful outcropping that runs from Missouri through Arkansas is a popular destination.

Exit 23 of I-55
Lake Poinsett State Park [12]
South of Jonesboro
Rates and Discounts - See Pg. 18

(870) 578-2064

http://www.arkansasstateparks.com/lakepoinsett/

Camp Accommodations

26 wooded sites (4A, 22 B) with water/electric. Amenities include dump station, showers, flush toilets, Visitor's Center, Interpretive Programs, nature & hiking trails. Interpreters lead trail walks, kayak/canoe tours, watchable wildlife outings and Dutch oven cooking workshops.

Directions
25 miles from I-55. From Exit 23 drive 13 miles northwest on Hwy 63 to Hwy 14 then 10 miles west to Hwy 163 then 2 miles south to the park entrance.

Points of Interest -

Downtown Jonesboro is filled with gift shops, restaurants, and art galleries. Arkansas State University offers one of the mid-South's finest museums & a fine arts center. Check out the Forum Civic Center and Theatre, known for its special productions as well as its art galleries.

Exit 20
Tar Camp [13]
South of Little Rock
COE Rate: $19
America/Beautiful Rate: $10

(501) 397-5101

http://www.recreation.gov

Camp Accommodations

Located on the Arkansas River by Pool 5 Lock and Dam, there are 53 shaded sites with concrete pads for RVs up to 98 feet, with electric and water hookups. The majority are river front. Amenities include a dump station, ADA restrooms, flush toilet, potable water, hot showers, & pet friendly.

Directions

5 miles from I-530. From Exit 20 go east on Hwy 46 through town for 0.9 miles to N. Brodie St. Go left for 2 blocks then turn right. Follow River Rd for 4 miles east to Tar Camp Park.

Points of Interest -

South of Little Rock. Discover the city by 'Little Rocks Tour' bus. Little Rock is the place to be with the bustling River Market District featuring restaurants, shops, bars, & museums. The Clinton Presidential Center is a significant addition to Little Rock.

Exit 46
Rising Star [14]
East of Pine Bluff
COE Rate: $8-$13
America/Beautiful Rate: $4-$7

(807) 534-0451

http://www.recreation.gov/

Camp Accommodations

24 paved sites for RVs up to 90 feet, most located along the Arkansas River shore, 20 with electric & water hookups. Amenities include a dump station, ADA restroom, flush toilet, potable water, hot showers, and watchable wildlife opportunities.

Directions

12 miles from I-530. From Exit 46 take Hwy 65 south for 8 miles then left for 4 miles on Blankenship Road to Rising Star Campground.

Points of Interest -

Visit Pine Bluff, the 'City of Murals.' Enjoy The Arts and Science Center, which features theatrical performances and workshops. Pine Bluff has the only museum dedicated to the history of band music and instruments. Visit the Arkansas Railroad Museum and the Martha Mitchell Home.

Exit 34
Lake Fort Smith State Park [15]
North of Fort Smith
Rates and Discounts - See Pg. 18

(479) 369-2469

www.arkansasstateparks.com/park-finder/parks.aspx?id=18

Camp Accommodations

There are 30 campsites (20 AAA, 10 B) with water/electric, some pull throughs, and a dump station. Amenities include a swimming pool, marina, hiking trails, and Visitor Center with exhibits, and outdoor patio featuring a native stone, wood-burning fireplace and lake view.

Directions

2 miles from I-540. From Exit 34 go southeast for 0.8 miles on Hwy 282 to Hwy 71. Take Hwy 71 south for 1.5 miles to Lake Fort Smith Rd. Turn left into the park entrance.

Points of Interest -

Sightsee the Fort Smith riverfront and Belle Grove Historic District (blocks of architecture from the past 130 years). Walk the downtown riverfront areas & you'll find boutiques, cafes and clothing stores from consignment to elegant antique shops including an old west cowboy store.

Exit 53
Devils Den State Park [16]
South of Fayetteville
Rates and Discounts - See Pg. 18

(479) 761-3325

http://www.arkansasstateparks.com/park-finder/parks.aspx?id=4

Camp Accommodations

The Park's renowned natural beauty and lush oak-hickory forest hold 93 campsites (44AAA, 12B, 13C, 24D). Amenities include a swimming pool, hiking trails (guided hikes available), and Visitor Center with restaurant, Interpretive Programs, and exhibits.

Directions

17 miles from I-540. From Exit 53 go 17 miles southwest on Hwy 170 to the park (**RVs over 26 feet are advised not to use Exit 45 and Hwy 74 - a mountainous road**).

Points of Interest -

RVers can explore one or more of the Park's many caves and crevices. Nearby, Fayetteville is a unique mix of college town, outdoor-lovers delight, cultural/arts center, & home to the University of Arkansas; and recognized by Forbes magazine as a top five smaller town.

Exit 83
Horseshoe Bend Camp [17]
East of Bentonville/Rogers
COE Rate: $16
America/Beautiful Rate: $8

(479) 925-2561

http://www.recreation.gov

Camp Accommodations

There are 2 campgrounds with 136 RV sites up to 100 feet long, many along the shore of Beaver Lake with electric, some are pull through. Amenities include a dump station, ADA restrooms, flush toilet, marina, fishing, hiking, potable water, hot showers, and pet friendly. Closed winters.

Directions

11 miles from I-540. From Exit 83 take Hwy 94 east (W New Hope Rd.) for 5.3 miles to Monte NE Rd. Bear right, go 1.6 miles to Hwy 94 Rd. Turn left, go 0.8 miles to Panorama Rd. Turn right, go 3.2 miles to the Camp.

Points of Interest -

Visit Bentonville and enjoy Opera in the Ozarks, the Northwest Arkansas Symphony, Walton Arts Center and Arends Arts Center, which hosts both national and international plays and concerts. Discover downtown Roger's many historically significant buildings with an historic aura.

CALIFORNIA

The State Parks System has a very helpful and comprehensive website -

http://www.parks.ca.gov/

Some, but not all State parks, accept reservations. Call the Park you are interested in for details. Many campgrounds fill-up months ahead so plan in advance. Of the almost 120 State Parks less than 15 currently can accommodate an RV of 36 feet or more.

Be advised that the basic California length law for vehicles is 40 feet unless specifically exempted. The California Vehicle Code (CVC) does allow motorhomes over 40 feet in length, up to 45 feet, on certain routes. Over-length motorhomes are allowed on interstates and on those State routes that can accommodate them.

Over-length motorhomes may travel on virtually every State route EXCEPT those signed with a 30-foot kingpin-to-rear-axle (KPRA) advisory sign.

In light of the State's RV length law many State Parks are restrictive on RV lengths over 35-40 feet so there are a limited number of State Parks listed in this chapter. On the other hand the California Counties have an exceptional collection of RV friendly parks, a number of which are cataloged here. The strong presence of National Forests (NF) shows in the list of some of the campgrounds noted here.

As you might expect the State Park Camps are higher priced ($35-$62), while county parks fall in the $16-$27 range. As is typical for other states the Federal campgrounds represent the fee bargain at $5-$18 with an America the Beautiful card.

[1] Guajome County Park N33 14.829 W117 16.348	[9] Burnt Rancheria N32 51.655 W116 25.252
[2] San Onofre State Beach N33 22.444 W117 33.735	[10] Cottonwood Camp N33 44.889 W115 49.482
[3] Bolsa Chica State Beach N33 41.558 W118 02.657	[11] Mayflower County Park N33 40.250 W114 32.038
[4] Los Alamos Camp N34 42.198 W118 48.337	[12] Dos Picos County Park N32 59.944 W116 56.473
[5] Kern River County Park N35 26.730 W118 55.193	[13] Lake Elsinore County Park N33 40.594 W117 22.423
[6] Dos Reis County Park N37 49.805 W121 18.646	[14] Table Mountain N34 22.882 W117 41.408
[7] Sycamore Grove N40 09.364 W122 12.251	[15] Calico Ghost Town N34 56.485 W116 52.011
[8] Antlers N40 53.155 W122 22.847	[16] Loggers Campground N39 27.841 W120 07.833

NOTES:

California

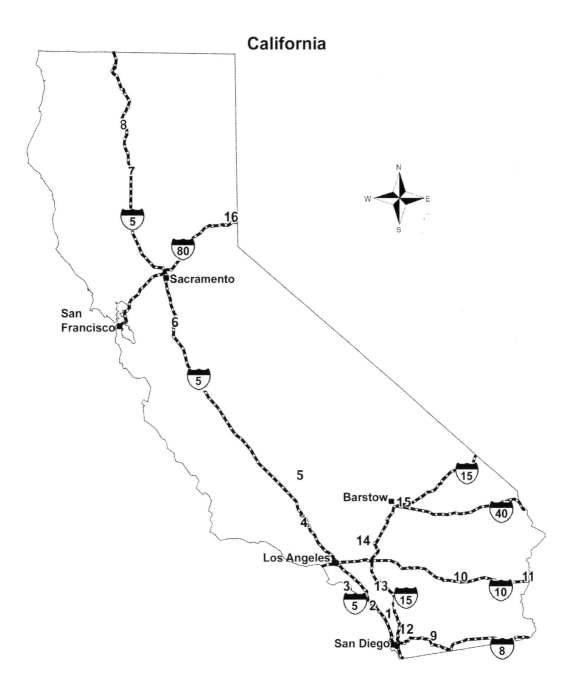

Exit 54
Guajome County Park [1]
In City of Oceanside
County Rate: $24

(760) 724 4489

http://www.sdcounty.ca.gov/parks/
Camping/guajome.html

Camp Accommodations

There are 35 shaded and paved sites with electric/water that will accommodate RVs up to 45 feet. Advance registrations advised. The camp is pet friendly and does require a $1 pet fee.

Directions

7 miles from I-5. From Exit 54 drive east on Hwy 76 for 8 miles to Guajome Lake Rd. Turn right on Guajome Lake Rd. and proceed to the park main entrance on your right..

Points of Interest -

The Park is located in the coastal community of Oceanside and has good access to San Diego County activities. The Park ponds attract migratory birds. Five miles of park trails wander through woodland, chaparral, wetland, and mixed grassland habitats.

Exit 71
San Onofre State Beach [2]
San Mateo Campground
Near San Clemente
State Rate: $35

(949) 492-4872

http://www.parks.ca.gov/?
page_id=647

Camp Accommodations

Located on the outer edge of San Clemente there are 157 shaded sites, up to 36 feet. Amenities include a dump station, fire pit and picnic table. Hookup sites are available with electricity, water, showers, and flush toilets.

Directions

1.5 mile from I-5. From Exit 71 (Exit Basilone) turn toward the ocean and follow Old Pacific Hwy for 1.5 mile. Turn right on to Beach Club Rd. to the Park.

Points of Interest -

The campground is just inland from the sandy beaches of San Onofre State Beach. A 1.5-mile nature trail connects the campground to the well known surf of Trestles Beach. View wetland habitats, which host some rare and even endangered species.

Exit 107
Bolsa Chica State Beach [3]
In Huntington Beach
State Rate: $50-$65

(714) 846-3460

 http://www.parks.ca.gov/?
page_id=642

Camp Accommodations

Located between Seal Beach and the Huntington Beach City Pier there are 55 sites, with a maximum RV length of 40 feet. Hookup sites are available with electricity and water. Amenities include ADA access, a dump station, showers, flush toilets, and picnic table.

Directions

17 mi. from I-5. From Exit 107 go west on Hwy 22 (Garden Grove Fwy) for 9.3 mi. to the Hwy 405 merge. Exit south on Bolsa Chica Rd., go south 4.4 mi. to Warner Ave. Turn west for 1.4 mi. to Pacific Coast Hwy 1, then south 2.3 mi. to the Park.

Points of Interest -

The camp is a popular place for surf fishing and bare-handed fishing for California grunion. The beach extends 3 miles from Seal Beach to Huntington Beach City Pier. There is a bikeway. Watchable wildlife options are also available. Bolsa Chica Ecological Reserve is close by.

Exit 195
Los Alamos Camp [4]
North of Santa Clarita
Angeles NF Rate: $14
America/Beautiful Rate: $7

(877) 444-6777

http://www.forestcamping.com/dow/
pacficsw/angcmp.htm#los alamos

Camp Accommodations

93 sites, 19 pull-through, up to 46 feet, dry camping, roads and some parking aprons are paved. Amenities include shade trees, dump station, family friendly, ADA toilets, pet friendly. NO utilities, no reservations.

Directions

4 miles from I-5. From Exit 195 turn southwest on Smokey Bear Rd. to Pyramid Lake Rd. Go 1.5 miles south on Pyramid Lake Rd. Turn right at sign and go 2 miles north on Hard Luck Rd. to campground.

Points of Interest -

Visit the Vista Del Lago Visitor Center and Pyramid Lake. Just south, in Santa Clarita enjoy the golf courses, wine lounges, fine dining, excellent retail shopping, music events, and a rich western heritage. Also visit Mentryville, the William S. Hart Museum, and the Oak of the Golden Dream.

Exit 257
Kern River County Park [5]
East of Bakersfield
County Rate: $10-$22

(661) 872-5149

http://www.co.kern.ca.us/parks/kern-river-camp.asp

Camp Accommodations

There are 50 paved sites on 28 landscaped acres, some sites are shaded, all are pull throughs with a 70 foot maximum. Amenities include patios, some shaded, picnic tables, fire rings, restrooms, showers, drinking water, is pet friendly, and a dump station. NO reservations.

Directions

33 miles from I-5. From Exit 257 follow Hwy 58 east. Go 20.6 miles on Hwy 58. At Hwy 99 continue straight, now on Hwy 178, for 7 miles to Fairfax Rd. Turn left for 2.2 miles to Alfred Harrell Hwy. Turn right, go 3.2 miles to the camp.

Points of Interest -

Enjoy Bakersfield, its proximity to Sequoia National Forest and largest collection of Basque restaurants in the US. Visit the California Living Museum (CALM) California's Premier Native Zoo/Garden. CALM, a teaching zoo, displays & interprets native animals, plants, fossils, and artifacts.

Exit 463
Dos Reis County Park [6]
South of Stockton
County Rate: $20

(209) 953-8800

http://www.mgzoo.com/parks/dos-reis-park.htm

Camp Accommodations

On the San Joaquin River, there are 26 paved RV sites, 4 pull throughs, up to 60 feet, full hook-ups. Amenities include shower facilities, fire ring, picnic table with lattice shade cover, horseshoe pit, boating, fishing, pet friendly, and a dump station (fee). Reservations available.

Directions

2 miles from I-5. From Exit 463 go west to the frontage road, Matheny Rd., then 0.5 miles north to Dos Reis Rd. Turn west for 1 mile to the park.

Points of Interest -

Stockton is close by with many sightseeing venues plus opportunities to enjoy music, theater, dance, literary events, and other cultural and entertainment programs. The City has its own symphony and opera company and hosts the popular Asparagus Festival.

Exit 649
Sycamore Grove [7]
Southeast of Red Bluff
Mendocino NF Rate: $16-$25
America/Beautiful Rate:
$8-$13

(530) 527-1196

http://www.fs.fed.us/r5/mendocino/
recreation/rbluff/

Camp Accommodations

30 paved sites, 12 pull throughs, up to 41
feet long, some with electricity. The grassy
camp has some shade. Amenities include
tables, grills, drinking water, flush toilets,
showers, wheelchair friendly, hiking, fishing, no dump station. NO reservations.

Directions

3 miles from I-5. From Exit 649 go east
on Hwy 36 (Antelope Blvd) 0.3 miles, turn
south on Sale Lane for 2.2 miles to the
park.

Points of Interest -

In Red Bluff visit Gaumer's Mineral Museum & find gems, minerals, fossils, Native American carvings, and a mining exhibit. The Kelly-Griggs House Museum is a
trip into the past - walk through this classic
Victorian home decorated with pioneer,
early Chinese & Native American artifacts.

Exit 702
Antlers [8]
North of Redding
Shasta NF Rate: $16-$30
America/Beautiful Rate:
$8-$15

(530) 275-8113

http://www.recreation.gov/

Camp Accommodations

45 paved spacious sites up to 40 feet, the
camp is heavily forested with pine and
Manzanita. Amenities include a picnic table, fire rings, grills, water spigots, fishing,
water sports, and toilets. NO utilities.

Directions

1 mile from I-5. From Exit 702 go east
to the Antlers Rd. frontage road, then right
for 1 mile to the park.

Points of Interest -

In Redding walk the Sundial Bridge at Turtle Bay. Explore nature's underground
works, thousands of years in the making,
at Lake Shasta Caverns. Visit Lassen Volcanic National Park. In 1914 the volcano
erupted, beginning a 7-year cycle of spo-
radic volcanic outbursts.

Exit 47 of I-8
Burnt Rancheria [9]
Northeast of Pine Valley
Cleveland NF Rate: $19
America/Beautiful Rate: $9

(619) 473-0120

http://www.recreation.gov/

Camp Accommodations

The 49 paved sites are heavily wooded and up to 50 feet long. The camp was upgraded in 2009. Amenities include table, fire ring, ADA restrooms, showers, & pet friendly. Firewood is available for purchase. NO utilities.

Directions

10 miles from I-8. From Exit 47 take Sunrise Hwy S1 northeast for 10 miles to Milepost 23. Stop at entrance for campground information and site location.

Points of Interest -

The San Diego State University Observatory sponsors 'Star Parties' for campers. Enjoy a hike along the Desert View Nature Trail and interpretive programs held in the amphitheater. Visit the old country Our Lady of the Pines Catholic Church. San Diego is an hour drive away.

Exit 168 of I-10
Cottonwood Camp [10]
East of Indio
Joshua Tree NP Rate: $10
America/Beautiful Rate: $5

(760) 367-5541

http://www.joshua.tree.national-park.com/camping.htm

Camp Accommodations

There are 62 spread out sites surrounded by the wide open desert rock and scrub terrain. Amenities include water, flush toilets, tables, fire grates, and a dump station, no reservations. You need to bring your own firewood. NO utilities.

Directions

4 miles from I-10. From Exit 168 take Cottonwood Spring Rd. north for 4 miles to the park entrance for campground information and site location.

Points of Interest -

A highlight of Cottonwood is the night sky. The desert environment allows for especially good views of the moon over the nearby mountains. With its mild winter climate and interesting rock formations, plants and wildlife, Joshua Tree National Park is excellent for hiking.

Exit 241 of I-10
Mayflower County Park [11]
West of Quartzsite
County Rate: $18-$22

(760) 922-4665

http://www.riversidecountyparks.org/locations/regional-parks/mayflower/

Camp Accommodations

152 RV sites, mostly grassy and shaded, many pull through, with sites clustered around utility poles. Amenities include electricity/water, periodic honey wagon service, picnic area, shuffleboard, horseshoes, boat launch to Colorado River, pet friendly. No reservations.

Directions

7 miles from I-10. From Exit 241 go north on Hwy 95 (Intake Blvd.) for 4 miles, then east on 6th Ave. for 3 miles to Colorado River Rd., then left into the park.

Points of Interest -

The Blythe Intaglios, a group of gigantic figures are found on the ground 15 miles north of Blythe, the largest is 171 feet. The figures are believed to be between 450 and 2,000 years old. On hikes, keep your eye out for the Chuckwalla, a stocky wide-bodied lizard up to 16 inches long!

Exit 17
Dos Picos County Park [12]
Northeast of San Diego
County Rate: $24

(760) 789-2220

http://www.sdcounty.ca.gov/parks/
Camping/dos_picos.html

Camp Accommodations

57 sites, some pull through, electric/
water, RVs up to 40 feet. The secluded
atmosphere of the shady park is a product
of the ranchland & steep rocky slopes,
which make it well suited for campers.
Amenities include restrooms, showers, is
pet friendly, and has reservations.

Directions

18 miles from I-15. From Exit 17 go
east on Scripps Poway Pkwy. for 8.6
miles to Hwy 67. Turn north for 7.5
miles to Mussey Grade Rd. Turn right for
2 mile to Dos Picos Park Rd. and follow
this 1 mile to the park.

Points of Interest -

In San Diego there are over 30 museums.
With 15 museums and 9 theatres and performing arts centers, Balboa Park is San
Diego's cultural heart. Visit, for example,
the Timken Museum of Art, San Diego
Opera or the Air and Space Museum or try
a show at The Old Globe.

Exit Lake Elsinore/Central Ave.
Lake Elsinore County Park [13]
South of Carona
County Rate: $20-$35

(800) 416-6992
www.rockymountainrec.com/camp/
elsinore-campground.htm

Camp Accommodations

There are 120 RV sites situated among
walnut, pine and deciduous trees providing ample shade with electric/water & limited sewer sites. Amenities include flush
toilets, showers, laundry, pet friendly,
dump station, propane for sale, convenience store, and advanced registration.

Directions

3 miles from I-15. Take the Lake Elsi-
nore/Central Ave Exit southwest toward
the lake. Turn right onto Collier (Hwy 74).
Go 0.5 miles. Turn left on Riverside Dr. for
2.2 miles to the park entrance on the left.

Points of Interest -

It is hard to know what to recommend. You
are surrounded by outdoor activities, historic sites, Hollywood, Los Angeles, Dis-
neyland.

Where to start?

Exit Hwy 138/Wrightwood
Table Mountain [14]
West of Wrightwood
Angeles NF Rate: $20-$40
America/Beautiful Rate: $10-$20

(760) 249-3526

http://www.recreation.gov/

Camp Accommodations

There are 39 spacious, paved sites, up to
50 feet. Amenities include ADA toilets, fire
pits, water spigots, grills, & bear boxes.
Activities include sightseeing, mountain
views, hiking, picnicking, and nature study.

Directions

18 miles from I-15. From Hwy 138/
Wrightwood Exit go west 8.4 miles on
Hwy 138 to Hwy 2, then left 8.8 miles,
to Big Pines. Turn north (right) on Table
Mountain Rd for 0.7 mile to the camp-
ground.

Points of Interest -

Visit Hesperia in the Mojave Desert. Hesperia has many unique restaurants. See
the Radio Control Model Aircraft Park. Enjoy watching or flying radio controlled aircraft (free admission). Dozens of movies
were filmed in Victorville at The New Re-
flections concert venue Downtown.

Exit Ghost Town Road of I-15
Calico Ghost Town [15]
Northeast of Barstow
County Park Rate: $25-$30 (includes admission to the Ghost Town)

(760) 254-2122

http://www.co.san-bernardino.ca.us/parks/calico.htm

Camp Accommodations

There are 265 RV sites, 46 electric/water, 58 electric, balance dry, situated in a desert environment. Amenities include showers, restrooms, grills, fire rings, tables, 3 dump stations, many restaurants, shops, and attractions.

Directions

3 miles from I-15. Take the Ghost Town Road Exit. Drive north for 3.4 miles on Ghost Town Rd. to the camp on your left.

Points of Interest -

An authentic silver mining town where hundreds of mines, 22 saloons, mercantile stores, & The U.S. Borax Co. left their mark. Events & living history are hallmarks of Calico (first preserved by Walter Knott, Knott's Berry Farm Founder). Knott donated Calico to the County in 1966.

Exit 194 of I-80
Loggers Campground [16]
North of Truckee
Tahoe NF Rate: $21
America/Beautiful Rate: $11

(530) 587-9281

http://www.recreation.gov/

Camp Accommodations

200 paved, wooded sites, up to 50 feet, 2 pull throughs, many near Stampede Reservoir, dry camping. Amenities include ADA toilets, dump station, fire pits, grills, water spigots, firewood, reservations.

Directions

9 miles from I-80. From Exit 194 take Hirshdale Rd. 0.5 miles northeast to Boca. Bare right on Cty Rd 894Aa1 (Stampede Meadows Rd). Go 6.6 miles to Cty Rd. 261 (Dog Valley Rd.). Turn left, go 2 miles to campground.

Points of Interest -

Truckee is an historically rich mountain town. The Donner Party ordeal is Truckee's most famous historical event. See a lot of the old west and discover some excellent shopping and restaurants. Visit the National Automobile Museum and the Sheppard Fine Arts Gallery.

COLORADO

With many Colorado State Parks close to Interstate roads it is not surprising that most entries for this state come from the Colorado State Parks System.

Attracting over 11 million visitors per year, Colorado's 42 State Parks are a vital cornerstone in Colorado's economy and quality of life, offering some of the highest quality outdoor recreation destinations in the state. You can find those parks at their website -

http://parks.state.co.us/

State Park advanced reservations are

available at:

http:// coloradostateparks.reserveamerica.com/

A few notes you should be aware of -
1. Do not bring firewood from out of state.
2. All state camps require a $6-$8 per day per vehicle pass.

We generally found most National lands to be too remote and inaccessible for most sizable RVs.

The parks listed here vary in site size from 16 to over 363 with the 105 being the average number for the locations selected. Basic campground fees were typically in the $8 to $22 range.

[1] **Trinidad Lake State Park**
N37 09.003 W104 34.247
[2] **Lathrop State Park**
N37 36.071 W104 49.998
[3] **Lake Pueblo State Park**
N38 14.852 W104 43.375
[4] **Cheyenne Mountain State Park**
N38 44.283 W104 48.529
[5] **Cherry Creek State Park**
N39 38.838 W104 49.738
[6] **St. Vrain State Park**
N40 09.649 W104 59.912
[7] **Boyd Lake State Park**
N40 25.797 W105 03.509
[8] **Highline Lake State Park**
N39 16.192 W108 50.171

[9] **Saddlehorn Camp**
N39 07.277 W108 43.917
[10] **Rifle Gap State Park**
N39 38.096 W107 44.045
[11] **Gore Creek**
N39 37.631 W106 16.486
[12] **Heaton Bay**
N39 36.245 W106 04.689
[13] **Bear Creek Lake Park**
N39 39.219 W105 10.611
[14] **Jackson Lake State Park**
N40 22.725 W104 05.370
[15] **North Sterling State Park**
N40 45.830 W103 16.037D

NOTES:

Colorado

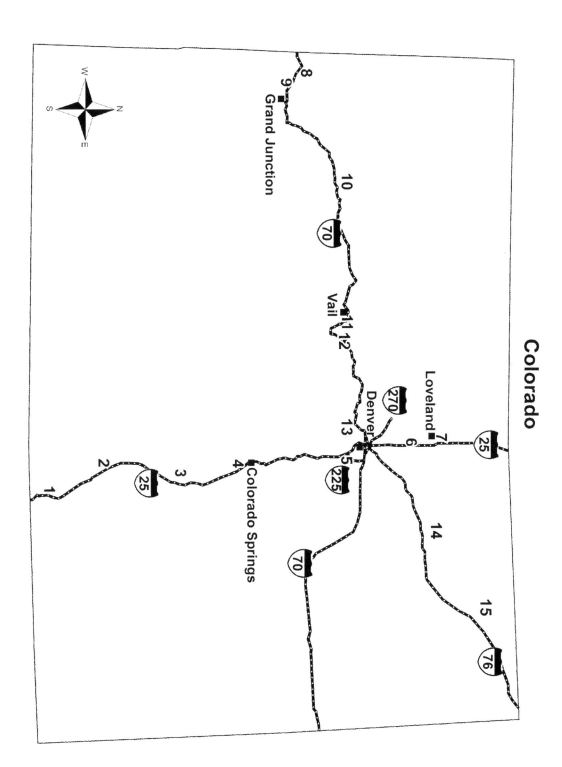

Exit 13
Trinidad Lake State Park [1]
West of Trinidad
State Rate: $14-$22

(719) 846-6951

http://parks.state.co.us/parks/
trinidadlake

Camp Accommodations

73 sites, 8 pull throughs, 5 ADA, utility options up to full hook-ups. Amenities include restrooms, showers, dump station,
potable water, picnic table, fire pit, firewood, pet friendly, Visitor's Center and
Interpretive Programs. Activity options are
biking, fishing, hiking, and wildlife viewing.

Directions

5 miles from I-25. From Exit 13 go east
on West Main St. to the first four-way stop,
turn left onto Nevada. At the next four-way
stop turn left on to Hwy 12 for 4 miles to
the Park.

Points of Interest -

The camp is a beautiful mountain setting
in southern Colorado, on a mesa approximately 200 feet above the lake. Ride the
free Trinidad trolley and discover winding
brick streets, historic architecture, art history, archaeology and museums. Musical
and gallery events occur year around.

Exit Walsenburg Hwy 160
Lathrop State Park [2]
West of Walsenburg
State Rate: $14-$18

(719) 738-2376

http://parks.state.co.us/parks/lathrop

Camp Accommodations

95 paved sites, many pull throughs, 4
handicapped, and all have electricity.
Amenities include restrooms, showers,
water fill-ups, dump station, picnic table,
fire pit, firewood available, & pet friendly.
There is a Visitor's Center & Interpretive
Programs. Activities include biking, fishing,
hiking, & wildlife viewing.

Directions

3 miles from I-25. From Exit Walsenburg
Hwy 160, go west on Hwy 160 for 3 miles
to the Park.

Points of Interest -

The Spanish Peaks tower over Colorado's
first State Park, which is close by Martin
and Horseshoe Lakes. Drive the scenic
'Highway of Legends,' which begins near
the campground and wends its way
through some of Colorado's most interesting historic locales and beautiful scenery.

Exits 94 or 101
Lake Pueblo State Park [3]
West of Pueblo
State Rate: $14-$22

(719) 561-9320

http://parks.state.co.us/Parks/
lakepueblo

Camp Accommodations

363 paved, spacious sites, many pull
throughs, and ADA sites, up to full hookups. Amenities include restrooms, showers, water fill-ups, dump station, picnic
table, fire pit, firewood, pet friendly, Visitor's Center & Interpretive Programs, biking, fishing, hiking, & wildlife viewing.

Directions

10 miles from I-25. From Exit 94 go
west/north on Hwy 45 for 5 miles to Hwy
96, then 4 miles west to park. From Exit
101 go 3 miles west on Hwy 50, then Hwy
45 south 4 miles to Hwy 96 & 4 miles west
to the park.

Points of Interest -

A popular park, but so large there is never
a crowded feeling. Pueblo, 'America's
Home of Heroes' (as proclaimed by the
Congress) hosts National Medal of Honor
Day. Pueblo is also home to the State Fair
and the National Hot Rod Association's
Rocky Mountain Street Rod Nationals.

Exit 135
Cheyenne Mountain State Park [4]
South of Colorado Springs
State Rate: $22

(719) 576-2016

http://parks.state.co.us/Parks/
cheyennemountain

Camp Accommodations

34 RV sites in a beautiful location, full hook-ups, 8 pull throughs, 1 ADA site. Amenities include restrooms, showers, picnic table, fire pit, firewood available, and pet friendly. There is a Visitor's Center & Interpretive Programs. Activities include biking, fishing, hiking, & wildlife viewing.

Directions

4 miles from I-25. From Exit 135 go west 2 miles on Hwy 83 to Hwy 115, then south 2 miles to Nelson Blvd (Fort Carson, Gate 1 is on the left). Turn right onto JL Ranch Heights and into the park.

Points of Interest -

Tour the Air Force Academy. Drive up Pikes Peak or to the Garden of the Gods Park, Seven Falls, or Cave Of The Winds. There are a number of military installations and the U. S. Olympic Training Center. Colorado Springs is home to many cultural, educational, & historical attractions.

Exits 199/200
Cherry Creek State Park [5]
In Southeast Denver
State Rate: $14-$22

(303) 690-1166

http://parks.state.co.us/parks/
cherrycreek/

Camp Accommodations

122 paved sites, 80+ feet long, 50+ pull throughs, 2 ADA, up to full hook-ups. Amenities include restrooms, showers, dump station, picnic table, fire pit, firewood, pet friendly, Visitor's Center and Interpretive Programs. Activity options are biking, fishing, hiking, and wildlife viewing.

Directions

5 miles from I-25. From Exit 199 or 200 go east on I-225 for 4 miles to Hwy 83 (S. Parker Rd.). Exit south and go 1 mile to the Park.

Points of Interest -

This modern park has a mature, grassy and tree landscape, lake and so many amenities you could stay busy with all the park has to offer. However, Denver beckons and is close by. The park can be a great base camp for exploring a city with so much to see and do.

Exit 240
St. Vrain State Park [6]
(aka Barbour Ponds)
East of Longmont
State Rate: $14-$22

(303) 678-9402

http://parks.state.co.us/Parks/StVrain

Camp Accommodations

78 RV sites, many waterfront, up to 40-42 feet long, primarily pull throughs, 1 ADA, and utility options up to full hook-ups. Amenities include restrooms, showers, dump station, picnic table, fire pit, firewood available, pet friendly. Activity options are biking, fishing, hiking, & wildlife viewing.

Directions

2 miles from I-25. From Exit 240 take Hwy 119 west for 1 mile then turn north and go 1 mile on County Rd. 7 and Weld County Rd. 24 1/2 to the Park.

Points of Interest -

You are a short drive from Boulder, Longmont, Loveland and Greeley. Boulder - Pearl St.; Longmont - The Community Theater; Loveland - bronze sculpture artists using three foundries, many art galleries and annual sculpture show; Greeley - James Michener Library.

Exit 257 of I-25
Boyd Lake State Park [7]
East of Loveland
State Rate: $20

(970) 669-1739

http://parks.state.co.us/Parks/
BoydLake/

Camp Accommodations

130 paved pull through, spacious electric sites along Boyd Lake, 2 ADA. Amenities include restrooms, showers, water fill-ups, dump station, picnic table, fire pit, firewood available, and pet friendly, Visitor's Center & Interpretive Programs. Activities include biking, fishing, hiking, & wildlife viewing.

Directions

6 miles from I-25. From Exit 257 go west on Hwy 34 for 4 miles to Madison Ave., then north for 2 miles to Cty Rd 24E. Turn east and follow signs to the park.

Points of Interest -

Loveland is a magnet for bronze sculpture artists. You'll find many art galleries and an annual sculpture show. The park is a good base for visiting Rocky Mountain National Park. In Estes Park, lunch at the magnificent Stanley Hotel, which inspired Steven King's 'The Shining.'

Exit 15 of I-70
Highline Lake State Park [8]
Northwest of Grand Junction
State Rate: $14

(970) 858-7208

http://parks.state.co.us/Parks/
highlinelake

Camp Accommodations

27 shaded, grassy sites, some 60+ feet long, many pull throughs, 1 ADA site, dry camping, potable water, dump station. Amenities include restrooms, showers, picnic table, fire pit, firewood available, pet friendly. Activity options are biking, fishing, hiking, and wildlife viewing.

Directions

8 miles from I-70. From Exit 15 go north on Hwy 139 for 6 miles to Q Rd. Turn west for just over a mile to 11 8/10 Rd., then north for a mile to the Park.

Points of Interest -

An ideal base for discovering the Grand Junction area. Bird watchers should note that The Audubon Society has designated the park an important bird area. Enjoy a dramatic red rock landscape & the wine country environment of Grand Junction with great shops, restaurants, & galleries.

Exits 19 of I-70
Saddlehorn Camp [9]
Colorado National Monument
West of Grand Junction
NM Rate: $10

(970) 858-3617

http://www.nps.gov/colm/
planyourvisit/campgrounds.htm

Camp Accommodations
There are 80 sites for RVs up to 40 feet, one is handicapped, some pull-throughs, no reservations. There is self-registration at the entrance. This is a dry camping destination. Amenities include restrooms, water (during the summer), picnic table, stand-up grill, and is pet friendly.

Directions

7 miles from I-70. From Exit 19 go south on Hwy 340 for 3 miles to the Park entrance at Rimrock Dr. Turn right and follow the road 4 miles to the campground, which is near the Visitor's Center.

Points of Interest -

Deep canyons, red rock & stone sculptures characterize this spectacle. Colorado National Monument is one of the grand landscapes of the American West. Towering monoliths exist within a vast plateau-and-canyon panorama. Climb to the top of Independence Monument - 450 feet high!

Exit 90
Rifle Gap State Park [10]
West of Glenwood Springs
State Rate: $14-$22

(970) 625-1607

http://parks.state.co.us/Parks/
RifleGap/

Camp Accommodations

88 spacious sites, many waterfront, 80+ feet long on concrete, pull throughs, 6 ADA, up to full hook-ups. Amenities include restrooms, showers, dump station, picnic table, fire pit, Visitor's Center, firewood, pet friendly, Interpretive Programs, biking, fishing, hiking, & wildlife viewing.

Directions

9 miles from I-70. From Exit 90 take Hwy 13 for 3 miles north through Rifle and to Hwy 325. Turn right on Hwy 325 and go 6 miles to Rifle Gap Rd. on left, into the Park.

Points of Interest -

Rifle is one of the top outdoor sports towns in the country. Enjoy the world's largest hot springs swimming pool in Glenwood Springs. You'll find both the Roaring Fork and Colorado Rivers so river rafting is very popular; or just enjoy lunch on the veranda of the historic Hotel Colorado.

Exit 180
Gore Creek [11]
East of Vail
White River NF Rate: $16
America/Beautiful Rate: $8

(970) 827- 5715

www.forestcamping.com/dow/
rockymtn/wrcmp.htm#gore creek

Camp Accommodations

22 wooded, gravel sites, up to 55 feet long, some pull throughs. Sites are spacious but access turns are tight for bigger RVs, no reservations, a dry camping destination. Amenities include vault toilet, fire rings, tables, water spigot, & pet friendly.

Directions

3 miles from I-70. From Exit 180 (East Vail Entrance) turn south and follow Bighorn Rd. southeast, go 3 miles to campground sign. Turn left into campground at Gore Creek Campground.

Points of Interest -

The closest camp to Vail. Vail Valley, home to Vail & Beaver Creek ski resorts, is a beautiful destination. The streets of Vail are closed to autos. You can walk or ride the free shuttle in the midst of an alpine village with world class views, shops, restaurants, and entertainment.

Exit 203
Heaton Bay [12]
Between Frisco and Dillon
White River NF Rate: $17
America/Beautiful Rate: $9

(970) 513-6669

http://www.recreation.gov/

Camp Accommodations

There are 59 paved sites for RVs, some over 90 feet long, many with electricity, one is handicapped, with some pull-throughs, and reservations available. Amenities include ADA restrooms, water spigots, firewood available, picnic table, grill, and is pet friendly.

Directions

1 mile from I-70. From Exit 203 on the south side of I-70, take County Rd. 7 (Dillon Dam Rd.) northeast 1 mile to the campground on the east (right) side of the road.

Points of Interest -

The towns of Frisco, Dillon, and Breckenridge are close, as are the ski areas of Copper Mountain, Keystone & others. The area is a skier's delight but there is much to see and do year around with unlimited sightseeing, shopping, large outlet malls, restaurants and après-ski destinations.

Exit 251 of I-70
Bear Creek Lake Park [13]
Southwest Denver
City of Lakewood Park Rate: $18

(303) 697-6159

http://www.lakewood.org/comres/
page.cfm?
ID=641&BearCreekLakePark/

Camp Accommodations

There are 47 sites, up to 50 feet   long, mostly pull through sites for RVs, all with electric hook-ups, no reservations. Amenities include restrooms, water spigots, dump station, showers, picnic table, stand-up grill, and is pet friendly.

Directions

6 miles from I-70. From Exit 251 go south on Hwy 470 for 5 miles to Hwy 8 (Morrison Rd.). Exit east to the Bear Creek Lake Regional Park, immediately on the right.

Points of Interest -

Very convenient to Bandimere Speedway and Red Rocks Amphitheatre, a must visit location. Consider visiting William Frederick Hayden Park on Green Mountain. Denver also beckons and is close by. The park can be a great base camp for exploring a city with so much to see and do.

Exit 66 of I-76
Jackson Lake State Park [14]
✦ **North of Wiggins**
State Rate: $14-$22

(970) 645-2551

http://parks.state.co.us/parks/jacksonlake

Camp Accommodations

228 large, electric RV sites, some waterfront, some shaded, up to 60+ feet long, ample pull throughs, 1 ADA site. Amenities include restrooms, showers, dump station, picnic table, fire pit, Visitor's Center, firewood, pet friendly. Activities are Interpretive Programs, biking, fishing, hiking, & wildlife viewing.

Directions

11 miles from I-76. From Exit 66 go north on Hwy 39 (becomes Cty Rd 5) for 7.6 miles, then west on Cty Rd. Y5/10 for 1.5 miles to Cty Rd 3, then north for 1.5 miles into the Park.

Points of Interest -

In Ft. Morgan take the Pioneer Trail Scenic & Historic Byway north to Pawnee Buttes, a key setting in James Michener's novel, *Centennial.* Hike the trails of Pawnee National Grassland. See the Rainbow Arch Bridge just north of town, a rare example of this style of bridge architecture.

Exit 125 of I-76
North Sterling State Park [15]
North of Sterling
State Rate: $14-$22

(970) 522-3657

http://parks.state.co.us/Parks/
northsterling

Camp Accommodations

135 large, dry or electric sites, many waterfront, 90+ feet long, ample pull throughs, 1 ADA. Amenities include restrooms, showers, dump station, picnic table, fire pit, Visitor's Center, firewood, pet friendly, Interpretive Programs, biking, fishing, hiking, & wildlife viewing.

Directions

21 mi. from I-76. From Exit 125 go west on Chestnut 1.6 mi. Turn right at 3rd (Hwy 138), go north, merging with Broadway. Go 9 mi. to Hwy 113. Turn left for 1.7 mi. to Cty Rd. 46. Go west for 8 mi. to the 'T.' Turn right 0.2 mi. to the Park on the left.

Points of Interest -

Enjoy majestic bluffs & expansive views of the high plains. Sterling, the 'Queen City of the Plains,' is close by the Overland Trail and is home to The Overland Tail Museum. Sterling, each summer, hosts the annual Logan County Fair, a typical old-time county fair.

CONNECTICUT

There are 17 public campgrounds in total in Connecticut, 14 of which are State Parks or Forests. The State lands are overseen by the Connecticut Department of Environmental Protection (DEP).

DEP regulations state -

TRAILERS AND RV's EXCEEDING 35' IN LENGTH ARE NOT PERMITTED IN STATE PARKS.

(DEP) has a toll free telephone (1-877-668-2267) and on-line system to reserve campsites (Reserve America) at state park and forest campgrounds. There is a fee for all online reservations.

The official camping season is April 17 - September 30. However, some campgrounds are open on a restricted basis prior to Memorial Day Weekend or after Labor Day. Pets are prohibited in State Park camping areas. Pets are permitted at the Salt Rock Campground, and State Forest campgrounds. Fires are permitted in designated fireplaces. Ground fires are strictly prohibited at all State campgrounds. Except as specifically authorized, no firearms, archery equipment or other weapons may be possessed in any campground or recreation area.

RHODE ISLAND

There are 6 public Campgrounds in total in Rhode Island, 5 of which are State Parks, Ponds or Recreation Areas. The Rhode Island Department of Environmental Management (RI DEM) provides oversight.

The RI DEM uses ReserveAmerica to provide its online reservation system. There is a fee for this. Reservations are also available through the call center or walk-in camping. The parks are all pet friendly.

Non-resident camping fees are:

- Water/Electric-$25
- Full Hook-up-$35
- Second Car-$6

---

[1] West Thompson Lake (CT)
N41 57.255 W71 53.651

[2] Fishermen's State Park (RI)
N41 22.773 W71 29.290
[3] George Washington Campground (RI)
N41 55.185 W71 45.298

NOTES:

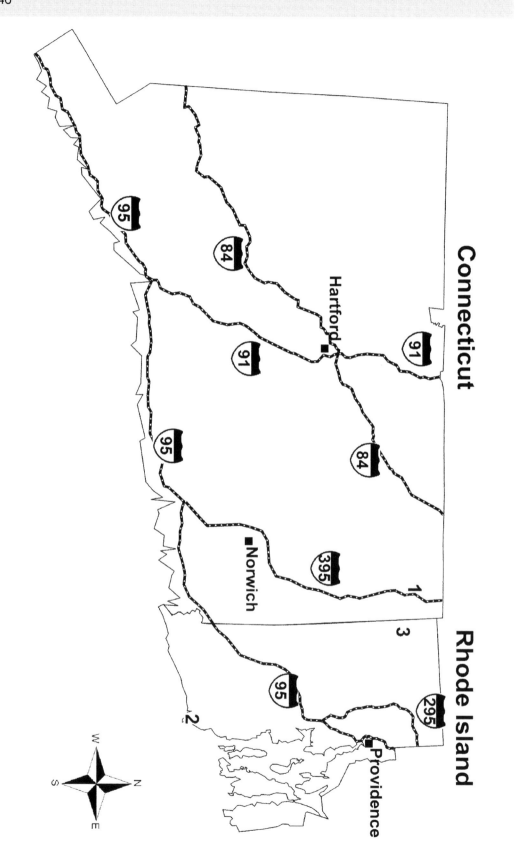

Exit 99 of I-395 (Connecticut)
West Thompson Lake [1]
West of Thompson
COE Rate: $15-$30
America/Beautiful Rate: $8-$15

(860) 923-3121

www.reserveamerica.com/campground

Camp Accommodations

24 shady RV sites up to 45 feet, near West Thompson Lake, with water/electricity, 1 handicapped. Amenities include ADA restrooms, showers, potable water, dump station, picnic table, fire pit, firewood available, and pet friendly. Activity options are biking, fishing, and hiking.

Directions

4 miles from I-395. From Exit 99 go east on Hwy 200 one mile, then south on Hwy 193 for 2 miles. Go north on Reardon Rd. 1/2 mile to the Park on the left.

Points of Interest -

Race car enthusiasts should visit Thompson, which has the highest banked race track, Thompson International Speedway, in New England. The speedway holds one of the biggest race programs in New England - "The World Series of Auto Racing", 14 divisions and 600 cars will show up.

Exit 9 of I-95 (Rhode Island)
Fishermen's State Park [2]
South of Warwick
State Rates: See Page 47

(401) 789-8374

http://
rhodeislandstate-
parks.reserveamerica.com/

Camp Accommodations

147 ample and shaded RV sites, many near water, up to 50 feet long, many pull throughs, with full hook ups. Amenities include, restrooms, picnic tables, showers, fireplaces, firewood for sale, fishing and swimming nearby.

Directions

22 miles from I-95. From Exit 9 go 10 miles south on Hwy 4 to Hwy 1, then south for 8 miles, to Rte. 108, then south 4 miles along Hwy 108 to the Park.

Points of Interest -

Visitors will find neatly trimmed grass and tree lined paths. You will be close to popular state beach areas like Roger Wheeler, Salty Brine, and Scarborough. You are a short drive from tourist mecca's such as Newport & Wickford. The camp is 1 mile from the Block Island Ferry Dock.

Exit 7 of I-295 (Rhode Island)
George Washington Campground [3]
Northwest of Providence
State Rates: See Page 47

(401) 568-2013

http://
rhodeislandstate-
parks.reserveamerica.com/

Camp Accommodations

45 ample, shaded, gravel sites, many near water, up to 45 feet, 1 pull through. This is a dry camping park. Amenities include, restrooms, picnic tables, showers, and water spigots, fishing, swimming, boating, hiking, biking, and watchable wildlife.

Directions

14 miles from I-295. From Exit 7 follow Hwy 44 (Putnam Pike) west approximately 14 miles to the camp entrance on your right.

Points of Interest -

Providence is a top travel destination. Visit Roger Williams Park, comprised of waterways, walks, a Botanical Center, a Carousel Village, and Museum of Natural History and Planetarium. History buffs will be attracted to rich and varied architecture, which ranges from Colonial to Modern.

DELAWARE

Camping is available at five Delaware state parks. The campgrounds are open from March 1 through November 30. You can learn more at the State Parks website -
www.destateparks.com

You may make a reservation up to 7 months or as little as 1 day in advance of your visit. Reservations at -

http://www.delaware.reserveworld.com/ index.cfm? CFID=3654297&CFTOKEN=51998137

All of the campgrounds provide drinking water outlets, modern shower and sanitary facilities, and sewage dumping stations. Campsites are equipped with a picnic table and may include a fire ring (campfire regulations). Many have electric and water hookups.

MARYLAND

The National Geographic Magazine calls Maryland's extraordinary public lands "America in Miniature." Maryland has the Appalachian Mountains, Chesapeake Bay, marshland on the Eastern Shore, and the Atlantic Ocean. You can learn more at -

http://www.dnr.state.md.us/ publiclands/pfwma2.html

There are 25 State Parks that have campgrounds, of which 11 have sites which will accommodate RVs of 35 feet or more and 16 of which have hook ups, and reservations are available. Most of Maryland's State Forests and National Parks supply equipment rentals for boating, canoeing, and kayaking, Camping season is generally mid-April through mid-October.

---

[1] **Lums Pond State Park (DE)**
      N39 32.898 W75 43.090
[2] **New Germany State Park (MD)**
      N39 37.839 W79 07.721
[3] **Rocky Gap State Park (MD)**
      N39 41.755 W78 39.047
[4] **Cunningham Falls State Park (MD)**
      N39 34.925 W77 26.167

[5] **Patapsco Valley-Hollofield State Park (MD)**
      N39 17.692 W76 47.243
[6] **Greenbelt Park (DC)**
      N38 59.748 W76 53.708
[7] **Elk Neck State Park (MD)**
      N39 28.829 W75 59.103
[8] **Little Bennett County Campground (MD)**
      N39 14.793 W77 17.453

NOTES:

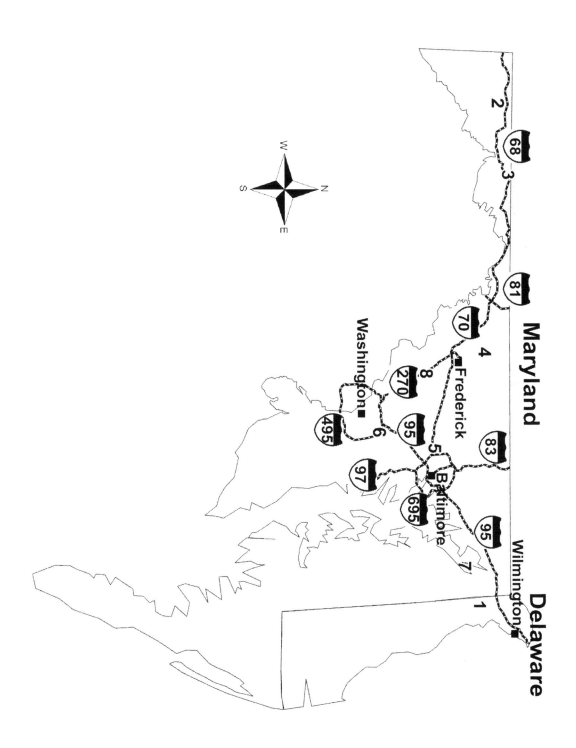

Exit 1 of I-95 (Delaware)
Lums Pond State Park [1]
South of Glasgow
State Rate: $25-$28

(302) 368-6989

http://www.destateparks.com/
camping/lums-pond/index.asp#cnorth

Camp Accommodations

There are 68 shaded sites adjoining Lums Pond, some waterfront, which will accommodate 40-45 foot RVs, some pull throughs, sites are well spaced, and 6 have electric hookups. Amenities include showers, dump station, picnic tables, grills, fishing, biking, hiking, and pet friendly.

Directions

8 miles from I-95. From Exit 1 take Hwy 896/301 south for 6.2 miles. Turn east (left) on Hwy 71 (Red Lion Rd.) for 1.4 miles to the Park entrance.

Points of Interest -

The camp is within the Brandywine Valley, where the Du Pont mansions and gardens at Longwood, Winterthur, Hagley and Nemours attract millions of visitors from around the world. The camp is also a good stopover for those going down the eastern shore.

Exit 22 of I-68 (Maryland)
New Germany State Park [2]
West of Frostburg
State Rate: $20

(301) 895-5453

http://www.dnr.state.md.us/
publiclands/western/newgermany.html

Camp Accommodations

39 reservable, dry camp sites, up to 35 feet, plus 9 overflow campsites. Amenities include dump station, picnic table, fire ring, grills, swimming, boat rental, camp fire programs, snack bar, nature center, fishing, hiking, historic interests. NO pets, minimum stay is 2 nights.

Directions

5 miles from I-68. From Exit 22 go south on Chestnut Ridge Rd. for 3 miles to New Germany Rd. Continue south (left) for 2 miles to the Park.

Points of Interest -

Located in the forested peaks and valleys of the Blue Ridge and Allegheny Mountains. Visit Frostburg, a historic main street community. Ride the Western Maryland Scenic Railroad or tour the Thrasher Carriage Museum, where costumed docents transport you back in time.

Exit 50 of I-68 (Maryland)
Rocky Gap State Park [3]
Northeast of Cumberland
State Rate: $25-$30

(301) 722-1480

http://www.dnr.state.md.us/
publiclands/western/rockygap.html

Camp Accommodations

278 wooded, lakeside sites, up to 45 feet, some ADA, electricity. Amenities include a dump station, potable water, picnic table, fire ring, bathhouses with hot water, nature center, private swimming beach, camp store, biking, hiking, canoeing/kayaking, Interpretive Programs, pet friendly.

Directions

Adjoins I-68. From Exit 50 go north directly into the Park entrance.

Points of Interest -

The Chesapeake and Ohio Canal's towpath is a favorite of hikers, joggers, and bicyclists. Go on the 'All Aboard For Cumberland' National Register of Historic Places Travel Itinerary, which explores Cumberland's past through 27 historic places listed in the National Register.

Exit 52 of I-70 (Maryland)
Cunningham Falls State Park [4]
North of Frederick
State Rate: $25-$30

(301) 271-7574

http://www.dnr.state.md.us/
publiclands/western/
cunninghamfalls.html

Camp Accommodations

171 gravel sites, up to 35 feet, electricity, some ADA, in two camping areas (Manor and Houck). Amenities include dump station, showers, potable water, restrooms, table, fire ring. A camp store offers groceries, camping supplies and souvenirs.

Directions

13 **or** 19 miles from I-70. From Exit 52 go north on Hwy 15 for 13 miles to the **Manor Camp** crossover left turn. **Or** continue 3 more miles to Thurmont, turn west on Hwy 77 for 4 miles, then left on Catoctin Hollow Rd. to **Houck Camp**.

Points of Interest -

In the Catoctin Mountains the camp area is known for its history and scenic beauty, as well as its 78-foot waterfall. In Frederick discover a great American main street. Scenic byways lead to wineries & orchards. You are an hour from Washington, Baltimore, Gettysburg and Antietam.

Exit 87 of I-70 (Maryland)
Patapsco Valley-Hollofield State Park [5]
West Side of Baltimore
State Rate: $25

(410) 461-5005

http://www.dnr.state.md.us/
publiclands/central/
patapscovalley.html

Camp Accommodations
There are 73 shaded, reservable, dry camp sites, some for RVs up to 40 feet, some electric hook ups, some handicapped. Amenities include dump station, showers, potable water, restrooms, table, fire ring, pet friendly.

Directions

4 miles from I-70. **If your RV is over 11' 1" high, you must enter the park by the Hwy 40 east-bound entrance.** From Exit 87 go south for 2 miles on Hwy 29. Turn east on Hwy 40 for 2 miles to the park.

Points of Interest -

A great location for exploring Baltimore and area attractions. See the Elkridge Furnace and forge in the park. In Baltimore see baseball at Camden Yards or tour the inner harbor of Washington. Go to Ellicott City and visit the B&O Railroad Museum - The Birthplace of American Railroading!

Exit 23 of I-95 (District of Columbia)
Greenbelt Park [6]
Northwest Side of
Washington D. C.
NP Rate: $16
America/Beautiful Rate: $8

(301) 344-3948

www.recreation.gov/

Camp Accommodations
There are 100 shaded, reservable, dry camp sites, some for RVs up to 35 feet, some pull throughs, 1 ADA site. Amenities include dump station, showers, restrooms, hiking, biking, and is pet friendly.

Directions

1 mile from I-95. From Exit 23 take Hwy 201 (Kenilworth Avenue) south 1/2 mile. Turn left on Hwy 193 (Greenbelt Rd.) 1/4 mile to the park entrance on the right.

Points of Interest -

The camp is known for its safe, peaceful surroundings in an urban setting, plus great National Park Service hospitality. The campground is located in suburban Maryland just ten miles from Washington, D.C. The camp is 1.5 mi. from the Washington D.C. Metro Rapid Transit System.

Exit 100 of I-95 (Maryland)
Elk Neck State Park [7]
South of North East Town
State Rate: $25-$35 (Seniors , 62+, camp half price, Sun-Thur)

(410) 287-5333

http://www.dnr.state.md.us/
publiclands/central/elkneck.html

Camp Accommodations

268 shaded sites, up to 40 feet, some full hook ups, several ADA, pull throughs. Amenities include dump station, showers, potable water, restrooms, table, fire ring, canoeing, hiking, biking. A camp store offers groceries, pet friendly.

Directions

12 miles from I-95. From Exit 100 take Hwy 272 south, through the Town of North East, for 12 miles to the Park.

Points of Interest -

Located on a peninsula with beaches, marshlands & bluffs. Walk to the scenic Turkey Point Lighthouse with a view of the Elk River and Chesapeake Bay. Downtown North East offers antique shops, stores, & restaurants. St. Mary Anne's Episcopal Church dates to the 1700's.

Exit 18 of I-270 (Maryland)
Little Bennett County Campground [8]
South of Frederick
CP Rate: $31

(301) 528-3430

www.montgomeryparks.org/
enterprise/park_facilities/
little_bennett/
little_bennett_campground.shtm

Camp Accommodations

91 shaded, gravel, large, reservable sites, some 70+ feet, 25 electric, some pull throughs, 2 ADA. Amenities include dump station, showers, restrooms, table, fire ring, hiking, biking, closed winters, is pet friendly.

Directions

2 miles from I-270. From Exit 18 go northeast on Hwy 121 (Clarksburg Rd.) 1/2 mile to Hwy 355 (Frederick Rd.). Turn left, go 1 mile to the park entrance on the right.

Points of Interest -

Civil War sites & historic monuments are nearby. If you are planning a visit to the Nation's Capital, be sure to ask staff for information on public transportation, including Metrorail service. In Frederick discover a great American main street. Scenic byways lead to wineries & orchards.

There are 160 State Parks, many of which will accommodate RVs. The State Park System represents over 50% of public campgrounds in the state, the balance being primarily county parks. State Park RV campsites range in length from 20 to 76 feet. Most campsites maintain a soft gravel pad and each is equipped with water and electricity. Most parks have a centrally located dump station. Some parks offer pull through and waterfront locations.

Florida state parks are open from 8 a.m. until sundown 365 days a year. Pets are welcome overnight in all the camping parks except Oscar Scherer State Park, where restrictions have been placed on some sites.

Camping fees range from $16.00 to $42.00 per night.

Visitors to Florida State Parks can reserve campsites as much as 11 months in advance, by dialing 1-800 326-3521. If you prefer, you can make your reservation online at:

www.ReserveAmerica.com

Reservations in advance are always a good idea in Florida!

[1] **Lake Louisa State Park**
N28 27.386 W81 43.263
[2] **Wekiwa Springs State Park**
N28 42.568 W81 27.768
[3] **Blue Springs State Park**
N28 57.142 W81 20.010
[4] **Big Lagoon State Park**
N30 19.313 W87 24.222
[5] **Blackwater River State Park**
N30 42.483 W86 52.956
[6] **Rocky Bayou State Park**
N30 29.762 W86 25.967
[7] **Falling Waters State Park**
N30 43.783 W85 31.683
[8] **Florida Caverns State Park**
N30 48.507 W85 12.742
[9] **Three Rivers State Park**
N30 44.362 W84 56.211
[10] **Suwannee River State Park**
N30 22.650 W83 09.952
[11] **Ocean Pond**
N30 14.364 W82 25.120
[12] **John Pennekamp Coral Reef State Park**
N25 07.646 W80 24.575
[13] **Lone Pine Key**
N25 25.033 W80 38.814
[14] **Markham Park**
N26 07.601 W80 21.590

[15] **Collier-Seminole State Park**
N25 59.534 W81 35.390
[16] **Koreshan State Historic Site Park**
N26 25.868 W81 48.885
[17] **Lake Manatee State Park**
N27 28.514 W82 20.920
[18] **Alafia River State Park**
N27 46.867 W82 08.734
[19] **Hillsborough River State Park**
N28 08.674 W82 13.463
[20] **Lake Griffin Park**
N28 51.450 W81 54.182
[21] **Paynes Prairie Preserve State Park**
N29 31.146 W82 17.892
[22] **O'Leno State Park**
N29 55.181 W82 36.514
[23] **Stephen Foster Folk Culture Center State**
N30 19.794 W82 45.616
[24] **St. Lucie South**
N27 06.680 W80 17.041
[25] **Sebastian Inlet State Park**
N27 51.366 W80 26.779
[26] **Jetty Park Campground**
N28 24.330 W80 35.693
[27] **Anastasia State Park**
N29 52.835 W81 17.170
[28] **Fort Clinch State Park**
N30 40.077 W81 26.056

NOTES:

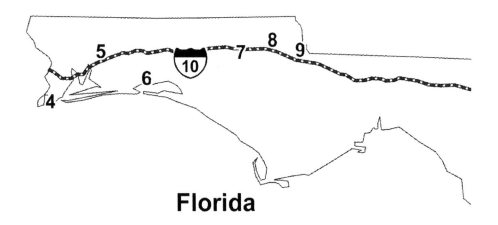

Florida

55

Florida

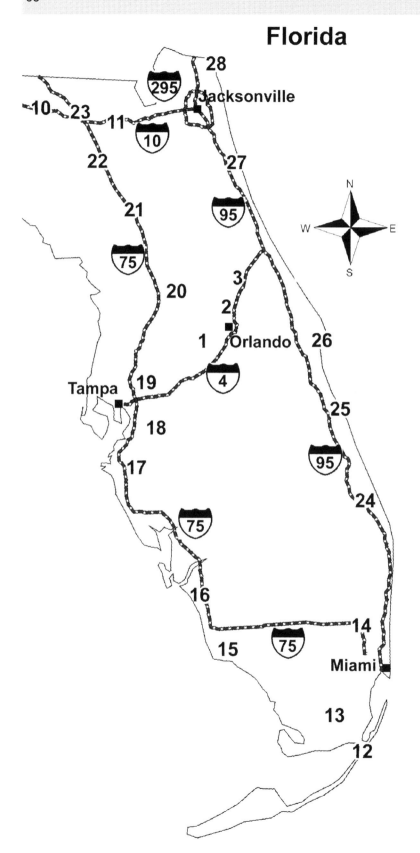

Exit 55
Lake Louisa State Park [1]
West of Orlando
State Rate: $24

(352) 394-3969

http://www.floridastateparks.org/
lakelouisa/default.cfm

Camp Accommodations

54 sites, up to 70 feet, 16 pull throughs, with electric/water, some sewer, along paved roads, 3 are handicapped, many waterfront. Amenities include ADA restrooms, showers, dump station, camp host, picnic tables, grills, firewood, fishing, biking, hiking, watchable wildlife, pet friendly.

Directions

16 miles from I-4. From Exit 55 go north on Hwy 27/25 for 16 miles to the entrance on the left.

Points of Interest -

The Park is noted for its beautiful lakes, rolling hills, and scenic landscapes. Lake Louisa is in a chain of 13 lakes connected by the Palatlakaha River. If you park at the highest park point at night you may see the fireworks shows from Walt Disney World Theme Park near by.

Exit 94
Wekiwa Springs State Park [2]
North of Orlando
State Rate: $24

(407) 884-2008

http://www.floridastateparks.org/
wekiwasprings/default.cfm

Camp Accommodations

54 well spaced, shaded sites with electric/water along paved roads, 50 feet long, 2 are handicapped. Amenities include ADA restrooms, showers, dump station, camp host, picnic tables, grills, firewood, fishing, biking, hiking, swimming, watchable wildlife, butterfly garden, & pet friendly.

Directions

5 miles from I-4. From Exit 94 go west on Hwy 434 for 1/2 mile. Turn right on Wekiva Springs Rd. and go 4 miles to the entrance on the right.

Points of Interest -

At the Wekiwa River headwaters, vistas offer a glimpse of what Central Florida looked like when Timucuan Indians inhabited the area. You should see wildlife in the park, which Rvers will enjoy. You are located less than an hour from most Central Florida attractions, many in Orlando.

Exit 114
Blue Springs State Park [3]
West of Orange City
State Rate: $24

(386) 775-3663

http://www.floridastateparks.org/
bluespring/default.cfm

Camp Accommodations

Park among Sand Pine Scrub in one of 46 sites with electric, up to 45 feet, 2 are ADA. Amenities include ADA restrooms, showers, dump station, water faucets, convenience store, picnic tables, grills, firewood, fishing, biking, hiking, swimming, watchable wildlife, and pet friendly.

Directions

7 miles from I-4. From Exit 114 go northwest on Hwy 472 for 3 miles. Turn south on Hwy 17/92 for 2 miles to West French Avenue (in Orange City). Turn west (right) about 2 miles to the Park.

Points of Interest -

Manatee viewing is possible in winter. Visit the 1872 Thursby House, that sits atop an ancient Timucuan shell midden (centuries of Timucuan oyster shell and debris accumulation). The House is a historic plantation home, now a museum. It was an early site for Florida orange crop shipping.

Exit 7
Big Lagoon State Park [4]
South of Pensacola
State Rate: $20

(850) 492-1595

http://www.floridastateparks.org/biglagoon/
default.cfm

Camp Accommodations

68 sites with electric/water, 50+ feet long, 2 are handicapped. Amenities include ADA restrooms, showers, dump station, water faucets, campground host, picnic tables, grills, firewood, fishing, biking, hiking, swimming, watchable wildlife, and pet friendly.

Directions

20 miles from I-10. From Exit 7 go south on Hwy 297 for 3.2 miles to Hwy 90. Turn right, go 1.1 miles to Hwy 173 (Blue Angel Pkwy). Turn left, proceed for 10 miles to Hwy 292 (Sorrento Rd). Turn right, go 5 miles to the Gulf Beach Hwy. Turn left, go 1.2 miles to the Park.

Points of Interest -

Enjoy the Great Florida Birding Trail. Visit Pensacola, America's first settlement. The flags of five nations have flown over the city in past centuries, their cultural and historic influence remains evident to this day. As the Cradle of Naval Aviation, Pensacola also boasts a proud military history.

Exits 31 or 45
Blackwater River State Park [5]
Northeast of Pensacola
State Rate: $20

(850) 983-5363

http://www.floridastateparks.org/
blackwaterriver/

Camp Accommodations

There are 27 shaded sites, up to 50 feet long, with full hook ups, along paved roads, 3 are handicapped. Amenities include ADA restrooms, showers, dump station, camp host, picnic tables, grills, firewood, fishing, biking, hiking, nature programs, watchable wildlife, pet friendly.

Directions

11 or 13 mi. from I-10. East bound, Exit 31. Go 1 mi. north on Hwy 87 then east on Hwy 90 for 7 mi. to Harold. Go north on Deaton Bridge Rd 3 mi. to Park. West bound, Exit 45. Go 1/2 mi. north to Hwy 90, then west 9 mi. to Harold. Turn north as noted above.

Points of Interest -

The park is certified as a Registered State Natural Feature - possessing exceptional value in illustrating the natural history of Florida. The river is one of the purest sand-bottom rivers in the nation. This is a popular park for swimming, fishing, and canoe/kayaking.

Exits 56 or 70
Rocky Bayou State Park [6]
East of Niceville
State Rate: $16

(850) 833-9144

www.floridastateparks.org/rockybayou/
default.cfm

Camp Accommodations

38 spacious, shaded sites, up to 50 feet, water views, electric/water, paved roads, 4 are ADA on concrete. Amenities include ADA restrooms, showers, dump station, camp host, picnic tables, grills, firewood, ice, fishing, biking, hiking, swimming, watchable wildlife, pet friendly.

Directions

20 or 21 miles from I-10. East bound, Exit 56, take Hwy 85 south 15.7 mi. Go east on Hwy 20 for 4.3 miles to Park. West bound, Exit 70, take Hwy 285 south for 17.4 mi. Go east on Hwy 20 for 3.4 mi. to the Park.

Points of Interest -

See Destin, on a peninsula separating the Gulf of Mexico from Choctawhatchee Bay & experience Florida's Emerald Coast. Originally a fishing village, it is a popular tourist destination. The city claims the biggest Florida fishing fleet & is known for white beaches & emerald-colored waters.

Exit 120
Falling Waters State Park [7]
South of Chipley
State Rate: $18

(850) 638-6130

http://www.floridastateparks.org/
fallingwaters/default.cfm

Camp Accommodations

19 pine forest shaded sites, up to 45 feet, with electric/water, along paved roads, 5 are pull throughs. Amenities include ADA restrooms, showers, dump station, camp host, picnic tables, grills, firewood, fishing, biking, hiking, nature programs, watchable wildlife, and is pet friendly.

Directions

2.5 miles from I-10. From Exit 120 go south on Hwy 77 for 0.7 mile. Turn east on State Park Rd for 1.8 mile to the Park.

Points of Interest -

The park has a beautiful waterfall (the highest in Florida) and lots of trails to explore. Impressive trees and fern-covered sinkholes line Sink Hole Trail, the boardwalk that leads campers to the waterfall. Also enjoy beautiful native and migrating butterflies in the butterfly garden.

Exit 142
Florida Caverns State Park [8]
North of Marianna
State Rate: $20

(850) 82-9598

www.floridastateparks.org/floridacaverns/
default.cfm

Camp Accommodations

28 wooded, well spaced sites, up to 40 feet, with electric/water, paved roads, 2 ADA. Amenities include ADA restrooms, showers, dump station, camp host, picnic tables, grills, firewood, Visitors Center, 9 hole golf course, fishing, biking, hiking, swimming, watchable wildlife, pet friendly.

Directions

8 miles from I-10. From Exit 142, turn north on Hwy 71 for 2 miles to Hwy 90. Go west 3 miles to Hwy 166 (Jefferson St, then Caverns Rd). Go north for 3 miles to Park.

Points of Interest -

Find the only Florida state park offering cave tours to the public. The cave has impressive formations of stalactites, stalagmites, soda straws, flowstones, & draperies. Visit Marianna, the city that dishes out an ice cream cone for under $2. Visit historic Russ House.

Exit 158
Three Rivers State Park [9]
West of Tallahassee
State Rate: $16

(850) 482-9006

http://www.floridastateparks.org/
threerivers/default.cfm

Camp Accommodations

26 shaded sites, up to 50 feet, electric/water, 3 pull throughs, gravel roads, 3 ADA/paved, turns a bit tight. Amenities include ADA restrooms, showers, dump station, camp host, picnic tables, grills, firewood, fishing, biking, hiking, nature programs, watchable wildlife, pet friendly.

Directions

8 miles from I-10. From Exit 158 go 5 miles north on Hwy 286 into Sneads to Hwy 90. Go west 0.5 miles to River Road. Turn north for 2.2 miles to the park.

Points of Interest -

Looking for trees dripping with Spanish moss, lovely shrubbery, shade trees, a great view of the water, wildlife and birds? This camp is for you. Situated on Lake Seminole where the Chattahoochee and Flint Rivers converge, this is a great camp to relax, walk, fish, read, or take that nap.

Exit 275 of I-10
Suwannee River State Park [10]
West of Live Oak
State Rate: $22

(386) 362-2746

http://www.floridastateparks.org/
suwanneeriver/default.cfm

Camp Accommodations

There are 24 shaded sites, up to 55 feet long, with electric/water, 2 pull throughs, along gravel roads, 1 ADA/paved site. Amenities include ADA restrooms, showers, dump station, camp host, picnic tables, grills, firewood and ice, hiking, pet friendly.

Directions

5 miles from I-10. From Exit 275 go northwest on Hwy 10/90 for 6 miles to the park.

Points of Interest -

Historic landmarks show the importance of the Suwannee River to Florida history. Along the Suwannee, long mounds of earthworks built during the Civil War guard incursions by Union Navy gunboats. Remnants include one of the State's oldest cemeteries, and a paddle-wheel shaft.

Exit 324 of I-10
Ocean Pond [11]
North of Olustee
Osceola NF Rate: $8-$16
America/Beautiful Rate: $4-$8

(386) 752-2577
www.forestcamping.com/dow/
southern/osccmp.htm#ocean%20pond

Camp Accommodations

67 shaded, paved, waterfront sites close to Ocean Pond, up to 65 feet long, many with electric/water. Amenities include ADA restrooms and showers, dump station, potable water, interpretive trail, fishing, boating, sailing, swimming, pet friendly.

Directions

9 miles from I-10. From Exit 324 go 6.5 miles east on Hwy 10/90 to Cty Rd. 250/266 (Forest Rd.), just before Olustee. Turn north for 2.5 miles to the camp.

Points of Interest -

Visit the Olustee Battlefield Historic State Park, which commemorates Florida's largest Civil War battle in 1864. Over 10,000 cavalry, infantry, and artillery troops fought a five-hour battle in a pine forest near Olustee. The Battlefield Park and Interpretive Center are open daily.

Exit 5 of I-75
John Pennekamp Coral Reef
State Park [12]
North of Key Largo
State Rate: $36

(305) 451-1202
www.floridastateparks.org/pennekamp/

Camp Accommodations

42 shaded sites, up to 55 feet long, 3 ADA, some are narrow, with electric/water, along paved roads. Amenities include ADA restrooms, showers, dump station, camp host, picnic tables, grills, Visitor's Center, Interpretive Programs, fishing, biking, hiking, swimming, pet friendly.

Directions

25 mi. from Florida's Turnpike. From Exit 5 of I-75 go south on the Florida's Turnpike for 39.5 miles to its terminus at Hwy 1. Continue south 25 miles on Hwy 1 to the Park at Mile Marker 102.5, just north of Key Largo.

Points of Interest -

The majority of the distance from I-75 is Interstate grade road. This park is said to be one of the main attractions near Key Largo. Be sure to take a boat, or glass-bottom boat tour, out to the coral reef as it is the coral reefs & marine life that bring most visitors to the park.

Exit 5
Lone Pine Key [13]
(see [12] for 1st leg of directions)
West of Homestead
Everglades NP Rate: $16
America/Beautiful Rate: $8

(800) 365-2267

http://www.everglades.national-park.com/
camping.htm

Camp Accommodations

108 shaded, spacious sites, big rig accessible, dry camping, paved roads, some pull throughs. Amenities include restrooms and showers, dump station, potable water, picnic tables, fire ring, biking, is pet friendly.

Directions

15 mi. from Florida's Turnpike terminus. At Hwy 1 immediately go west on Palm Dr. 1.6 mi. to 192nd Ave., then south 2 mi. to Hwy 9336 (Ingram Hwy) & west on 9336, 10 mi. to the camp road. Turn left, go 1.3 mi. to camp.

Points of Interest -

The unique Everglades ecosystem begs you to slow down & look around. Look for Mahogany Hammock, with the largest Mahogany tree in the U. S. The 'Artist in Residence Program' offers artists the opportunity to live & work in this unique environment for a period of up to one month.

Exit 15
Markham Park [14]
West of Ft. Lauderdale
County Rate: $35

(954) 389-2000

http://www.broward.org/parks/
camping.htm

Camp Accommodations

50 shaded and spacious sites, paved roads, some pull throughs. Amenities include full hookups, picnic tables, grills, restrooms, showers, enclosed dog park/walk, boating, swimming pool, is pet friendly, great view of the Everglades, reservations by phone.

Directions

3 miles from I-75. From Exit 15 go west on to Royal Palm Blvd, but immediately turn at the first right on Weston Rd. Go north 3 miles to Hwy 84. Proceed straight into the Park.

Points of Interest -

In Ft. Lauderdale, you'll find the Riverwalk Arts and Entertainment District. The brick-lined promenade features the Broward Center for the Performing Arts, Museum of Discovery and Science, Florida Grand Opera, Ft. Lauderdale Historical Center, Stranahan House and Museum of Art.

Exit 101
Collier-Seminole State Park [15]
Southeast of Naples
State Rate: $22

(239) 394-3397

http://www.floridastateparks.org/
collierseminole/default.cfm

Camp Accommodations

91 shaded sites, up to 55 feet long, with electric/water, along paved roads, 1 pull through, 6 handicapped. Amenities include ADA restrooms, showers, dump station, camp host, picnic tables, grills, firewood, fishing, biking, hiking, nature programs, watchable wildlife, and is pet friendly.

Directions

16 miles from I-75. From Exit 101 go south on Cty Rd 951 (Collier Rd.) for 7 miles to Hwy 41 Turn east, go 9 miles. The Park will be on the right just past Cty Rd. 92.

Points of Interest -

The park has a wealth of vegetation & wildlife typical of the Everglades and a forest of tropical trees. Although rare elsewhere, the Florida royal palm is common here. The restaurants of Marco Island will delight with fresh seafood and island creations. Explore the Ten Thousand Islands.

Exit 123
Koreshan State Historic Site Park [16]
South of San Carlos Park
State Rate: $26

(239) 992-0311

www.floridastateparks.org/koreshan/
default.cfm

Camp Accommodations

42 shaded sites, up to 40 feet long, 3 ADA, some are narrow, with electric/water, along paved roads. Amenities include ADA restrooms, showers, dump station, camp host, picnic tables, grills, Visitor's Center, Interpretive Programs, fishing, biking, hiking, swimming, pet friendly.

Directions

2 miles from I-75. From Exit 123 go west 2.2 miles on Corkscrew Road. After crossing Hwy 41/45 look for entrance to park on right.

Points of Interest -

Cyrus Teed brought followers to Estero in 1894 to build New Jerusalem for his new faith, Koreshanity. The colony faded and deeded the land to the State. Tour Founders House, Planetary Court, and Bamboo Landing. Contact the Park Curator for more information.

Exit 220
Lake Manatee State Park [17]
East of Bradenton
State Rate: $22

(941) 741-3028

www.floridastateparks.org/lakemanatee/
default.cfm

Camp Accommodations

54 shaded sites, up to 60 feet, electric/water, 4 ADA. Amenities include ADA restrooms, showers, dump station, camp host, picnic tables, grills, firewood, fishing, biking, hiking, nature programs, watchable wildlife, potluck lunches, community game days, coffee clutches, pet friendly.

Directions

9 miles from I-75. From Exit 220 go 9 miles east on Hwy 64, just past Dam Rd, to the park on your left.

Points of Interest -

Try the award winning Bradenton Riverfront Theatre. Visit South Florida Museum, Bishop Planetarium & Parker Manatee Aquarium. Shop the Village of Arts - studios, galleries & small restaurants, mostly catering to the arts. One of the Top 10 cities in the country for working artists.

Exit 240
Alafia River State Park [18]
Southeast of Tampa
State Rate: $22

(813) 72-5320

www.floridastateparks.org/alafiariver/
default.cfm

Camp Accommodations

16 shaded, paved sites, 55 feet long, electric/water, 9 pull throughs, 2 ADA, some sites with paved patios and water views. Amenities include ADA restrooms, showers, dump station, camp host, picnic tables, grills, fishing, biking, hiking, nature programs, watchable wildlife, pet friendly.

Directions

20 miles from I-75. From Exit 240 go east on Hwy 674 for 15 miles. Turn north on Cty Rd. 39 for 5 miles to the park entrance on the right.

Points of Interest -

Tampa/St. Petersburg are close. Try Heritage Park, St. Petersburg Museum of History, Salvador Dali Museum, Old Hyde Park Village, Sunken Gardens, Florida Holocaust Museum, and much more. See <http://www.tampaguide.com/Todo/TodoCat22.asp>

Exit 265
Hillsborough River State Park [19]
Northeast of Tampa
State Rate: $22

(813) 987-6771

www.floridastateparks.org/
hillsboroughriver/default.cfm

Camp Accommodations

100 shaded, paved sites, up to 60 feet, electric/water, paved roads, 6 pull through, 7 ADA. Amenities include ADA restrooms, showers, dump station, camp host, picnic tables, grills, firewood, Interpretive Center, fishing, biking, hiking, nature programs, watchable wildlife, and is pet friendly.

Directions

11 miles from I-75. From Exit 265 take Fowler Ave 1.5 miles east to Hwy 301. Go northeast on Hwy 301 for 9.5 miles to the park entrance on the left.

Points of Interest -

Fort Foster, a replica of an 1837 fort from the Second Seminole War, is located on the park grounds. Tampa - St. Petersburg are close by. For a list of activities go to entry [18] and/or see -
<http://www.tampaguide.com/Todo/TodoCat22.asp>

Exit 329
Lake Griffin Park [20]
North of Leesburg
State Rate: $18

(352) 360-6760

www.floridastateparks.org/lakegriffin/
default.cfm

Camp Accommodations

There are 36 shaded, buffered sites, up to 40 feet long, 2 ADA, with full or electric/water hook ups, 6 pull throughs. Amenities include ADA restrooms, showers, dump station, camp host, picnic tables, grills, firewood, Interpretive Programs, nature tails, fishing, pet friendly.

Directions

17 miles from I-75. From Exit 329 go east 13.5 miles on Hwy 44 to Leesburg. Turn north on Hwy 27/25 for 3.5 miles to park on the right.

Points of Interest -

The Park is located within an hour of central Florida attractions & theme parks. Visit Leesburg, the 'Lakefront City.' Lake Griffin, in the world-renowned Harris Chain of Lakes, is one of central Florida's largest freshwater lakes and is host to the Bassmasters Tournament.

Exit 374
Paynes Prairie Preserve State Park [21]
South of Gainesville
State Rate: $18

(352) 466-3397

www.floridastateparks.org/paynesprairie/
default.cfm

Camp Accommodations

31 ample, shaded sites with a private feel, 50+ feet long, with electric/water, 2 ADA sites. Amenities include ADA restrooms, showers, dump station, camp host, Visitor's Center, picnic tables, grills, firewood, fishing, biking, hiking, nature programs, watchable wildlife, pet friendly.

Directions

2 miles from I-75. From Exit 374 go east on Cty Rd. 234 for 1.4. Turn left on Hwy 441 and go 0.6 miles to Savannah Blvd. and the Park on the right.

Points of Interest -

In a 22,000-acre preserve, the Park is in one of the most significant natural and historic areas in Florida. In 1774, noted artist and naturalist William Bartram called it the "great Alachua Savannah." Gainesville has much to offer in museums, historic sites, live theater, and shopping.

Exit 414 of I-75
O'Leno State Park [22]
North of Gainesville
State Rate: $18

(386) 454-1853

www.floridastateparks.org/oleno/
default.cfm

Camp Accommodations

50 shaded sites, up to 50 feet, recent site & road improvements, 1 pull through, electric/water, 2 ADA sites. Amenities include ADA restrooms, showers, dump station, campground host, picnic tables, grills, museum, fishing, biking, hiking, nature programs, watchable wildlife, pet friendly.

Directions

6 miles from I-75. From Exit 414 go 6 miles south on Hwy 41 to Sprite Loop and the park entrance on the left.

Points of Interest -

Enjoy a rustic 1930's Civilian Conservation Corps era atmosphere on the banks of the scenic Santa Fe River. Discover nearby Cross Creek, the home of author Marjorie Kinnan Rawlings, who wrote The Yearling and Cross Creek, both made into movies.

Exit 439 of I-75
Stephen Foster Folk Culture
Center State Park [23]
North of I-10
State Rate: $20

(386) 397-2733

www.floridastateparks.org/stephenfoster/

Camp Accommodations

39 shaded, ample sites, up to 100 feet, electric/water, 13 pull through, ALL ADA accessible. Amenities include ADA restrooms, showers, dump station, camp host, picnic tables, grills, Interpretive Programs, fishing, biking, hiking, nature programs, watchable wildlife, and is pet friendly.

Directions

4 miles from I-75. From Exit 439 travel east on Hwy 136 for 3 miles. Turn left on Hwy 25/41. Park entrance is on the left.

Points of Interest -

On the legendary Suwannee River, the Park honors the memory of American composer Stephen Foster. A wide variety of artisans populate Craft Square monthly. Tour the Museum and Carillon Tower. Participate in workshops and retreat events or get involved as a crafter or demonstrator.

Exit 101 of I-95
St. Lucie South [24]
South of Stuart
COE Rate: $20-$24
America/Beautiful Rate: $10-$12

(772) 287-1382

www.reserveamerica.com/camping/
St_Lucie_South_Fl/r/campground

Camp Accommodations

9 shaded, cement pad, riverfront sites, up to 46 feet long, dry or electric/water, 1 handicapped site. Amenities include ADA restrooms and showers, paved roads, dump station, attendant, potable water, fishing, boating, pet friendly.

Directions

2 miles from I-95. From Exit 101 go 0.5 mile south on Hwy 76 to Locks Rd. Turn right, drive 1.3 miles to the camp.

Points of Interest -

Enjoy the view of boats and manatees passing through the lock and dam as they travel the Okeechobee Waterway. Visit the City of Stuart, known as the 'Sailfish Capital of the World,' because of the many sailfish found in the ocean off Martin County. Charter a boat, catch your own!

Exit 156
Sebastian Inlet State Park [25]
North of Vero Beach
State Rate: $28

(321) 984-4852

www.floridastateparks.org/sebastianinlet/
default.cfm

Camp Accommodations

43 shaded, waterfront sites up to 40 feet
long, with electric/water, 3 ADA sites.
Amenities include ADA restrooms, showers, dump station, camp host, Interpretive
Programs, picnic tables, grills, firewood,
fishing, biking, hiking, nature programs,
watchable wildlife, pet friendly.

Directions

18 miles from I-95. From Exit 156 go
east 2.2 miles on Cty Rd. 512 (Fellsmere
Rd). Turn south then east on Cty Rd. 510.
Go 8.5 miles, crossing over the Indian
River to Hwy A1A. Turn north for 7 miles
to the Park.

Points of Interest -

You are in the premier saltwater fishing
spot on Florida's east coast. Three miles
of beautiful beaches provide opportunities
for swimming, snorkeling, shelling, & sunbathing. Visit the McLarty Treasure Museum featuring the history of the Survivors'
& Salvagers' Camp of the 1715 Fleet.

Exit 205
Jetty Park Campground [26]
Cape Canaveral
Port Authority Rate: $32-$47

(321) 783-7111

http://www.portcanaveral.com/recreation/
beaches.php

Camp Accommodations

126 ample and shaded RV sites, may
paved, full utilities, some pull throughs.
Amenities include hot showers, laundry,
grills, picnic tables, playground, picnic pavilion, bait & tackle shop, beach snack bar,
camp store, dump stations and 24 hour
security, pet friendly.

Directions

14 miles from I-95. From Exit 205 go 12
miles east on Hwy 528 (Beachline Expressway), which merges into Hwy A1A, to
the George J. King Blvd. Exit and go east
1.7 miles to the park entrance.

Points of Interest -

Watch giant cruise ships come in with the
dolphins. When NASA launches Shuttles,
Jetty Park is an ideal watch site. One of
this park's best features is the 1,200 foot
Malcolm E. McLouth Fishing Pier
(accessible to the physically challenged).
Cocoa Beach is just a few minutes drive.

Exit 311
Anastasia State Park [27]
South of St. Augustine
State Rate: $28

(904) 461-2033

www.floridastateparks.org/anastasia/
default.cfm

Camp Accommodations

101 shaded, ample sites up to 40 feet, electric/water, paved roads, 5 ADA accessible. Amenities include ADA restrooms, showers, dump station, camp host, picnic tables, grills, Interpretive Programs, fishing, biking, hiking, nature programs, watchable wildlife, and is pet friendly.

Directions

9 miles from I-95. From Exit 311 travel northeast 3.6 miles on Hwy 207 to Hwy 312. Turn east on Hwy 312, go 3.6 miles to Hwy A1A. Travel 1.5 miles north to the park entrance on the right.

Points of Interest -

At the park, shop the Farmer's Market on Saturday. St. Augustine is the oldest European established city in the U.S. There is much to see - St. Augustine Lighthouse, Avero House, Castillo de San Marcos National Monument, Old St. Johns County Jail, & Zorayda Castle to name a few.

Exit 373
Fort Clinch State Park [28]
At Fernandina Beach
State Rate: $26

(904) 277-7274

www.floridastateparks.org/fortclinch/
default.cfm

Camp Accommodations

51 ample sites up to 48 feet, near water, electric/water, paved roads, 1 ADA. Amenities include ADA restrooms, showers, dump station, camp host, picnic table, grill, Visitors Center, Interpretive Programs, fishing, biking, hiking, nature programs, watchable wildlife, & pet friendly.

Directions

16 miles from I-95. From Exit 373 travel mostly east, finally north, 15 miles in all, on Hwy 200/A1A. In Fernandina the street name is 8th St. At Atlantic (A1A) turn east (right) for 1 mile to the Park.

Points of Interest -

Enjoy hiking in the maritime hammock, explore Atlantic beaches, or experience the Living History Program, available daily at the well preserved 19th century Historic Fort Clinch. Special events occur monthly. Fernandina Beach has a historic district with Victorian homes and shops.

GEORGIA

Forty-one Georgia State Parks offer over 2,700 campsites, many of which are curved, RV pull-thru sites for large RVs. Rates average around $23 per night. Sites offer electrical and water hookups, grills or fire rings, and picnic tables. Sewage hook-ups are provided only at select sites at Florence Marina, Gordonia-Alatamaha, Hart and Victoria Bryant state parks.

Campgrounds offer modern comfort stations with hot showers, flush toilets and electrical outlets. All campgrounds have dump stations, and several offer cable TV hookups. Most state parks have laundry facilities and sell camping supplies, offer accessible campsites, fishing piers, nature trails and picnic areas. Pets are welcome in campgrounds if kept on a six-foot leash and attended at all times. Every Tuesday the State Park website will show which campsites are available for the upcoming weekend.

You can get details at -

www.georgiastateparks.org/

Reservations are accepted up to 11 months in advance (to the day) of your arrival date. Go to -

www.georgiastateparks.org/reservations/

Seniors, 62 and older receive a 20% campground discount. The daily (entrance) fee is $5 and RVers pay only one fee for the duration of the stay.

[1] Little Ocmulgee State Park N32 05.513 W82 53.078	**[10] Georgia Veterans State Park** N31 58.082 W83 54.737
[2] George L. Smith State Park N32 32.686 W82 07.512	**[11] Indian Springs State Park** N33 14.719 W83 55.229
[3] John Tanner State Park N33 36.111 W85 10.005	**[12] McKinney Campground** N34 06.895 W84 41.552
[4] Hard Labor Creek State Park N33 39.582 W83 36.121	**[13] R. Shaefer Heard Campground** N32 55.304 W85 09.376
[5] A.H. Stephens Historic Park N33 33.477 W82 53.815	**[14] Fort Yargo State Park** N33 59.098 W83 44.015
[6] Big Hart Campground N33 36.881 W82 30.772	**[15] Tugaloo State Park** N34 30.115 W83 04.938
[7] Petersburg Campground N33 39.593 W82 15.634	**[16] Crooked River State Park** N30 50.438 W81 33.711
[8] Cloudland Canyon State Park N34 48.930 W85 29.376	**[17] Fort McAllister Historic Park** N31 53.143 W81 12.695
[9] Reed Bingham Historic Park N31 09.683 W83 32.380	**[18] F.D. Roosevelt State Park** N32 50.334 W84 48.893

NOTES:

67

Georgia

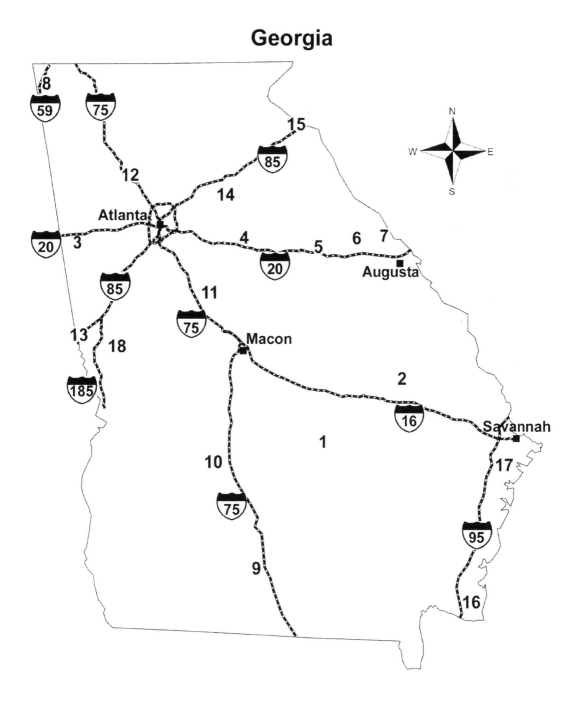

Exit 51 of I-16
Little Ocmulgee State Park [1]
South of Dublin
State Rate: $23-$25
Senior Discount Rate: $18-$20

(229) 868-7474

http://gastateparks.org/info/liocmulgee/

Camp Accommodations
(see chapter introduction)

There are 54 shaded sites, up to 40 feet long, electric/water, some sewer sites, dump station, some pull throughs, cable TV. Amenities include golf course, tennis, fishing, boating, miniature golf, Visitor's Center, Park events, Wi-Fi, pet friendly.

Directions

28 miles from I-16. From Exit 51 go south on Hwy 319/441 for 28 miles to the entrance on the right, just before entering McRae.

Points of Interest -

The lodge restaurant is said to offer a good meal. Visit Dublin, known for its St Patrick's festival, also tour the Laurens Museum originally built by Andrew Carnegie as a library. Check out the Statue of Liberty replica, one-twelfth actual size, in downtown McRae's Liberty Square.

Exit 104 of I-16
George L. Smith State Park [2]
North of Metter
State Rate: $21-$23
Senior Discount Rate: $17-$18

(478) 763-2759

http://gastateparks.org/info/georgels/

Camp Accommodations
(see chapter introduction)

There are 20 shaded RV sites along a beautiful lake filled with huge cypress trees. Sites are up to 40 feet long, electric/water, dump station, some pull throughs, 1 ADA site. Amenities include fishing, boating, birding, pet friendly.

Directions

15 mi. from I-16. From Exit 104 go 1.6 miles north on Hwy 23/121 to Hwy 46 in Metter. Turn left for 3 blocks to Hwy 23 (College St). Turn north on Hwy 23 for 11.3 miles to George L. Smith Rd, then right 2 miles to the Park.

Points of Interest -

The Park is known for the Parrish Mill. You can observe cane ground & cooked into syrup. Hikers have 7 miles of trails, & look for the lumbering Gopher Tortoise, Georgia's state reptile. In Statesboro visit the Georgia Southern University Museum and Georgia Southern Botanical Garden.

Exit 11 of I-20
John Tanner State Park [3]
Northwest of Carrollton
State Rate: $22-$24
Senior Discount Rate: $18-$19

(770) 830-2222

http://gastateparks.org/info/jtanner/

Camp Accommodations
(see chapter introduction)

29 shaded, large gravel sites, up to 40 feet, electric/water, dump station, some pull throughs. Amenities include miniature golf, horseshoes, hiking, fishing, boating, largest sand swimming beach of any Georgia State Park, cable TV, pet friendly.

Directions

7 miles from I-20. From Exit 11 go south on Hwy 27 for 1.3 miles to Bowdon Junction Rd. Turn right, go 3 miles to Hwy 16. Go left, drive 1.6 miles, then right on Tanner Beach Rd 0.7 mile to the Park.

Points of Interest -

Explore shops, restaurants & galleries of historic Carrollton. Visit Pickett's Mill, one of the best preserved Civil War battlefields in the nation. Travel roads used by Federal and Confederate troops, see earthworks constructed by these men, and walk the same ravine where hundreds died.

Exit 105
Hard Labor Creek State Park [4]
Northwest of Madison
State Rate: $23-$25
Senior Discount Rate:$18-$20

(706) 557-3001

http://gastateparks.org/info/hardlabor/

Camp Accommodations
(see chapter introduction)

There are 26 shaded, large gravel sites, up to 60 feet long, electric/water, dump station, some pull throughs, 1 ADA. Amenities include an observatory, hiking, laundry, fishing, boating, golf, pet friendly.

Directions

5 miles from I-20. From Exit 105 go north on Newborn for 2.5 miles (bare left at Hawkins Ave), crossing Hwy 12/278 (Atlanta Hwy) to E. Dixie Hwy. Turn left, go one block, turn right on Fairplay St. Go 2.6 miles into the Park.

Points of Interest -

The Park is best known for The Creek Golf Course, used by the pros for practice before Augusta. It is one of Georgia's best golf values, with special rates for seniors. Visit historic Madison, with the largest designated historic district in Georgia. It is the City Sherman refused to burn!

Exit 148
A.H. Stephens Historic Park [5]
North of Crawfordville
State Rate: $21-$23
Senior Discount Rate: $17-$18

(706) 456-2602

http://gastateparks.org/info/ahsteph/

Camp Accommodations
(see chapter introduction)

There are 20 shaded, large and secluded sites, up to 60 feet long, electric/water, dump station, some pull throughs. Amenities include, fishing, boating, pet friendly.

Directions

4 miles from I-20. **Due to low bridge, especially if your RV is taller than 12' 10",** from Exit 148 go 2.2 miles on Hwy 22, cross Hwy 278. Turn right onto MLK Jr. Dr. Go 1 mile (keeping left), then turn left on Alexander St. to park.

Points of Interest -

Tour Liberty Hall, home of Confederate Vice President Alexander Stephens & governor of Georgia. The Park features a Confederate museum with one of the finest collections of Civil War artifacts in Georgia. Stephens' home is renovated to 1875 style, furnished and open for tours.

Exit 172
Big Hart Campground [6]
Northwest of Augusta
COE Rate: $16-$20
America/Beautiful Rate: $8-$10

(706) 595-8613

www.recreation.gov/

Camp Accommodations

32 shaded and spacious, lakefront sites, 60+ feet long, dry or electric/water, 28 pull throughs. Amenities include showers, dump station, attendant, potable water, swimming, fishing, boating, pet friendly.

Directions

8.5 miles from I-20. From Exit 172 go north 6 miles on Hwy 78 to Russell Landing Rd. Turn right and travel east 2.5 miles to campground.

Points of Interest -

Nearby Augusta is Georgia's second oldest city. Known as the South's "Garden City," it is full of history, atmosphere & Southern charm. Discover Augusta's tree-lined streets & majestic antebellum mansions. Enjoy dozens of shops, restaurants, cultural attractions & entertainment.

Exit 183 of I-20
Petersburg Campground [7]
Northwest of Augusta
COE Rate: $14-$22
America/Beautiful Rate: $7-$11

(706) 541-9464

www.reserveamerica.com/campground

Camp Accommodations

93 shaded lakefront sites, up to 45 feet long, dry or electric/water, 54 pull throughs, 2 ADA, most sites near water with great views. Amenities include showers, dump station, potable water, swimming, fishing, boating, pet friendly.

Directions

13 miles from I-20. From Exit 183 go north on Hwy 221 for 11.5 miles to Petersburg Rd. Turn left, go 1 miles to the campground.

Points of Interest -
Nearby Augusta is Georgia's second oldest city. Known as the South's "Garden City," it is full of history, atmosphere & Southern charm. Discover Augusta's tree-lined streets & majestic antebellum mansions. Enjoy dozens of shops, restaurants, cultural attractions & entertainment.

Exit 11 of I-59
Cloudland Canyon State Park [8]
Southwest of Chattanooga, TN
State Rate: $23-$25
Senior Discount Rate: $18-$20

(706) 657-4050

http://gastateparks.org/info/cloudland/

Camp Accommodations
(see chapter introduction)

There are 60 shaded, large gravel sites, up to 40 feet long, electric/water, dump station, some pull throughs, 2 ADA sites. Amenities include hiking, tennis, disc golf, fishing, gift shop, pet friendly.

Directions

7 miles from I-59. From Exit 11 go southeast 2 blocks to Main St. Turn right, go 2 blocks to Hwy 136 (Lafayette St.) Turn left on Hwy 136, go 6.2 miles to Cloudland Canyon Park Rd. Turn left in to the Park.

Points of Interest -
Don't miss the Lookout Mountain scenery. Visit Dalton's Prater's Mill, listed on the National Register of Historic Places. Its heritage runs back to the days of the Cherokee Indians. At the Tunnel Hill Heritage Center, one of the South's oldest railroad tunnels still stands.

Exit 39 of I-75
Reed Bingham Historic Park [9]
West of Adel/Sparks
State Rate: $23-$25
Senior Discount Rate: $18-$20

(229) 896-3551

http://gastateparks.org/info/reedbing/

Camp Accommodations
(see chapter introduction)

There are 39 shaded, large gravel sites, up to 50 feet long, electric/water, dump station, some pull throughs, 1 ADA. Amenities include, hiking, fishing, boating, miniature golf, pontoon boat tours, swimming, cable TV, pet friendly.

Directions

6 miles from I-75. From Exit 39 go 5.4 miles west on Hwy 37 to Reed Bingham Rd. Turn right, go 0.9 miles in to the Park.

Points of Interest -
Rvers can see abundant wildlife, rare and endangered species. Volunteers can assist with Gopher Tortoise Management projects and may witness hatching of tortoises. In winter, thousands of "buzzards", large black vultures and turkey vultures, roost in the trees and soar overhead.

Exit 101
Georgia Veterans State Park [10]
West of Cordele
State Rate: $23-$25
Senior Discount Rate: $18-$20

(229) 276-2371

http://gastateparks.org/info/georgiavet/

Camp Accommodations
(see chapter introduction)

There are 72 shaded, large gravel sites, up to 50 feet long, electric/water, dump station, some pull throughs, 2 ADA. Amenities include, hiking, fishing, boating, golf, disc golf, model airplane flying field, cable TV, pet friendly.

Directions

10 miles from I-75. From Exit 101 go 10 miles west on Hwy 30/280 through Cordele to Cannon Rd. Turn left into the Park.

Points of Interest -

The park museum has Revolutionary through Gulf War items. The golf course and lake make this one of Georgia's most popular parks. The SAM Shortline Excursion Train covers Cordele-Plains via the park. Riders see a telephone museum and President Jimmy Carter's boyhood farm.

Exits 188 or 205
Indian Springs State Park [11]
North of Forsyth
State Rate: $23-$25
Senior Discount Rate: $18-$20

(770) 504-2277

http://gastateparks.org/info/indspr/

Camp Accommodations
(see chapter introduction)

There are 26 shaded, large gravel RV sites, up to 50 feet long, electric/water, dump station, some pull throughs, 2 ADA. Amenities include, hiking, fishing, boating, miniature golf, swimming, cable TV, pet friendly.

Directions

15 miles from I-75. **Northbound**, take Exit 188, proceed north on Hwy 42 15 mi. to Spring Rd & the Park. **Southbound**, take Exit 205, go east 8.6 mi. on Hwy 16 to Jackson; then south 5.2 miles on Hwy. 23/42 to Spring Rd and the Park.

Points of Interest -

In Macon, see the Georgia Music Hall of Fame - country, big band & southern rock; or Hay House - William Butler Johnston was Confederate treasurer, but the mansion he built is the real treasure; or Tubman African American Museum - Georgia's largest African American museum.

Exit 278
McKinney Campground [12]
North of Atlanta
COE Rate: $20-$24
America/Beautiful Rate: $10-$12

(678) 721-6700

http://www.recreation.gov

Camp Accommodations

150 shaded and spacious, lakefront sites, 50 feet long, dry or electric/water, 35 pull throughs. Amenities include showers, dump station, attendant, potable water, swimming, fishing, boating, pet friendly.

Directions

4 miles from I-75. From Exit 278 go north 2.7 miles on Glade Rd. to Kings Camp Rd. Turn left and go west 0.7 mile to McKinney Campground Rd. Turn south (left) 0.5 mile to the campground.

Points of Interest -

In Cartersville experience the Cowboy way at the Booth Western Art Museum - a two-time award winner for best attraction. Very new is the Smithsonian Affiliate Tellus: Northwest Georgia Science Museum. Or just shop, enjoy and have lunch in historic downtown Cartersville.

Exit 2
R. Shaefer Heard Campground [13]
Southwest of LaGrange
COE Rate: $22
America/Beautiful Rate: $11

(706) 645-2404

www.recreation.gov/campgroundDetails.do?
contractCode=NRSO&parkId=71370

Camp Accommodations

117 shaded and spacious, lakefront sites, 65 feet long, electric/water, 7 pull throughs, 10 with decks, wide paved roads. Amenities include showers, dump station, attendant, potable water, swimming, fishing, boating, tennis, pet friendly.

Directions

5 miles from I-85. From Exit 2 go west 1.3 miles on Hwy 18 (10th Av.) to Ave. E (Westpoint Rd). Turn north (right) and travel 3.3 miles on Hwy 29 to the campground road (just past Reed Rd) on the left.

Points of Interest -

Visit LaGrange, a classic Georgia town known as the 'City Of Elms and Roses.' Classic antebellum homes proudly attest to the rich history of LaGrange. In Pine Mountain you can experience the thrill of a steeplechase. The city is also the gateway to Callaway Gardens.

Exit 126
Fort Yargo State Park [14]
East of Lawrenceville
State Rate: $23-$25
Senior Discount Rate: $18-$20

(770) 867-3489

http://gastateparks.org/info/ftyargo/

Camp Accommodations
(see chapter introduction)

There are 31 shaded, large gravel RV sites, up to 50 feet long, electric/water, dump station, some pull throughs, 1 ADA. Amenities include, hiking, fishing, boating, miniature and disc golf, tennis, pet friendly.

Directions

10.5 miles from I-85. From Exit 126 go 9.6 miles southeast on Hwy 211 to Winder. At Hwy 81 (Broad St.) turn right for 1 mile to the park on the left.

Points of Interest -

You are close to Athens, Atlanta, and Stone Mountain. Stone Mountain is well-known for the enormous bas-relief on its north face, the largest in the world. Three figures of the Confederate States of America are carved there: Stonewall Jackson, Robert E. Lee, and Jefferson Davis.

Exit 173
Tugaloo State Park [15]
At South Carolina State Line
State Rate: $23-$25
Senior Discount Rate: $18-$20

(706) 356-4362

http://gastateparks.org/info/tugaloo/

Camp Accommodations
(see chapter introduction)

There are 37 shaded, water view, gravel RV sites, up to 35 feet long, electric/water, dump station, some pull throughs. Amenities include, hiking, fishing, boating, miniature golf, horseshoes, cable TV, tennis, pet friendly.

Directions

7.5 miles from I-85. From Exit 173 turn south on Hwy 17 toward Lavonia, go 1.1 miles to Hwy 59. Turn left, follow Hwy 59 1.1 miles to Hwy 328. Bare left on Hwy 328, go 4 miles to Tugaloo Park Rd. Turn right, drive 1.3 miles in to the Park.

Points of Interest -

Most of Tugaloo's campsites offer spectacular views of 55,600-acre Lake Hartwell in every direction. Visit the Ty Cobb Museum in Royston that honors the Baseball Hall of Fame player. The museum contains art, memorabilia, film, video, books and historical archives of Cobb.

Exit 3 of I-95
Crooked River State Park [16]
East of Kingsland
State Rate: $22-$24
Senior Discount Rate: $18-$19

(912) 882-5256

http://www.gastateparks.org/info/crookriv/

Camp Accommodations
(see chapter introduction)

50 shaded, large gravel sites, up to 50 feet long, electric/water, dump station, some pull throughs, 3 ADA. Amenities include, hiking, fishing, boating, Nature Center, miniature golf, cable TV, pet friendly.

Directions

12 miles from I-95. From Exit 3 go east 5.6 miles on Hwy 40 to Spur 40 (Charlie Smith Sr. Hwy). Turn north and go 6.3 miles to the park.

Points of Interest -

Birding enthusiasts will enjoy the large bird blind that provides close views. Visitors may venture to the nearby ruins of the tabby (a mixture of limestone, sand, and sea shells) "McIntosh Sugar Works" mill. Closeby is the ferry and visitor center for Cumberland Island National Seashore.

Exit 90 of I-95
Fort McAllister Historic Park [17]
South of Savannah
State Rate: $22-$24
Senior Discount Rate: $18-$19

(912) 727-2339

http://gastateparks.org/info/ftmcallister/

Camp Accommodations
(see chapter introduction)

There are 49 shaded, large gravel sites, up to 65+ feet long, electric/water, dump station, some pull throughs, 2 ADA. Amenities include, hiking, fishing, boating, pet friendly.

Directions

10 miles from I-95. From Exit 90 go 6.4 miles southeast on Hwy 144 to Spur 144 (Fort McAllister Rd.). Turn left, go 3.2 miles to the Park.

Points of Interest -

The park is the home of the best preserved earthwork fortification of the Confederacy. The park's Civil War museum contains exhibits and artifacts. Enjoy Savannah, one of the most beautiful cities in the world. The Historic District of Savannah is a must visit location.

Exit 34 of I-185
F.D. Roosevelt State Park [18]
East of Pine Mountain
State Rate: $23-$25
Senior Discount Rate: $18-$20

(706) 663-4858

http://gastateparks.org/info/fdr/

Camp Accommodations
(see chapter introduction)

There are 59 shaded, large gravel sites near 2 lakes, up to 40 feet long, electric/water, dump station, some pull throughs, 1 ADA. Amenities include, hiking, fishing, boating, pet friendly.

Directions

11 miles from I-185. From Exit 34 go east 6.5 miles on Hwy 18. Southwest of Pine Mountain go straight on Hwy 354 for 3.8 miles to Hwy 190. Turn west (right) 0.3 miles to the Park entrance.

Points of Interest -

The Park is close to Callaway Gardens & the town of Pine Mountain. In addition, visit the FDR Little White House or take in one of the local festivals. Spend a day in downtown Pine Mountain's and Chipley Village's shops, with boutiques & antiques, from fine art to handcrafted birdhouses.

IDAHO

There are 26 Idaho State Parks. Detailed information is available at -

http://parksandrecreation.idaho.gov/parks/index.aspx

You can register online up to 9 months in advance at -

http://idahostateparks.reserveamerica.com/

Discounts may be available on reservations and/or use fees for currently registered Idaho RV sticker holders, disabled Idaho veterans, low income Idahoans, and senior citizens. Discounts are only available on reservations made through the call center (1-888-922-6743) or may be claimed when registering at the park.

Those 62 or older will receive 50% off camping fees within select Idaho State Parks. The discount is valid mid-week on stays Monday – Thursday (excluding holidays).

Standard Campsite $12 - $14. Any campsite, tent or RV.

Serviced Campsite/ W or E $16 - $18. Any campsite, tent or RV with water or electricity.

Serviced Campsite /W, E $20 - $22. Any campsite, tent pad or RV with water and electricity.

Serviced Campsite /W, E, SWR $22 - $24. Any campsite, tent pad or RV, with water, electricity, and sewer.

Towed vehicles are not considered to be an extra vehicle. Pets are welcome in most parks, but you must keep them on a leash no longer than six feet, or confined to your RV.

---

[1] **Scout Mountain Campground**
N42 41.503 W112 21.541
[2] **Stoddard Creek Campground**
N44 25.064 W112 12.809
[3] **Three Island Crossing State Park**
N42 56.718 W115 19.077

[4] **Lake Walcott State Park**
N42 40.515 W113 29.011
[5] **Massacre Rocks State Park**
N42 40.692 W112 59.135
[6] **Beauty Creek Campground**
N47 36.408 W116 40.092

NOTES:

Idaho

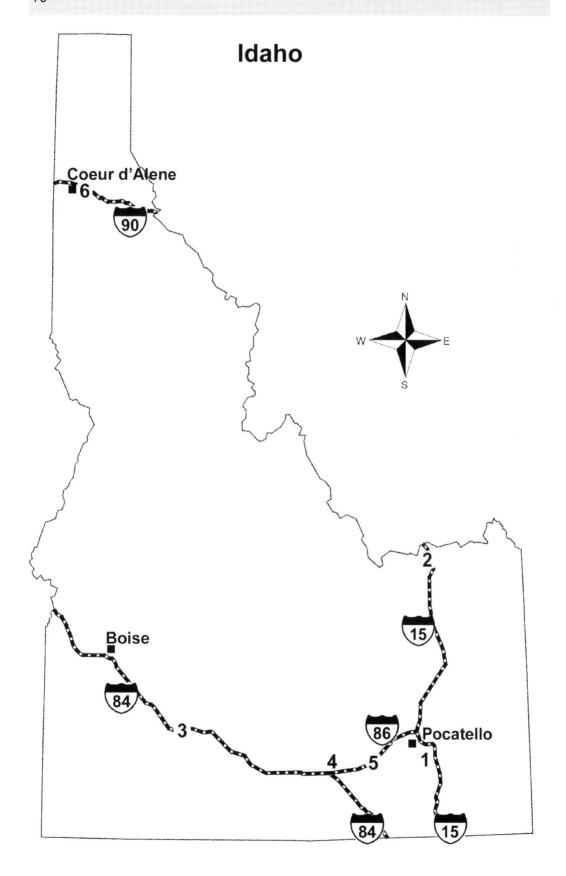

Exit 63 of I-15
Scout Mountain Campground [1]
South of Pocatello
Caribou NF Rate: $10
America/Beautiful Rate: $5

(208) 236-7500

http://www.recreation.gov/

Camp Accommodations

13 shaded sites, some paved, up to 70 feet, dry camping, 3 ADA, 3 pull through. Amenities include ADA vault toilets, potable water, grills, picnic tables, fire rings, biking, nature trails, firewood, watchable wildlife, pet friendly. NO utilities.

Directions

14 mi. from I-15. From Exit 63 go south 0.3 mi. to Portneuf Rd. Go east 2 mi. to Bannock Hwy then south 5 mi. to E. Fork of Mink Creek Rd. Turn left, go 6 mi. up to campground.

Points of Interest -

The road to the camp is paved all the way. There are switchbacks but RVs should be OK. In Pocatello, you can find rodeos, a casino, attend an Indian Pow Wow, seek out historic sites or see living history with a Fur Traders Encampment reliving the daily routine of the fur trader era.

Exit 184 of I-15
Stoddard Creek Campground [2]
North of Dubois
Targhee NF Rate: $10
America/Beautiful Rate: $5

(208) 374-5422

http://www.recreation.gov/

Camp Accommodations

21 shaded sites, some 50 feet long, dry camping, 2 pull through. Amenities include ADA vault toilets, potable water, grills, picnic tables, fire rings, biking, nature trails, watchable wildlife, pet friendly. NO utilities.

Directions

1 mile from I-15. From Exit 184 go west on Stoddard Creek Rd. (FR 002) 1 mile to the Stoddard Creek Camp Ground Rd. (FR 003). Turn left into the campground.

Points of Interest -

Drive to Craters of the Moon National Monument and St. Anthony Sand Dunes, near St. Anthony. This 10,600 acre area of clear, shifting, white quartz sand is known for its unique beauty, recreation opportunities, and is home to one of the largest herds of wintering elk in the United States.

Exit 121 of I-84
Three Island Crossing State Park [3]
South of Glenns Ferry
State Rate: $20-$22
Senior Discount Rate: $10-$11

(208) 366-2394

www.parksandrecreation.idaho.gov/
parks/threeislandcrossing.aspx

Camp Accommodations

There are 82 shaded and ample sites, some 65+ feet long, 1 ADA, some river views, electric/water, some sewer, dump station, some pull throughs. Amenities include host, ADA restrooms, bath house, grills, tables, fishing, pet friendly.

Directions

2 miles from I-84. From Exit 121, turn south and follow 1st Ave for 0.7 miles. Go left on Commercial Ave for 0.5 miles then right on Madison Ave. Drive 1 mile to the park entrance.

Points of Interest -

The Park is home to The Oregon Trail History & Education Center. Within walking distance is the Carmela Winery and Golf Course. Just south of town is Hagerman Fossil Beds National Monument, with the largest concentration of Hagerman Horse fossils in North America.

Exit 211 of I-84
Lake Walcott State Park [4]
Northeast of Rupert
State Rate: $16-$20
Senior Discount Rate: $8-$10

(208) 436-1258

www.idahostateparks.reserveamerica.
com/camping/Lake_Walcott/r/
campground

Camp Accommodations

23 shaded, ample RV sites, some 90+ feet long, some water views, electric/water, dump station. Amenities include host, ADA restrooms, bath house, grills, tables, biking, walking paths, fishing, pet friendly.

Directions

16 miles from I-84. From Exit 211 go northeast on Hwy 24, following it through Rupert, 10.4 miles in all to 400 North Rd. (Minidoka Dam Rd.), just past Acequia. Turn right for 5.3 miles to the campground.

Points of Interest -

Drive to Craters of the Moon National Monument. Try the Shoshone Ice Caves, a natural wonder. Guides explain the geologic, volcanic, and historical background in these large lava ice caves. A museum contains Indian artifacts, gems, and minerals of local and world interest.

Exit 28 of I-86
Massacre Rocks State Park [5]
Southwest of American Falls
State Rate: $20
Senior Discount Rate: $10

(208) 548-2672

www.parksandrecreation.idaho.gov/
parks/massacrerocks.aspx

Camp Accommodations

There are 42 shaded and ample sites, some 100 feet long, 1 ADA, some river views, electric/water, dump station, some pull throughs. Amenities include host, ADA restrooms, bath house, grills, fire ring, tables, fishing, hiking, pet friendly.

Directions

1 mile from I-86. From Exit 28, turn to the northwest side of the Interstate. Take the frontage road right for 1 mile to campground.

Points of Interest -

The Park, along The Oregon Trail, has excellent vistas. Visit Register Rock, two miles from the park, that holds the signatures of Oregon Trail emigrants who stopped for an evening of rest before continuing on their journeys. Discover the "Gate of Death" & "Devil's Gate."

Exit 22 of I-90
Beauty Creek Campground [6]
East of Coeur d'Alene
Coeur d'Alene NF Rate: $14
America/Beautiful Rate: $7

(208) 765-7287

www.forestcamping.com/dow/northern/
coercmp.htm#beauty%20creek

Camp Accommodations

14 shaded paved sites, up to 40 feet long, dry camping. Amenities include ADA vault toilets, potable water, grills, picnic tables, fire rings, biking, nature trails, watchable wildlife, pet friendly. NO utilities, NO reservations.

Directions

3 miles from I-90. From Exit 22 go south on Hwy 97 for 2.4 mile to Beauty Creek Rd. Turn left, go 0.7 miles to the campground.

Points of Interest -

The campground is 1/2 a mile from Lake Coeur d'Alene. The lake is very large with much to do - rent paddle boats, take a ferry or sea plane ride, go parasailing, or just swim and relax. Go horseback riding or try a cattle drive outing; or kayaking, perhaps even white water rafting!

ILLINOIS

State and COE Parks dominate the countryside. There are 81 State Parks with RV camp sites. The Army Corps of Engineers also has a number of campgrounds that Rvers will find appealing.

The Illinois Department of Natural Resources does not charge an entrance fee to any of their campgrounds. The fee schedule listed below is for all sites with RV category camping. Generally, throughout the state, camping is available year round weather permitting. Camp roads are usually paved, sites typically are gravel.

Campground reservations are maintained by each site, there is no statewide system. Contact the park for more information about making a reservation. E-mail reservations are not accepted.

The fee schedule is:

Class AA: $25 - Showers, electricity, sewer, and vehicular access.

Class A: $20 - Showers, electricity, and vehicular access.

Class B/E: $18 - Electricity and vehicular access.

Class B/S: $10 -Showers and vehicular access.

Class C: $8 - Vehicular access without showers access.

P = $2-$5/day Premium.

For Memorial Day, July 4th, and Labor Day there is a $10/day premium. All Discounts apply only to Illinois residents. The reservation fee surcharge is $5.

Note - with the large number of Interstate Roads in close proximity in Illinois, a number of the parks can easily be reached from more than one Interstate highway.

---

[1] Ferne Clyffe State Park
N37 31.954 W88 57.986
[2] Starved Rock State Park
N41 19.278 W89 00.648
[3] Shabbona Lake State Recreation Area
N41 45.666 W88 52.184
[4] Rock Cut State Park
N42 22.193 W88 58.699
[5] Sangchris Lake State Park
N39 39.317 W89 29.279
[6] Giant City State Park
N37 36.266 W89 11.653
[7] Gun Creek Campground
N38 04.686 W88 55.833
[8] Dam West Campground
N38 37.923 W89 21.647
[9] Lithia Springs Camp
N39 26.062 W88 45.626

[10] Kankakee River State Park
N41 12.248 W87 58.750
[11] Ramsey Lake State Park
N39 09.566 W89 07.500
[12] Fox Ridge State Park
N39 24.166 W88 08.091
[13] Siloam Springs State Park
N39 53.749 W90 57.305
[14] Clinton Lake State Park
N40 09.794 W88 47.266
[15] Moraine View State Park
N40 24.808 W88 43.654
[16] Kickapoo State Park
N40 08.323 W87 45.185
[17] Fisherman's Corner
N41 34.006 W90 23.767
[18] Johnson Sauk Trail Park
N41 19.777 W89 53.455
[19] Morrison-Rockwood State Park
N41 50.474 W89 58.004

NOTES:

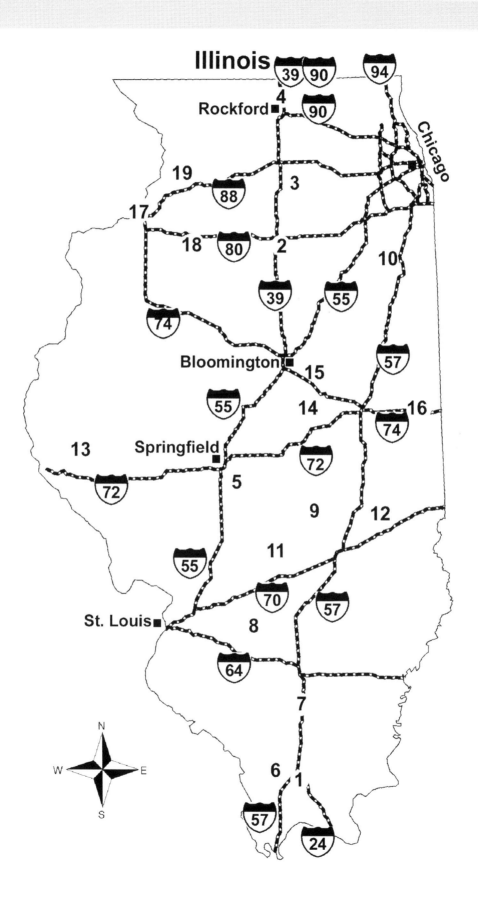

Exit 7 of I-24
Ferne Clyffe State Park [1]
South of Goreville
State Rate: $8-$20

(618) 995-2411

http://dnr.state.il.us/lands/LandMgt/
PARKS/R5/FERNE.HTM

**Camp Accommodations
(see chapter introduction)**

59 ample **Class A & C** shaded sites, 40+ feet long, gravel pads, some pull throughs, dump station. Amenities in the Deer Ridge camp include picnic tables, grills, potable water, showers, flush toilets, hiking, fishing, pet friendly. NO reservations.

Directions

3 miles from I-24. From Exit 7 turn west for 2.4 miles on Cty Hwy 12 to Hwy 37 (S Broadway). Turn left (south) and go 0.6 miles to park entrance.

Points of Interest -

The Park is known as an outstanding natural scenic spot, walkers will enjoy the experience. The Park is a great base for exploring the southern Illinois region, from the Tunnel Hill State Bike Trail in Vienna, to Golconda on the Ohio River, and The Garden of the Gods south of Harrisburg.

Exits 54 or 59 of I-39
Starved Rock State Park [2]
South of LaSalle
State Rate: $25

(815) 667-4726

http://dnr.state.il.us/lands/Landmgt/
PARKS/i&m/east/starve/park.htm

**Camp Accommodations
(see chapter introduction)**

133 well spaced **Class A/P** shaded sites, 100 reservable (by mail), 40+ feet, dump station. Amenities include picnic tables, grills, potable water, showers, flush toilets, hiking, Visitors Center/Lodge, pet friendly.

Directions

5.5 mi. from I-39. **Northbound**, from Exit 54 go east 2.1 mi. on Walnut to Ed Hand (Hwy 23). Turn north for 1 mi. to Hwy 71. Turn east (right) for 1.3 mi. to Hwy 178. Turn north for 0.8 mi. to the Park. **Southbound**, from Exit 59 go 2.2 mi. east on I-80 to Exit 81. Turn south on Hwy 178 for 3.2 mi. to Park.

Points of Interest -

What makes this park unique are the 18 canyons formed by glacial meltwater & stream erosion, which slice through tree-covered, sandstone bluffs for 4 mi. The park is best known for its fascinating rock formations. Walkers & photographers will enjoy the sites. Eat a meal at the lodge.

Exit 87 of I-39
**Shabbona Lake State
Recreation Area [3]**
South of DeKalb
State Rate: $25

(815) 824-2106

http://dnr.state.il.us/lands/Landmgt/
PARKS/R1/SHABBONA.HTM

**Camp Accommodations
(see chapter introduction)**

150 **Class A/P** shaded sites, 40 reservable (by mail), 9 ADA, some waterfront, dump station. Amenities include picnic tables, fire rings, potable water, ADA showers/toilets, hiking, fishing, pet friendly.

Directions

7 miles from I-39. From Exit 87 take Hwy 30 east 5.5 miles toward Shabbona. Before town turn right on Preserve Road. Go 1.6 mile to the Park.

Points of Interest -

The 1,550 acres of Park land is rolling prairie and features a 319 acre man-made fishing lake. In Shabbona, you'll find some great restaurants, shopping at stores that take you back to another time, and history to keep you busy learning for hours.

Exit Hwy 173 Exit of I-39/90
Rock Cut State Park [4]
North Side of Rockford
State Rate: $10-$20

(815) 885-3311

http://dnr.state.il.us/lands/Landmgt/
PARKS/R1/ROCKCUT.HTM

Camp Accommodations
(see chapter introduction)

240 spacious **Class A/P & B/S/P** shaded sites, 28 reservable (by mail), 2 ADA, 40+ feet long, dump station. Amenities include picnic tables, grills, potable water, ADA showers/toilets, hiking, biking, swimming, watchable wildlife, pet friendly.

Directions

0.5 miles from I-39/90. From Hwy 173 Exit (at mile marker 70) go 0.6 miles west to the Park.

Points of Interest -

Rockford is home to many quality antique stores, intriguing curiosities, boutiques and plain old junk shops. Some examples - Fire Station Antique Mall, Angela's Attic on Gardner, and Roscoe Antiques. Or visit homes located within the eight historic neighborhoods of Rockford's urban core.

Exits 82 or 96A of I-55
Sangchris Lake State Park [5]
Southeast of Springfield
State Rate: $8-$20

(217) 498-9208

http://dnr.state.il.us/Lands/Landmgt/
PARKS/R4/SANGCH.HTM

Camp Accommodations
(see chapter introduction)

There are 190 **Class A, B/S & C** shaded sites (19 reservable), 40+ feet long, some ADA, dump station. Amenities include picnic tables, grills, potable water, showers, flush toilets, hiking, fishing, boating, pet friendly.

Directions

13-15 mi. from I-55. **Northbound,** from Exit 82 go east on Hwy 104 for 6 mi. to Cty 37. Turn north 5.5 mi. to New City Rd (Cty 9). Turn right 3.4 mi. to the Park. **Southbound,** from Exit 96A, take Hwy 29 south 4.1 mi. to Rochester. Go right at Walnut (Hwy 37). Go south 5.7 mi. to New City Rd then left 3.4 mi. to the Park.

Points of Interest -

Springfield has many historic sites, museums, and memorials. Some examples include several notable Veteran's Memorials, Abraham Lincoln Library and Museum, Frank Lloyd Wright's Lawrence Memorial Library, State Capital, Lincoln Tomb, and Shea's Gas Station Museum.

Exit 40 of I-57
Ferne Clyffe State Park [1]
South of Goreville
State Rate: $8-$20

(618) 995-2411

http://dnr.state.il.us/lands/LandMgt/
PARKS/R5/FERNE.HTM

Camp Accommodations
(see chapter introduction)

59 ample **Class A & C** shaded sites, 40+ feet long, gravel pads, some pull throughs, dump station. Amenities in the Deer Ridge camp include picnic tables, grills, potable water, showers, flush toilets, hiking, fishing, pet friendly. NO reservations.

Directions

5 miles from I-57. From Exit 40 go east for 3.2 mi. on Hwy 13 (Goreville Rd.) to Goreville. Turn south on Hwy. 37. Go 1.7 mi. to the park entrance.

Points of Interest -

The Park is known as an outstanding natural scenic spot, walkers will enjoy the experience. The Park is a great base for exploring the southern Illinois region, from the Tunnel Hill State Bike Trail in Vienna, to Golconda on the Ohio River, and The Garden of the Gods south of Harrisburg.

Exit 45
Giant City State Park [6]
South of Carbondale
State Rate: $20

(618) 457-4836

http://dnr.state.il.us/Lands/Landmgt/
PARKS/R5/GC.HTM

Camp Accommodations
(see chapter introduction)

There are 85 **Class A** shaded sites, 40+ feet long, dump station. Amenities include picnic tables, grills, potable water, showers, flush toilets, fishing, boating, hiking, rock climbing, pet friendly. NO reservations.

Directions

16 mi. from I-57. From Exit 45 go northwest on Hwy 148 for 2.4 mi.. Turn left on Grassy Rd. Follow Grassy Rd for 4.3 mi. Turn left at the 'Y', staying on Grassy for 4.4 more mi. to Giant City Rd. Turn south on Giant City Rd 4.5 mi. to the Park.

Points of Interest -

Hike the Giant City Nature Trail, home of the "Giant City Streets" formed 12,000 years ago by huge bluffs of sandstone. Man made highlights of the Park include the new Visitor Center. Enjoy the rustic beauty of the Lodge with a meal. Drive the Southern Illinois Wine Trail.

Exit 77
Gun Creek Campground [7]
North of Benton
COE Rate: $16
America/Beautiful Rate: $8

(618) 629-2338

http://www.recreation.gov/

Camp Accommodations

101 shaded sites, 60+ feet, some waterfront, electric/water, dump station, 2 pull throughs, 6 ADA sites. Amenities include ADA toilets, potable water, grills, picnic tables, fire rings, biking, trails, fishing, boating, watchable wildlife, pet friendly.

Directions

1 mile from I-57. From Exit 77 go 0.3 miles west on Hwy 154. Go south for 0.3 miles to Gun Creek Trail. Turn right on Golf Course Drive, go 0.5 miles to the campground.

Points of Interest -

Activities include the Rend Lake Visitor Center, Ranger-led programs, educational programs, environmental education, and Rend Lake Wildlife Refuge. Auto touring and "Watchable Wildlife" viewing opportunities abound at the lake. Rend Lake is one of the best areas for birding.

Exit 116
Dam West Campground [8]
North of Carlyle
COE Rate: $24
America/Beautiful Rate: $12

(618) 594-4410

http://www.recreation.gov/

Camp Accommodations

109 shaded, ample, gravel sites, up to 100 feet, some waterfront, electric/water, 24 sewers, dump station, 1 ADA sites. Amenities include ADA toilets, potable water, grills/rings, tables, biking, trails, fishing boating, watchable wildlife, pet friendly.

Directions

24 miles from I-57. From Exit 116 go 22 miles west on Hwy 50 to Carlyle. Go north on Hwy 127 for 1.3 mile to William Rd. Turn east, go 0.6 mile to Lake Road (Cty Rd 1430 N), turn north 0.3 miles to the campground.

Points of Interest -

Carlyle Lake is the largest in-land lake in Illinois, with much to offer. You will also be 50 miles from St. Louis. Some area museums of note include the Bock Sculpture Museum, American Farm Heritage Museum, Pioneer Log Cabin Village, and Lewis and Clark Interpretive Center.

Exit 190 of I-57
Lithia Springs Camp [9]
West of Mattoon
COE Rate: $18-$22
America/Beautiful Rate: $9-$11

(217) 774-3951

www.reserveamerica.com/camping/
Lithia_Springs_Il/r/campground

Camp Accommodations

115 shaded, large, gravel sites, 85+ feet long, many waterfront, electric/water, 11 full hook ups, dump station, 1 ADA site. Amenities include ADA toilets, potable water, grills/rings, tables, biking, fishing boating, watchable wildlife, pet friendly.

Directions

27 miles from I-57. From Exit 190 go 24 miles west on Hwy 16. East of Shelbyville turn north on Cty Rd. 2200E for 1.5 miles to Cty Rd. 1500N, then west 1.5 miles to the campground.

Points of Interest -

A favorite trip is the Amish destination of Rockome Gardens, north of Mattoon, with Elvan's Soda Fountain, Enchanted Cave, Horse Powered Sawmill, & Blacksmith Shop. Master craftsmen and artisans demonstrate century-old traditions like pottery, candle making, baking and candy making.

Exit 315 of I-57
Kankakee River State Park [10]
Northwest of Kankakee
State Rate: $8-$25

(815) 933-1383

http://dnr.state.il.us/Lands/Landmgt/
PARKS/R2/KANKAKEE.HTM

Camp Accommodations
(see chapter introduction)

There are 260 **Class AP, B/E/P & C** shaded, ample sites, 40+ feet long, dump station, reservations taken. Amenities include picnic tables, grills, potable water, showers, flush toilets, hiking, fishing, canoeing, pet friendly.

Directions

9 mi. from I-57. From Exit 315 go south 0.5 mile to Armour Rd. Turn right, go 2 miles to Hwy. 102. Turn west (right), go 7 miles to the Park entrance.

Points of Interest -

The park puts you within an hour of the southern suburbs of Chicago as well as the Indiana state line. Frank Lloyd Wright designed two houses in the Riverview section of Kankakee - The B. Harley Bradley House & Stable and the Warren Hickox House, both still stand today.

Exit 50 of I-64
Dam West Campground [8]
North of Carlyle
COE Rate: $24
America/Beautiful Rate: $12

(618) 594-4410

http://www.recreation.gov/

Camp Accommodations

109 shaded/ample/gravel sites, 90+ feet, some waterfront, electric/water, 24 sewers, dump station, 1 ADA. Amenities include ADA toilets, potable water, grills/rings, tables, biking, trails, fishing, boating, watchable wildlife, pet friendly.

Directions

18 miles from I-64. From Exit 50 go 16.8 miles north on Hwy 127 to the north side of Carlyle. Turn east (right) on William Rd, go 0.6 mile to Lake Rd (Cty Rd 1430 N), turn north 0.3 miles on Lake Rd to the Camp.

Points of Interest -

Carlyle Lake is the largest in-land lake in Illinois, with much to offer. You will also be 50 miles from St. Louis. Some area museums of note include the Bock Sculpture Museum, American Farm Heritage Museum, Pioneer Log Cabin Village, and Lewis and Clark Interpretive Center.

Exit 63 of I-70
Ramsey Lake State Park [11]
North of Vandalia
State Rate: $8-$20

(618) 423-2215

http://dnr.state.il.us/Lands/Landmgt/
PARKS/R5/RAMSEY.HTM

Camp Accommodations
(see chapter introduction)

There are 155 ample **Class A, B/E & C** shaded sites, 40+ feet long, some waterfront, dump station, some reservable. Amenities include picnic tables, grills, potable water, showers, flush toilets, hiking, fishing, boating, pet friendly.

Directions
14 miles from I-70. From Exit 63 go 12.8 miles north on Hwy 51. Just north of Ramsey turn west on Cty Rd. 2900 (Ramsey Lake Rd.) for 1.4 mile to the Park.

Points of Interest -
Vandalia, significant in State history, is the oldest existing Capitol, and served the State from 1819-1839. You can tour The Vandalia State House, which is also notable for its association with Abraham Lincoln, who served in the House of Representatives. The building is downtown.

Exit 119 of I-70
Fox Ridge State Park [12]
South of Charleston
State Rate: $20

(217) 345-6416

http://dnr.state.il.us/Lands/Landmgt/
PARKS/R3/FOX/FOX.HTM

Camp Accommodations
(see chapter introduction)

There are 43 large and shady **Class A** sites, 40+ feet long, dump station, some reservable. Amenities include picnic tables, grills, potable water, showers, flush toilets, hiking, fishing, boating, nature trails, pet friendly.

Directions
11 miles from I-70. From Exit 119 go 11 miles north on Hwy 130 to the Park entrance at State Park Rd.

Points of Interest -
Tour Lincoln Log Cabin Historic Site. West of the Park, the site preserves the 1840s farm of Thomas and Sarah Bush Lincoln, father & stepmother of our 16th president. Close by is the Moore Home Historic Site, where Lincoln bid his stepmother farewell before assuming the Presidency.

Exit 20 of I-72
Siloam Springs State Park [13]
East of Quincy
State Rate: $10-$20

(217) 894-6205

http://dnr.state.il.us/Lands/Landmgt/
PARKS/R4/SILOAMSP.HTM

Camp Accommodations
(see chapter introduction)

There are 182 **Class A & B/EP** shaded sites, 40+ feet long, some pull throughs, dump station. Amenities include picnic tables, grills, potable water, showers, flush toilets, hiking, fishing, canoeing, pet friendly. NO reservations.

Directions
19 mi. from I-72. From Exit 20 go 7.7 mi. north on Cty Rd. 4/24. Turn right on Cty 22 (400 N) for 1 mi., then left on Cty Rd 2500 for 0.5 mi. to Hwy 104. Go right 3.5 mi. to Road 2873 (Siloam Rd.). Turn left, go 5.8 mi. to the park entrance.

Points of Interest -
Visit The Old Carthage Jail, where the Mormon leader, Joseph Smith Jr., and his brother Hyrum, were killed by an angry mob in 1844. See The Nauvoo Temple of the Church of Jesus Christ of Latter-day Saints. Relax at Baxter's Winery, the oldest Winery in Illinois, in Nauvoo.

Exit 156 of I-72
Clinton Lake State Park [14]
West of Champaign
State Rate: $10-$25

(217) 935-8722

http://dnr.state.il.us/Lands/Landmgt/
PARKS/R3/CLINTON.HTM

**Camp Accommodations
(see chapter introduction)**

There are 308 spacious **Class AA, A, & B/S** shaded sites, 40+ feet long, dump station, reservations. Amenities include picnic tables, grills, potable water, showers, flush toilets, hiking, fishing with accessible piers, canoeing, pet friendly.

Directions

12 mi. from I-72. From Exit 156 go 7.5 miles north on Hwy 48 to Hwy 10. Turn west, go 2 miles to Hwy 14 (Friends Creek Rd.). Go north on Cty 14 for 2.5 miles to the park entrance.

Points of Interest -

This is a good choice for a quiet, beautiful, & enjoyable location. There is easy access to the lake for fishing or boating & nature trails nearby for walking. Nevertheless you are within 30 minutes drive of Champaign-Urbana, Decatur or Bloomington-Normal if you want to sightsee or shop.

Exit 149 of I-74
Moraine View State Park [15]
East of Bloomington
State Rate: $20

(309) 724-8032

http://dnr.state.il.us/Lands/Landmgt/
PARKS/R3/MORAINE.HTM

**Camp Accommodations
(see chapter introduction)**

There are 137 ample **Class A** shaded sites, some lake front, 40+ feet long, some concrete ADA sites, dump station, some reservable. Amenities include picnic tables, grills, potable water, showers, flush toilets, hiking, fishing, boating, pet friendly.

Directions

7 miles from I-74. From Exit 149 take Chestnut (Cty 21) north 0.5 miles to Hwy 150. Turn left, follow Hwy 150 north for 0.6 miles through LeRoy to N West St. Turn north, still on Cty 21 (2600 East Rd), going 5.2 miles in all to E 900 Rd N. Turn right, go 2.1 miles to the park.

Points of Interest -

The road around the lake is a great walking/biking loop. Bloomington has the Bloomington Center for the Performing Arts & McLean County Museum of History You are in Illinois wine country, with several of Illinois' finest wineries located just a short drive from Bloomington-Normal.

Exit 210 of I-74
Kickapoo State Park [16]
West of Danville
State Rate: $8-$20

(217) 442-4915

http://dnr.state.il.us/Lands/Landmgt/
PARKS/R3/KICKAPOO.HTM

**Camp Accommodations
(see chapter introduction)**

There are around 90 **Class A** shaded sites, 40+ feet long, dump station. Amenities include picnic tables, grills, potable water, showers, flush toilets, hiking, fishing, boating, nature trails, pet friendly. NO reservations.

Directions

4.2 mile from I-74. From Exit 210 go 2.2 miles southwest on Hwy 150 to 1000 East Rd. Turn north, go 2 miles to Kickapoo Park Rd. Turn right in to the Park.

Points of Interest -

Hikers, wildflower enthusiasts, and wildlife lovers will enjoy this park. Visit the Danville Vermilion County War Museum; the downtown area has many antique, collectible and specialty shops. In Rossville the Depot Museum, built by the C&EI railroad in 1903, features railroad memorabilia.

Exit 1 of I-80
Fisherman's Corner [17]
Northeast of Moline
COE Rate: $16-$18
America/Beautiful Rate: $9

(815) 259-3628

http://www.recreation.gov/

Camp Accommodations

29 shaded, paved sites, 45 feet long, close to the Mississippi River, electric, dump station. Amenities include ADA toilets, potable water, grills, picnic tables, fire rings, biking, nature trails, fishing, boating, watchable wildlife, pet friendly.

Directions

2 mile from I-80. From Exit 1 go 2 mile southwest on Hwy 84 to the camp entrance.

Points of Interest -

Moline is part of the Quad Cities area. Of note is The John Deere Pavilion, which contains exhibits celebrating the history of the agricultural implements industry in the Midwest and showcases a variety of past and present John Deere plows, tractors, combines, and other machinery.

Exit 33 of I-80
Johnson Sauk Trail Park [18]
North of Kewanee
State Rate: $20

(309) 853-5589

http://dnr.state.il.us/Lands/Landmgt/
PARKS/R1/JOHNSON.HTM

Camp Accommodations
(see chapter introduction)

There are 70 **Class A** shaded sites, 40+ feet long, dump station. Amenities include picnic tables, grills, potable water, showers, flush toilets, hiking, fishing, canoeing, pet friendly. NO reservations.

Directions

7 miles from I-80. From Exit 33 go 5.6 miles south on Hwy 78 to N 1200th Ave. Turn left, go 1.2 miles to the park entrance.

Points of Interest -

Tour the Park's feature - a 1910 round barn. One of the largest round barns in the country, this architectural marvel is 80 feet high & 85 feet in diameter, with a 16-foot wide silo inside! Round barns originally were built by religious groups as they "left no corners for the devil to hide."

Exit 26 of I-88
Morrison-Rockwood State Park [19]
North of Morrison
State Rate: $10-$20

(815) 772-4708

http://dnr.state.il.us/lands/landmgt/
PARKS/R1/MORRISON.HTM

Camp Accommodations
(see chapter introduction)

There are 92 ample **Class A & B/S** shaded sites, some pull throughs, 40+ feet long, dump station. Amenities include picnic tables, grills, potable water, showers, flush toilets, hiking, fishing, boating, pet friendly. NO reservations.

Directions

11 miles from I-88. From Exit 26 take Hwy 78 north 6 miles in to Morrison. Turn left at Hwy 30 for 1.5 miles. Turn north on Hwy 78, go 1 mi. to Damen Rd. Turn right for 1.1 mi. to Crosby Rd. Turn left, go 1 mile to the Park.

Points of Interest -

Visit Ronald Reagan's birthplace in Tampico and tour the Ronald Reagan Birthplace and Museum. Then drive to Dixon and visit President Regan's boyhood home. The home is open to the public and operated by the Ronald Reagan Boyhood Home Foundation.

INDIANA

The Indiana Department of Natural Resources website has helpful information relevant to RV camping. Go to -

www.in.gov/dnr/parklake/

Online reservations for campgrounds can be found at

www.indiana.reserveworld.com/

Many campgrounds are seasonal and may not be available for the dates you select. Reservations may be made up to 6 months in advance.

You may bring firewood from a non-quarantined Indiana county into the camp-

ground. You must present a receipt or other proof of purchase. Don't move firewood. Burn all hardwood before you leave your campsite no matter where the wood came from.

Camping fees are -
Water/Electric-
$24.48 (Sun-Wed)
$34.68 (Thur-Sat)
Electric-
$17.34 (Sun-Wed)
$25.50 (Thur-Sat)
Non-Electric -
$10.20 (Sun-Wed)
$13.26 (Thur-Sat)

[1] **Harmonie State Park**
N38 05.415 W87 56.656
[2] **Warrick Country Lynnville Park**
N38 11.591 W87 19.733
[3] **Celina Lake Campground**
N38 11.927 W86 36.223
[4] **Charlestown State Park**
N38 26.964 W85 38.777
[5] **Muscatatuck County Park**
N38 59.377 W85 36.969
[6] **Brown County State Park**
N39 10.606 W86 16.232
[7] **Ouabache State Park**
N40 43.515 W85 07.365

[8] **Johnny Appleseed Campground**
N41 06.730 W85 07.136
[9] **Chain O' Lakes State Park**
N41 20.482 W85 24.138
[10] **McCormicks Creek State Park**
N39 16.992 W86 43.572
[11] **Whitewater Memorial State Park**
N39 36.724 W84 56.538
[12] **Turkey Run State Park**
N39 52.925 W87 12.115
[13] **Indiana Dunes State Park**
N41 39.391 W87 03.757

NOTES:

88

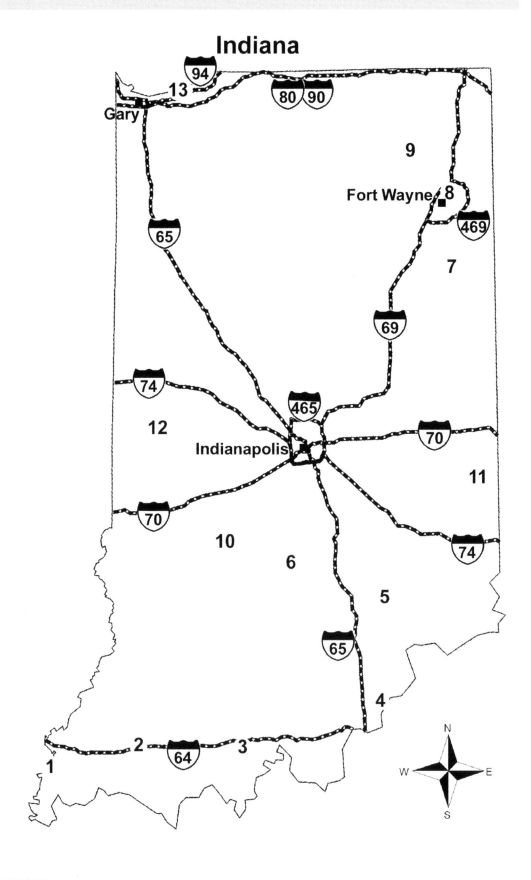

Exit 4
Harmonie State Park [1]
Northwest of Evansville
State Rate: $17-$26

(812) 682-4821

http://www.in.gov/dnr/
parklake/2981.htm

Camp Accommodations

There are 200 ample and shaded sites, up to 40 feet long, gravel pads, paved roads, electric, some pull throughs, 6 ADA, dump station, reservations available. Amenities include picnic tables, grills, firewood, ice, potable water, showers, flush toilets, walking, fishing, swimming pool, pet friendly.

Directions

11 mi. from I-64. From Exit 4 turn south for 10 miles on Hwy 69 to Hwy 269 (Cty Rd 325N). Turn right for 1 miles to the park entrance.

Points of Interest -

Two communal living experiments give the RVer a chance to visit Historic New Harmony which retains some of the colorful history for public interest. Here, utopian experiments - The Harmonists of the Rappite Community and the Owen Community - originated in New Harmony in the 1800's.

Exit 39
Warrick Country Lynnville Park [2]
West of Lynnville
County Rate: $20

(812) 922-5144

http://www.visitwarrick.com/outdoor/
lynnville/

Camp Accommodations

There are 24 shaded sites, 40+ feet long, some narrow, gravel pads, paved roads, water/electric, some pull throughs. Amenities include showers, flush toilets, accessible fishing, pet friendly. NO reservations.

Directions

2 mi. from I-64. From Exit 39 turn north for 0.2 mile on Hwy 61 to Hwy 68. Turn west and go just under 2 miles to the park entrance on the right.

Points of Interest -

Visit the Park's Wahnsiedler Observatory and home of the Evansville Astronomical Society. Spend some quality night time gazing at the stars. Check out the observatory's two telescopes: a 14 inch Celestron Schmitt-Cassegrain reflector and a 12.5 inch Cave Newtonian reflector.

Exit 79 of I-64
Celina Lake Campground [3]
South of St. Croix
Hoosier NF Rate: $17-$20
America/Beautiful Rate: $9

812) 843-4891

www.recreation.gov/

Camp Accommodations

23 wooded sites, up to 51 feet, electric, 1 ADA site. Amenities include ADA toilets, showers, potable water, grills, picnic tables, fire rings, biking, boating, fishing, nature trails, watchable wildlife, pet friendly. A dump station is at Tipsaw Recreation Area 3 miles south on Hwy 37.

Directions

3 miles from I-64. From Exit 79 go 2 miles south on Hwy 37 to Cty Rd. 501. Turn right, go 0.3 miles to Cty Rd. 502. Turn left into the campgrounds.

Points of Interest -

Swimming is excellent at Tipsaw Lake Beach, with its excellent swimming beach, modern bathhouse/showers, dressing facilities, and restrooms. Drive to Holiday World, an hour away. It's a great place to walk, enjoy the sights, food & take in some of the shows and other entertainment.

Exit 9 of I-65
Charlestown State Park [4]
North of Louisville, KY
State Rate: $17-$35

(812) 256-5600

http://www.in.gov/dnr/
parklake/2986.htm

Camp Accommodations

There are 192 ample and shaded sites, both water/electric and electric, 9 ADA sites, some up to 40 feet long, gravel pads, paved roads, dump station, reservations available. Amenities include picnic tables, grills, potable water, showers, flush toilets, walking, fishing, pet friendly.

Directions

9 miles from I-65. From Exit 9 go northeast on Hwy 331 for 1 mile to Hwy 403. Turn right, go 5.6 miles to Hwy 3. Turn right, go 1.2 mile to Hwy 62. Turn left and proceed 1 mile to the Park on the right.

Points of Interest -

The park has 200 foot overlooks above the Ohio River. This area is known for its diversity of topography, which will interest walkers, as well as excellent watchable wildlife - birders can seek out the 70+ species of birds. Of course Louisville is a 25 minute drive for sightseers and shoppers.

Exit 50
Muscatatuck County Park [5]
East of Seymour
County Rate: $16-$23

(812) 346-2953

http://www.muscatatuckpark.com/
camping.htm

Camp Accommodations

There are 26 shaded sites, 60+ feet long, gravel pads, paved roads, full hook ups or water/electric, some pull throughs, dump station, reservations available. Amenities include fire ring, picnic table, showers, flush toilets, accessible fishing, firewood available, pet friendly.

Directions

13 miles from I-65. From Exit 50 turn east for 12.4 miles on Hwy 50 to Hwy 3/7. Turn south and go 1.2 mile to the park entrance on the right.

Points of Interest -

Two Wildlife Refuges, 2 State Fish & Wildlife Areas, a State Forest & a State Nature Preserve surround the Park. The local towns are rich in history. Vernon is a Historic District. Enjoy "Indiana's best mid-19th century towns," with antique shops, festivals, herb farms & quaint dining.

Exit 68 of I-65
Brown County State Park [6]
West of Bloomington
State Rate: $17-$35

(812) 988-6406

http://www.in.gov/dnr/
parklake/2988.htm

Camp Accommodations

429 shaded sites, water/electric or electric, many ADA sites, 40+ feet long, pull throughs, gravel pads, paved roads, dump station, reservations available. Amenities include picnic tables, grills, potable water, showers, flush toilets, biking, walking, fishing, lodge, swimming pool, pet friendly.

Directions

18 miles from I-65. **You must use the West Entrance.** From Exit 68 go 16 miles west on Hwy 46, through Gnaw Bone, to Nashville. Turn south on Hwy 46 for 2.3 miles to the West Entrance.

Points of Interest -

This is the largest Indiana State park, with 15,776-acres. The Ogle Hollow Nature Preserve contains a self-guided nature trail. Naturalist services are available year-round. Visit the Abe Martin Lodge and Restaurant. Nashville features specialty shops, art galleries, and historic homes.

Exit 86 of I-69
Ouabache ('Wabash') State Park [7]
South of Ft. Wayne
State Rate: $17-$26

(260) 824-0926

http://www.in.gov/dnr/
parklake/2975.htm

Camp Accommodations

There are 124 shaded paved sites, up to 40 feet long, electric, 6 ADA, dump station, reservations available. Amenities include picnic tables, grills, potable water, showers, flush toilets, walking, fishing, swimming pool, pet friendly.

Directions

16.5 mi. from I-69. From Exit 86 go east onto Hwy 224, then immediately turn right on Hwy 116. Drive 13 miles to Bluffton. Turn left on Hwy 124 for 1.8 miles to Hwy 201. Turn south (right) for 1.6 mile on 201 to the Park.

Points of Interest -

The park area was occupied by the Miami Indians along the Wabash. In Fort Wayne see world-class art venues and museums. Check out the renowned Vera Bradley bags & DeBrand Fine Chocolates. Use the largest public genealogical collection in America; enjoy world-class arts & theatre.

Exit 109 of I-69
Johnny Appleseed Campground [8]
North side of Fort Wayne
County Rate: $18

(260) 425-5745

www.fortwayneparks.org/

Camp Accommodations

There are 36 shaded sites, 40+ feet long, gravel pads, electric, some pull throughs, dump station. Amenities include fire ring, picnic table, showers, flush toilets, fishing, boating, pet friendly. NO reservations.

Directions

4 miles from I-69. From Exit 109 turn southeast a block to Hwy 33/930, Coliseum Blvd. Turn left, go 3.8 miles to N Harry Baals Dr and the park entrance, on the right.

Points of Interest -

See Fort Wayne world-class art venues & museums. Check out the renowned Vera Bradley bags & DeBrand Fine Chocolates, made here. Use the largest public genealogical collection in America. Enjoy world-class arts and theatre. Enjoy a touring Broadway show, concert, or dine out.

Exit 129 of I-69
Chain O' Lakes State Park [9]
Northwest of Ft. Wayne
State Rate: $13-$26

(260) 636-2654

http://www.in.gov/dnr/parklake/2987.htm

Camp Accommodations

There are 380 shaded and spacious sites, up to 40+ feet long, electric, dump station, reservations available. Amenities include picnic tables, grills, potable water, showers, flush toilets, boat rentals, beach, concessions store, walking trails, nature center, fishing, pet friendly.

Directions

20.5 mi. from I-69. From Exit 129 go west on Hwy 8 for 7.1 miles to Hwy 3. Turn south 1 mile to E Baseline Rd. Turn west again for 10.6 miles to Hwy 9. Turn south for 0.7 miles to the E 75 S Rd. Turn left, go 1.1 miles to the Park.

Points of Interest -

Paddle the chain of lakes, hike trails, or attend a nature program in the park's 'old schoolhouse' nature center. Visit the Auburn Cord Duesenburg Museum. Area sights include the Mid America Windmill Museum, Old Jail Museum, and Indiana Historic Radio Museum.

Exit 41 of I-70
McCormicks Creek State Park [10]
South of Cloverdale
State Rate: $17-$26

(812) 829-2235

http://www.in.gov/dnr/
parklake/2978.htm

Camp Accommodations

189 shaded sites, electricity, 5 ADA, up to 40 feet long, pull throughs, gravel pads, paved roads, dump station, reservations available. Amenities include picnic tables, grills, potable water, showers, flush toilets, biking, walking, fishing, lodge, Interpretive Naturalist, swimming pool, pet friendly.

Directions

20 miles from I-70. From Exit 41 go 18.3 miles south on Hwy 231 to Spencer. Turn east on Hwy 46 for 1.7 miles to the Park entrance on your left.

Points of Interest -

Indiana's first State Park is noted for manicured grounds, unique limestone formations, & scenic waterfalls. At the Saddle Barn go on trail/hayrides. Play racquetball, handball, basketball, volleyball or use the shuffleboard courts in the Recreation Center, then enjoy a meal at the Canyon Inn.

Exit 151 of I-70
Whitewater Memorial State Park [11]
South of Richmond
State Rate: $10-$26

(765) 458-5565

http://www.in.gov/dnr/
parklake/2962.htm

Camp Accommodations

There are 236 shaded sites, up to 40 feet long, electric or dry, some pull through, 8 ADA, dump station, reservations available. Amenities include picnic tables, grills, potable water, showers, flush toilets, Interpretive Naturalist, walking, fishing, swimming, canoeing, pet friendly.

Directions

19 mi. from I-70. From Exit 151 turn south on Hwy 27 for 17 miles to Liberty. In Liberty, continue 1.8 miles south on Hwy 101 to the Park entrance on the right.

Points of Interest -

Ride the Whitewater Valley Railroad. Visit historic Metamora, observe a horse-drawn canal boat at the Whitewater Canal State Historic Site. Take a short cruise on the Ben Franklin, which passes through the Duck Creek Aqueduct, believed to be the only structure of its kind still in existence.

Exit 15 of I-74
Turkey Run State Park [12]
Southwest of Crawfordsville
State Rate: $17-$26

(765) 597-2635

http://www.in.gov/dnr/parklake/2964.htm

Camp Accommodations

There are 213 shaded sites, 40+ feet long, electricity, some pull through, 6 ADA, dump station, reservations available. Amenities include picnic tables, grills, potable water, showers, flush toilets, Interpretive Naturalist, Saddle Barn, walking, fishing, swimming, Inn and restaurant, wireless internet, pet friendly.

Directions

19 mi. from I-74. From Exit 15 turn south on Hwy 41 for 17.3. Turn east on Hwy 47 for 1.7 miles to the Park entrance on the left.

Points of Interest -

Enjoy the Park's geologic wonders and woodlands. Explore sandstone ravines, stands of aged forests, and scenic views along Sugar Creek. Dine at Turkey Run Inn's Narrows Restaurant, one of the finest in the area. Relax by the fireplace after a hike. Don't miss Billie Creek Village.

Exit 31 of I-80/90
Exit 26 of I-94
Indiana Dunes State Park [13]
North of Chesterton
State Rate: $17-$26

(219) 926-1952

http://www.in.gov/dnr/parklake/2980.htm

Camp Accommodations

140 shaded spacious sites, concrete pads, 6 ADA, 40+ feet long, electric, dump station, reservations available. Amenities include picnic tables, grills, potable water, showers, flush toilets, beach, walking trails, nature center, fishing, pet friendly. Early reservations are a good idea.

Directions

6 mi. from I-80/90. From Exit 31 go north 6 miles on Hwy 49 (Cty Rd 25) to the Park.

2.5 mi. from I-94. From Exit 26 go north 2.5 miles on Hwy 49 (Cty Rd 25) to the Park.

Points of Interest -

This campground is an adventure in itself. The grounds & trails are great for bikes or walking. There are different trails over the dunes, one with an interesting wooden stairs, great for photographs. Walk up, along, down the dunes. Walk the Lake Michigan beach, Chicago on the horizon.

IOWA

Half of Iowa State Park campsites can be reserved in advance. Reservations can be made 24 hours a day, 7 days a week, up to 3 months in advance, online at

www.reserveiaparks.com

Reservations can also be made M-F 8:00 am to 4:30 pm CDT, call 1-877-IAPARKS. If you can't find an answer about state parks on the web pages or are experiencing problems with website links send your question(s) to:

sandra.sampson@dnr.iowa.gov

RV camp fees, during the peak season (May 1 to September 30) per night are:

Modern electrical - $16
Modern, non-electric - $11
Non-modern, electric - $14
Non-modern, non-electric- $9
Water/sewer - add $3

(**Modern** - camping area which has showers and flush toilets. **Non-modern** - camping area in which no showers are provided, containing only pit-type latrines or flush toilets. Water may or may not be available to campers.)

There are no park entrance fees. It is in direct violation of the USDA APHIS quarantine for you to bring firewood from quarantined states into Iowa. You may bring your dog to the park as long as it is on a leash no more than 6 feet in length.

There is also an excellent Country Park System in Iowa, with over 40 parks with substantial campgrounds. You can find these parks by visiting -

http://www.mycountyparks.com

[1] **Waubonsie State Park**
N40 40.845 W95 40.912
[2] **Wilson Island State Recreation Area**
N41 29.503 W96 00.574
[3] **Lewis & Clark State Park**
N42 01.597 W96 09.715
[4] **Nine Eagles State Park**
N40 35.298 W93 45.254
[5] **Lake Ahquabi State Park**
N41 17.743 W93 34.952
[6] **Cherry Glen Campground**
N41 43.905 W93 40.792
[7] **Briggs Woods County Park**
N42 25.917 W93 48.092
[8] **Clear Lake State Park**
N43 06.657 W93 23.316

[9] **Prairie Rose State Park**
N41 36.004 W95 12.704
[10] **Lake Anita State Park**
N41 25.962 W94 45.705
[11] **Rock Creek State Park**
N41 45.635 W92 50.202
[12] **Sugar Bottom**
N41 46.538 W91 33.519
[13] **West Lake County Park**
N41 31.191 W90 41.286
(14) **Squaw Creek County Park**
N42 01.210 W91 33.367
(15) **Black Hawk County Park**
N42 33.752 W92 28.655

NOTES:

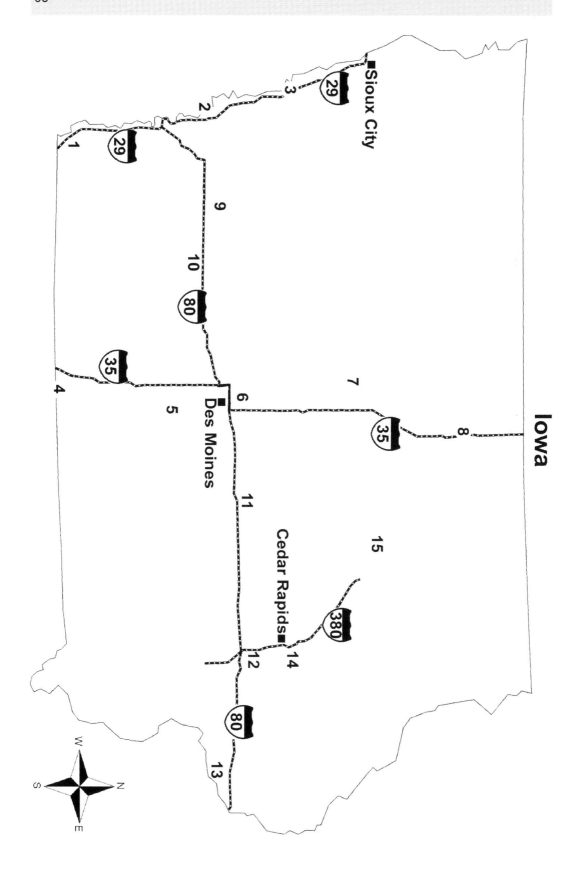

Exit 10
Waubonsie State Park [1]
Southeast of Percival
State Rate: $9-$16

(712) 382-2786

http://www.iowadnr.gov/parks/
state_park_list/waubonsie.html

**Camp Accommodations
(see chapter introduction)**

40 shaded campsites, 24 with electrical hookups, 60+ feet, some pull through, gravel, dump station, reservations available. Amenities include picnic tables, grills, potable water, showers and restrooms, biking, walking, fishing, pet friendly.

Directions

5.5 miles from I-29. From Exit 10 go 5.3 miles east on Hwy 2 to Hwy 239, turn right in to the Park.

Points of Interest -

The Park is in the "Loess Hills," a landform found only along the Missouri River & in China. Interpretive Trails provide visitors a chance to learn of the important plants and trees there, as well as enjoy the views. Waubonsie State Park is a site on the national Lewis & Clark Historical Trail.

Exit 72
Wilson Island State Recreation Area [2]
North of Council Bluffs
State Rate: $9-$16

(712) 642-2069

http://www.iowadnr.gov/parks/
state_park_list/wilson_island.html

**Camp Accommodations
(see chapter introduction)**

135 shaded, spacious sites, 2 ADA, 63 electric, 60+ feet, some pull through, gravel, dump station, reservations available. Amenities include tables, grills, potable water, showers/restrooms, firewood, biking, walking, fishing, pet friendly.

Directions

6 miles from I-29. From Exit 72 turn west and follow DeSoto Ave. for 6 miles to the Park.

Points of Interest -

Quiet, shady and spacious campsites are some of the Park's assets. Just north is the Bertrand (sunken paddleboat sternwheeler) Museum and The DeSoto National Wildlife Refuge. Both are terrific places to visit. The sights of Council Bluffs and Omaha are close by.

Exit 112
Lewis & Clark State Park [3]
North of Onawa
State Rate: $9-$19

(712) 423-2829

http://www.iowadnr.gov/parks/
state_park_list/lewis_clark.html

**Camp Accommodations
(see chapter introduction)**

There are 100 shaded, electric sites, 12 full hookup, 60+ feet, some pull through, gravel, dump station, reservations available. Amenities include picnic tables, grills, potable water, showers/restrooms, biking, walking, fishing, pet friendly.

Directions

1.5 miles from I-29. From Exit 112 go 1.5 miles west on Hwy 175 to Hwy 324. Turn north in to the Park.

Points of Interest -

Lewis and Clark State Park is perfect for a hike. You can view the full-sized reproduction of Lewis and Clark's keelboat/barge, "Best Friend." Blue Lake is great for a variety of water sports, the beach is a fine place for sunbathing, swimming or reading your book.

Exit 4
Nine Eagles State Park [4]
Southeast of Davis City
State Rate: $9-$16

(641) 442-2855

http://www.iowadnr.gov/parks/
state_park_list/nine_eagles.html

**Camp Accommodations
(see chapter introduction)**

68 shaded sites, 28 electric, 1 ADA, 60+
feet, some pull through, gravel, dump station, reservations available. Amenities include picnic tables, grills, potable water,
showers and restrooms, biking, walking,
fishing, boating, fishing, pet friendly.

Directions

10 miles from I-35. From Exit 4 go 3.9
miles east on Hwy 69. Turn south on Cty
Rd J66 for 5.6 miles to the Park entrance
on the left.

Points of Interest -
Wooded hills & valleys make this one of
southern Iowa's most scenic parks. Enjoy
9 miles of trails meandering through
wooded hills & valleys. The beach offers
swimming & is a great place for swimmers
and sunbathers. For local flavor Lamoni,
Davis City, Pleasanton & Leon are close.

Exit 56
Lake Ahquabi State Park [5]
South of Des Moines
State Rate: $6-$16

(515) 961-7101

http://www.iowadnr.gov/parks/
state_park_list/lake_ahquabi.html

**Camp Accommodations
(see chapter introduction)**

141 lake view sites, 85 electric, 1 ADA,
60+ feet, some pull through, gravel, dump
station, reservations available. Amenities
include tables, grills, potable water, show-
ers/restrooms, biking, swimming beach,
walking, fishing, boating, pet friendly.

Directions

20 miles from I-35. From Exit 56 go 13.3
mi. east on Hwy 92 to Indianola. Turn
south on Hwy 65/69 for 5.1 mi. to the intersection where Hwy 65 turns east. Turn
west (right) for 1 mi. on Cty Rd. 58 to
118th Ave. Go north 0.6 mi. to the Park.

Points of Interest -
In Indianola visit The National Balloon Museum. Exhibits provide a comprehensive
understanding of ballooning and its history. The town square provides an array of
unique shops and restaurants. Dine inside
or on the patio and enjoy the ambiance of
both the present day & not so distant past.

Exit 90
Cherry Glen Campground [6]
North of Des Moines
COE Rate: $16
America/Beautiful Rate: $8

(515) 964-8792

www.recreation.gov/

Camp Accommodations

125 shaded, electric sites, 3 ADA, 3 full
hookups, 60+ feet, dump station, reservations available. Amenities include, tables,
grills, potable water, ADA showers/
restrooms, biking, fishing, pet friendly.

Directions

7 miles from I-35. From Exit 90 turn
west and follow Hwy 160 (Oralabor Rd),
which becomes Hwy 415, for 6.1 miles.
Turn west (left) on 94th Ave for 0.6 miles
to the Park.

Points of Interest -
Try the 24 mile paved Neal Smith Trail
which runs from Des Moines to Big Creek
State Park, and connects the campground
to all recreation areas on the east side of
the lake. It is designated as a National
Recreation Trail and is used for biking,
hiking, jogging, walking, & in-line skating.

Exit 142
Briggs Woods County Park [7]
South of Webster City
County Rate: $16-$20

(515) 832-9570
www.conservation.hamiltoncountyiow
a.com/park.asp?
IDWebPage=2&IDSite=1

Camp Accommodations
(see chapter introduction)

There are 81 shaded sites, 51 electric, 30 full hookup, 40+ feet, some pull through, gravel. Amenities include picnic tables, grills, ADA showers and restrooms, biking, walking, fishing, pet friendly.

Directions

15.5 miles from I-35. From Exit 142 go 12.2 miles west on Hwy 20 to Hwy 17. Turn south 2.3 miles to Briggs Wood Trail. Turn left for 0.9 miles to the Park.

Points of Interest -

The Park, located in the heart of some of the most fertile land in the world, has a 62 acre lake and 18 hole golf course, which is one of Iowa's most challenging golf courses. There are numerous multi-recreational trails, including one going to Webster City, a great bike outing.

Exit 193
Clear Lake State Park [8]
South side of Clear Lake
State Rate: $9-$16

(641) 357-4212

http://www.iowadnr.gov/parks/
state_park_list/clear_lake.html

Camp Accommodations
(see chapter introduction)

200 shaded, gravel, campsites, 95 electric, 2 ADA, 60+ feet, some pull through, dump station, reservations available. Amenities include picnic tables, grills, potable water, showers/restrooms, biking, walking, fishing, boating, pet friendly.

Directions

3 miles from I-35. From Exit 193 go 1 mile west on Hwy 106 (255 St.). Turn south on Hwy 107 (S. 8th St.) for 1.5 miles, then turn west on 27th Ave. for 0.5 mile. Turn left on S Shore Dr, then an immediate right in to the Park entrance.

Points of Interest -

This is one of the most popular parks in the state. Clear Lake's premier attraction is the Surf Ballroom, best known as the site of Buddy Holly's last concert in 1959. Year around, the Ballroom hosts a variety of musical acts, ranging from rock and roll, to jazz, the blues & traditional big bands.

Exit 46
Prairie Rose State Park [9]
North of Avoca
State Rate: $6-$19

(712) 773-2701

www.iowadnr.gov/parks/
state_park_list/prairie_rose.html

Camp Accommodations
(see chapter introduction)

97 lake view, shaded, spacious sites, 8 full hookups, 77 electric, paved roads, 1 ADA, 60+ feet, dump station, reservations available. Amenities include tables, grills, potable water, showers/restrooms, biking, swimming, beach, fishing, pet friendly.

Directions

7.5 miles from I-80. From Exit 46 go 7.5 miles north on Cty Hwy M47 (York Rd.) to the Park entrance on your left.

Points of Interest -

The terraced hillside provides wonderful views of the lake and the surrounding hills. An interpretive trail winds along the shoreline and provides opportunities to observe a variety of plants and wildlife. The Prairie Rose beach provides good swimming and sunbathing.

Exit 70
Lake Anita State Park [10]
South of Anita
State Rate: $6-$19

(712) 762-3564

www.iowadnr.gov/parks/state_park_list/
lake_anita.html

Camp Accommodations
(see chapter introduction)

144 shaded sites, some waterfront, 40 full hookups, 52 electric, paved roads, 2 ADA, 60+ feet, dump station, reservations available. Amenities include tables, grills, potable water, showers and restrooms, biking, swimming, beach, fishing, pet friendly.

Directions

4.5 miles from I-80. From Exit 70 go south on Hwy 148 (through Anita) for 4.5 miles in total to the Park entrance on your right.

Points of Interest -

The Park is one of the most popular recreation facilities in the region. Using the self-guided nature trail provides an opportunity to learn about many of the shrubs and trees found in southwest Iowa. Lake Anita also offers a 4-mile walking trail which winds around the entire lake.

Exit 173
Rock Creek State Park [11]
Northeast of Kellogg
State Rate: $6-$19

(641) 236-3722

www.iowadnr.gov/parks/state_park_list/
rock_creek.html

Camp Accommodations
(see chapter introduction)

196 shaded sites, some waterfront, 101 electric, paved roads, 2 ADA, 60+ feet, dump station, reservations available. Amenities include tables, grills, potable water, showers/restrooms, biking, swimming, beach, walking, fishing, pet friendly.

Directions

9 miles from I-80. From Exit 173 go north on Hwy 224 (through Kellogg) for 5.3 miles to Cty Rd. F27. Turn east for 3.5 miles, crossing over the lake, to the Park entrance on your right.

Points of Interest -

Migrating ducks take refuge at Rock Creek - the concentrations of teal, bluebills and mallards offer an excellent bird watching opportunity. Kellogg features the five-building Kellogg Museum, with a one-room schoolhouse, country church, factory/bank museum, and blacksmith shop.

Exit 239
Sugar Bottom [12]
North of Iowa City
COE Rate: $14-$24
America/Beautiful Rate: $7-$12

(319) 338-3543

http://www.recreation.gov/

Camp Accommodations

233 shaded electrical sites, 3 ADA, 13 full hookups, 60+ feet, 13 pull throughs, some waterfront, dump station, reservations available. Amenities include ADA facilities, tables, grills, potable water, showers/restrooms, biking, fishing, pet friendly.

Directions

9 mi. from I-80. From Exit 239 turn north on I-380 for 4 mi. to Exit 4. Go east 2.1 mi. on Penn Street to Front St. Turn left, go 3 mi. (Front becomes Mehaffey). Just after crossing Mehaffey Bridge, turn right into the Park.

Points of Interest -

Iowa City, Coralville, & North Liberty have much to see, such as the Antique Car Museum of Iowa, Herbert Hoover Presidential Museum, and Riverside Theater. There are also a number of vineyards and wineries. Visit the Devonian Fossil Gorge, a 375-million-year-old fossilized ocean floor.

Exit 290
West Lake County Park [13]
West of Davenport
County Rate: $15-$18

(563) 328-3281

www.scottcountyiowa.com/conservation/west_lake.php

Camp Accommodations
(see chapter introduction)

There are 150 ample, shaded sites, some full hookup, 40+ feet, some pull through, some paved pads. Amenities include picnic tables, grills, ADA showers and restrooms, biking, walking, fishing, pet friendly. NO reservations.

Directions

6 miles from I-80. From Exit 290 go 4 miles south on I-280 to Exit 4. Go west on 160th St. 0.6 miles to 110th Ave (Cty. Rd. Y48). Turn south 1.3 miles to the Park entrance on the left.

Points of Interest -

Davenport offers theatre, symphony, riverboats, gaming, Mississippi Valley Blues Festival, Quad City Air Show, & world famous Bix Beiderbecke Memorial Jazz Festival. The Figge Art Institution which holds a magnificent collection of paintings/prints by American Regionalist Grant Wood.

Exit 4
Sugar Bottom [12]
North of Iowa City
COE Rate: $14-$24
America/Beautiful Rate: $7-$12

(319) 338-3543

http://www.recreation.gov/

Camp Accommodations

233 shaded electric sites, 3 ADA, 13 full hookups, 60+ feet, 13 pull throughs, some waterfront, dump station, reservations available. Amenities include ADA facilities, tables, grills, potable water, showers/restrooms, biking, fishing, pet friendly.

Directions

6 mi. from I-380. From Exit 4 go east 2.3 mi. on Penn Street to Front St. Turn left, go 3 mi. (Front turns into Mehaffey). Just after crossing Mehaffey Bridge, turn right into the Park.

Points of Interest -

Iowa City, Coralville, & North Liberty have much to offer, such as the Antique Car Museum of Iowa, Herbert Hoover Presidential Museum, & Riverside Theater. There are a number of vineyards and wineries. Visit the Devonian Fossil Gorge, a 375-million-year-old fossilized ocean floor.

Exit 24
Squaw Creek County Park [14]
East of Cedar Rapids
County Rate: $19

(319) 377-5954

www.mycountyparks.com/County/Linn/Park/Squaw-Creek-Park.aspx

Camp Accommodations
(see chapter introduction)

There are 61 ample, shaded sites, electric/water, 40+ feet, some pull through, paved roads, gravel pads. Amenities include picnic tables, grills, ADA showers and restrooms, biking, walking, fishing, pet friendly. NO reservations.

Directions

6 miles from I-380. From Exit 24 go 6 miles east on Hwy 100. Just before you reach Hwy 13/151 turn right on Banner Dr. into the Park and Golf Course.

Points of Interest -

In Cedar Rapids visit Brucemore. The Queen Anne-style mansion/estate has exhibits, music festivals, outdoor theatre, garden walks and holiday events. See the National Motorcycle Museum, Duffy's Collectible Cars Museum, and the Silos and Smokestacks National Heritage Area.

Exit 72
Black Hawk County Park [15]
Northwest of Cedar Falls
County Rate: $20

(319) 433-7275

www.mycountyparks.com/County/Black-Hawk/Park/Black-Hawk-Park.aspx

Camp Accommodations
(see chapter introduction)

197 ample, shaded sites, 21 full hook up, 176 electric/water, 40+ feet, some pull through, paved roads, gravel pads. Amenities include picnic tables, grills, ADA showers/restrooms, biking, fishing, pet friendly.

Directions

12.5 miles from I-380. Follow I-380 as it ends at Exit 72 and becomes Hwy 218. Follow Hwy 218 for 9.7 miles (through Waterloo) to Exit 189. Turn west on Lone Tree Rd. for 2.7 miles to the Park.

Points of Interest -

Bike to Cedar Falls. Take time to visit Heritage Farm, a Percheron horse farm & enjoy a horse drawn wagon ride. See the Cedar Valley Arboretum and Botanical Gardens; Cedar Falls Raceway (a 1/4 mile drag strip with 350' concrete launch pads) and the Hearst Sculpture Gardens.

KANSAS

The Kansas Department of Wildlife and Parks manages 24 state parks. You will find information and a helpful brochure at -
www.kdwp.state.ks.us/news/State-Parks/About-State-Parks

The Parks are pet friendly but pets must be restrained by a leash no longer than 10 feet. Reservation requests are accepted by telephone, mail or in-person (CAMPSITE RESERVATION CAN NOT BE MADE ONLINE). Phone reservations require a credit card payment. A reservation fee includes a reservation charge, one night's camping fee and utilities, if needed. You may be charged a Park entrance fee to camp.

The Corps of Engineers provides a number of good campgrounds, with almost half of the Interstate accessible locations listed in this chapter.

[1] **El Dorado State Park**
N37 49.981 W96 47.136
[2] **Riverside East -**
John Redmond Reservoir
N38 14.978 W95 45.227
[3] **Eisenhower State Park**
N38 32.140 W95 44.846
[4] **Hillsdale State Park**
N38 39.889 W94 53.250
[5] **Cedar Bluff State Park - North**
N38 48.761 W99 43.593

[6] **Wilson Lake - Lucas Camp**
N38 58.159 W98 30.174
[7] **West Rolling Hills**
N39 03.582 W96 56.347
[8] **Clinton State Park**
N38 56.496 W95 21.224
[9] **Cheney State Park - West**
N37 43.139 W97 50.070
[10] **Hillsboro Cove**
N38 21.757 W97 06.453
[11] **Venango Campground**
N38 38.009 W97 59.270

NOTES:

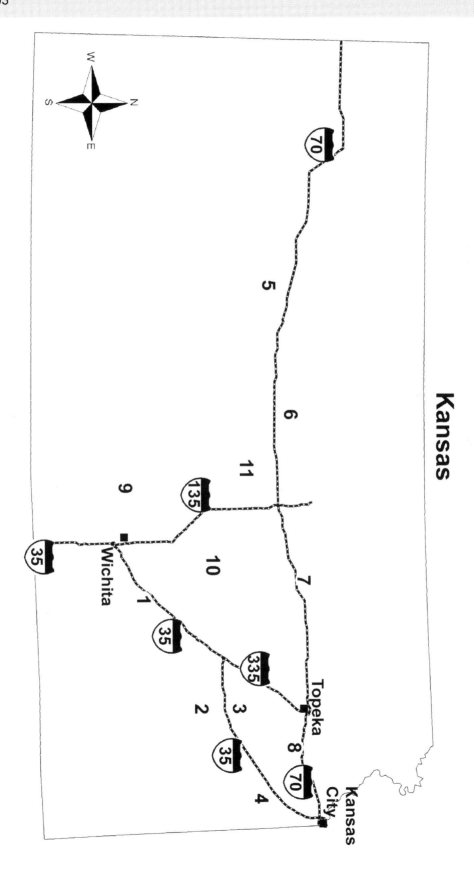

Kansas

Exit 71
El Dorado State Park [1]
East of El Dorado
State Rate: $18-$22

(316) 321-7180

http://kdwp.state.ks.us/news/State-Parks/Locations/El-Dorado

Camp Accommodations

128 full hook-ups, 352 water/electric, graveled, 40+ feet large sites, some waterfront, mostly shaded, many pull through, paved roads. Amenities include ADA accessible, picnic table, fire ring or grill, shower house, dump station, hiking, fishing, boating, beach, pet friendly.

Directions

8 miles from I-35. From Exit 71 turn east for 6.1 miles on Hwy 54/254 to Bluestem Rd. Turn north for 1.7 miles to Shady Creek Access Rd and the park entrance on your right.

Points of Interest -

El Dorado provides an opportunity to relive the Kansas oil boom at the Butler County History Center and Kansas Oil Museum. Some of that history is captured in works at the Coutts Memorial Museum of Art. Fine art galleries, upscale shops, and dining out complete the day.

Exit 155
Riverside East -
John Redmond Reservoir [2]
North of Burlington
COE: $15
America/Beautiful Rate: $8

(620) 364-8613

http://www.recreation.gov/

Camp Accommodations

43 shaded sites, mostly riverfront, 60+ feet long, water/electric, some pull through, dump station, reservations available. Amenities include showers, flush toilets, fishing, Interpretive Trail, pet friendly.

Directions

13 miles from I-35. From Exit 155 turn south for 11.8 miles on Hwy 75 to New Strawn. Turn west on 16th (Lake St.) for 0.3 miles to Embankment Rd. Bear left, go 1 mile to the campground.

Points of Interest -

The spillway area close to the camp is one of the most popular fishing areas on the reservoir. Starting in the middle of the park is a two-mile hiking trail, providing numerous year around wildlife observation and photography opportunities. Burlington main street is 3 miles south.

Exit 155
Eisenhower State Park [3]
Northeast of Emporia
State Rate: $18-$22

(785) 528-4102

http://kdwp.state.ks.us/news/State-Parks/Locations/Eisenhower

Camp Accommodations

25 full hook-up, 109 water/electric, 83 electric, graveled, large sites, 60+ feet, some waterfront, mostly shaded, pull throughs, paved roads. Amenities include ADA accessible, picnic table, fire ring or grill, shower house, dump station, hiking, fishing, boating, beach, pet friendly.

Directions

11 mi. from I-35. From Exit 155 turn north for 8.2 miles on Hwy 75 to Hwy 278. Go west for 3 miles to the Park entrance on your left.

Points of Interest -

Go to Ike's General Store in Doud Campground to pay campground fees. Emporia is notable for structures on the National Register of Historic Places such as the Old Emporia Public Library, Finney (Warren Wesley) House, & the Granada Theater (known as the Fox Theater).

Exit 207 of I-35
Hillsdale State Park [4]
Southwest of Olathe
State Rate: $18-$22

(913) 783-4507

http://kdwp.state.ks.us/news/State-Parks/Locations/Hillsdale

Camp Accommodations

160 water/electric, graveled sites, 40+ feet, some waterfront, mostly shaded, pull throughs, paved roads. Amenities include ADA accessible, picnic table, fire ring or grill, shower house, dump station, hiking, fishing, boating, beach, model airplane flying field, pet friendly.

Directions

10 miles from I-35. From Exit 207 turn south for 9.7 miles on Gardener Rd, which becomes Tontzville Rd, crosses the lake, then becomes Harmony Rd, to 255th St (Lake Rd). Go right for 0.3 mi. to the Park entrance.

Points of Interest -

See the John Brown Museum in Osawatomie, a stop on the Underground Railroad. In Olathe visit the Mahaffie Stagecoach Stop and Farm, Ernie Miller Park and Nature Center, or Heritage Park. In Louisburg check out the Powell Observatory or take in a show at the Middle Creek Opry.

Exit 135 of I-70
Cedar Bluff State Park - North [5]
South of Wakeney
State Rate: $18-$22

(785) 628-8614

http://kdwp.state.ks.us/news/State-Parks/Locations/Cedar-Bluff

Camp Accommodations

There are 5 campgrounds, 10 full hook-up, 91 water/electric, 20 electric, 40+ feet, mostly shaded, paved roads/pads. Amenities include ADA accessible, dump station, picnic table, fire ring or grill, shower house, dump station, hiking, fishing, boating, beach, pet friendly.

Directions

13 miles from I-70. From Exit 135 turn south for 13 miles on Hwy 147 to the park entrance on your right.

Points of Interest -

Threshing Machine Canyon, site of an 1850s Indian attack on a wagon train bearing a threshing machine, is west of the park. In the historic canyon, you find carvings dating to the mid 1800s. For a stunning view, drive to the top of the 150-foot tall, cedar covered limestone bluffs.

Exit 206 of I-70
Wilson Lake - Lucas Camp [6]
North of Wilson
COE: $8-$16
America/Beautiful Rate: $4-$8

(785) 658-2551

http://www.recreation.gov/

Camp Accommodations

There are 103 shaded sites, mostly lakefront, 60+ feet long, water/electric or electric only, 32 pull throughs, dump station, reservations available. Amenities include showers, flush toilets, fishing, hiking, swimming, pet friendly.

Directions

9 mi. from I-70. From Exit 206 turn north for 8 miles on Hwy 232 to Hwy 181. Turn west for 1 mile to the campground on the right.

Points of Interest -

The Wilson Lake area has 3 other excellent campgrounds as well. You will pass Wilson State Park and Sylvan (COE) on the way to Lucas. From Wilson State Park you can drive west to Minooka (COE). The three provide over 200 additional sites and can accommodate large RVs.

Exit 290
West Rolling Hills [7]
Northwest of Junction City
COE: $12-$19
America/Beautiful Rate: $6-$9

(785) 238-5714

http://www.recreation.gov/

Camp Accommodations

62 shaded, ample sites, mostly lakefront, 60+ feet long, electric or dry, 3 pull throughs, 2 ADA, dump station, reservations available. Amenities include showers, flush toilets, fishing, hiking, swimming, pet friendly.

Directions

5 miles from I-70. From Exit 290 turn north on Milford Lake Rd. for 4.3 miles to Hwy 244. Turn east for 0.3 mile to the campground on the left.

Points of Interest -

The Milford Lake area has 3 other excellent campgrounds within 5 miles of Rolling Hills - Milford State Park, Curtis Creek and Farnum Creek (both COE). See the U. S. Calvary Museum, Custer House, and 1st Infantry Division Museum in Fort Riley's historic main post district.

Exit 197 of I-70 Kansas Turnpike
Clinton State Park [8]
Southwest of Lawrence
State Rate: $18-$22

(785) 842-8562

http://kdwp.state.ks.us/news/State-Parks/Locations/Clinton

Camp Accommodations

There are 2 campgrounds with 240 water/electric graveled sites, 40+ feet, some waterfront, mostly shaded, paved roads. Amenities include ADA accessible, picnic table, fire ring or grill, shower house, dump station, hiking, fishing, boating, archery, disc golf, beach, pet friendly.

Directions

5 mi. from I-70 Turnpike. From Exit 197 turn south on Hwy 10 for 4 miles to 2nd exit (N 1400 Rd). Turn right, then right again at E 900th Rd. Turn left at N 1415 Rd, go 1 mile to the Park entrance.

Points of Interest -

Lawrence claims one of the most beautiful downtowns in the U.S. The 'Gallery Walk' is memorable. See the Black Jack Battlefield, site of the Battle of Black Jack, 1856. Visit Atchison, birthplace of Amelia Earhart. Her grandparents' Victorian home (where Earhart was born) is a museum.

Exit 6 of I-135 or Exit 7 of I-235
Cheney State Park - West [9]
West of Wichita
State Rate: $18-$22

(316) 542-3664

http://kdwp.state.ks.us/news/State-Parks/Locations/Cheney

Camp Accommodations

There are 3 campgrounds with 90 water/electric, shaded, large sites, 40+ feet, pull throughs, paved roads/pads. Amenities include ADA accessible, dump station, picnic table, fire ring or grill, shower house, dump station, hiking, fishing, boating, beach, pet friendly.

Directions

26 or 31 miles. From Exit 6 of I-135 turn west for 26 miles or 21 miles from Exit 7 of I-235 on Hwy 400 to Hwy 251. Go north 3.4 miles to 21st, turn west for 2.5 miles to the park entrance on your right.

Points of Interest -

The Park contains one of the top U. S. sailing lakes. The Ninnescah Center there is "headquarters" for sailing. A marina on the East Shore offers supplies & services for boaters/anglers. The Wildlife Area adjacent to the park provides a variety of wildlife watching & nature photography.

Exit 60
Hillsboro Cove [10]
East of McPherson
COE: $15-$17
America/Beautiful Rate: $8

(620) 382-2101

http://www.recreation.gov/

Camp Accommodations

There are 52 shaded sites, some lakefront, up to 50 feet long, water/electric or electric only, 8 pull through, dump station, reservations available. Amenities include flush toilets, fishing, hiking, swimming, pet friendly.

Directions

28 mi. from I-135. From Exit 60 turn east on Hwy 56 for 27.7 miles. Turn left on Nighthawk Rd, then right on 200th for 0.3 miles to the campground on the left.

Points of Interest -

The nearby communities of Hillsboro and Marion offer many opportunities for visitors, with festivals, art and craft events scheduled throughout the year. The shopping and dining choices in the towns, as well as a welcoming atmosphere will give you a small town's comfort and feel.

Exit 78
Venango Campground [11]
Southwest of Salina
COE: $12-$18
America/Beautiful Rate: $6-$9

(785) 546-2294

http://www.recreation.gov/

Camp Accommodations

There are 205 shaded sites, some lakefront, 65+ feet long, electric or electric/water, 17 pull throughs, some ADA, dump station, reservations available. Amenities include showers, flush toilets, hiking, swimming, pet friendly.

Directions

27 miles from I-135. From Exit 78 turn southwest on Hwy 81 Bus for 4.5 miles to Lindsborg. Continue west on Hwy 4 for 16.1 miles to Hwy 141. Turn north for 5.2 miles to Venango Rd. Turn left, go 0.6 miles the campground.

Points of Interest -

Notable area sites include taking in a Salina Symphony performance at the Stiefel Theatre for the Performing Arts. Also visit the Eisenhower Presidential Library and Museum in Abilene. The Coronado-Quivira Museum in Lyons focuses on Spanish explorers, and the Santa Fe Trail.

KENTUCKY

Wherever you travel in Kentucky, you are never far from one of the 52 Kentucky State Parks. Thirty-two of the Parks offer nearly 3,000 improved camp sites. Find them at -

http://parks.ky.gov/explore/exploreCamping.htm

Kentucky State Parks offer nearly 300 miles of trails suitable for all levels of enjoyment. The state parks oversee 15 marinas that offer pontoon and fishing boat rentals. All 17 resort parks have themed restaurants that serve both regional and specialty dishes. With 19 State Park golf courses, there is sure to be something for everyone. Several parks are equipped with seasonal riding stables. The parks operate more than two dozen swimming pools and 11 lake beaches. Leashed pets are allowed in park campgrounds and on many trails.

You can reserve a Kentucky State Parks campsite up to a year in advance with a credit card. Reservations are allowed for stays of up to two weeks. There is no Park general admission fee. There is a Senior Discount of 10 percent on lodging and camping fees with proof of age for those 62 and older. Get reservations at -

http://parks.ky.gov/reservations/campgrounds/

There is an online reservation fee (around $8) and a Holiday Premium fee ($2-$8). Parks prohibit the importation of firewood by campers from any state outside of Marshall County.

[1] Kentucky Dam Village State Resort Park N37 00.733 W88 16.903	**[7] Tailwater - Barren River Lake** N36 53.162 W86 07.701
[2] Hurricane Creek N36 55.212 W87 58.502	**[8] Mammoth Cave -** **Headquarters Campground** N37 07.778 W86 04.016
[3] Taylorsville Lake Park N38 02.023 W85 13.823	**[9] General Butler State Resort** N38 40.009 W85 08.625
[4] Kentucky Horse Resort Campground N38 08.474 W84 30.814	**[10] Big Bone Lick State Park** N38 53.342 W84 44.855
[5] Twin Knobs N38 05.747 W83 29.464	**[11] Grove Recreation Area** N36 56.414 W84 13.032
[6] Grayson Lake State Park N38 12.740 W83 00.916	

NOTES:

109

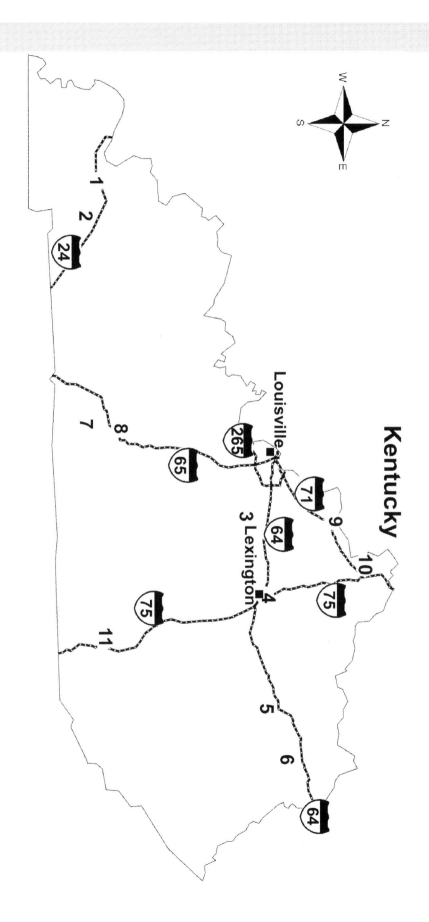

Exit 27 of I-24
Kentucky Dam Village
State Resort Park [1]
East of Paducah
State Rate: $21-$23
Senior Discount: $19-$21

(270) 362-4271

http://parks.ky.gov/findparks/
resortparks/kd/

Camp Accommodations

214 shaded, paved sites, 60+ feet, water/
electric, dump station, reservations available. Amenities include shower/restrooms,
fire rings, grills, tables, golf, biking, hiking,
fishing, swimming pool, store, pet friendly.

Directions

3 miles from I-24. From Exit 27 turn east
for 2 miles on Hwy 62. Exit north (left) on
Hwy 282 (Gilbertsville Hwy) for 0.7 miles
to the camp registration.

Points of Interest -

This is one of Kentucky's most popular
resort campgrounds. The Village Inn
Lodge and Harbor Lights Restaurant provide a nice view of the Tennessee River
and the marina. In Paducah visit the Low-
ertown Arts District, National Quilt Museum, and the River Discovery Center.

Exit 56 of I-24
Hurricane Creek [2]
South of Eddyville
COE Rate: $16-$22
America/Beautiful Rate: $8-$11

(270) 522-8821

http://www.recreation.gov/

Camp Accommodations

44 shaded sites, 1 ADA, some lakefront,
up to 40 feet long, water or water/electric,
11 pull throughs, dump station, reservations available. Amenities include showers, flush toilets, potable water, fishing,
swimming, pet friendly.

Directions

8 miles from I-24. From Exit 56 turn
south for 1.2 miles on Hwy 139 to Hwy
276 (Hurricane Rd.). Turn west (right) for 6
miles to Hwy 274. Turn right, go 0.5 miles
to Hurricane Camp Rd and the campground on the left.

Points of Interest -

You are close to 'Land Between the Lakes
National Recreation Area,' the largest
inland peninsula in the U.S.A., which offers hunting, fishing, horseback riding,
plus motorcycle/ATV trails. You'll find
many restaurants and resorts. 'Patti's
1880's Settlement' is a unique destination.

Exit 35 of I-64
Taylorsville Lake Park [3]
East of Louisville
State Rate: $21-$23
Senior Discount: $19-$21

(502) 477-8713

http://parks.ky.gov/findparks/recparks/
tl/

Camp Accommodations

42 spacious, gravel sites, 60+ feet, 2 ADA,
water/electric, dump station, 3 pull
throughs, reservations available. Amenities include shower/restrooms, fire rings,
grills, picnic tables, biking, hiking, fishing,
nature programs, store, pet friendly.

Directions

14 miles from I-64. From Exit 35 go
south for 5.8 miles on Hwy 53 to South-
ville. Turn right on Hwy 44, go 6.2 miles to
Hwy 248. Turn left, go 2 miles to Park Rd
and the park on the right.

Points of Interest -

The trail system in this park is multi-use for
hikers, mountain bikers, and horseback
riders. In Taylorsville visit the Sanctuary
Arts Center, enjoy it's characters, storytell-
ers, music makers, and artists. The art
center offers classes, and art works of
every kind - from quilts to sculpture!

Exit 75
Kentucky Horse Resort Campground
[4]
North of Lexington
State Rate: $22-$27
Senior Discount: $20-$24

(800) 370-6416

www.kyhorsepark.com/index.php

Camp Accommodations

260 spacious, paved sites, all are 55 feet, water/electric, two dump stations, reservations available. Amenities include two bathhouse/laundrys, fire rings, grills, picnic tables, firewood, tennis, volleyball, biking, swimming pool, grocery store, pet friendly.

Directions

3 miles from I-64. From Exit 75 go 2 miles north on I-75 to Exit 120. Turn east on Cty Rd. 1973 for 1 mile to Campground Rd and the park on the left.

Points of Interest -

If you are into horses or just want to see what the thoroughbred horse community is all about, this is the place to go. Visit the Kentucky Horse Park at a discounted rate. Go to the Hall of Champions, International Museum of the Horse, American Saddlebred Museum, etc.

Exit 133
Twin Knobs [5]
Southwest of Morehead
Daniel Boone NF: $18-$28
America/Beautiful Rate: $9-$14

(606) 784-8816

http://www.recreation.gov/

Camp Accommodations

64 shaded, spacious, paved sites, 13 ADA, some lakefront, up to 70 feet long, from dry to full hookups, dump station, reservations available. Amenities include ADA showers, flush toilets, potable water, fishing, hiking, pet friendly.

Directions

9 miles from I-64. From Exit 133 turn south for 9 miles on Hwy 801 to Twin Knobs Rd and the campground on the right.

Points of Interest -

The camp has a lot to offer for all interests and activities. Paved walkways make walking and exploring easier across the 10 camping loops. Photographers will like the views of Cave Run Lake and the wind surfers. Enjoy the large sandy beach, partake in the Interpretive Programs.

Exit 172
Grayson Lake State Park [6]
South of Grayson
State Rate: $20-$22
Senior Discount: $18-$20

(606) 474-9727

http://parks.ky.gov/findparks/recparks/gl/

Camp Accommodations

71 spacious, shaded, paved sites, water/electric, 60+ feet, 2 pull throughs, dump station, reservation available. Amenities include showers/restrooms, fire rings, grills, tables, firewood, ice, golf course, biking, fishing, hiking, store, pet friendly.

Directions

11 miles from I-64. From Exit 172 go 11.2 miles south on Hwy 7 in to the park. Turn right at Grayson Lake State Park Rd.

Points of Interest -

The rolling terrain presents challenging play for golfers on a 18 hole course that encircles the lake. Hidden Cove was rated #4 by Golf Digest in 2005. For non-golfers the Beech-Hemlock Forest Trail is an opportunity to discover the distinctive plants, rock formations, and wildlife of the park.

Exit 38 of I-65
Tailwater - Barren River Lake [7]
South of Smiths Grove
COE Rate: $17
America/Beautiful Rate: $8

(270) 622-7732

http://www.recreation.gov/

Camp Accommodations

There are 45 shaded sites, 1 ADA, most riverfront, 65+ feet long, water/electric, 2 pull throughs, 2 ADA, dump station, reservations available. Amenities include showers, flush toilets, potable water, fishing, hiking, pet friendly.

Directions

14.5 miles from I-65. From Exit 38 turn south for 11.2 miles on Hwy 101 to Hwy 1533 (Meader-Port Oliver Rd.). Turn left for 3.1 miles to Hwy 252. Turn left, go 0.2 miles to Riverbend Rd and the campground on the left.

Points of Interest -

Camping options include Baileys Point (COE) and Barren River Lake State Park. In Bowling Green visit Aviation Heritage Park, Historic Railpark & Train Museum. Take an Historic Walking Tour. Downtown offers restaurants, shops, memorial sites, Fountain Square Park & Circus Square.

Exit 48 of I-65
Mammoth Cave
Headquarters Campground [8]
North of Park City
NP Rate : $17
America/Beautiful Rate: $8

(270) 758-2180

http://www.nps.gov/maca/
planyourvisit/camping.htm

Camp Accommodations

50 RV shaded sites, 2 ADA, up to 40 feet long, many pull throughs, dump station, reservations available. Amenities include showers, flush toilets, potable water, store, hiking, fishing, pet friendly. NO utilities.

Directions

3 miles from I-65. From Exit 48 turn north for 3 miles on Hwy 255 (Mammoth Cave Parkway) into the park. Follow signs to Headquarters.

Points of Interest -

Tour part of the world's longest known cave system, with more than 367 miles explored. Plan your cave tour in advance and buy reserve tickets. Other park activities include nature walks, evening programs, surface hikes, canoeing, horseback riding, and bicycling.

Exit 44 of I-71
General Butler State Resort Park [9]
Southeast side of Carrollton
State Rate: $22-$24
Senior Discount: $20-$22

(502) 732-4384

http://parks.ky.gov/findparks/
resortparks/gb/

Camp Accommodations

105 shaded sites, 45+ feet, paved, water/electric, dump station, 5 pull throughs, reservations available. Amenities include shower/restrooms, fire rings, grills, tables, golf, nature programs, biking, hiking, fishing, swimming pool, store, pet friendly.

Directions

2 miles from I-71. From Exit 44 turn north for 1.8 miles on Hwy 227 to General Butler Park Rd and the park on the left.

Points of Interest -

Enjoy the General Butler Lodge and Two Rivers Restaurant. Visit the Butler-Turpin State Historic House, built in 1859, which recalls one of Kentucky's foremost military families from Colonial times, American Revolution, War of 1812, Mexican War and the Civil War.

Exit 175 of I-71/75
Big Bone Lick State Park [10]
South of Cincinnati
State Rate: $22-$24
Senior Discount: $20-$22

(859) 384-3522

http://parks.ky.gov/findparks/recparks/bb/

Camp Accommodations

There are 60 shaded, paved sites, water/
electric, 45+ feet, dump station, reservation available. Amenities include showers,
restrooms, fire rings, grills, picnic tables,
firewood, ice, golf course. biking, fishing,
hiking, store, pet friendly.

Directions

8 miles from I-71/75. From Exit 175 go
7.6 miles southwest on Hwy 338
(Richwood then Beaver Rd.) to the park.

Points of Interest -

Designated as a National Natural Landmark, the park is significant for its combination of salt springs and late Pleistocene
bone beds, where the mammoth, mastodon, ground sloth and bison roamed. Walk
recreated grasslands/wetlands/savannas
leading to a "bog" diorama.

Exit 25 of I-75
Grove Recreation Area [11]
West of Corbin
Daniel Boone NF Rate: $15
America/Beautiful Rate: $8

(606) 528-6156

http://www.recreation.gov/

Camp Accommodations

There are 44 shaded sites, 1 ADA, most
riverfront, 50 feet long, water/electric,
dump station, reservations available.
Amenities include showers, flush toilets,
potable water, fishing, hiking, pet friendly.

Directions

11 miles from I-75. From Exit 25 turn
southwest for 4.7 miles on Hwy 25W to
Hwy 1193 (Bee Creek Rd.). Turn right for
2.8 miles to Grove Rd. Turn right, follow
Grove Rd. for 3 miles to the campground.

Points of Interest -

See nearby Cumberland Falls and enjoy
the "Niagara of the South", the 125-foot
fall's curtain of water drops 60 feet. In Corbin go to Harland Sanders Museum &
Café and dine where it all began - at Colonel Sander's original restaurant. Tour the
Corbin Railroad Museum.

Exit 120 of I-75
**Kentucky Horse Resort Campground
[4]**
North of Lexington
State Rate: $22-$27
Senior Discount: $20-$24

(800) 370-6416

www.kyhorsepark.com/index.php

Camp Accommodations

260 spacious, paved sites, all are 55 feet,
water/electric, dump stations, reservations
available. Amenities include two bath-
house/laundry units, fire rings, grills, picnic
tables, firewood, tennis/volleyball courts,
biking, swimming pool, store, pet friendly.

Directions

1 mile from I-75. From Exit 120 turn east
on Cty Rd. 1973 for 1 mile to Campground
Rd and the park on the left.

Points of Interest -

If you are into horses or just want to see
what the thoroughbred horse community is
all about, this is the place to go. Visit the
Kentucky Horse Park at a discounted rate.
Go to the Hall of Champions, International
Museum of the Horse, American Saddlebred Museum, etc.

LOUISIANA

Each of the 20 Louisiana State Parks is located in a high recreation potential area. You can hike, fish, bike and enjoy birding and nature trails. Most State Parks feature a waterfront location, campsites and picnic areas. Any pet brought in to a State Park must be on a leash (not to exceed 5 feet in length). See the state website for more details and information -

http://www.crt.state.la.us/parks/iparkslisting.aspx

Visitors who hold an America the Beautiful Pass (or already have a Golden Age/Golden Access Passport) are entitled to a 50% reduction on camping fees at Louisiana State Parks. Parks may have $1 per person entrance fee (waived for people 62 and older).

Reservations can be made 11 months to the day in advance online at -

www.reserveamerica.com/la/state/campgrounds/r/campgroundDirectoryList.do?contractCode=LA

or call the reservation center at (877) 226-7652.

[1] Sam Houston Jones State Park N30 18.043 W93 14.669	**[6] Chicot State Park, North Loop** N30 47.379 W92 17.269
[2] Bayou Segnette State Park N29 54.013 W90 09.327	**[7] Indian Creek Recreation Area** N31 06.817 W92 28.228
[3] Fontainebleau State Park N30 20.729 W90 01.354	**[8] Kincaid Camp** N31 15.494 W92 37.915
[4] Beaver Dam N32 40.575 W93 18.349	**[9] Tickfaw State Park** N30 23.451 W90 37.658
[5] Lake Claiborne State Park N32 42.780 W92 55.401	

NOTES:

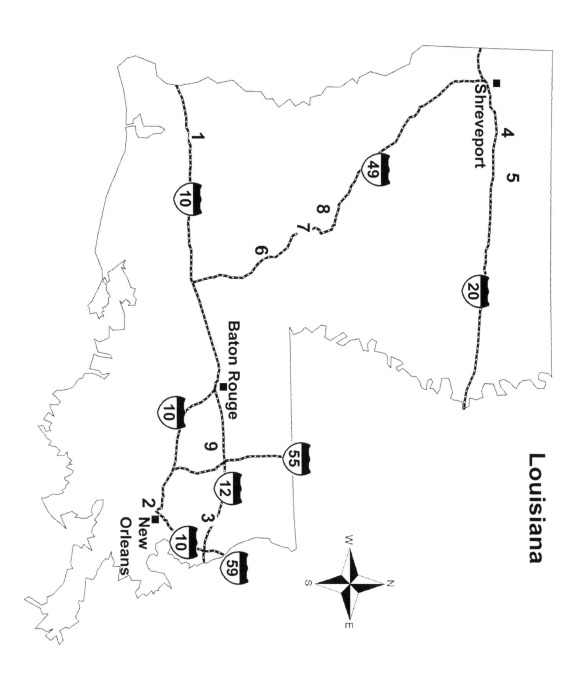

Louisiana

Exit 27 of I-10
Sam Houston Jones State Park [1]
North of Lake Charles
State Rate: $16-$18
America/Beautiful Rate: $8-$9

(337) 855-2665

http://www.crt.state.la.us/parks/
iShjones.aspx

Camp Accommodations

62 shaded, gravel sites, 60+ feet, by lagoon, 2 ADA, full hook-up or water/electric, 7 pull through, paved roads, dump station. Amenities include restroom/shower, grill, fire ring, picnic table, biking, hiking, pet friendly.

Directions

5 miles from I-10. From Exit 27 go 5 miles north on Hwy 378 to the entrance, Sam Houston Jones Parkway, on your left.

Points of Interest -

The area is known as the "Festival Capital," with over 75 annual festivals, there is something going on nearly every weekend. In Lake Charles visit the Charpentier Historical District, the Port of Lake Charles, Millennium and Adventure Cove Parks for dining, shopping, entertainment.

Exit 234 of I-10
Bayou Segnette State Park [2]
South of New Orleans
State Rate: $18
America/Beautiful Rate: $9

(504) 736-7140

http://www.crt.state.la.us/parks/
ibyusegne.aspx

Camp Accommodations

98 large paved sites, up to 50 feet, 3 ADA, water/electric, dump station. Amenities include restroom/shower, grill, fire ring, picnic table, biking, boardwalks, swimming, Wi-Fi, Interpretive Programs, pet friendly.

Directions

12 miles from I-10. From Exit 234 go 12 miles south on Expressway 90 (Pontchartrain Expressway, then Westbank Expressway). The Park will be on your left at Drake Dr. (blinking yellow light). Avoid rush hours.

Points of Interest -

Camp in the scenic bayou. Just 20-30 minutes from New Orleans and the French Quarter, a multitude of recreational opportunities awaits visitors. Also go to a Mississippi River Road Plantation, or the Louisiana State Museum. Check out the park wave pool!

Exit 65 of I-12
Fontainebleau State Park [3]
North shore of Lake Pontchartrain
State Rate: $12-$18
America/Beautiful Rate: $6-$9

(985) 624-4443

http://www.crt.state.la.us/parks/
iFontaine.aspx

Camp Accommodations

163 shaded, large paved sites, 70+ feet, 2 ADA, water/electric, a few with sewer or dry, 19 pull through, dump station. Amenities include restroom/shower, grill, fire ring, picnic table, biking, fishing, swimming, pet friendly.

Directions

6.5 miles from I-12. From Exit 65 follow Hwy 59 south for 3.6 miles to Hwy 190. Turn left, go 2.6 miles to Group Campground Rd on the right.

Points of Interest -

The Park has beautiful views! Enjoy the beach, boardwalk and the pier. See **[2]** for New Orleans suggestions. Another option would be the Global Wildlife Center, the largest free-roaming wildlife preserve of its kind in the country, with over 4,000 exotic, endangered animals.

Exit 47 of I-20
Beaver Dam [4]
North of Minden
Kisatchie N F Rate: $10
America/Beautiful Rate: $5

(318) 927-2061

http://www.forestcamping.com/dow/
southern/kisacmp.htm#beaver%
20dam

Camp Accommodations

28 shaded, paved sites, some lake view, 40+ feet, water/electric, dump station. Amenities include restroom/shower, grill, fire ring, picnic table, fishing, biking, hiking, pet friendly.

Directions

9 mi. from I-20. From Exit 47 go 1.6 mi. north on Hwy 7 to Hwy 79. Go right for 0.5 mi. to Hwy 159. Go left for 4.6 mi. to Cty Rd. 111 (Caney Lake Rd), then left 2.4 mi. to Caney Lake camp sign, turn left on NF 810 to the camp.

Points of Interest -

The Minden red-bricked Main Street generates nostalgic images of a time gone by. The old-time charm extends to restaurants and quaint shops. Minden has an historic residential district, adjoining downtown. Visit the near by Germantown Colony and Museum.

Exit 67 of I-20
Lake Claiborne State Park [5]
North of Arcadia
State Rate: $16-$18
America/Beautiful Rate: $8-$9

(318) 927-2976

http://www.crt.state.la.us/parks/
iClaiborn.aspx

Camp Accommodations

87 shaded sites, many lakefront, 40+ feet, 2 ADA, 12 pull through, water/electric, dump station. Amenities include restroom/shower, grill, fire ring, picnic table, biking, hiking, Interpretive Programs, pet friendly.

Directions

17 miles from I-20. From Exit 67 go 7.6 miles northwest to Athens. Turn east, then bear north, on Hwy 518 for 8.2 miles to Hwy 146. Go east (right) 1 mile to the Park entrance.

Points of Interest -

Visit the Bonnie and Clyde Historic Site, near Arcadia, marking the last hours of the infamous outlaws. Tour Poverty Point Historic Site (East of Monroe), a very significant archaeological find, a complex of Native American ceremonial mounds built between 1700 and 700 B.C

Exit 46 of I-49
Chicot State Park, North Loop [6]
North of Opelousas
State Rate: $16
America/Beautiful Rate: $8

(337) 363-2403

http://www.crt.state.la.us/parks/
ichicot.aspx

Camp Accommodations

100 shaded sites, 60+ feet, 7 pull through, water/electric, dump station. Amenities include restroom/shower, grill, fire ring, picnic table, biking, swimming pool, Wi-Fi, lodge, Interpretive Programs, pet friendly.

Directions

11 miles from I-49. From Exit 46 go 7.1 miles west on Hwy 106 to Hwy 3042. Turn south on Hwy 3042 for 4 miles to the main entrance on the left.

Points of Interest -

Visit the Acadian town of Ville Platte ("flat town"). Cajun traditions/cultural are found in the spoken French, music & food. Opelousas was the Confederate Civil War capital of Louisiana and boyhood home of Jim Bowie. Don't miss the "Rendez-vous des Cajuns" live radio show in Eunice.

Exit 73 of I-49
Indian Creek Recreation Area [7]
Southeast of Woodworth
LA Dept of Ag. Rate: $12

(318) 487-5058

http://townofwoodworth.com/
recreation/indiancreek.html

Camp Accommodations

101 shaded, paved sites, 40+ feet, water/electric, dump station. Amenities include restroom/shower, grill, fire ring, picnic table, fishing, biking, swimming, hiking, pet friendly.

Directions

6 miles from I-49. From Exit 73 go 2.5 miles southwest on Hwy 3265 (Robinson Bridge Rd.) to just east of Woodworth. Turn south on Indian Creek Rd for 1.2 miles to Camp Ground Rd. Turn left and go 2.1 miles to the Park.

Points of Interest -

In Alexandria/Pineville, attractions include the Alexandria Museum of Art, Frogmore Cotton Plantation and Gins, Louisiana Maneuvers and Military Museum, Tunica-Biloxi Indian Museum, Alexandria Antique Mall, and many restaurants.

Exit 86 of I-49
Kincaid Camp [8]
West of Alexandria
Kisatchie N F Rate: $15
America/Beautiful Rate: $8

(318) 793-9427

http://www.forestcamping.com/dow/
southern/kisacmp.htm#kincaid

Camp Accommodations

40 shaded, paved sites, 60+ feet, water/electric, dump station. Amenities include restroom/shower, grill, fire ring, picnic table, fishing, biking, hiking, pet friendly.

Directions

21 miles from I-49. From Exit 86 go 2 miles west on Hwy 165 to Hwy 28, then west for 12.7 miles to Hwy 121. Turn south for 0.3 miles to Kincaid/Valentine Lakes sign. Turn left, go 4 miles to Forest Rd. 200. Go left for 2.4 miles to the camp.

Points of Interest -

In Alexandria/Pineville, attractions include the Alexandria Museum of Art, Frogmore Cotton Plantation and Gins, Louisiana Maneuvers and Military Museum, Tunica-Biloxi Indian Museum, Alexandria Antique Mall, and many restaurants.

Exit 26 of I-55
Tickfaw State Park [9]
West of Springfield
State Rate: $16
America/Beautiful Rate: $8

(225) 294-5020

http://www.crt.state.la.us/parks/
itickfaw.aspx

Camp Accommodations

30 shaded, large, paved sites, 70+ feet, 2 ADA, water/electric, dump station. Amenities include restroom/shower, grill, fire ring, picnic table, biking, fishing, swimming, store, Wi-Fi, pet friendly.

Directions

13 miles from I-55. From Exit 26 go west for 5.4 miles on Hwy 22 to Springfield. Continue west on Hwy 1037 (Blood River Rd.) for 6.2 miles to Patterson Road, then bear left for 1.2 miles to the park entrance.

Points of Interest -

Ponchatoula is said to be "America's Antique City," with the quality of the antiques and collectibles combined with the experience of the dealers. Try the "Swamp Walk," a boardwalk into the Joyce Wildlife Management Area Swamp, one of the largest uninhabited swamps in Louisiana.

119

MAINE

Maine's State Park system is as varied as the state's landscape. In Maine, there are more than 30 state parks dedicated to the visitor's enjoyment. Twelve state parks and the Allagash Wilderness Waterway provide camping opportunities. In addition to campground fees there is a per person day use fee, varying from $1-$7. After Labor Day most facilities are closed for the season. The Maine State Parks website is -

http://www.maine.gov/doc/parks/index.html

Make camping reservations at-
http://www.maine.gov/doc/parks/reservations/maps.html

State parks sites offer a number of accommodations for people with disabilities and special needs - reserved parking spaces; wheelchair ramps; beach wheelchairs; hardened surfaces on trails and walkways; accessible restrooms; roll-in showers; benches in showers and changing rooms; TTY; and easy-to-reach campsites. Each park or historic site is rated by the state for overall ease of access.

Pets must be on a leash not exceeding four feet in length and must not be left unattended. Pets are not allowed on beaches or in the Sebago Lake State Park campground.

Acadia National Park is an exceptional RV campground destination so 2 campgrounds, either near or in the Park, were added even though the locations exceed the 'within 30 minutes of an Interstate' guideline.

[1] **Sebago Lake State Park**
N43 56.526 W70 32.778
[2] **Lake St. George State Park**
N44 23.884 W69 20.861
[3] **Lamoine State Park**
N44 27.332 W68 17.855
[4] **Blackwoods Campground**
N44 18.804 W68 12.849
[5] **Bradbury Mountain State Park**
N43 53.982 W70 10.724

NOTES:

Maine

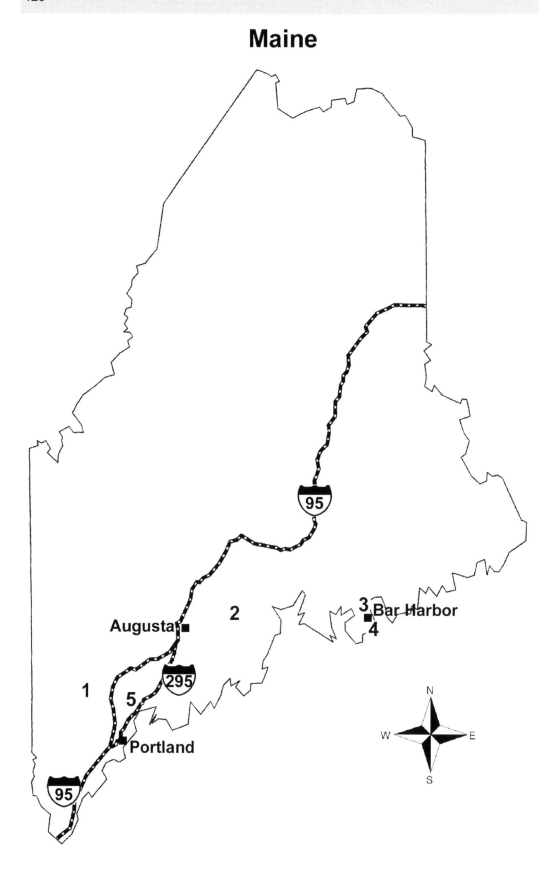

Exit 63
Sebago Lake State Park [1]
Sebago Lake - North Shore
State Rate: $15-$25

(207) 693-6613

http://www.maine.gov/cgi-bin/online/
doc/parksearch/index.pl

Camp Accommodations

250 shaded sites, some lakefront, up to 40 feet, water/electric, dump station, generally accessible facilities. Amenities include reservations, restroom/shower, fire ring, picnic table, fishing, biking, hiking, no pets allowed.

Directions

17 miles from I-95. From Exit 63 turn southwest on Hwy 202 (Gray Rd.) for 6.4 miles to Hwy 302. Turn northwest (right) on 302 for 10.2 miles. Turn left on State Park Rd into the Park.

Points of Interest -

Ride the Songo River Queen or Point Sebago Princess on Sebago-Long Lake. Visit the South Casco boyhood home/museum of Nathaniel Hawthorne. Enjoy auctions, antiquing, craft fairs and bazaars. Bridgton is a haven for old books, antiques, china, porcelain, Shaker items and quilts.

Exit 109
Lake St. George State Park [2]
East of Augusta
State Rate: $15-$25

(207) 589-4255

http://www.maine.gov/cgi-bin/online/
doc/parksearch/index.pl

Camp Accommodations

38 shaded sites, some lakefront, up to 40 feet, dry camping, potable water, dump station, somewhat accessible facilities, reservations available. Amenities include restroom/shower, grill, fire ring, picnic table, fishing, biking, hiking, pet friendly.

Directions

28 miles from I-95. From Exit 109 turn east on Hwy 202 (Western Ave.) for 3 miles, where the road joins with Hwy 3. Now follow Hwy 3 for 25 miles to the Park, just north of Sherman's Corner.

Points of Interest -

Visit Belfast, where the decades long presence of artists, artisans, studios and galleries is a big reason it is called "the funkiest little town in Maine." You will find most any type of art here, from contemporary photographic art and sea glass jewelry, to more traditional paintings.

Exit 182
Lamoine State Park [3]
Southeast of Ellsworth
State Rate: $15-$25

(207) 667-4778

http://www.maine.gov/cgi-bin/online/
doc/parksearch/index.pl

Camp Accommodations

62 shaded sites, up to 40 feet, 1 ADA, dry camping, medium accessibility, reservations available. Amenities include restroom/shower, potable water, grill, fire ring, picnic table, biking, fishing, hiking, kayaking, firewood, pet friendly.

Directions

37 miles from I-95. From Exit 182 go 4.6 miles east on I-395 to exit 6. Go southeast (right) for 23 miles on Hwy 1a to Ellsworth. Continue on Hwy 1 for 2 miles to Hwy 184. Turn right on Hwy 184 for 7.7 miles to the Park on your right.

Points of Interest -

In the heart of Down East Maine, this oceanfront park is located in one of the most sought-after vacation regions in the state. The Park's location provides easy access to Bar Harbor, Acadia National Park, rockbound islands, and area lighthouses.

Exit 182 of I-95
Blackwoods Campground [4]
Southeast of Ellsworth
Arcadia NP Rate: $10
America/Beautiful Rate: $5

(207) 288-3338

www.nps.gov/acad/planyourvisit/
blackwoodscampground.htm

Camp Accommodations

40 shaded sites, up to 35 feet, dry camping, some ADA, dump station, pull throughs, reservations available. Amenities include restrooms, potable water, grill, fire ring, picnic table, biking, hiking, firewood, pet friendly.

Directions

54 miles from I-95. From Exit 182 go 4.6 miles east on I-395 to exit 6. Go southeast (right) for 23 miles on Hwy 1a to Ellsworth. Continue on Hwy 1 for 1 mile. Bear right onto Hwy 3 and go 25 miles to the Park.

Points of Interest -

Acadia's carriage roads, designed by John D. Rockefeller so he could travel via horse and carriage, provide you an excellent way to explore Acadia by auto, horseback or bicycle. The system features 17 stone-faced bridges spanning streams, waterfalls, cliffs, & roads. Each bridge is unique.

Exit 22 of I-295
Bradbury Mountain State Park [5]
Northwest of Freeport
State Rate: $11-$19

(207) 688-4712

http://www.maine.gov/cgi-bin/online/
doc/parksearch/index.pl

Camp Accommodations

35 shaded sites, up to 35 feet, 2 ADA, dry camping, medium accessibility, reservations available. Amenities include restroom/shower, potable water, grill, fire ring, picnic table, biking, hiking, pet friendly.

Directions

5 miles from I-295. From Exit 22 turn northwest on Hwy 125 to Durham Rd. turn left, go 0.2 miles to Pownal Rd. Go right for 4.2 miles (becomes Elmwood). Turn right on Hwy 9 (Hallowell Rd) for 0.6 mile to the Park.

Points of Interest -

Sculpted by a glacier, Bradbury Mountain is the park's outstanding natural feature. A trail on top offers wonderful views of the coast. In Freeport, a beautiful coastal village, find over 200 outlets, designer shops, eclectic boutiques, great restaurants, casual cafes, and L.L.Bean.

MASSACHUSETTS

Public campgrounds in Massachusetts are essentially limited to the State Park System. For folks with larger rigs, 35-40 feet is generally the length limit. Massachusetts State Park camping information can be found at -

www.mass.gov/dcr/recreate/camping.htm

Camping fees at Department of Conservation & Recreation campgrounds are:

Coastal Campground
- Out Of State Resident - $17 a night
- MA Resident - $15 a night

Inland Campground
- Out Of State Resident - $14 a night
- MA Resident - $12 a night

Advanced reservations are available for 28 state forests and park campgrounds. Reservations may be made as early as six months prior to the date of arrival, and as late as one day prior to arrival. The reservation transaction charge is $9.25 per reservation. Call (877) 422-6762 or go online to ReserveAmerica at -

http://www.reserveamerica.com/mapHome.do?topTabIndex=1

Pets are allowed but must be leashed (10 foot maximum) at all times. There may be areas posted off-limits to pets.

[1] **October Mountain State Forest**
N42 20.178 W73 14.036
[2] **Tolland State Forest**
N42 08.680 W73 02.996
[3] **Wells State Park**
N42 08.482 W72 02.496
[4] **DAR State Forest**
N42 27.376 W72 47.448

[5] **Harold Parker State Forest**
N42 36.649 W71 05.436
[6] **Salisbury Beach State Reservation**
N42 50.507 W70 49.361
[7] **Pearl Hill State Park**
N42 39.274 W71 45.457
[8] **Scusett Beach State Reservation**
N41 46.680 W70 30.345

NOTES:

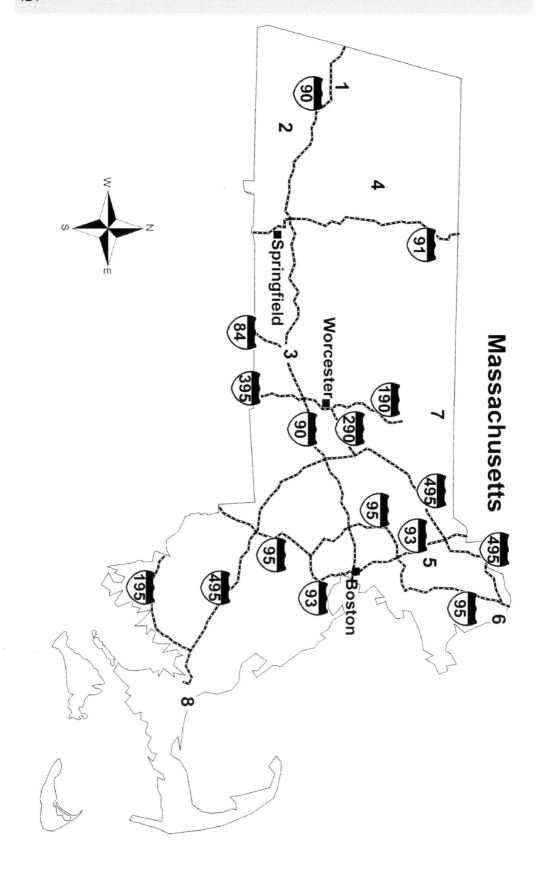

Exit 2 of I-90
October Mountain State Forest [1]
North of Lee
State Rate: $12-$14

(413) 243-1778

http://www.mass.gov/dcr/parks/
western/octm.htm

Camp Accommodations

23 ample, accessible sites, some pull through, up to 35 feet, dry camping, dump station, reservations available. Amenities include ADA restroom/ shower, potable water, hosts, fishing, hiking, boating, pet friendly.

Directions

3.5 miles from I-90. From Exit 2 follow Hwy 20 northwest 1.1 mile through Lee to Center St. Turn right, go 0.3 miles, bear left on Columbia St. for 0.8 miles. Go straight at the merge onto Bradley St. Go 1.1 miles (becomes Woodland Rd), following brown signs to the campground.

Points of Interest -

The name "October Mountain" is attributed to writer Herman Melville. You are in the midst of the Berkshire Region, with the Appalachian Trail close by. Visit Tanglewood in Lenox and Stockbridge, home of the annual Tanglewood Music Festival or Jazz Festival. Also see **[2]** below.

Exit 3 of I-90
Tolland State Forest [2]
West of Westfield
State Rate: $12-$14

(413) 269-6002

http://www.mass.gov/dcr/parks/
western/toll.htm

Camp Accommodations

44 sites on a scenic, wooded peninsula, up to 35 feet, 1 ADA, dry camping, dump station, reservations available. Amenities include ADA restroom/ showers, potable water, hosts, fishing, beach/swimming, boating, hiking, pet friendly.

Directions

22 miles from I-90. From Exit 3 go 1.5 miles south on Hwy 10/202 to Hwy 20. Go west for 5.8 miles to Hwy 23 (Blandford). Turn left & go 11.8 miles (through East Otis). A mile past the East Otis townline, go left on West Shore Rd for 1.7 miles, then left 1.3 miles on Tolland Rd. to the camp.

Points of Interest -

In the southern Berkshires, browse The Mews, off Main Street in Stockbridge. This cluster of unique shops includes many local artists' designs. Visit the Hancock Shaker Village, Berkshire Museum and the Norman Rockwell Museum. Also see **[1]** above.

Exit 9 of I-90
Exit 3A of I-84
Wells State Park [3]
North of Sturbridge
State Rate: $12-$14

(508) 347-9257

http://www.mass.gov/dcr/parks/
central/well.htm

Camp Accommodations

48 sites, some waterfront, up to 35 feet, many pull through, dry camping, dump station, reservations available. Amenities include ADA restroom/ showers, potable water, hosts, fishing, swimming, hiking, pet friendly.

Directions

2.5 miles from I-84/90. From either Interstate Exit, follow Hwy 131/20 for 1.4 miles east to Hwy 49. Turn north (left) on Hwy 49. Go 0.9 mile to the Park entrance on the left.

Points of Interest -

Visit Old Sturbridge Village. Discover rural New England life of the 1700s and 1800s. 'OSV,' on 200+ acres of historical land features over 40 reproduction, reconstructed buildings reminiscent of centuries-old New England. The Village is the largest outdoor living history in the northeast.

Exit 19 of I-91
DAR State Forest [4]
Northwest of Northampton
State Rate: $12-$14

(413) 268-7098

http://www.mass.gov/dcr/parks/
western/darf.htm

Camp Accommodations

34 accessible sites, 2 ADA, up to 28 feet, dry camping, dump station, reservations available. Amenities include ADA restroom/shower, potable water, hosts, fishing, hiking, boating, fire wood, Nature Center, pet friendly.

Directions

15.5 miles from I-91. From Exit 19 in Northampton follow Hwy 9 west and northwest for 13.9 miles to just past Goshen. Turn right onto Hwy 112 and continue for 0.7 miles to Moore Hill Rd. Turn right, go 0.8 miles to the Park entrance.

Points of Interest -

In 1851, opera singer Jenny Lind, the "Swedish Nightingale", called Northampton the "Paradise of America." Today the city is an arts destination, named "Number One Best Small Arts Town" by author John Villani & one of the "Top 25 Arts Destinations" by AmericanStyle magazine.

Exit 41 of I-93
Harold Parker State Forest [5]
Northwest of Danvers
State Rate: $12-$14

(978) 475-7972

http://www.mass.gov/dcr/parks/
northeast/harp.htm

Camp Accommodations

25 accessible, shaded sites, 2 ADA, up to 40 feet, dry camping, dump station, reservations available. Amenities include ADA restroom/shower, potable water, hosts, fishing, hiking, boating, Interpretive Programs, swimming, pet friendly.

Directions

4.5 miles from I-93. From Exit 41 go 2.6 miles northeast on Hwy 125. Turn right on Harold Parker Rd and go 1.5 miles to Jenkins Rd. Turn right on Jenkins Rd, go 0.2 miles to the Park entrance on the right.

Points of Interest -

From the Park you are within an hour of most of the sites and activities that the Boston metropolitan area has to offer. The 3,000 acre Park forest offers 35 miles of hiking and biking trails, which provide wonderful seclusion and a sylvan break from the activities of the day.

Exit 47 of I-95
Harold Parker State Forest [5]
Northwest of Danvers
State Rate: $12-$14

(978) 475-7972

http://www.mass.gov/dcr/parks/
northeast/harp.htm

Camp Accommodations

25 accessible, shaded sites, 2 ADA, up to 40 feet, dry camping, dump station, reservations available. Amenities include ADA restroom/shower, potable water, hosts, fishing, hiking, boating, Interpretive Programs, swimming, pet friendly.

Directions

9 miles from I-95. From Exit 47 go 4.1 miles northwest on Hwy 114. Just past Middleton bear left on Forest Rd (becomes Marblehead St.), go 3.7 miles to Haverhill St. Turn right, go 1 mile (becomes Jenkins) to the Park entrance.

Points of Interest -

From the Park you are within an hour of most of the sites and activities that the Boston metropolitan area has to offer. The 3,000 acre Park forest offers 35 miles of hiking and biking trails, which provide wonderful seclusion and a sylvan break from the activities of the day.

Exit 58 of I-95
Salisbury Beach State Reservation [6]
East of Salisbury
State Rate: $22-$24

(978) 462-4481

http://www.mass.gov/dcr/parks/
northeast/salb.htm

Camp Accommodations

405 sites, 2 ADA, up to 40 feet, electricity/water, dump station, reservations available. Amenities include ADA restroom/shower, hosts, Interpretive Programs, fishing, hiking, boating, swimming, pet friendly.

Directions

4 miles from I-95. From Exit 58 follow Hwy 110 east for 2 miles to Salisbury and the intersection with Hwy 1. Turn north 0.2 miles, then turn right on Hwy 1a (Beach Rd.) and follow it 2 miles to the Park entrance (State Beach Rd.) on the right.

Points of Interest -

Salisbury Beach is one of the state's most popular beaches stretching for miles along the Atlantic. On the beach, over-the-dune boardwalks, a new playground, and pavilion area make this a popular ocean destination. There are also many coastal towns south and north to visit and enjoy.

Exit 8 of I-190
Pearl Hill State Park [7]
North of Fitchburg
State Rate: $12-$14

(978) 597-8802

http://www.mass.gov/dcr/parks/
northeast/phil.htm

Camp Accommodations

43 shaded sites, 11 ADA, 3 pull through, up to 35 feet, dry camping, reservations available. Amenities include ADA restroom/showers, potable water, hosts, fishing, hiking, boating, swimming, pet friendly.

Directions

16 miles from I-190. From Exit 8 go 1.9 mile west on Hwy 2 to exit 32. Go north onto Hwy 13 for 10 miles to Hwy 119 in Townsend. Turn left on Hwy 119, go 2.1 miles to New Fitchburg Rd. Turn left, go 1.8 miles to the park entrance on the right.

Points of Interest -

Leominster has over 20 antique shops and every Thursday there is an auction. Visit the Fitchburg Art Museum - 14 galleries with American and European paintings, prints, drawings, ceramics and decorative arts as well as Greek, Roman, Asian and pre-Columbian antiquities.

Exit 1 of I-495
Scusset Beach State Reservation [8]
On the Cape Cod Canal
State Rate: $20-$22

(508) 888-0859

http://www.mass.gov/dcr/parks/
southeast/scus.htm

Camp Accommodations

92 shaded sites, all ADA, up to 40 feet, electricity/water, dump station, reservations advised. Amenities include ADA restroom/shower, potable water, hosts, fishing, hiking, swimming, pet friendly, no fires or grills.

Directions

15.5 miles from I-495. From Exit 1 continue east 10 miles on Hwy 25 to Hwy 6 exit. Go east on Hwy 6 for 3.5 miles to the Hwy 3/6 rotary. Go east on Meetinghouse Lane (becomes Scusset Beach Rd) for 2 miles to the camp.

Points of Interest -

Scusset Beach is located on Cape Cod Bay, with 1.5 miles of frontage along the east end of the Cape Cod Canal. It is a popular swimming, salt water angling and ship watching area. Bicycling along the canal is also fun. You are at the gateway to Cape Cod too!

MICHIGAN

Michigan is predominately populated with State Park and National Forest campgrounds. There are around 125 State Park and Forest as well as over 60 National Forest campgrounds statewide. It can be said that you are never more than half an hour from a Michigan State Park, State Forest or National Forest Campground. Of this wide selection, those most accessible by Interstate and suitable for RVs are complied in this chapter.

The Michigan Department of Natural Resources and Environment is responsible for the State's Parks and Forest, and can be found at -

http://www.michigan.gov/dnr/0,1607,7-153-10365---,00.html

Reservations for campsites may be made up to 6 months in advance of your arrival date. The reservation fee is $8. Annual or daily permits are required, as well as towed duplicate vehicle permits/fees. The Michigan Department of Natural Resources State Park Campground and Harbor Reservation page can be found at -

http://www.midnrreservations.com/

In Michigan:

Modern Campgrounds provide a modern restroom/shower building, pressurized water spigots and a dump station. Each campsite has electrical service available.

Semi-Modern Campgrounds provide electrical service or access to a modern restroom building. In areas that offer electrical service, vault toilets are provided, as well as potable water provided by hand pumps or pressurized spigots. Dump stations are not typically provided.

Rustic Campgrounds provide vault toilets and hand pumps or pressurized spigots for water. Showers, electricity and sanitation stations are not provided.

Many parks require as much as 100 feet of electric extension cord. With few exceptions, pets are welcomed in Michigan state parks and recreation areas. Pets are not allowed on designated beaches or areas used for wading or swimming. Always keep your pet on a leash not to exceed six feet in length.

The western end of the Michigan Upper Peninsula is not shown on the map as there is no Interstate in that region.

[1] **Sleepy Hollow State Park**
N42 55.747 W84 24.461

[2] **Metamora-Hadley Recreation Area**
N42 56.702 W83 21.425

[3] **Lakeport State Park**
N43 07.466 W82 29.837

[4] **Sterling State Park**
N41 55.206 W83 20.292

[5] **Pontiac Lake Recreation Area**
N42 41.199 W83 29.390

[6] **Seven Lakes State Park**
N42 49.006 W83 38.886

[7] **Bay City State Recreation Area**
N43 40.041 W83 54.451

[8] **South Higgins Lake State Park**
N44 25.383 W84 40.684

[9] **Hartwick Pines State Park**
N44 44.120 W84 40.179

[10] **Burt Lake State Park**
N45 24.083 W84 37.151

[11] **Wilderness State Park**
N45 44.739 W84 53.999

[12] **Foley Creek Campground**
N45 55.979 W84 44.982

[13] **Brimley State Park**
N46 24.759 W84 33.364

[14] **Warren Dunes State Park**
N41 54.080 W86 35.690

[15] **Fort Custer Recreation Area**
N42 20.072 W85 20.302

[16] **Waterloo Portage Lake**
N42 19.513 W84 14.497

[17] **Hoffmaster State Park**
N43 08.411 W86 16.291

[18] **Ionia State Recreation Area**
N42 55.783 W85 08.045

[19] **Proud Lake Recreation Area**
N42 33.560 W83 31.745

[20] **Van Buren State Park**
N42 20.074 W86 18.249

[21] **Holland State Park**
N42 46.415 W86 12.475

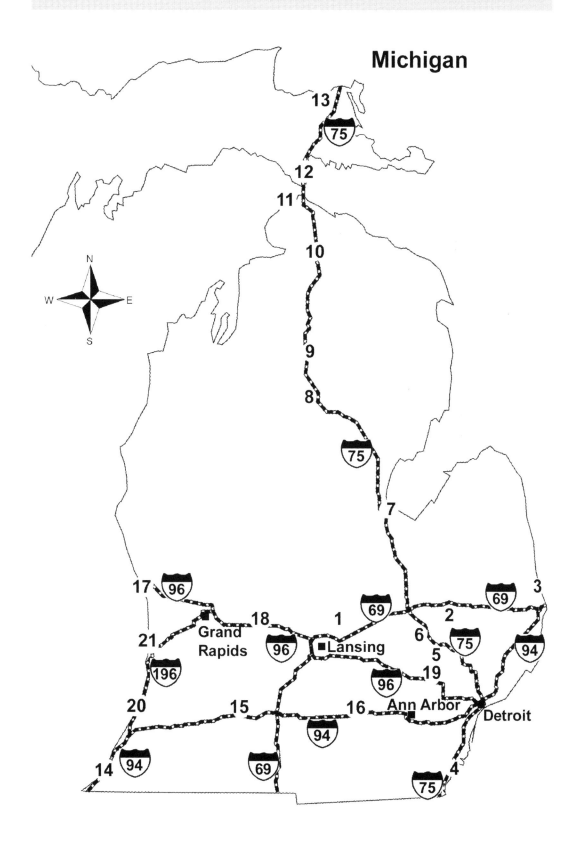

Exit 89 of I-69
Sleepy Hollow State Park [1]
North of Lansing
State Rate: $19

(517) 651-6217

http://www.michigandnr.com/
parksandtrails/Details.aspx?
id=495&type=SPRK

Camp Accommodations

181 paved, shaded sites, 45 feet, electricity, dump station, reservations available. Amenities include modern restrooms/showers, potable water, fire ring, picnic table, swimming, fishing, biking, pet friendly.

Directions

14 miles from I-69. From Exit 89 go north on Hwy 127 for 8 miles to Price Rd. Turn east on Price for 6 miles to the Park entrance at State Park Rd.

Points of Interest -

Possible destinations in the Greater Lansing area include Curwood Castle, Abrams Planetarium, Kresge Art Museum, Cooley Gardens, Michigan Women's Historical Center, and the Meridian Historical Village. For food/beverages try Uncle John's Cider Mill or the Michigan Brewing Company.

Exit 155 of I-69
Metamora-Hadley Recreation Area [2]
Southeast of Flint
State Rate: $23

(810) 797-4439

http://www.michigandnr.com/
parksandtrails/details.aspx?
id=472&type=SPRK

Camp Accommodations

214 shaded sites, 50 feet, electricity, dump station, paved roads, many lake front, reservations. Amenities include modern restrooms/showers, potable water, camp store, fire ring, table, swimming, fishing, biking, pet friendly.

Directions

8 miles from I-69. From Exit 155 go 5 miles south on Hwy 24. Turn west on Cty. Hwy. 62 (Pratt Rd.) for 2.3 miles to Herd Rd. Turn south for 0.7 miles to the Park entrance.

Points of Interest -

In Flint visit the Buick Gallery, housing the world's largest collection of vintage Buicks, automotive memorabilia and research archives. At Crossroads Village wander through 35 historic buildings and shops. Ride the Genesee Belle Riverboat for a scenic cruise on Mott Lake. Also see **[6]**.

Exit 274 of I-69/I-94
Lakeport State Park [3]
North of Port Huron
State Rate: $23

(810) 327-6224

http://www.michigandnr.com/
parksandtrails/Details.aspx?
id=466&type=SPRK

Camp Accommodations

250 sites, 50 feet, some lake view, some paved, 20 pull through, electricity, dump station, reservations available. Amenities include modern restrooms/showers, potable water, fire ring, table, swimming, biking, pet friendly.

Directions

9.5 miles from I-69. From Exit 274 go 9.5 miles north on Hwy 25. Just north of Burtchville, bear right at the south side of the Park on M-25, Lakeshore Rd., to the campground.

Points of Interest -

In Port Huron tour the retired Coast Guard Cutter Bramble and the Huron Lightship. Watch freighters close up at Great Lakes Maritime Center. Find out why antique collectors treasure Marine City. Stroll the world's longest wooden freshwater boardwalk in St. Clair.

Exit 15
Sterling State Park [4]
East of Monroe on Lake Erie
State Rate: $33

(734) 289-2715

http://www.michigandnr.com/
parksandtrails/Details.aspx?
id=497&type=SPRK

Camp Accommodations

256 shaded sites, 8 ADA, many water view, 50 feet, electricity, dump station, reservations available. Amenities include modern restrooms/showers, potable water, fire ring, picnic table, swimming, fishing, biking, pet friendly.

Directions

2 miles from I-75. From Exit 15 go northeast for 0.7 mile on Dixie Hwy. Turn right on State Park Rd. for 1 mile to the Park entrance.

Points of Interest -

The Park is in Monroe County, one of Michigan's oldest communities. Historic treasures abound giving Monroe County both national and global appeal. With Lake Erie and the River Raisin, the area is Michigan's top visitor destination. Learn more at - http://www.monroeinfo.com/

Exit 93
Pontiac Lake Recreation Area [5]
Northwest of Pontiac
State Rate: $18

(248) 666-1020

http://www.michigandnr.com/
parksandtrails/details.aspx?
id=196&type=SPCG

Camp Accommodations

176 shaded sites, 40 feet, electricity, dump station, reservations available. Amenities include modern restrooms/showers, potable water, fire ring, picnic table, shooting range, biking, pet friendly.

Directions

6.5 miles from I-75. From Exit 93 go southeast 1.5 mi. on Dixie Hwy to White Lake Rd. Turn south for 1.7 mi. to Anderson Rd. Turn west for 0.5 mi. to White Lake Rd. (not **Old** White Lake). Turn left for 2.2 mi. to Teggerdine Rd. Turn south 0.5 mi. to Maceday Rd and the campground.

Points of Interest -

Visit Pontiac, known for the Arts, Beats & Eats Festival, a summer festival featuring an art show, musical concert venues, and a sampling of food from numerous regional restaurants. Pontiac participates in the annual Woodward Dream Cruise celebrating Woodward's hot-rod history.

Exit 101
Seven Lakes State Park [6]
South of Flint
State Rate: $19

(248) 634-7271

http://www.michigandnr.com/
parksandtrails/Details.aspx?
id=492&type=SPRK

Camp Accommodations

70 sites, some waterfront, 40 feet, electricity, 4 ADA, dump station, reservations available. Amenities include modern restrooms/showers, potable water, fire ring, picnic table, swimming/beach, biking, pet friendly.

Directions

5 mi. from I-75. From Exit 101 go west on Grange Hall Rd for 4.1 miles to Fish Lake Rd. Turn north 0.8 mile to the Park entrance on you left.

Points of Interest -

Flint's dramatic history as the birthplace of General Motors comes to life at Sloan Museum. The museum's newest gallery takes visitors on a fascinating journey through Flint in the 20th century - from the birth of General Motors to the present. Visit Durand Union Station. Also see [2].

Exit 168
Bay City State Recreation Area [7]
North of Saginaw
State Rate: $19-$21

(989) 684-3020

http://www.michigandnr.com/
parksandtrails/details.aspx?
id=99&type=SPCG

Camp Accommodations

193 shaded sites, 50 feet, 2 ADA, electricity, dump station, reservations available. Amenities include modern restrooms/showers, potable water, fire ring, picnic table, Visitors Center, Interpretive Programs, biking, fishing, pet friendly.

Directions

5 miles from I-75. From Exit 168 go 5 miles east on Beaver Rd. to the Park.

Points of Interest -

The Park has one of the largest remaining freshwater, coastal wetlands on the Great Lakes (the Tobico Marsh). You will be on Saginaw Bay with paved trails, a boardwalk, 2 observation towers, multiple observation platforms and photo opportunities.

Exit 239
South Higgins Lake State Park [8]
South of Grayling
State Rate: $25-$29

(989) 821-6374

http://www.michigandnr.com/
parksandtrails/details.aspx?
id=496&type=SPRK

Camp Accommodations

400 shaded sites, 50 feet, some lake view, 18 pull through, electricity, dump station, reservations available. Amenities include modern restrooms/showers, potable water, fire ring, table, fishing, swimming, biking, pet friendly.

Directions

6.5 miles from I-75. From Exit 239 turn southwest but, just after the off ramp, immediately turn right on Cty Rd 103 (Robinson Lake Rd.). Go 3.2 miles to Higgins Lake Rd. Turn south 3.1 miles to State Park Dr and the Park.

Points of Interest -

The area is a sanctuary for those who enjoy the outdoors. When you're here, you enter "River Time Zone"– where time has no meaning. The morel beckons visitors to this area during the spring. Crawford County has ample state & federal property which may be mushroom hunted at will.

Exit 259
Hartwick Pines State Park [9]
North of Grayling
State Rate: $25-$33

(989) 348-7068

http://www.michigandnr.com/
parksandtrails/details.aspx?
id=126&type=SPCG

Camp Accommodations

100 shaded, paved sites, 6 ADA, 50 feet, 36 pull through, electricity, dump station, reservations available. Amenities include modern restrooms/showers, potable water, fire ring, table, fishing, swimming, biking, pet friendly.

Directions

2 miles from I-75. From Exit 259 go 2 miles northeast on Hwy 93 (Hartwick Pines Rd.) to State Park Dr. and the entrance on your left.

Points of Interest -

Visit the Park logging museum. Forest hikes are special along the Old Growth Pine Trail of 300 year old trees. Gaylord, Michigan's Alpine Village, offers a quaint setting and much shopping. Enjoy weekend entertainment, a twice weekly farmers market & vast array of events & activities.

Exit 310
Burt Lake State Park [10]
Southeast side of Indian River
State Rate: $24-$26

(231) 238-9392

http://www.michigandnr.com/
parksandtrails/details.aspx?
id=107&type=SPCG

Camp Accommodations

306 shaded sites, some paved, 5 ADA, 45 feet, electricity, dump station, reservations available. Amenities include modern restrooms/showers, potable water, fire ring, picnic table, swimming, fishing, biking, pet friendly.

Directions

1 mile from I-75. From Exit 310 go west, 0.4 mile, then south 0.3 mile on Hwy 68 to State Park Dr and the Park entrance on your right.

Points of Interest -

In Indian River visit the 55 foot Cross In The Woods. Go to Ocqueoc Falls, on the Ocqueoc Falls Bicentennial Pathway. There are two falls. See one of only three known surviving examples of deck truss highway bridges in Michigan, built in 1937.

Exit 337
Wilderness State Park [11]
West of Mackinaw City
State Rate: $27

(231) 436-5381

http://www.michigandnr.com/
parksandtrails/details.aspx?
id=240&type=SPCG

Camp Accommodations

250 shaded sites, 45 feet, electricity, dump station, reservations available. Amenities include modern restrooms/showers, potable water, fire ring, picnic table, shooting range, biking, pet friendly.

Directions

10 mi. from I-75. From Exit 337 turn south on Hwy 108 (Nicolet), but immediately turn right on Trails End Rd. Go 2.5 miles to the shoreline and Wilderness Park Dr. Turn south, follow Wilderness Park Dr for 7.5 miles to the camp at Swamp Line Rd.

Points of Interest -

Explore the Park's 10,000 acres, 26 miles of beautiful Lake Michigan shoreline, and numerous trails. Discover Mackinaw City, one of Michigan's top tourist destinations and gateway to Mackinac Island. Check out the 'Icebreaker Mackinaw' Maritime Museum and McGulpin Point Lighthouse.

Exit 352
Foley Creek Campground [12]
North of St. Ignace
Hiawatha NF Rate: $14
America/Beautiful Rate: $7

(906) 292-5549

http://www.recreation.gov/

Camp Accommodations

48 sites, 60+ feet, dry camping, reservations. Amenities include restrooms, potable water, berry picking, firewood, fire ring, picnic table, biking, watchable wildlife, pet friendly.

Directions

2 mi. from I-75. From Exit 352 go east to Mackinac Trail Rd. Turn south 2.2 miles to the Park entrance on you left.

Points of Interest -

St. Ignace, the third oldest continuously inhabited settlement in the United States, has a variety of activities including restaurants, golfing, shady beaches, shopping, and ferry service to Mackinac Island. Explore the Straits of Mackinac Lighthouses, and Father Marquette National Memorial.

Exit 386 of I-75
Brimley State Park [13]
West of Sault Ste. Marie
State Rate: $21-$23

(906) 248-3422

http://www.michigandnr.com/
parksandtrails/details.aspx?
id=414&type=SPRK

Camp Accommodations

237 shaded sites, 50 feet, 24 pull through, electricity, dump station, reservations available. Amenities include modern restrooms/showers, potable water, fire ring, picnic table, biking, fishing, beach house, pet friendly.

Directions

10.5 miles from I-75. From Exit 386 go 7.2 miles west on Hwy 28 to Hwy 221. Turn north for 2.5 miles to W. 6 Mile Road. Turn east 0.8 miles to S. Park St. and the Park entrance.

Points of Interest -

Tahquamenon Falls, two national fish hatcheries, the Tower of History, the Museum of Ship Valley Camp, the Soo Locks, Sault Ste. Marie, the Coast Guard Station, the International Bridge and the Mackinaw Bridge are all within the local area.

Exits 12 or 16 of I-94
Warren Dunes State Park [14]
South of Benton Harbor
State Rate: $25-$27

(269) 426-4013

http://www.michigandnr.com/
parksandtrails/details.aspx?
id=504&type=SPRK

Camp Accommodations

182 sites, 50 feet, some pull through, electricity, dump station, reservations available. Amenities include modern restrooms/showers, potable water, fire ring, table, beach house, swimming, biking, pet friendly (except beach).

Directions

2 miles from I-94. From Exit 12 turn west on Sawyer Rd. for 0.3 miles to the Red Arrow Hwy. Turn northeast (right) for 1.4 miles to State Park Rd. and the entrance. From Exit 16 turn west to the Red Arrow Hwy. Go 2.2 miles south to the entrance.

Points of Interest -

The Park's roads were paved in 2009. A sampling of near by southwest Michigan destinations includes the Silver Beach Carousel Museum, Box Factory for the Arts, Fort St Joseph Museum, Horn Archaeological Museum, Krasl Art Center, & Michigan Flywheelers Museum.

Exit 92 of I-94
Fort Custer Recreation Area [15]
West of Battle Creek
State Rate: $21

(269) 731-4200

http://www.michigandnr.com/
parksandtrails/details.aspx?
id=448&type=SPRK

Camp Accommodations

219 shaded, sites, many paved, 11 ADA, 40+ feet, electricity, dump station, reservations available. Amenities include modern restrooms/showers, potable water, fire ring, picnic table, fishing, swimming, biking, pet friendly.

Directions

9 miles from I-94. From Exit 92 go 4 miles northeast on Hwy 37 to Hwy 96. Turn northwest, go 5.2 miles on Hwy 96 to Fort Custer Dr. Turn south (left) into the Park.

Points of Interest -

Area attractions include the American Museum of Magic; the Arcadia Brewing Company; Cherry Creek Wine Cellar; Cornwell's Turkeyville, USA; the Critchlow Alligator Sanctuary; Historic Adventist Village; the Southern Exposure Herb Farm; and the Marshall Postal Museum.

Exit 147 of I-94
Waterloo Portage Lake [16]
Northeast of Jackson
State Rate: $22-$24

(734) 475-8307

http://www.dnr.state.mi.us/
parksandtrails/Details.aspx?
id=234&type=SPCG

Camp Accommodations

136 shaded sites, some paved, 7 ADA, 45 feet, 2 pull through, electricity, dump station, reservations. Amenities include modern restrooms/ showers, potable water, fire ring, table, swimming, fishing, biking, pet friendly.

Directions

3 miles from I-94. From Exit 147 go north on Race Rd. for 2 miles to Seymore Ave. Turn east and go 1 mile to the Park entrance on your left.

Points of Interest -

Jackson is ringed with a number of vineyards and wineries. Enjoy Cascade Falls, all manmade - 500 feet in length, a vertical height of 64 feet, total width of 60 feet, 6 fountains, 16 Falls (11 are illuminated), 1,230 Colored Electric Lights, and a 2,000 gallon per minute flow rate.

Exit 1 of I-96
Hoffmaster State Park [17]
South of Muskegon
State Rate: $27-$29

(231) 798-3711

http://www.michigandnr.com/
parksandtrails/details.aspx?
id=457&type=SPRK

Camp Accommodations

293 shaded sites, 50 feet, electricity, 8 pull throughs, dump station, reservations available. Amenities include modern restrooms/showers, potable water, fire ring, picnic table, Visitor Center, swimming/beach, biking, pet friendly.

Directions

6 mi. from I-96. From Exit 1 turn south for 2.5 miles on Hwy 31 to Pontaluna Rd. Go west for 2.7 miles. As you approach the shoreline Pontaluna turns northwest and becomes Lake Harbor. Go 0.6 miles to the Park entrance on your left.

Points of Interest -

Try the Park's Dune Climb Stairway with an observation deck and panoramic view of the dunes and Lake Michigan. In Muskegon visit the Hackley & Hume Historic site (homes of a famous lumber baron), Fire Barn Museum, and Scolnik House (Historic Depression Era House).

Exit 64 of I-96
Ionia State Recreation Area [18]
East of Grand Rapids
State Rate: $19

(616) 527-3750

http://www.michigandnr.com/
parksandtrails/details.aspx?
id=461&type=SPRK

Camp Accommodations

100 sites, 5 ADA, 45 feet, electricity, reservations available. Amenities include restrooms, potable water, fire ring, picnic table, biking, swimming/beach, watchable wildlife, pet friendly.

Directions

4 mi. from I-96. From Exit 64 go 3.5 miles north on Jordan Lake Rd. to the Park entrance.

Points of Interest -

Grand Rapids touts its walkable downtown for shopping and food, all within a 1/2 mile radius, with riverwalks, bridges, and unique architecture. Visit the Grand Rapids Art Museum and Gerald R. Ford Presidential Museum. Try the Opera or treat yourself to the Symphony Pops.

Exit 159 of I-96
Proud Lake Recreation Area [19]
Northwest of Farmington Hills
State Rate: $20

(248) 685-2433

http://www.dnr.state.mi.us/
parksandtrails/Details.aspx?
id=487&type=SPRK

Camp Accommodations

130 shaded sites, 2 ADA, 50 feet, electricity, dump station, reservations. Amenities include modern restrooms/showers, potable water, fire ring, table, swimming, fishing, hiking, wildflower identification, nature study, biking, pet friendly.

Directions

5 miles from I-96. From Exit 159 go 4.3 miles north on Wixom Rd. Turn east on Glengary Rd. for 0.5 miles to the Park entrance, Proud Lake Rec Rd, on your left.

Points of Interest -

The Park, on the scenic Huron River, offers more than 20 miles of trails covering several diverse habitats. In spring, hepatica (liverwort), marsh marigold, violets and many other wildflowers abound. Guided interpretive walks and other nature activities are offered.

Exit 18 of I-196
Van Buren State Park [20]
North of Benton Harbor
State Rate: $21-$23

(269) 637-2788

http://www.michigandnr.com/
parksandtrails/details.aspx?
id=227&type=SPCG

Camp Accommodations

220 shade or sun sites, 45 feet, electricity, dump station, reservations available. Amenities include modern restrooms/showers, potable water, fire ring, table, beach house, swimming, biking, pet friendly (except beach).

Directions

3.5 miles from I-196. From Exit 18, turn north on Hwy 140 for 0.2 miles to 14th Ave. Turn west for 0.8 mi. to the Five Star Hwy (Ruggles). Turn south 1.4 mi., bear right at the Blue Star Hwy, & continue on the Five Star Hwy for 1.1 mi. to the park.

Points of Interest -

Visit South Haven, a one-of-a-kind Michigan Beach and resort town. Don't miss South Haven's World-Famous Lighthouse, a great photo opportunity. Antiquing, museums, wineries, beach sights and walks all are good choices in this area. Also try a Lake Michigan boat cruise.

Exit 44 of I-196
Holland State Park [21]
West of Holland
State Rate: $27-$33

(616) 399-9390

http://www.michigandnr.com/
parksandtrails/details.aspx?
id=458&type=SPRK

Camp Accommodations

211 paved sites, 45 feet, electricity, 18 ADA, 2 pull though, dump station, reservations. Amenities include modern restrooms/showers, potable water, fire ring, table, beach house, swimming, biking, pet friendly (except beach).

Directions

14 mi. from I-196. From Exit 44 go 7 miles north on Hwy 31. Exit at Lakewood and go west. Along the way Lakewood will become Douglas, then Ottawa Beach. Go 7.2 miles in all to the Park.

Points of Interest -

Visit Holland! Spring is for tulips, making it one of the best times to visit the many parks, gardens, and Dutch attractions. In summer, enjoy the beaches, ride the trails, or sail on Lake Michigan. Autumn brings a harvest of orchards, fall color, and the area's renowned Farmer's Market.

MINNESOTA

The Minnesota Parks and Recreation Division oversees 66 parks, six recreation areas, and eight waysides that contain examples of Minnesota's most scenic lands. You can explore specifics about these resources at -

http://www.dnr.state.mn.us/index.html

All vehicles entering a state park must display a valid Minnesota State Park vehicle permit (annual and day permits can be purchased at a park). The park system is working to make facilities accessible to people of all abilities. You should call the specific state park you are planning to visit for up-to-date information on accessibility. Gathering firewood in a park is not permitted, however, firewood can be purchased at the park office. Pets are welcome in state parks but must be kept on a leash of not more than six feet and must be personally attended at all times.

RV reservations can be made up to one year in advance. You can search by date to find the perfect time for your overnight stay. Typically, 30% of campsites in parks and state recreation areas are only rented on a first-come, first-serve basis. Reservations can be made by phone, 8 a.m. to 8 p.m., seven days a week at (866) 857-2757 [TDD (866) 672-8213]. For online reservations go to -

http://www.stayatmnparks.com/

Fees are -

Standard campsites: $12-$24

Electricity: add $4

Water and Sewer: add $4

Reservation fee: $8.50

There are also some excellent County and Town Parks. While the County/Town fees are a bit higher, they are comparable to the State Parks, after miscellaneous State fees are added.

[1] **Myre - Big Island State Park**
N43 38.190 W93 18.526
[2] **Rice Lake State Park**
N44 05.535 W93 03.862
[3] **Nerstrand - Big Woods State Park**
N44 20.498 W93 06.484
[4] **Lebanon Hills Regional Park**
N44 46.375 W93 11.241
[5] **Interstate Park**
N45 23.692 W92 40.073
[6] **Banning State Park**
N46 10.275 W92 50.887
[7] **Moose Lake State Park**
N46 26.180 W92 44.149
[8] **Indian Point Campground**
N46 43.326 W92 11.112

[9] **Blue Mounds State Park**
N43 43.046 W96 11.515
[10] **Adrian Municipal Park**
N43 38.424 W95 56.416
[11] **Pihl's Park**
N43 38.460 W93 43.851
[12] **Whitewater State Park**
N44 03.779 W92 02.595
[13] **Great River Bluffs State Park**
N43 56.355 W91 24.546
[14] **Buffalo River State Park**
N46 52.175 W96 28.421
[15] **Lake Carlos State Park**
N46 00.021 W95 20.153

NOTES:

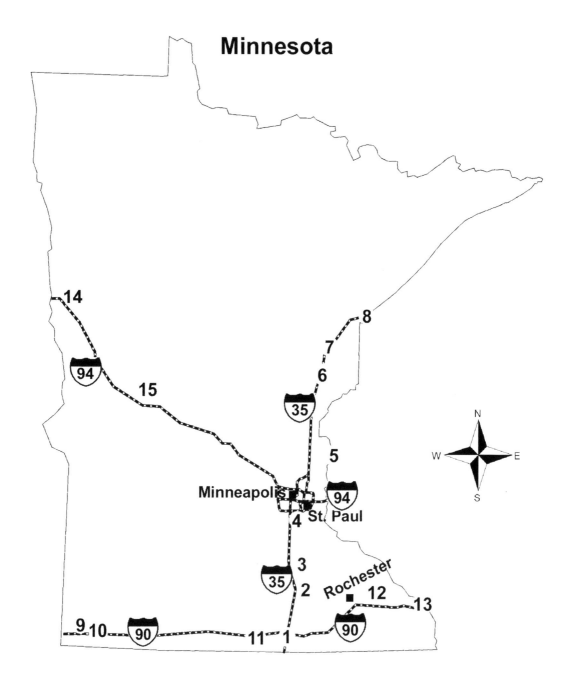

Minnesota

Exit 11
Myre - Big Island State Park [1]
Southeast of Albert Lea
State Rate: $18-$22

(507) 379-3403

http://www.dnr.state.mn.us/
state_parks/myre_big_island/
index.html

Camp Accommodations

93 sites, wooded or prairie settings, 40+ feet, 32 electric, dump station, reservations available. Amenities include ADA restroom/showers, fire ring, table, potable water, hiking, biking, gift shop, firewood, pet friendly.

Directions

2 miles from I-35. From Exit 11 go east for 0.5 mile on Cty Rd. 46 to Cty Rd. 38. Turn south 1.5 miles to the campground.

Points of Interest -

Albert Lea, "The Land Between the Lakes," is between Fountain & Albert Lea Lake. Take a tour on the Pelican Breeze II Cruise Boat. Tour Historical Museum/ Village, Albert Lea Art Center & Story Lady Doll/Toy Museum. Shop historic downtown specialty, craft, gift and antique shops.

Exit 42
Rice Lake State Park [2]
East of Owatonna
State Rate: $18-$22

(507) 455-5871

http://www.dnr.state.mn.us/
state_parks/rice_lake/index.html

Camp Accommodations

44 sites, 1 ADA, 2 loops - wooded or open settings, 40+ feet, 16 electric, reservations available. Amenities include ADA restroom/showers, fire ring, picnic table, potable water, hiking, biking, lake access, canoeing, pet friendly.

Directions

10 miles from I-35. From Exit 42 go east and south on Hoffman Dr. for 1.2 miles. Turn east (left) on Cty Rd. 19 (Rose St.). Go 9 miles to Cty. Rd. 40. Turn south into the Park.

Points of Interest -

Stroll through the Historic Owatonna Downtown Retail District of specialty shops and boutiques. Shop at Cabela's, the second most popular tourist attraction in Minnesota. Experience what life was like in Owatonna at the turn of the 20th Century at the Village of Yesteryear.

Exit 56
Nerstrand - Big Woods State Park [3]
Northeast of Faribault
State Rate: $18-$22

(507) 333-4840

http://www.dnr.state.mn.us/
state_parks/nerstrand_big_woods/
index.html

Camp Accommodations

51 sites, 2 ADA, wooded or open, 45 feet, 27 electric, 1 pull through, dump station, reservations available. Amenities include ADA restroom/ showers, fire ring, table, potable water, hiking, biking, pet friendly.

Directions

12.5 miles from I-35. From Exit 56 go 2.6 miles east on Hwy 60. Turn left on Shumway Ave. for one block then bear right on Cty. Rd. 20 (St Paul Ave.). Go 3.7 miles to Cty. Rd. 27. Turn right, go 3.4 miles to Hall Ave. Turn north for 1 mile to Cty Rd 88. Go east 1.7 miles to the Park.

Points of Interest -

Visit Northfield & find a vibrant, welcoming atmosphere. The college presence creates an active open atmosphere few other small communities can offer. Discover outlets for your arts, history or nature curiosities. When you are ready to wine, dine and relax, enjoy one-of-a-kind restaurants.

Exit north of Exit 87 @ I-35E/I-35W split
Lebanon Hills Regional Park [4]
South of Eagan (next to the MN Zoo)
County Rate: $25-$30

(651) 688-1376

http://www.co.dakota.mn.us/
LeisureRecreation/CountyParks/
Locations/LebanonHills/Campground.htm

Camp Accommodations

93 shaded sites, 3 ADA, up to 40 feet, electric/full hook-up, dump station. Amenities include ADA restroom/ showers, fire ring, picnic table, potable water, hiking, biking, canoeing, Interpretive Trails, gift shop, hosts, store, firewood, pet friendly.

Directions

7 miles from I-35. At I-35E/I-35W split take I-35E northeast 5.1 miles to Exit 93. Go east for 0.6 mile on Cliff Rd. to Johnny Cake Ridge Rd. Turn south 1.2 mile to the campground on the left.

Points of Interest -

The Park is on the south edge of Minneapolis and St. Paul and provides a gateway to all the Twin Cities have to offer. You are adjacent to the Minnesota Zoo, near Fort Snelling State Park, and convenient to the Mall of America. For a scenic outing drive east to Afton to antique and for ice cream.

Exit 135
Interstate Park [5]
Northeast of Forest Lake
State Rate: $20-$24

(651) 465-5711

http://www.dnr.state.mn.us/
state_parks/interstate/index.html

Camp Accommodations

37 sites, up to 35 feet, 2 ADA, 22 electric, reservations available. Amenities include ADA restroom/ showers, fire ring, picnic table, potable water, hiking, biking, river access, pet friendly.

Directions

19 miles from I-35. From Exit 135 go east 0.2 miles on Viking to Hwy 61 (Forest). Turn south 0.3 miles to Hwy 98 (Wyoming). Go east 5 miles to Hwy. 8. Proceed 13.7 miles northeast on Hwy. 8 to the campground entrance on the right.

Points of Interest -

Interstate is a lovely state park in the Dalles of the St. Croix. Two hundred foot basalt sheer cliffs with huge rock resembling human profiles are the hallmark. The glacier-carved Dalles includes Devil's Chair, Lion's Head and Turk's Head. Enjoy the quaint towns on the St. Croix River.

Exit 195
Banning State Park [6]
North of Sandstone
State Rate: $18-$22

(320) 245-2668

http://www.dnr.state.mn.us/
state_parks/banning/index.html

Camp Accommodations

33 ample and shaded sites, 40+ feet, 11 electric, reservations available. Amenities include ADA restroom/ showers, fire ring, picnic table, potable water, hiking, biking, river access, pet friendly.

Directions

Adjoins I-35. From Exit 195 go east 0.3 miles on Hwy 23 to Banning Park Rd on your right.

Points of Interest -

Sandstone is well known as home of the "Midwest Country Music Theater," aired on RFD TV. Enjoy live performances throughout the year. The History & Art Center (on the National Registry), contains quarry artifacts and exhibits of the Great Hinckley Fire and the Railroad of by-gone days.

Exit 214 of I-35
Moose Lake State Park [7]
Southeast of Moose Lake
State Rate: $18-$22

(218) 485-5420

http://www.dnr.state.mn.us/
state_parks/moose_lake/index.html

Camp Accommodations

33 shaded sites, 2 ADA, 45 feet, 20 electric, reservations available. Amenities include ADA restroom/showers, potable water, hiking, biking, fire ring, picnic table, firewood, canoeing, pet friendly.

Directions

0.5 miles from I-35. From Exit 214 go east for 0.5 mile on Cty Rd. 137 to the campground on the right.

Points of Interest -

Duluth is within an hour of the Park, where there is much to see and do. Visit the Great Lakes Aquarium, Lake Superior & Mississippi Railroad excursion and museum, Renegade Theater Company, S.S. William A. Irvin Ore Boat Museum, Tweed Museum of Art. Take a lake cruise.

Exit 251 of I-35
Indian Point Campground [8]
South of Duluth
County Rate: $25-$32

(218) 628-4977
www.indianpointcampground.com/
ip_home.html

Camp Accommodations

74 shaded sites, some riverfront, 45 feet, electric/full hook-up, some pull through, dump station, reservations available. Amenities include restroom/showers, fire ring, picnic table, hiking, biking, hosts, Wi-Fi, pet friendly.

Directions

2 miles from I-35. **Northbound,** from Exit 251a (Cody St) go 0.3 miles to 63rd Ave. Turn right, go 0.6 miles to Hwy 23 (Grand Ave). Turn right, go 1.0 miles to 75th Ave. (Pulaski St.). Turn left to the campground. **Southbound**, from Exit 251b (Grand Ave) go 1.2 miles to 75th Ave. (Pulaski St). Turn left to campground.

Points of Interest -

There is much to see and do in Duluth such as the Great Lakes Aquarium, Lake Superior & Mississippi Railroad excursion and museum, Renegade Theater Company, S.S. William A. Irvin Ore Boat Museum, Tweed Museum of Art. Take a lake cruise.

Exit 12 of I-90
Blue Mounds State Park [9]
North of Luverne
State Rate: $18-$22

(507) 283-1307

http://www.dnr.state.mn.us/
state_parks/blue_mounds/index.html

Camp Accommodations

73 shaded sites on paved roads, 2 ADA, 40 feet, 40 electric, dump station, reservations available. Amenities include ADA restroom/showers, potable water, hiking, biking, fire ring, picnic table, swimming, canoe, Visitor Center, pet friendly.

Directions

6.5 miles from I-90. From Exit 12 go 5.4 miles north on Hwy 75 to Cty Rd. 20. Turn east for 1.1 mile into the park.

Points of Interest -

Enjoy the Park's natural features. The Sioux quartzite cliff rises 100 feet above the plains. Get close up with bison (fenced) grazing on the prairie. Walk the rolling hills among a sea of prairie grasses & flowers swaying in the wind. Don't miss the annual Luverne dachshund races!

Exit 26
Adrian Municipal Park [10]
North of Adrian
Town Rate: $14-$23

(507) 483-2820

http://www.adrian.govoffice2.com/
index.asp?Type=B_LOC&SEC=
{37BF5E1E-0906-41FC-9285-
598A01179A51}

Camp Accommodations

100 shaded sites, 40+ feet, 100 electric/water, pull throughs, dump station. Amenities include ADA restroom/showers, fire ring, picnic table, pool, biking, hosts, cable, Wi-Fi, pet friendly.

Directions
0.5 miles from I-90. From Exit 26 go 0.2 miles south to Franklin St. Turn right, go 0.3 miles to the campground.

Points of Interest -
Visit Luverne. Go to Blue Mounds State Park. The Sioux quartzite cliff rises 100 feet above the plains. Get close up with bison (fenced) grazing on the prairie. Walk the rolling hills among a sea of prairie grasses & flowers swaying in the wind. See [9].

Exit 138
Pihl's Park [11]
South of Wells
County Rate: $18-$20

(507) 553-5864

http://wells.govoffice.com/index.asp?
Type=B_BASIC&SEC={A8A1DFF5-
F9BD-4FC5-892B-7D73C15CD627}

Camp Accommodations

30 shaded, gravel sites, up to 40 feet, 30 electric, 3 pull through, dump station. Amenities include ADA restroom/showers, fire ring, picnic table, pool, biking, disc golf, fishing, boating, hosts, pet friendly.

Directions
1.5 miles from I-90. From Exit 138 go 1.2 miles south on Hwy 22 to the Park entrance on the right.

Points of Interest -
Albert Lea, "The Land Between the Lakes," is between Fountain & Albert Lea Lake. Take a tour on the Pelican Breeze II Cruise Boat. Tour the Historical Museum/Village, Albert Lea Art Center & Story Lady Doll/Toy Museum. Shop historic downtown specialty, craft, gift & antique shops.

Exit 233
Whitewater State Park [12]
North of St. Charles
State Rate: $20-$24

(507) 932-3007

http://www.dnr.state.mn.us/
state_parks/whitewater/index.html

Camp Accommodations

104 open and grassy to wooded and secluded sites, 40 feet, 2 ADA, 47 electric, 5 pull through, dump station, reservations available. Amenities include ADA restroom/showers, fire ring, picnic table, potable water, hiking, biking, river access, pet friendly.

Directions
8 miles from I-90. From Exit 233 go 8 miles north on Hwy 74 through St. Charles to the Park.

Points of Interest -
Rochester, the "Best Small City in America," is home to the renowned Mayo Clinic & the largest IBM complex under one roof. There are many upscale shops & nice restaurants. Drive to historic Mantorville to enjoy the Melodramas at the Opera House and have a steak at the Hubbell House.

Exit 266 of I-90
Great River Bluffs State Park [13]
(aka O. L. Kipp State Park)
South of Winona
State Rate: $16

(507) 643-6849

http://www.dnr.state.mn.us/
state_parks/great_river_bluffs/
index.html

Camp Accommodations

31 secluded sites, 2 ADA, 45 feet, dry camping, reservations available. Amenities include ADA restroom/ showers, potable water, hiking, biking, fire ring, picnic table, pet friendly.

Directions

2 miles from I-90. From Exit 266 turn north to Cty Rd. 3. Go right for 1 mile to Lynch Rd (Kipp Dr). Turn right into the Park. Drive 1 miles to the camp.

Points of Interest -

The bluff area is quite beautiful! The Park's King's Bluff trail offers a breathtaking view of the Mississippi River Valley. Drive north to Winona, on the Mississippi, and enjoy this riverfront town, or visit the National Eagle Center in Wabasha (of *Grumpy Old Men* fame).

Exit 6 of I-94
Buffalo River State Park [14]
East of Fargo - Moorhead
State Rate: $18-$22

(218) 498-2124

http://www.dnr.state.mn.us/
state_parks/buffalo_river/index.html

Camp Accommodations

44 shaded sites, 2 ADA, 40 feet, 35 electric, dump station, reservations available. Amenities include ADA restroom/showers, potable water, hiking, biking, fire ring, swimming/beach, fishing, picnic table, pet friendly.

Directions

10 miles from I-94. From Exit 6 go 2 miles north on Hwy 336 to Hwy 10. Turn east for 8.3 miles to the Cty Hwy 44 and the park entrance on the right.

Points of Interest -

Explore Fargo-Moorhead. Walk the Walk with more than 100 celebrity signatures, handprints and footprints in cement at the Celebrity Walk Of Fame. The Fargo Air Museum is home to the only flying F2G-1D Super Corsair in the world, and one of four flying Japanese Zero's in the world.

Exit 103 of I-94
Lake Carlos State Park [15]
North of Alexandria
State Rate: $20-$24

(320) 852-7200

http://www.dnr.state.mn.us/
state_parks/lake_carlos/index.html

Camp Accommodations

121 wooded or lakeview sites, 2 ADA, 45 feet, 81 electric, dump station, reservations available. Amenities include ADA restroom/showers, potable water, hiking, biking, fire ring, picnic table, swimming, fishing, pet friendly.

Directions

13.5 miles from I-94. From Exit 103 follow Hwy 29 through Alexandria. Go 11.8 miles in all to Cty. Rd. 38. Turn left and go into the Park for 1.5 miles to the campground.

Points of Interest -

In Alexandria, the Runestone Museum allows visitors to decide for themselves if the artifact is authentic - were the first visitors to America the Vikings in 1362? Enjoy summer stock theatre productions, or nationally known musicians. Eat at one of the restaurants situated on a lake marina.

MISSISSIPPI

Mississippi has one of the most diverse collections of parklands. Lands and park management is provided by the State as well as the Corp of Engineers, some Counties, the National Forest Service, and the National Park Service.

The Mississippi Department of Wildlife, Fisheries and Parks oversees the 21 State Parks but has given Reserve America primary responsibility for providing park information and oversight of reservations. Reservations can be made up to two years in advance. The website for the Parks, and where to make reservations is -

mississippistateparks.reserveamerica.com/

RV camping fees range from $16-$22. Sites are classified as follows -

Standard (electric and water): $16

Full Hook-up: $18

Premium (waterfront): $22

Pets are allowed but must be on a leash up to 6 feet long.

[1] **Davis Bayou Campground** N30 23.831 W88 47.746	[9] **Holmes County State Park** N33 01.643 W89 55.211
[2] **Shepard State Park** N30 22.356 W88 37.566	[10] **Hugh White State Park** N33 48.198 W89 43.732
[3] **Roosevelt State Park** N32 19.144 W89 39.967	[11] **Wallace Creek Campground** N34 09.992 W89 53.771
[4] **Marathon Lake** N32 12.295 W89 21.842	[12] **John W. Kyle State Park** N34 24.749 W89 48.663
[5] **Twiltley Branch Campground** N32 29.722 W88 48.791	[13] **Hernando Point** N34 44.277 W90 04.486
[6] **Percy Quin State Park** N31 11.496 W90 29.810	[14] **Paul B. Johnson State Park** N31 08.093 W89 13.807
[7] **Lake Lincoln State Park** N31 40.401 W90 20.470	[15] **Clarkco State Park** N32 06.241 W88 42.219
[8] **Timberlake Campground** N32 23.146 W90 02.374	

NOTES:

Mississippi

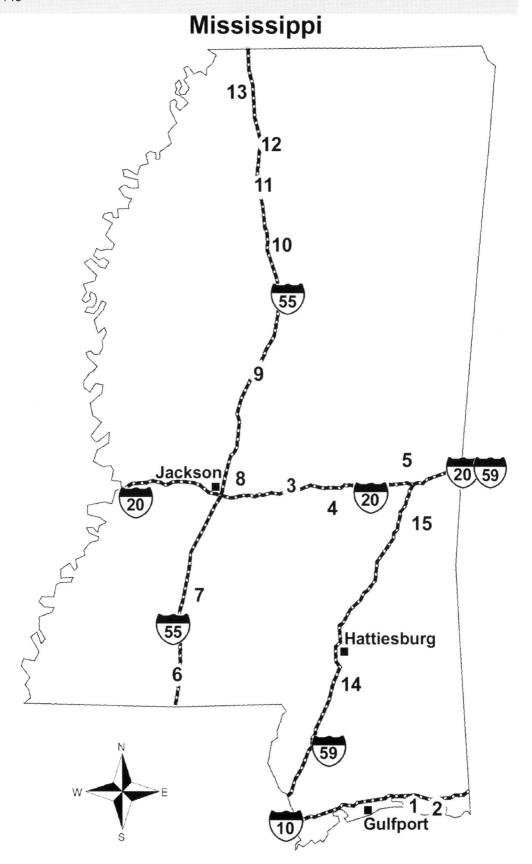

Exit 50 of I-10
Davis Bayou Campground [1]
In Ocean Springs
Gulf Islands NPS Rate: $16
America/Beautiful Rate: $8

(228) 875-3962

http://www.nps.gov/guis/planyourvisit/
davis-bayou-area.htm

Camp Accommodations

51 shaded, spacious, paved sites, 2 ADA, 45 feet, water/electric. Amenities include ADA restrooms/showers, fire ring, table, fishing, biking, hiking, Visitor Center, Ranger led tours, pet friendly.

Directions

8 mi. from I-10. From Exit 50 go 2.7 miles south on Hwy 609 to Hwy 90 (Bienville Blvd.). Turn east and go 3 miles to Gulf Island National Seashore Parkway (G.I.N.S. Pkwy). Turn south and follow the road 2.4 miles to the campground.

Points of Interest -

Explore Ocean Springs, the 'City of Discovery.' This community is one of the most sought out destinations on the Mississippi Gulf Coast for culture, history, beaches and entertainment. The quaint downtown will be the first attraction that lures you to the city.

Exit 61 of I-10
Shepard State Park [2]
East of Pascagoula
State Rate: $16

(228) 497-2244

mississippistate-
parks.reserveamerica.com/ms/Shepard/
Campground/r/campgroundDetails.do?
contractCode=MS&parkId=156849

Camp Accommodations

29 shaded (all standard) sites, 40 feet, 4 pull through, dump station, reservations available. Amenities include modern restrooms/showers, fire ring, picnic table, disc golf, biking, pet friendly.

Directions

8 miles from I-10. From Exit 61 go south for 3 miles on Gautier Vancleave Rd. to Hwy 90. You are advised to call for the best 'final miles' directions.

Points of Interest -

With some of the nation's most pristine natural resources, some species found in the Pascagoula River can be found nowhere else in the U.S. For bird-watchers, the Audubon Center in Moss Point can point you to the best sites. You are a few miles away from casino action in Biloxi.

Exit 77 of I-20
Roosevelt State Park [3]
South of Morton
State Rate: $16-$22

(601) 732-6316

mississippistateparks.reserveamerica.com/ms/
Roosevelt_State_Park/Campground/r/
campgroundDetails.do?
contractCode=MS&parkId=154848

Camp Accommodations

109 shaded (22 premium, 87 standard, some full) sites, some paved, 40 feet, dump station, reservations available. Amenities include modern restrooms/showers, fire ring, table, pool, fishing, biking, hiking, store, pet friendly.

Directions

0.6 miles from I-20. From Exit 77 go north for 0.6 miles on Hwy 13 to Park Rd. and the entrance on the left.

Points of Interest -

Visit Jackson, the 'City with Soul.' There are many museums, attractions, Civil War and Civil Rights venues. Stir your soul with great blues, gospel, and jazz. Bring your appetite and savor "down home" southern cooking and gourmet Southern Fusion. Ride the Fondern Trolley.

Exit 88 of I-20
Marathon Lake [4]
South of Forest
Bienville NF Rate: $20
America/Beautiful Rate: $13

(601) 469-3811

http://www.forestcamping.com/dow/
southern/biencmp.htm#marathon

Camp Accommodations

34 shaded, paved sites, 45 feet, water/electric, dump station. Amenities include ADA restrooms/showers, potable water, fire ring, table, fishing, biking, hiking, pet friendly.

Directions

14 miles. from I-20. From Exit 88 turn north and immediately go right on Erle Johston Dr for 1 mile to Hwy 501. Go southeast for 9.5 miles to Morton Marathon Rd. Turn east (left), go 1.5 miles to Smith Cty Rd 506 and continue 1.6 miles to Shopping Center Rd 520. Turn 0.4 miles to camp on left.

Points of Interest -

In Meridian, ride the Dentzel Carousel (a National Historic Landmark), in operation since 1909. Tour the Jimmy Rodgers Museum. Both are in Highland Park. Then set out to find 50 brightly decorated carousel horses around town and created by local artists. Also see [5].

Exit 150 of I-20
Twiltley Branch Campground [5]
North of Meridian
COE Rate: $10-$18
America/Beautiful Rate: $5-$9

(601) 626-8068

http://www.recreation.gov/

Camp Accommodations

64 shaded, gravel sites, dry/standard/premium, many lakefront, all ADA, 45+ feet, 4 pull through, dump station. Amenities include ADA restrooms/showers, potable water, fire ring, table, fishing, biking, hiking, pet friendly.

Directions

15.5 miles from I-20. From Exit 150 go 13 miles north on Hwy 19 to Collinsville. Turn east on West Lauderdale Rd. for 1 mile. Turn right on Hamrick Rd., go 1.1 miles to Barrett Rd. Turn south (right) for 0.4 mile to the campground.

Points of Interest -

For Meridian, download the Tour Guide for all kinds of ideas for things to do and see, great pictures too! (*http://www.visitmeridian.com/pdf/Merdian_Tour_Guide.pdf*). Visit the Causeyville General Store, opened in 1895 as a general store and gristmill. Also see [4].

Exit 15 of I-55
Percy Quin State Park [6]
South of McComb
State Rate: $16-$22

(601) 684-3938

mississippistateparks.reserveamerica.com/ms/
Percy_Quin/Campground/r/
campgroundDetails.do?
contractCode=MS&parkId=155847

Camp Accommodations

100 shaded (20 premium, 80 standard, some full) paved sites, 40 feet, dump station, reservations available. Amenities include modern restrooms/showers, fire ring, table, golf, fishing, biking, hiking, swimming, store, pet friendly.

Directions

3.5 miles from I-55. From Exit 15 go west for 1.5 miles on Hwy 24 to Hwy 48. Turn south for 2 miles to Percy Quin Dr. Turn west into the Park.

Points of Interest -

McComb was selected as "The Hospitality City" of "The Hospitality State" three years running. Antiquing is popular here, with 8 shops to explore. Magnolia has 2 historic districts, one with three of Mississippi's premier Queen Anne residences and an antebellum Greek Revival cottage.

Exit 51
Lake Lincoln State Park [7]
East of Wesson
State Rate: $16-$22

(601) 643-9044

mississippistateparks.reserveamerica.com/
camping/Lake_Lincoln/r/
campgroundDetails.do?
page=details&contractCode=MS&parkId=15585
3&topTabIndex=CampingSpot

Camp Accommodations

71 shaded (22 premium, 49 standard, some full) sites, 45+ feet, dump station, reservations. Amenities include restrooms/showers, fire ring, table, fishing, biking, hiking, swimming, pet friendly.

Directions

10 miles from I-55. From Exit 51 go east 1.6 miles on Sylvarena, then left on Lowery Rd for 1.7 miles to Hwy 51. Turn south for 1 mile to Bahala Rd. Turn east, go 0.4 miles to Hardy St. and turn south. Go 0.7 mile to Timberlane Rd. Turn east, go 2.2 miles to Sunset Rd. Turn south again for 2 miles to the Park.

Points of Interest -

Stop in Crystal Springs, once know as the 'Tomatopolis of the World.' Visit the Tomato Museum and Art Gallery, Robert Johnson Blues Museum, numerous antique shops, or join in one of the many festivals held there each year. Learn more at *http://www.crystalspringsmiss.com/*

Exit 105
Timberlake Campground [8]
Northeast of Jackson
Water District Rate: $17-$24
Senior Discount: $2/night

(601) 992-9100

http://www.therez.ms/camping/
timberlake.html

Camp Accommodations

61 paved, shaded (22 premium, 39 standard, some full) sites, 40+ feet reservations available. Amenities include restrooms/showers, fire ring, table, water sports, pool, tennis, disc golf, Wi-Fi, biking, hiking, pet friendly.

Directions

7.5 miles from I-55. From Exit 105 go 1.7 miles east on Natchez Trace Pkwy to the Old Canton Rd exit. Turn south for 1.1 miles to Lake Harbour Dr. Turn east, go 4.5 miles (the road changes to Spillway Rd) to Northshore Pkwy. Turn left, go 0.2 miles to the campground on your left.

Points of Interest -

Visit Jackson, the 'City with Soul.' There are many museums, attractions, Civil War, and Civil Rights venues. Stir your soul with great blues, gospel, and jazz. Bring your appetite and savor "down home" southern cooking and gourmet Southern Fusion. Ride the Fondern Trolley.

Exit 150
Holmes County State Park [9]
South of Durant
State Rate: $16

(662) 653-3351

mississippistateparks.reserveamerica.com/ms/
Holmes_County/Campground/r/
campgroundDetails.do?
contractCode=MS&parkId=153824

Camp Accommodations

28 shaded (all standard) sites, 40 feet, 1 pull through, dump station, reservations available. Amenities include modern restrooms/showers, fire ring, picnic table, fishing, biking, hiking, bird watching, pet friendly.

Directions

1.2 miles from I-55. From Exit 150 go east for 1.2 miles on Hwy 424 (State Park Rd.) into the Park.

Points of Interest -

Kosciusko, one of "America's 100 Best Small Towns," & one of the "Top Sixty Prettiest Painted places in America" is Oprah Winfrey's birthplace. A downtown driving/walking tour through historic downtown features 28 historic homes, many on the National Register of Historic Places.

Exit 206
Hugh White State Park [10]
East of Grenada
State Rate: $16

(662) 226-4934

mississippistateparks.reserveamerica.com/ms/
Hugh_White/Campground/r/
campgroundDetails.do?
contractCode=MS&parkId=152812

Camp Accommodations

153 shaded (all standard) sites, 40 feet, dump station, reservations available. Amenities include modern restrooms/showers, fire ring, picnic table, fishing, biking, hiking, bird watching, firewood, ice, pet friendly.

Directions

7.5 miles from I-55. From Exit 206 go east on Hwy 8/333 (Sunset Dr.) into Grenada. Continue on Hwy 8 (now Lakeview Dr.) for 4.4 miles total. Turn left on Hwy 333 and Old Hwy 8 (while Hwy 8 goes straight). Follow Old Hwy 8 for 3 miles into the Park.

Points of Interest -

Outdoor enthusiasts will enjoy Grenada and all it has to offer from Grenada Lake to the Lofton Archery Classic and the National Fox Hunt. Grenada Lake is the largest body of water in Mississippi. In town, antiquing and downtown shopping will keep you busy.

Exit 233
Wallace Creek Campground [11]
South of Batesville
COE Rate: $10-$18
America/Beautiful Rate: $5-$9

(662) 563-4571

http://www.recreation.gov/

Camp Accommodations

99 shaded sites, standard/premium, many lakefront, 3 ADA, 45+ feet, pull throughs, dump station, reservations. Amenities include ADA restrooms/showers, potable water, fire ring, table, fishing, biking, hiking, pet friendly.

Directions

1.6 miles from I-55. From Exit 233 go east for 0.8 miles on Cty Rd 36. Go left on Cty Rd 38 (Enid Dam Rd) for 0.8 miles to the Park on your right.

Points of Interest -

Southern Living Magazine reported "A popular poster in Oxford Mississippi, proclaims, 'The Square is the Center of the Universe.' After a visit to this downtown's mecca of shops and restaurants, that statement is hard to deny." William Faulkner's home is nearby. Also see **[12]**.

Exit 252
John W. Kyle State Park [12]
East of Sardis
State Rate: $16-$22

(662) 487-1345

mississippistateparks.reserveamerica.com/
camping/John_W_Kyle_State_Park/r/
campgroundDetails.do?
page=details&contractCode=MS&parkId=15281
3&topTabIndex=CampingSpot

Camp Accommodations

199 shaded sites (16 premium, 183 standard, some full) 40 feet, dump station, reservations. Amenities include restrooms/showers, fire ring, table, golf, fishing, biking, pool, pet friendly.

Directions

7 miles from I-55. From Exit 252 go east and south for 7 miles on Hwy 315 to the campground on your right. Note the campground is on the Lower Lake.

Points of Interest -

Oxford, one of the South's crown jewels, is home to The University of Mississippi & hosts an array of athletic events, enlightening performing arts programs, scholarly presentations, museums & exhibits. Springtime brings the colors of blooming azaleas, wisteria & dogwood. See **[11]**.

Exit 271 of I-55
Hernando Point [13]
Southwest of Hernando
COE Rate: $12-$20
America/Beautiful Rate: $6-$10

(662) 562-6261

http://www.recreation.gov/

Camp Accommodations

76 shaded, standard sites, many lake view, 1 ADA, 45+ feet, dump station, reservations available. Amenities include ADA restrooms/showers, potable water, fire ring, table, fishing, biking, hiking, pet friendly.

Directions

9 miles from I-55. From Exit 271 go west on Hwy 306 for 0.8 miles to Hwy 51. Turn north for 3.1 miles to Wheeler Rd. Turn west for 5.1 miles to the end of Wheeler, which is the campground.

Points of Interest -

If you like Bar-B-Q then visit Southaven, whose Springfest is the largest barbecue contest in Mississippi. Southaven is home to the nationally famous 'Interstate Bar-B-Q.' Take in an event at the Desoto Civic Center, which hosts more than 1,000 events each year.

Exit 59 of I-59
Paul B. Johnson State Park [14]
South of Hattiesburg
State Rate: $16-$22

(601) 582-7721

mississippistateparks.reserveamerica.com/
camping/map_of_Paul_B_Johnson/r/
campgroundMap.do?
page=map&search=site&contractCode=MS&par
kId=156846&topTabIndex=CampingSpot

Camp Accommodations

125 shaded sites (14 premium, 111 standard, some full) 45+ feet, 2 ADA, many pull throughs, some paved, dump station, reservations available. Amenities include restrooms/showers, fire ring, table, fishing, biking, swimming, pet friendly.

Directions

11 miles from I-59. From Exit 59 go east for 3 miles on Hwy 98. Turn south on Hwy 49 for 7.5 miles to the campground on your right.

Points of Interest -

In Hattiesburg, visit the All-American Rose Garden at the University of Southern Mississippi (750 award-winning bushes). At the Historic Saenger Theater swing to the sounds of the theater's original 1929 pipe organ. Both are free. Shop for antiques, 'eclectibles' and bargains.

Exit 157 of I-59/I-20
Clarkco State Park [15]
South of Meridian
State Rate: $16-$22

(601) 776-6651

mississippistateparks.reserveamerica.com/ms/
Clarkco/Campground/r/campgroundDetails.do?
contractCode=MS&parkId=154842

Camp Accommodations

40 shaded (27 premium, 13 standard, all full hook up) sites, 40 feet, 1 pull through, dump station, reservations available. Amenities include modern restrooms/showers, fire ring, picnic table, fishing, biking, hiking, swimming, bird watching, store, disc golf, pet friendly.

Directions

22 miles from I-20/59. From Exit 157 go south for 22 miles on Hwy 45 to Hwy 145. Turn left, go 0.5 miles to the Park entrance on the right.

Points of Interest -

For Meridian, download the Tour Guide for all kinds of ideas for things to do and see, great pictures too! (*http://www.visitmeridian.com/pdf/Merdian_Tour_Guide.pdf*). Visit the Causeyville General Store, opened in 1895 as a general store and gristmill. Also see **[4].**

MISSOURI

Missouri State Parks and Historic Sites are administered by the Division of State Parks. Missouri's state park system, which on four occasions has been ranked as one of the top four state park systems in the nation, contains 85 state parks and historic sites, 39 of which offer camping opportunities. You can find details about the State Parks system at -

www.mostateparks.com/things.htm

To ensure that the state park system can be used and enjoyed by everyone, a major effort was undertaken to make facilities, activities and programs accessible to all persons, regardless of abilities. Facilities such as campgrounds, showers, picnic areas, fishing docks and other areas have been renovated to comply with the Americans with Disabilities Act.

Keep your pet on a leash, not longer than 10 feet, at all times. Pets are not allowed inside any park or historic site building, or in public swimming areas and beaches.

The Missouri state park system does not charge entrance fees. However, there are fees associated with camping, lodging, tours, museums and certain special events. Reservations are accepted in 35 of Missouri's 40 state park and historic site campgrounds and can be made online or by phone up to six months in advance or as close as two days. The reservation fee is $8.50. To make reservations visit -

www.mostateparks.com/campres.htm

Citizens, 65 years of age or older or persons with disabilities, are entitled to a reduced camping fee. An official document such as a driver's license certifying proof of age or disability must be presented when registering.

Campsite fees typically are -

Basic: $10 - $13

Electric: $17 - $21

Electric/Water: $17 - $23

Sewer/Electric/Water: $20 - $26

Senior/Disabilities Discount: $2

---

[1] **Weston Bend State Park**
   N39 23.638 W94 52.264
[2] **Lewis and Clark State Park**
   N39 32.328 W95 03.207
[3] **Big Lake State Park**
   N40 05.174 W95 20.549
[4] **Wallace State Park**
   N39 39.646 W94 12.798
[5] **Bennett Springs State Park**
   N37 44.275 W92 51.552
[6] **Lane Spring Recreation Area**
   N37 47.941 W91 48.932
[7] **Meramec State Park**
   N38 12.444 W91 06.132
[8] **Babler Memorial State Park**
   N38 37.050 W90 41.356

[9] **Trail of Tears State Park**
   N37 26.111 W89 29.083
[10] **Hawn State Park**
   N37 50.037 W90 14.432
[11] **Blue Springs Campground**
   N39 00.305 W94 21.062
[12] **Knob Noster State Park**
   N38 45.182 W93 34.645
[13] **Arrow Rock State Historic Site**
   N39 03.793 W92 56.789
[14] **Finger Lakes State Park**
   N39 04.615 W92 19.792
[15] **Graham Cave State Park**
   N38 54.531 W91 34.567

NOTES:

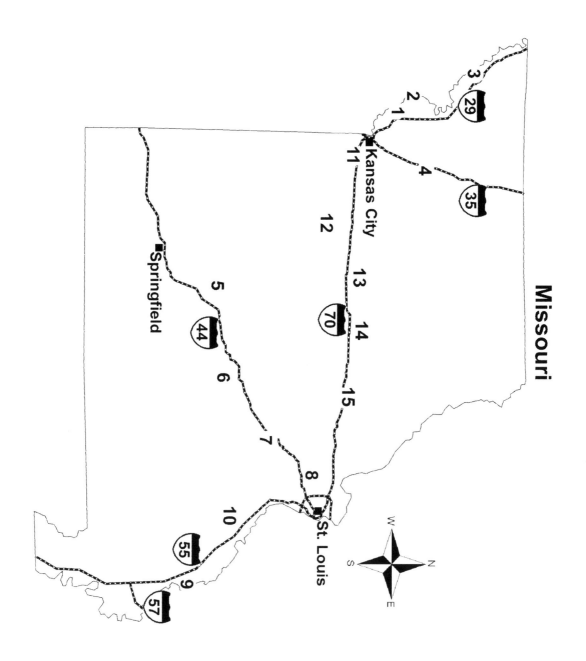

Exit 20
Weston Bend State Park [1]
West of Platte City
State Rate: $10-$21

(816) 640-5443

http://www.mostateparks.com/
westonbend.htm

Camp Accommodations

36 sites, 40 feet, 32 electric, 4 basic, 4 ADA, 2 pull through, dump station, reservations available. Amenities include ADA restroom/showers, grill, picnic table, potable water, hiking, biking, firewood, pet friendly.

Directions

5 miles from I-29. From Exit 20 turn west on Hwy 273 for 4.6 miles to Hwy 45. Turn south 0.4 miles to the Park Entrance.

Points of Interest -

Visit Weston, nestled among the high bluffs of the Missouri River and voted Kansas City's #1 Day Trip. Experience unique shopping in lovely pre-Civil War buildings. Enjoy the variety of shops, restaurants, pubs, brewery, wineries, entertainment and places to see in this historic town.

Exit 30
Lewis and Clark State Park [2]
Southwest of St. Joseph
State Rate: $10-$21

(816) 579-5564

http://www.mostateparks.com/
lewisandclark/camp.htm

Camp Accommodations

69 roomy, lake view sites, 45 feet, 62 electric, 7 basic, 4 ADA, 26 pull through, dump station, reservations available. Amenities include ADA restroom/showers, grill, picnic table, potable water, hiking, biking, swimming, fishing, firewood, pet friendly.

Directions

23 mi. from I-29. From Exit 30 go west 0.7 mi. on Cty Rd H to Hwy 371. Go north 3 mi. to Hwy 116. Go west, 15.2 mi. to Hwy 59. Go south, 2.2 mi. When Hwy 59 turns west, go straight on Hwy 45 for 1.1 mi. to Hwy 138. Turn west for 0.6 mi. to the Park.

Points of Interest -

St. Joseph, known as the city where the Pony Express began and Jesse James ended, was recently named the Top Western Town by True West Magazine. Visit some if its 13 museums and 50+ listings on the National Register of Historic Places. Also see [4].

Exit 79
Big Lake State Park [3]
Southwest of Mound City
State Rate: $10-$21

(660) 442-3770

http://www.mostateparks.com/
biglake.htm

Camp Accommodations

75 lake front/view sites, 40 feet, 57 electric, 18 basic, 4 ADA, 28 pull through, dump station, reservations available. Amenities include ADA restroom/showers, grill, table, potable water, restaurant, biking, swimming, fishing, firewood, pet friendly.

Directions

12.5 miles from I-29. From Exit 79 go 10 miles west on Hwy 159 to Hwy 111. Turn north for 2.4 miles to State Park Rd on your left.

Points of Interest -

Visit the Squaw Creek Wildlife Refuge. Squaw Creek has a ten-mile, self-guided auto tour route. This loop road provides an excellent opportunity to enjoy wildlife in a natural setting from the comfort of a vehicle and/or stop for wildlife observation and photography. There are three hiking trails.

Exit 48 of I-35
Wallace State Park [4]
South of Cameron
State Rate: $10-$21

(816) 632-3745

http://www.mostateparks.com/
wallace.htm

Camp Accommodations

77 paved sites, 45 feet, 42 electric, 35 basic, 4 ADA, 16 pull through, dump station, reservations available. Amenities include ADA restroom/ showers, grill, picnic table, potable water, fishing, hiking, biking, firewood, pet friendly.

Directions

2 miles from I-35. From Exit 48 turn southeast and go 0.4 miles on Hwy 69 to Hwy 121. Turn east and go 1.2 miles to the Park entrance.

Points of Interest -

With 11 antique shopping destinations and numerous specialty shops, St. Joseph should keep any serious collector/browser busy. St. Joseph's cultural arts, from a world-class art museum to a renowned symphony orchestra, will also give you much to enjoy. Also see [2].

Exit 129 of I-44
Bennett Springs State Park [5]
West of Lebanon
State Rate: $10-$26

(417) 532-4338

http://www.mostateparks.com/
bennett.htm

Camp Accommodations

191 paved sites, 45 feet, 48 full hook up, 128 electric, 15 basic, 12 ADA, 26 pull throughs, dump station, reservations available. Amenities include ADA restroom/showers, grill, picnic table, potable water, restaurant, rafting, fishing, hiking, Wi-Fi, pet friendly.

Directions

13.5 miles from I-44. From Exit 129 turn northwest and go 1.5 miles through Lebanon on Hwy 5. Continue straight on Hwy 64 for 12 miles. Turn into the Park on Hwy 64A on your left.

Points of Interest -

Car racing enthusiasts will want to check out the Lebanon I-44 Speedway and Midway Speedway. Other points of interest include the Gunter Farms Pumpkin Patch & Maze, Heartland Arena (horse/rodeo events), and the Laclede County Historical Society Museum and Old Jail.

Exit 184 of I-44
Lane Spring Recreation Area [6]
South of Rolla
Mark Twain NF Rate: $8-$15
America/Beautiful Rate: $4-$8

(573) 364-4621

http://www.fs.fed.us/r9/forests/
marktwain/recreation/sites/
lane_springs/flyer.php

Camp Accommodations

17 wooded, paved sites, 45+ feet, 6 electric, 2 pull throughs. Amenities include ADA restroom, grill, table, potable water, fishing, hiking, pet friendly.

Directions

13 miles from I-44. From Exit 184 turn southeast to Kings Hwy and go east 0.8 miles to Hwy 63. Turn south and go 11.5 miles to Cty Rd. 726 (Lake Springs Rd). Go right and follow signs to campground.

Points of Interest -

The Park has a shaded stone patio with benches overlooking Lane Spring. The beautiful surroundings have made it a popular spot for weddings. In Rolla see the Blue Bonnet Special Steam Train and visit the Edward L. Clark Museum. There also a number of local wineries.

Exit 226 of I-44
Meramec State Park [7]
East of Oak Grove and Sullivan
State Rate: $10-$26

(573) 468-6072

http://www.mostateparks.com/
meramec.htm

Camp Accommodations

209 shaded, sites, 45 feet, 21 full, 14 electric/water, 124 electric, 50 basic, 9 ADA, many pull throughs, dump station, reservations available. Amenities include ADA restroom/showers, grill, picnic table, potable water, hiking, biking, Visitor Center, pet friendly.

Directions

3 miles from I-44. From Exit 226 turn southeast on Hwy 185 for 3 miles to the Park Entrance.

Points of Interest -

The Park combines the beauty of the Meramec River and its surrounding bluffs, caves and forests. Guided tours of Fisher Cave, one of more than 40 caves in the park, are provided on a seasonal basis for a nominal fee. The Visitor Center offers a mix of educational exhibits.

Exit 264 of I-44
Babler Memorial State Park [8]
West of St. Louis
State Rate: $10-$21

(636) 458-3813

http://www.mostateparks.com/
babler.htm

Camp Accommodations

73 shaded, paved, sites, 45 feet, 43 electric, 30 basic, 5 ADA, dump station, reservations available. Amenities include ADA restroom/showers, grill, picnic table, potable water, hiking, biking, Interpretive Trails, pet friendly.

Directions

9.5 mi. from I-44. From Exit 264 turn north 7.7 miles on Hwy 109 to Babler Park Dr. Turn left for 1.9 miles to Guy Park Dr. Turn left into the Park.

Points of Interest -

At the Park you can spend a peaceful night camping and still be less than a hour from downtown St. Louis and all the city has to offer. You can discover the visitor options at <http://www.explorestlouis.com/visitors/index.asp>.

Exit 105 of I-55
Trail of Tears State Park [9]
Southwest of Mound City
State Rate: $10-$26

(573) 290-5268

http://www.mostateparks.com/
trailoftears.htm

Camp Accommodations

52 paved sites, 45 feet, 7 full hook up, 10 electric, 35 basic, 1 ADA, 8 pull through, dump station, reservations available. Amenities include ADA restroom/showers, grill, table, potable water, biking, swimming, fishing, hiking, pet friendly.

Directions

13 miles from I-55. From Exit 105 go 1 mile north on Hwy 61 to Hwy 177. Turn east (right), south later, for 11.5 miles to the Park entrance, Moccasin Springs Rd, on your left.

Points of Interest -

The Park is a memorial to the Cherokee Indians that lost their lives in a forced relocation. Visit Jackson, which Money magazine ranks 59th best small town in the United States. The National Park Service has also recognized Jackson's attractive uptown historic district.

Exit 150 of I-55
Hawn State Park [10]
East of Farmington
State Rate: $10-$21

(573) 883-3603

http://www.mostateparks.com/
hawn.htm

Camp Accommodations

45 paved sites, 45 feet, 26 electric, 19 basic, 4 ADA, dump station, reservations available. Amenities include ADA restroom/showers, grill, picnic table, potable water, fishing, hiking, biking, firewood, pet friendly.

Directions

14.5 miles from I-55. From Exit 150 turn west on Hwy 32. Go 11.2 miles to Hwy 144. Turn south and go 3.1 miles to the Park entrance.

Points of Interest -

Hawn is considered "the loveliest of all Missouri State Parks." Enjoy Farmington's historical sites - the Missouri Mines Historical Site and the Fort Davidson State Historic Site. Take a tour of vineyards or just relax with some delicious food and live music at one of the area's wineries.

Exit 15 of I-70
Blue Springs Campground [11]
Southeast of Kansas City
County Park Rate: $18-$25

(816) 503-4805

http://www.jacksongov.org/
content/3279/3798/
default.aspx#Jacomo

Camp Accommodations

82 gravel sites, 40 feet, 30 full hook up, 13 electric/water, 39 electric, 1 ADA, 6 pull throughs, dump station, reservations. Amenities include restroom/showers, grill, table, potable water, hiking, swimming, pet friendly.

Directions

3 miles from I-70. From Exit 15 turn south on I-470 and go 2.3 miles to Exit 14. Go 0.4 miles east on NE Bowlin Rd. Turn north into the Park.

Points of Interest -

At the Park you can spend a peaceful night camping and still be less than a hour from downtown Kansas City and all the city has to offer. You can discover the visitor options at <http://www.visitkc.com/things-to-do/index.aspx>

Exit 58 of I-70
Knob Noster State Park [12]
South of Concordia
State Rate: $10-$21

(660) 563-2463

http://www.mostateparks.com/
knobnoster.htm

Camp Accommodations

70 sites, 40 feet, 45 electric, 30 basic, 4 ADA, dump station, reservations available. Amenities include ADA restroom/showers, grill, picnic table, potable water, fishing, hiking, biking, Visitor Center, pet friendly.

Directions

18.5 miles from I-70. From Exit 58 turn south and follow Hwy 23. Go 18.5 miles to SE 10 Rd and the Park entrance on your right.

Points of Interest -

Sedalia is called the home of rails, trails, and ragtime. Depending on your timing, go to the Missouri State Fair, the foot-tapping Scott Joplin Festival, or just explore beautiful historic buildings (such as the Bothwell Lodge State Historic Site), museums and discover antique finds galore.

Exit 98
Arrow Rock State Historic Site [13]
East of Marshall
State Rate: $10-$26

(660) 837-3330

http://www.mostateparks.com/
arrowrock/camp.htm

Camp Accommodations

47 paved, shaded sites, 45 feet, 1 full, 34 electric, 12 basic, 3 ADA, 13 pull throughs, dump station, reservations available. Amenities include ADA restroom/showers, grill, picnic table, potable water, hiking, biking, firewood, pet friendly.

Directions

12.5 miles from I-70. From Exit 98 turn north to Hwy 41. Go west on Hwy 41 for 12.3 miles to the Park entrance on your right.

Points of Interest -

Walk to Arrow Rock Village, a National Historic Landmark. Limestone gutters line main street. Wooden sidewalks & overhead canopies line store fronts, recalling the grace of times past. Go to the Lyceum Theater, eat at the Huston Tavern. Visit the George Caleb Bingham Home.

Exit 128
Finger Lakes State Park [14]
North of Columbia
State Rate: $10-$21

(573) 443-5315

http://www.mostateparks.com/
fingerlakes.htm

Camp Accommodations

35 shaded, paved, sites, 45 feet, 16 electric, 19 basic, 1 ADA, dump station, reservations available. Amenities include ADA restroom/showers, grill, picnic table, potable water, hiking, biking, ATV activities, pet friendly.

Directions

9 miles from I-70. From Exit 128 turn north on Hwy 63 for 9 miles to E Peabody Rd, the Park entrance on your right.

Points of Interest -

Columbia's eclectic mix of restaurants, shops, art galleries, music venues, sporting events, and coffee houses means there's never a shortage of things to do. Twenty-five art galleries or museums and nine antique shops guarantee plenty of shopping or places to see.

Exit 170
Graham Cave State Park [15]
West of St. Louis
State Rate: $10-$21

(573) 564-3476

http://www.mostateparks.com/
grahamcave.htm

Camp Accommodations

52 paved sites, 35 feet, 18 electric, 345 basic, 1 ADA, 1 pull through, dump station, reservations available. Amenities include ADA restroom/showers, grill, table, potable water, biking, Interpretive Trails, pet friendly.

Directions

2 miles from I-70. From Exit 170 turn north and immediately turn left on Hwy TT. Go 2 miles to the Park entrance.

Points of Interest -

Graham Cave became historically significant when archaeologists discovered how long ago human occupancy had occurred. Archaeologists uncovered artifacts revealing human use of the cave dating back to as early as 10,000 years ago. The Park is an hour from St. Louis. See [8].

MONTANA

The State Park System is the responsibility of Montana Fish, Wildlife & Parks. At their main website you can plan your stay by searching for a park by name, nearest city, regional area, closest water body, activity, or facility. Go to -

http://fwp.mt.gov/parks/

You can select a cultural park (window into Montana's storied past and diverse culture), natural park (emphasis on natural beauty and scenic wonders), or recreational park (great for boating, fishing, swimming, water skiing, camping).

There is no park entrance fee for Montana residents. For those parks that charge an entrance fee, nonresidents must purchase a Day Pass ($5/vehicle) or Annual Pass ($25/first vehicle, $20/second vehicle). Additional fees are charged at state parks for camping, showers, some guided tours, and special events.

Campsites in Montana State Park Campgrounds are available on a first-come first-served basis. You use a self pay registration system once you find a campsite. Most camp sites include picnic table and fire ring. There are no utility hook-ups, except at Finley Point where there is electricity and water, and at Hell Creek, Cooney and Tongue River Reservoir where there is electricity. All campgrounds have vault toilets unless noted otherwise.

All pets must be on a leash not over 10 feet long. Pets are not permitted on swimming beaches, in sanitary facilities, or in any other area posted to exclude them.

Given the presence of ten forests across the state, there are also a number of National Forest Campgrounds.

[1] **Clark Canyon Recreation Area**
N44 59.748 W112 52.250
[2] **Bannack State Park**
N45 09.653 W112 59.614
[3] **Black Sandy State Park**
N46 44.718 W111 53.219
[4] **Cabin City Campground**
N47 22.540 W115 15.817
[5] **Sloway Campground**
N47 14.077 W115 01.581
[6] **Quartz Flat Campground**
N47 04.484 W114 45.902

[7] **Lewis & Clark Caverns State Park**
N45 49.351 W111 51.080
[8] **Pine Creek Campground**
N45 29.886 W110 31.473
[9] **Cooney State Park**
N45 26.540 W109 12.231
[10] **Tongue River Reservoir**
N45 06.097 W106 47.922
[11] **Makoshika State Park**
N47 05.414 W104 42.598

NOTES:

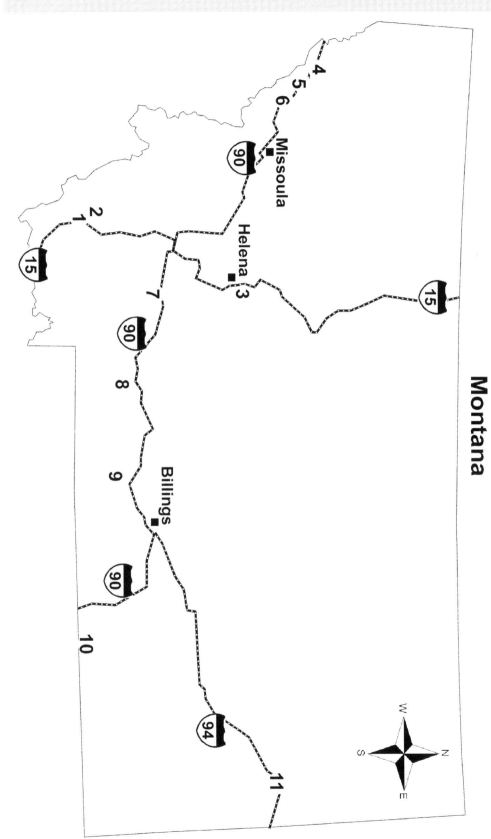

Montana

Exit 44
Clark Canyon Recreation Area [1]
Southwest of Grayling
Bureau of Reclamation Rate: $20
America/Beautiful Rate: $10

(406) 683-6472

http://www.usbr.gov/gp/mtao/
clarkcanyon/

Camp Accommodations

55 sunny, water view sites, 40+ feet, 40 full hook ups, 9 water/electric. Amenities include restrooms, potable water, picnic table, fishing, biking, hiking, pet friendly.

Directions

1.2 miles from I-15. From Exit 44 go west 1.2 miles on Hwy 324 to the campground on your left.

Points of Interest -

This is the site of Camp Fortunate, a significant spot along the Lewis and Clark Trail. It was here that Lewis and Clark met the Lemhi Shoshoni Tribe, and cached their canoes and supplies for the return trip. Sacagawea was reunited with her people here.

Exit 59
Bannack State Park [2]
West of Dillon
State Rate: $15

(406) 834-3413

http://fwp.mt.gov/parks/visit/
parkSiteDetail.html?id=281798

Camp Accommodations

14 sites, up to 35 feet, dry camping. Amenities include restrooms, potable water, fire ring, picnic table, firewood, Interpretive Programs, cultural events, Visitors Center, watchable wildlife, host, pet friendly. No electricity/sewer.

Directions

21 miles from I-15. From Exit 59 go west on Hwy 278 for 17.2 miles. Turn south at Bannack Bench Rd. and go 4 miles. The Park entrance is on the left.

Points of Interest -

The Park is a National Historic Landmark and the site of Montana's first major gold discovery in 1862. The Park is actually a preserved abandoned mining town managed by the state. Over 50 buildings line Main Street; the historic log & frame structures recall Montana's formative years.

Exit 200
Black Sandy State Park [3]
Northeast of Helena
State Rate: $15

(406) 495-3270

http://fwp.mt.gov/parks/visit/
parkSiteDetail.html?id=281944

Camp Accommodations

29 lake view sites, 2 ADA, up to 35 feet, dump station, dry camping. Amenities include restrooms, potable water, fire ring, picnic table, swimming, fishing, biking, hiking, host, pet friendly. No electricity/sewer.

Directions

8 miles from I-15. From Exit 200 go east for 5.1 miles on Hwy 453 (Lincoln Rd.) to Hauser Dam Rd. Turn north, then go 3.1 miles to the Park.

Points of Interest -

Yellow metal transformed remote 'Last Chance Gulch' into Montana's golden capital. The "Queen City of the Rockies" lives up to its nickname. Helena's nineteenth century architecture dazzles, its gold rush history compels, and its arts and culture reflect a richly talented community.

Exit 22
Cabin City Campground [4]
East of De Borgia
Lolo National Forest Rate: $7
America/Beautiful Rate: $4

(406) 822-4233

http://www.publiclands.org/explore/
site.php?id=2909

Camp Accommodations

24 wooded sites, up to 40 feet, dry camping. Amenities include ADA restroom, grill, picnic table, fishing, biking, hiking, pet friendly. No Utilities.

Directions

2.5 miles from I-90. From Exit 22 go east 1.6 miles, just past Cabin City, on 12 Mile Rd. (aka Mullan Gulch Rd or 2148). Bear left on 12 Mile Rd 353 for 0.3 miles to the campground entrance on your left.

Points of Interest -

Try a day trip to the Savenac Historic Tree Nursery in Haugan, MT (I-90, exit 16). It is one of the oldest U.S. Forest Service nurseries in the West. A self-guided tour provides insight to the nursery's history, and its importance to the area's recovery from the 1910 "Big Burn."

Exit 37
Sloway Campground [5]
South of St. Regis
Lolo National Forest Rate: $10
America/Beautiful Rate: $5

(406) 822-4233

http://www.forestcamping.com/dow/
northern/lolocmp.htm#sloway

Camp Accommodations

27 paved, wooded sites, up to 40 feet, 12 pull throughs, dry camping. Amenities include ADA restroom, potable water, grill, picnic table, host, fishing, biking, hiking, pet friendly. No Utilities.

Directions

2.5 miles from I-90 From Exit 37 turn west and immediately go left on the frontage road, Old US 10, for 2.5 miles to the campground.

Points of Interest -

The campground is popular for fly fishing enthusiasts and rafters, kayakers, and canoeists. Try a day trip to the Savenac Historic Tree Nursery in Haugan, MT (I-90, exit 16). It is one of the oldest U.S. Forest Service nurseries in the West. See **[4]** above.

Exit Mile Marker 58 Rest Area
Quartz Flat Campground [6]
North of Quartz
Lolo National Forest Rate: $10
America/Beautiful Rate: $5

(406) 822-4233

http://www.forestcamping.com/dow/
northern/lolocmp.htm#quartz_flat

Camp Accommodations

48 paved, partially shaded sites, 45+ feet, 6 pull throughs, dump station. Amenities include ADA restroom, potable water, grill, picnic table, fishing, biking, hiking, pet friendly. No electricity.

Directions

Adjoins I-90. From Rest Area to west side of I-90. **The tunnel from the westbound side has a 14 foot clearance.** Traffic noise.

Points of Interest -

Try a day trip to the Savenac Historic Tree Nursery in Haugan, MT (I-90, exit 16). It is one of the oldest U.S. Forest Service nurseries in the West. See **[4]** above.

Exit 256
Lewis & Clark Caverns State Park [7]
South of Cardwell
State Rate: $15

(406) 287-3541

http://fwp.mt.gov/parks/visit/
parkSiteDetail.html?id=281895

Camp Accommodations

20 shaded, spacious sites, 1 ADA, 45+ feet, some pull through, dump station. Amenities include restrooms/showers, potable water, fire ring, picnic table, firewood, hiking, biking, fishing, Interpretive Trail, Visitors Center, watchable wildlife, host, pet friendly. No electricity.

Directions

7.5 miles from I-90. From Exit 256 turn south and immediately go left on Hwy 2 for 7.5 miles to the Park entrance on your left.

Points of Interest -

This is Montana's first and best-known state park and showcases one of the most highly decorated limestone caverns in the Northwest The caverns tour is said to be worth your time to experience (there is a fee). Butte's vintage architecture and colorful past will draw you to make a visit.

Exit 333
Pine Creek Campground [8]
South of Livingston
Gallatin National Forest Rate: $13
America/Beautiful Rate: $7

(877) 646-1012

http://www.recreation.gov/

Camp Accommodations

25 wooded sites, 45+ feet, 21 ADA, 6 pull throughs, dry camping. Amenities include ADA restroom, potable water, grill, picnic table, fishing, biking, hiking, fishing, firewood, berry picking, watchable wildlife, pet friendly. No Utilities.

Directions

14 miles from I-90 From Exit 333 turn south, go 3.1 miles on Hwy 89 to E. River Rd. (Hwy 540). Turn left, go through Pine Creek, 7.7 mile in all to Luccock Park Rd. (FS Rd. 202). Turn left, go 2.7 miles to the campground on left.

Points of Interest -

Surrounded by majestic mountain ranges, Livingston is steeped in the history of Lewis & Clark, Calamity Jane & Yellowstone National Park. Enjoy a blend of shops, museums, galleries & restaurants - from cowboys to culture, from railroads to whitewater, from historic to contemporary.

Exit 434
Cooney State Park [9]
Southwest of Laurel
State Rate: $15-$20

(406) 445-2326

http://fwp.mt.gov/parks/visit/
parkSiteDetail.html?id=283293

Camp Accommodations

70 lake view sites, electricity, 45+ feet. Amenities include restrooms/showers, potable water, fire ring, picnic table, swimming, fishing, biking, hiking, host, pet friendly.

Directions

31 miles from I-90. From Exit 434 go south for 23 miles on Hwy 212 to Cooney Dam Rd in Boyd. Turn right, go west 8.2 miles to the Park.

Points of Interest -

Visit Billings and the land where General Custer fought the Sioux and Cheyenne, where Sitting Bull and Crazy Horse led their people through struggles and to victories, where the Lewis & Clark Expedition passed through, and where Calamity Jane raised a ruckus.

Exit 16 of I-90, in Wyoming
Tongue River Reservoir [10]
East of Aberdeen
State Rate: $15-$20

(406) 234-0900

http://fwp.mt.gov/parks/visit/
parkSiteDetail.html?id=283967

Camp Accommodations

90 sunny sites, many paved, 45+ feet, electricity, dump station. Amenities include restrooms, potable water, fire ring, picnic table, hiking, biking, fishing, watchable wildlife, host, store, pet friendly.

Directions

24 miles from I-90. From Exit 16 in Wyoming turn east on Hwy 339 for 1 mile to Hwy 338. Turn north for 21.5 miles. Along the way you will cross into Montana and the road will become Hwy 314. Turn right at Cty Hwy 180, go 1.5 miles into the Park.

Points of Interest -

Just north is the Little Bighorn Battlefield where the U.S. Army's 7th Cavalry fought the Sioux and Cheyenne in one of the Indians last armed efforts to preserve their way of life. Just south is Sheridan, one of Wyoming's jewels, with a fabled Western history and dramatic mountain vistas.

Exit 213 of I-94
Makoshika State Park [11]
South side of Glendive
State Rate: $15

(406) 377-6256

http://fwp.mt.gov/parks/visit/
parkSiteDetail.html?id=283890

Camp Accommodations

14 sunny, paved sites, 1 ADA, 40 feet, dry camping. Amenities include restrooms, potable water, fire ring, picnic table, hiking, biking, fishing, archery and rifle ranges, Interpretive Trail, Visitor Center, firewood, watchable wildlife, host, pet friendly. No Utilities.

Directions

3 mi. from I-94. From Exit 213 go south 0.5 mi. to W. Towne St. Turn left, go 1.1 mi. to Merrill. Turn right, go 0.3 mi., bearing left on Douglas to E. Berry, go 0.3 mi. to S. Taylor. Turn right, go 0.4 mi. to Snyder, go left, 0.3 mi. to the Park entrance.

Points of Interest -

To the Sioux Indians, Ma-ko-shi-ka meant bad earth or 'bad land.' As Montana's largest state park, the pine & juniper studded badland formations, one of the most geologically spectacular in the region, houses the fossil remains of such dinosaurs as tyrannosaurus rex and triceratops.

NEBRASKA

Nebraska's state system encompasses 87 areas across the state (State Parks, Recreation Areas, Historical Parks), 23 of which will accommodate RVs. You will find lands to suit virtually every outdoor taste, whether you're seeking the ultimate in modern conveniences in a picturesque outdoor setting or want to get back to nature amid the unspoiled beauty of the wilderness. The Park system is the responsibility of the Nebraska Game and Parks Commission (NGPC), whose website is -

http://www.ngpc.state.ne.us/parks/ guides/parksearch/findpark.asp

Relevant NGPC regulations state the following: (1) Dogs, cats and other pets are prohibited unless under physical restrictive control at all times. Leashes may not exceed six feet in length. Pets which become a nuisance shall be removed from the area. Pets are prohibited in public eating places and food stores, public buildings, and on designated swimming beaches; (2) The reservation of campsites designated as "reservable" in designated campgrounds is permitted through the NGPC reservation system.

NGPC has joined with ReserveAmerica to make reservations. The system includes easy-to-use maps, photographs and a shopping cart so users can reserve multiple arrival dates or multiple type of units. Users may go online to book reservations ($7 fee) up to 12 months in advance at:

www.ReserveAmerica.com

Reservations can also be made through the call center at (402) 471-1414.

A Nebraska State Park Permit is required when entering all state parks, state historical parks and state recreation areas. The daily fee is $4. All motor vehicles, operated within the boundaries of a designated fee area, must properly display a valid permit.

[1] **Lake McConaughy State Rec. Area**
N41 13.176 W101 40.289
[2] **Johnson Lake State Rec. Area**
N40 40.757 W99 49.798
[3] **Fort Kearny State Rec. Area**
N40 39.130 W98 59.366
[4] **Windmill State Rec. Area**
N40 42.441 W98 50.730
[5] **Mormon Island State Rec. Area**
N40 49.416 W98 22.666
[6] **Pawnee Lake State Rec. Area**
N40 51.034 W96 51.796
[7] **Eugene T. Mahoney State Park**
N41 00.967 W96 19.013
[8] **Two Rivers State Rec. Area**
N41 13.148 W96 20.969

NOTES:

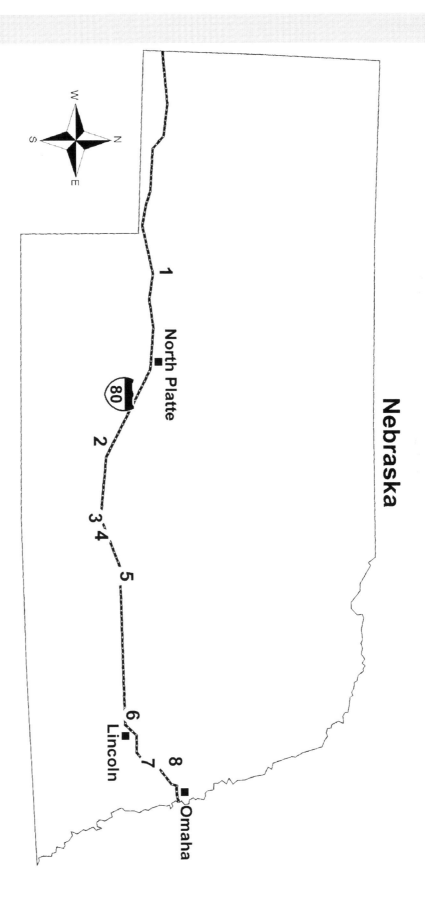

Exit 126
Lake McConaughy State Rec. Area [1]
North of Ogallala
State Rate: $12-$25

(308) 284-8800

http://www.ngpc.state.ne.us/parks/
guides/parksearch/addons/lakemac/
campground.asp#Areas

Camp Accommodations

There are three RV suitable camp-grounds:

Lake Ogallala - electric/water, paved

Lone Eagle - full service, water front

Little Thunder - full service, paved

Directions

10-13 miles from I-80. From Exit 126 go north and follow Hwy 61 for 10-13 miles to the campground of your choice.

Points of Interest -

Visit the website for details as to which camp you prefer. There is much to see and do in this large recreation area. In all there are over 200 sites, which accommo-date 45 foot RVs, with every combination of utilities/services available. Some have sewers and there is a dump station.

Exit 237
Johnson Lake State Rec. Area [2]
South of Lexington
State Rate: $17

(308) 785-2685

http://www.ngpc.state.ne.us/parks/
guides/parksearch/showpark.asp?
Area_No=94

Camp Accommodations

63 RV shaded sites, 42 feet, some paved, electricity, dump station. Amenities include showers/restrooms, potable water, picnic tables, grills, boat ramp, fishing, swimming/beach, accessible fishing piers, pet friendly.

Directions

8 miles from I-80. From Exit 237 go south for 8 miles on Hwy 283. Turn right on E Park Dr 25A into the Park.

Points of Interest -

Lexington offers numerous antique shops. Several century old homes have been re-stored to their original beauty. See the McCabe Aeroplane or "Baby Biplane" with its unique elliptical wing design at the Dawson County Historical Society Mu-seum.

Exit 279
Fort Kearny State Rec. Area [3]
South of Kearny
State Rate: $12-$17

(308) 865-5305

http://www.ngpc.state.ne.us/parks/
guides/parksearch/showpark.asp?
Area_No=98

Camp Accommodations

38 shaded RV sites, 45 feet, electric-ity/water, dump station. Amenities in-clude showers/restrooms, potable water, picnic tables, grills, fishing, swimming, bik-ing, hiking, archeological sites, watchable wildlife, pet friendly.

Directions

6 miles from I-80. From Exit 279, go south on Hwy 10 for 3 miles. Turn west on Hwy 50A for 2 miles to Rd 30. Turn north for 0.8 miles to the Park.

Points of Interest -

For Sandhill Crane viewing and photogra-phy go to Rowe Sanctuary. In Kearny visit the Trails and Rails Museum, Nebraska Firefighters Museum, Museum of Ne-braska Art, or Fort Kearney Museum. Tour the Cedar Hills Vineyard or Geo Spencer Vineyards.

Exit 285
Windmill State Rec. Area [4]
East of Kearny
State Rate: $12-$17

(308) 468-5700

http://www.ngpc.state.ne.us/parks/
guides/parksearch/showpark.asp?
Area_No=196

Camp Accommodations

32 shaded RV sites, 45 feet, electricity, some pull through, dump station.
Amenities include showers/restrooms,
potable water, picnic tables, grills, boating,
fishing, swimming/beach, biking, host,
watchable wildlife, pet friendly.

Directions

Adjoins I-80. From Exit 285 go north on
Hwy 10C (Lowell Rd) for 0.3 miles and
turn right in to the Park.

Points of Interest -

Windmill Crossing is where the Pawnee
Indians forded the Platte River during annual buffalo hunts. The old-time windmills
on site add much to the character of the
Park. They have all been restored to working order. For Sandhill Crane viewing and
photography go to Rowe Sanctuary.

Exit 312
Mormon Island State Rec. Area [5]
South of Grand Island
State Rate: $12-$17

(308) 385-6211

http://www.ngpc.state.ne.us/parks/
guides/parksearch/showpark.asp?
Area_No=123

Camp Accommodations

34 shaded RV sites, 45 feet, electricity, 8 pull through, dump station.
Amenities include showers/restrooms,
potable water, picnic tables, grills, boating,
fishing, swimming/beach, biking, walking,
host, watchable wildlife, pet friendly.

Directions

Adjoins I-80. From Exit 312 go north on
Hwy 34/281 for 0.2 miles and turn right in
to the Park.

Points of Interest -

The early spring Sandhill Crane viewing
and photography are excellent. In Grand
Island experience live thoroughbred racing
at Fonner Park. Explore the area's pioneer
heritage at Stuhr Museum. Try your hand
at clay or skeet shooting. Visit art galleries
and a myriad of shopping venues.

Exit 388
Pawnee Lake State Rec. Area [6]
West of Lincoln
State Rate: $12-$17

(402) 796-2362

http://www.ngpc.state.ne.us/parks/
guides/parksearch/showpark.asp?
Area_No=135

Camp Accommodations

68 shaded RV sites, 45 feet, mostly electric, dump station. Amenities include showers/restrooms, potable water, picnic tables, grills, boating, fishing, swimming/beach, biking, hiking, host, watchable wildlife, pet friendly.

Directions

7.5 miles from I-80. From Exit 388 go 0.5 miles south on Hwy 103. Go east on Hwy 6 for 4 miles. Turn north on NW. 98th St. for 2 miles to W. Adams St. Turn west for 0.9 miles to the Park.

Points of Interest -

Lincoln, the state capital, is home to many of the nation's prized historical monuments dating from 1900. Examples include the Germans from Russia Museum, the Home of William Jennings Bryan, or Historic Haymarket. The International Quilt Study Center & Museum is an excellent stop.

Exit 426
Eugene T. Mahoney State Park [7]
Southwest of Omaha
State Rate: $15

(402) 944-2523

http://www.ngpc.state.ne.us/parks/
guides/parksearch/showpark.asp?
Area_No=273

Camp Accommodations

149 shaded sites, 45 feet, all electric, dump stations. Amenities include showers/restrooms, potable water, tables, grills, boating, fishing, pool, biking, hiking, paddle boats, host, lodge/restaurant, Wi-Fi, pet friendly.

Directions

Adjoins I-80. From Exit 426 go northwest 0.5 miles and turn right, just before the Strategic Air & Space Museum, in to the Park.

Points of Interest -

Dine in the Lodge restaurant (with the scenic Platte River as a backdrop). Mahoney has many recreational activities - aquatic center, miniature golf, driving range, tennis, horseback rides, crafts, observation tower, and nature conservatory. Visit the Strategic Air & Space Museum.

Exit 445
Two Rivers State Rec. Area [8]
West of Omaha
State Rate: $7-$19

(402) 359-5165

http://www.ngpc.state.ne.us/parks/
guides/parksearch/showpark.asp?
Area_No=175

Camp Accommodations

200+ shaded, padded sites, 45 feet, 1 ADA, electric, some water, dump stations. Amenities include showers/restrooms, potable water, picnic tables, grills, accessible fishing, hiking, biking, swimming/beach, host, pet friendly.

Directions

15 miles from I-80. From Exit 445 go west 12.7 miles on Hwy 92/275 (becomes Center Rd.). Follow 92 when 275 turns north. Turn south for 1 mile on S 264th St to F St. Turn right for 1 mile to the Park entrance.

Points of Interest -

Omaha has the world's largest indoor rainforest - The Lied Jungle. Visit the Durham Western Heritage Museum or Joslyn Art Museum. Shop in the Old Market district, where restaurants, pubs and galleries line authentic cobblestone streets. Savor a legendary Omaha steak.

NEVADA

The Nevada Division of State Parks is responsible for the 25 park system, 16 of which have RV camping facilities. The website is -

http://parks.nv.gov/

There is no online registration system. Fees for an RV site are variable and determined by adding the sum of - Entrance fee ($6/vehicle) plus Camping fee (varies from $6 - $10) plus Utilities fee ($10).

Pets are welcome, but they must be kept on a leash of not more than six feet in length. They are not allowed in Visitor Centers.

[1] **Valley of Fire State Park**
    N36 25.814 W114 31.093
[2] **Washoe Lake State Park**
    N39 14.489 W119 45.795
[3] **Lahontan State Recreation Area**
    N39 22.668 W119 12.078

[4] **Rye Patch State Recreation Area**
    N40 28.130 W118 18.657
[5] **South Fork State Recreation Area**
    N40 39.836 W115 44.464
[6] **Angel Creek Campground**
    N41 01.725 W115 03.053

NOTES:

Nevada

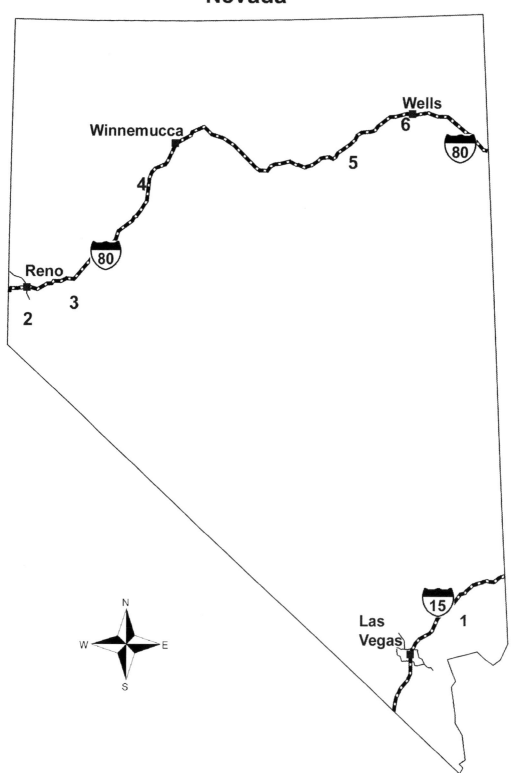

Exit 75 of I-15
Valley of Fire State Park [1]
Northeast of Las Vegas
State Rate: $14-$24

(702) 397-2088

http://parks.nv.gov/vf.htm

Camp Accommodations

73 shaded and spacious sites, 50 feet, electricity/water, some pull through, dump station. Amenities include restroom/showers, grill, picnic table, potable water, hiking, biking, Visitors Center, shop, pet friendly.

Directions

19 miles from I-15. From Exit 75 turn southeast on Hwy 169 (Valley of Fire Highway) for 19 miles into the Park.

Points of Interest -

There are many beautiful sites within the Park. Lake Mead National Recreation Area borders the park. Lost City Museum in Overton offers fine displays of Indian artifacts and reconstruction of the original pit dwellings and pueblo found in the Moapa Valley.

Exit 15 of I-80
Washoe Lake State Park [2]
South of Reno
State Rate: $14

(775) 687-4319

http://parks.nv.gov/wl.htm

Camp Accommodations

49 shaded sites, 45 feet, dry camping, dump station. Amenities include restroom/showers, grill, picnic table, potable water, hiking, biking, fishing, boating, watchable wildlife, pet friendly.

Directions

24 miles from I-80. From Exit 15 turn south on Hwy 395 for 17 miles to the East Lake Blvd. Turn left, go south 7 miles to the Park entrance on your right.

Points of Interest -

A day trip to Virginia City is a step back in time. The 19th century mining boom turned Virginia City and its grubby prospectors into instant millionaires. They built mansions, imported furniture & fashions from Europe & the Orient. Find it as it was then. See [3] & www.virginiacity-nv.org/

Exit 46 of I-80
Lahontan State Recreation Area [3]
South of Fernley
State Rate: $10

(775) 577-2235

http://parks.nv.gov/lah.htm

Camp Accommodations

Silver Spring Beach #7 area sites will accommodate RV rigs up to 60 feet, dry camping, dump station. Amenities include restroom/showers, grill, picnic table, potable water, hiking, biking, fishing, boating, watchable wildlife, pet friendly.

Directions

20 miles from I-80. From Exit 46 turn south, go 18 miles on Hwy 95 (which turns south again in Fernley). Go east on Fir Ave. for 2 miles into the Park. Drive to Silver Springs Beach #7.

Points of Interest -

Virginia City was a boisterous town with gold in every hill. The spirits of past Comstock characters still inhabit the places they built, and 150 years later romance thrives in this wondrous place. Learn about Mark Twain and his stint as reporter for the Territorial Enterprise. Also see [2].

Exit 129
Rye Patch State Recreation Area [4]
Southwest of Winnemucca
State Rate: $10

(775) 538-7321

http://parks.nv.gov/rp.htm

Camp Accommodations

46 shaded waterfront sites, 45 feet, dry camping, dump station. Amenities include restroom/showers, grill, picnic table, potable water, fishing, boating, swimming, hiking, biking, pet friendly.

Directions

1 mile from I-80. From Exit 129 turn west on Hwy 401 for 1 mile into the Park.

Points of Interest -

Winnemucca has much to offer, from 24-hour gaming opportunities, to a rich western history, to renowned Basque festivals and Basque dining. The annual festival in June hosts a variety of traditional Basque games including weight carrying, wood chopping, and Jota dancing.

Exit 301
South Fork State Recreation Area [5]
South of Elko
State Rate: $10

(775) 744-4346

http://parks.nv.gov/sf.htm

Camp Accommodations

25 water view sites, 30 feet, dry camping, dump station. Amenities include restroom/showers, grill, picnic table, potable water, fishing, boating, swimming, hiking, biking, pet friendly.

Directions

18 miles from I-80. From Exit 301 turn southeast 0.8 miles on Mountain City Hwy to Idaho St. Turn left for 1 mile to Hwy 227. Turn right for 7 miles to Hwy 228. Go south for 5.5 miles to Cty Rd. 715 (South Fork). Go right 3.5 miles to the Park.

Points of Interest -

Check out Elko . . . "Nevada with Altitude." You can take a gold mine tour or visit the Northeastern Nevada Museum with its new American Mastodon exhibit. Also see the Western Folklife Center, Headquarters for the *National Cowboy Poetry Gathering*. Wander around Elko Railroad Park.

Exit 351
Angel Creek Campground [6]
South of Wells
Humboldt NF Rate: $9-$12
America/Beautiful Rate: $5-$6

(775) 752-3357

http://www.recreation.gov/camping/
Angel_Creek_Nv/r/campground

Camp Accommodations

18 river view, paved sites, 45 feet, dry camping. Amenities include ADA restroom, grill, picnic table, potable water, biking, firewood, fishing, hiking, watchable wildlife, pet friendly.

Directions

9 miles from I-80. From Exit 351 go south and immediately turn right on Hwy 231 (Angel Lake Rd). Go 8 miles to Angel Creek. Turn left and go 1 mile to the campground.

Points of Interest -

Visit Wells - cows, cowboys and casinos! Explore Metropolis, a ghost town, with a fascinating history. The grandest hotel between Reno & Salt Lake, a business district with concrete sidewalks, and street lights all sprang up in 1911. The railroad laid track to the then booming town.

NEW HAMPSHIRE

The New Hampshire Division of Parks and Recreation oversees the State Park system. Visit their website for detailed information at -

http://www.nhstateparks.org/

There are nineteen State campgrounds. Fees vary from $25 - $50, depending on location, amenities and utilities available. Reservations are taken for all state park campgrounds through Reserveamerica, either online, at -

http://
newhampshirestate-
parks.reserveamerica.com/

or by calling 1-877-nhparks (1-877-647-

2757). The maximum reservation window is 11 months in advance. There is a non-refundable reservation fee of $8.75. New Hampshire residents age 65 and older are offered a $5 discount per nightly fee.

Pets are permitted at Bear Brook, Coleman, Deer Mountain, Dry River, Greenfield (designated area only), Lake Francis, Milan, Mollidgewock, Moose Brook, Pillsbury, Sunapee, and Umbagog campgrounds. Pets must be leashed and supervised at all times. No pets are permitted on the bathing beaches. Pets are not to be left unattended in any vehicle, camper, carrier or enclosure at any time.

The White Mountain National Forest also provides a number of campground opportunities.

[1] Pillsbury State Park
N43 14.014 W72 06.940
[2] Storrs Pond Recreation Area
N43 43.206 W72 15.641
[3] Pawtuckaway State Park
N43 04.792 W71 10.373
[4] Campton Campground
N43 52.260 W71 37.819
[5] Franconia Notch State Park (Lafayette Campground)
N44 08.341 W71 41.105

NOTES:

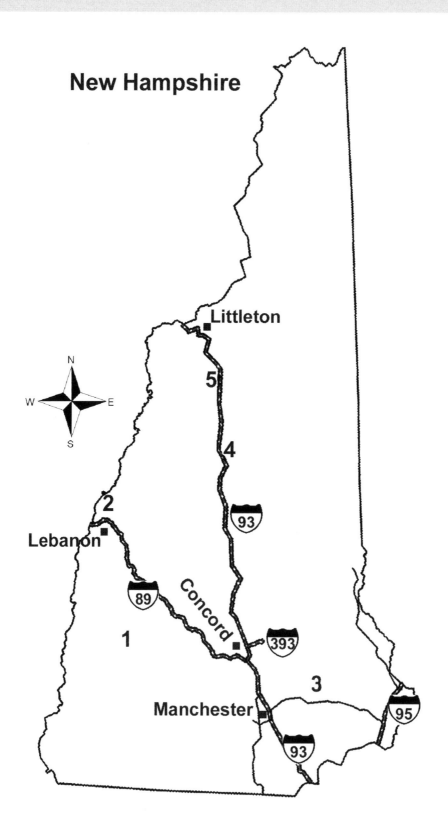

New Hampshire

Exit 5 of I-89
Pillsbury State Park [1]
South of Newport
State Rate: $16-$23

(603) 863-2860

www.nhstateparks.org/state-parks/
alphabetical-order/pillsbury-state-
park/campground-information.aspx

Camp Accommodations

14 wooded, water front RV sites, 38 feet, 1 ADA, reservations available. Amenities include restroom, fire ring, picnic table, potable water, hiking, biking, boating, firewood, watchable wildlife, pet friendly. No Utilities.

Directions

29 miles from I-89. From Exit 5 go 16 miles west on Hwy 9/202, past Hillsboro. Turn right on Hwy 31 for 13.5 miles to Pillsbury State Park Rd. Turn right in to the Park.

Points of Interest -

Concord and the surrounding region offers a diversity of destinations. Travel in the fast lane at a world class motor speedway or take a tour of the State House. Visit President Pierce's Manse, or enjoy a lively evening's entertainment at one of Concord's many fine performing arts facilities.

Exit 18 of I-89
Storrs Pond Recreation Area [2]
North of Hanover
County Park Rate: $34

(603) 643-2134

http://www.storrspond.org/

Camp Accommodations

11 wooded RV sites, 35 feet, electricity/water, reservations available. Amenities include restroom/showers, fire ring, picnic table, potable water, hiking, biking, pool, tennis.

Directions

7 miles from I-89. From Exit 18 go 5 miles north on Hwy 120 to Hwy 10 (Lyme Rd). Turn north (right), go 1 mile to Reservoir Rd. Turn right for 0.7 miles to the Campground.

Points of Interest -

The region is a part of what is known as "The Upper Valley." At the region's center are Hanover & Lebanon on the New Hampshire side of the river. Hanover is home to Dartmouth College (one of the Ivies and ninth oldest college in the nation) and enjoys a lively, traditional downtown.

Exit 7 of I-93
Pawtuckaway State Park [3]
East of Manchester
State Rate: $30-$32

(603) 895-3031

http://www.nhstateparks.org/state-
parks/alphabetical-order/
pawtuckaway-state-park/

Camp Accommodations

53 wooded, water front RV sites, 38 feet, 1 ADA, reservations available. Amenities include restroom/showers, fire ring, picnic table, potable water, hiking, biking, boating, watchable wildlife, store. No Pets, No Utilities.

Directions

18 mi. from I-93. From Exit 7 go 14 mi. east on Hwy 101 to exit 5. Go north 0.6 mi. on Hwy 107/156. Turn left then an immediate right on Hwy 156. Go 1.1 mi. to Harriman Rd. Turn left for 0.2 mi., then right on Mountain Rd. Go 2 miles to State Park Rd.

Points of Interest -

Manchester, recently nationally ranked among top cities by a number of different Magazines, is home to a majority of New Hampshire's major cultural institutions. Some examples are the Currier Museum, Palace Theatre, New Hampshire Symphony, the Tupelo Music Hall.

Exit 28
Campton Campground [4]
North of Plymouth
White Mountain NF Rate: $20
America/Beautiful Rate: $10

(603) 536-1315

http://www.recreation.gov/

Camp Accommodations

53 wooded, sites, 50 feet, 15 ADA, reservations available. Amenities include restroom/showers, fire ring, picnic table, potable water, hiking, biking, Interpretive Programs, watchable wildlife, pet friendly. No Utilities.

Directions

2 miles from I-93. From Exit 28 go 2 miles northeast on Hwy 49 to the campground on your left.

Points of Interest -

Plymouth, has a rich historical and cultural heritage. Nathaniel Hawthorne, Daniel Webster, Robert Frost, and the Pemigewasset Indians have all played their part in the history of Plymouth. Do the Heritage Trail to get a sense of the past and an appreciation of the town's history.

Exit 34A
Franconia Notch State Park (Lafayette Campground) [5]
South of Franconia
State Rate: $19-$25

(603) 823-9513

http://www.nhstateparks.org/state-parks/alphabetical-order/lafayette-campground/

Camp Accommodations

21 wooded RV sites, 30 feet, 1 ADA, reservations available. Amenities include restroom/showers, fire ring, table, potable water, hiking, biking, store. No Pets, No utilities.

Directions

Adjoins I-93. Accessible directly from Exit 34A, if southbound. If northbound on I-93 go 2.5 miles north to Exit 34B and backtrack 2.5 miles to the park.

Points of Interest -

There are a number of towns nearby, each with a unique flavor and traditional New England attractions. Try the Franconia Heritage Museum or Clark's Trading Post, home of Clark's Trained Bears and the White Mountain Central Railroad. Bretton Woods Lodge is also a special destination.

NEW JERSEY

With more than 430,000 acres, New Jersey's state parks and forests have much to offer and explore. Chances are there's one less than 30 miles away from your in-state location. The Parks are managed by the Division of Parks and Forestry. There website is -

http://www.state.nj.us/dep/parksandforests/parks/index.html

Sixteen state campgrounds will accommodate RVs, however, there are no hook ups. Pets are prohibited from all buildings, swimming beaches and swimming waters, non-designated pet friendly campsites and overnight facilities.

To make a reservation, contact the appropriate park, forest or recreation area office during normal business hours. Reservations can be made up to 11 months in advance of the reservation date in person at the area office; by mail using an overnight application form; or by telephone using a credit card. Campsites are typically around $20. Park entrance fees are $5 per vehicle.

[1] **Spruce Run Recreation Area**
N40 39.771 W74 56.324
[2] **Stephens State Park**
N40 52.300 W74 48.617
[3] **Turkey Swamp County Park**
N40 11.825 W74 17.896
[4] **Allaire State Park**
N40 09.732 W74 07.877

NOTES:

New Jersey

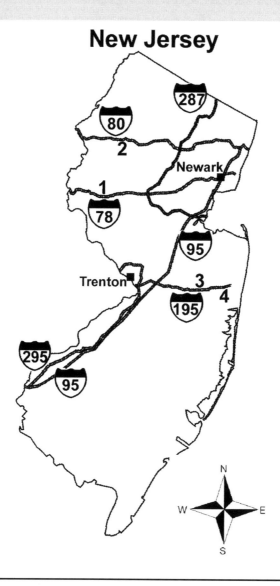

Interstate 78

Exit 17
Spruce Run Recreation Area [1]
North of Annandale
State Rate: $20

(908) 638-8572

http://www.state.nj.us/dep/
parksandforests/parks/
spruce.html#camp

Camp Accommodations

67 shaded sites, 38 feet, dump station, 3 pull throughs, reservations available. Amenities include ADA restroom/showers, fire ring/grill, picnic table, potable water, hiking, biking, boating, swimming. No Pets, No Utilities.

Directions

5 miles from I-78. From Exit 17 go north for 3.2 miles on Hwy 31 to Van Syckels Corner Rd. Turn left, go 1.5 miles to the Park entrance on the left.

Points of Interest -

Just north visit Oxford Furnace and Shippen Manor. The Furnace, built in 1741, was the third furnace in Colonial New Jersey and the first where iron ore was mined. On a hill overlooking the Furnace sits Shippen Manor, once the home of the ironmaster and now a Museum.

Exit 25 of I-80
Stephens State Park [2]
North of Hackettstown
State Rate: $20

(908) 852-3790

http://www.state.nj.us/dep/
parksandforests/parks/stephens.html

Camp Accommodations

11 shaded RV sites, up to 40 feet, reservations available. Amenities include restrooms, fire ring/grill, picnic table, potable water, hiking, biking, boating. No Pets, No Utilities.

Directions

8 miles from I-80. From Exit 25 bear right onto the off ramp to Continental and Kays Rd. for 1.8 miles to Cty Rd 604 (Waterloo Rd.). Turn left and go 5.7 miles to the camp on your left.

Points of Interest -

Explore Morris Canal & Waterloo Village. The Village is a 400-year old Lenape (Delaware) Indian village along the once prosperous Canal. The 19th-century restored Village contains a working mill complex with grist & sawmills, a general store, blacksmith and several historic houses.

Exit 22 of I-195
Turkey Swamp County Park [3]
North of Vista Center
CP Rate: $30-$33

(732) 462-7286

www.monmouthcountyparks.com/
page.asp?agency=133&Id=2522

Camp Accommodations

64 wooded RV sites, up to 40 feet, electric/water, all pull throughs, dump station, reservations available. Amenities include restrooms/showers, fire ring/grill, picnic table, potable water, biking, boating, pet friendly.

Directions

3.5 miles from I-195. From Exit 22 turn northeast for 2.4 miles on Jackson Mills Rd to Georgia Rd. Go left for 1 mile to the park entrance on your left.

Points of Interest -

At historic Longstreet Farm, in Holmdel Park, costumed interpreters share with visitors life as it was in rural Monmouth County during the 1890's. Go to the Creative Arts Center in Thompson Park, with pottery & ceramics studios, and classrooms for painting, drawing, & other crafts.

Exit 31 of I-195
Allaire State Park [4]
North of Lakewood
State Rate: $20

(732) 938-2371

http://www.state.nj.us/dep/
parksandforests/parks/allaire.html

Camp Accommodations

45 shaded sites, up to 40 feet, dump station, reservations available. Amenities include restrooms/showers, fire ring/grill, picnic table, potable water, hiking, biking, Visitors Center, Museum, Interpretive Center, store, No Pets, No Utilities.

Directions

1.5 miles from I-195. From Exit 31 turn north on Squankum Rd and immediately go right on Cty Rd 524 (Allaire Rd) for 1.3 miles to the Park on your right.

Points of Interest -

The Park is best known for its historic 19th-century iron making town, Allaire Village, and its antique steam trains on the Pine Creek Railroad. The Village was known as the Howell Works in the early 19th century, when it was a thriving industrial community producing pig & cast iron.

NEW MEXICO

New Mexico has 35 diverse State Parks to explore, including cool lakes, mountain forests, canyons, desert beauty, and fascinating historical sites, including dinosaur tracks! Information from the New Mexico State Parks Division can be found at -

http://www.emnrd.state.nm.us/PRD/

Facilities are available on a first come, first served basis with the exception of parks where the division has established a reservation program and a visitor has reserved the facility. Pet owners must restrain pets on leashes that are not more than 10 feet in length.

Primitive campsites offer no special facilities except a cleared area for camp-ing. Sites may include trash cans, chemical toilets or parking. Developed sites offer additional facilities such as electric and sewage hookups.

Camp sites fees are as follows -

Developed site - $10
Developed site with electricity - $14
Developed site with sewage - $14
Developed site with electric/sewage - $18
Electric hookup with annual permit - $ 4
Sewage hookup with annual permit - $ 4
Electric/sewage with annual permit - $ 8
Water hookup (where available) - No charge
Per vehicle entrance fee - $ 5

New Mexico campsites can be reserved from 1 day to 6 months in advance at -

http://www.newmexico.reserveworld.com/

You can also call (877) 664-7787 to make a reservation.

---

[1] **Rockhound State Park**
    N32 11.134 W107 36.786
[2] **Leasburg Dam State Park**
    N32 29.330 W106 54.888
[3] **Caballo Lake State Park**
    N32 54.429 W107 18.702
[4] **Elephant Butte Lake State Park**
    N33 10.846 W107 12.525
[5] **Cochiti Lake Campground**
    N35 38.542 W106 19.980
[6] **Field Tract Campground**
    N35 41.258 W105 41.672

[7] **Storrie Lake State Park**
    N35 39.463 W105 13.904
[8] **Sugarite Canyon State Park**
    N36 56.306 W104 22.732
[9] **McGaffey Campground**
    N35 22.232 W108 31.395
[10] **Bluewater Lake State Park**
    N35 18.094 W108 06.447
[11] **Santa Rosa Lake State Park**
    N35 01.810 W104 40.067
[12] **Ute Lake State Park**
    N35 21.356 W103 27.178

NOTES:

New Mexico

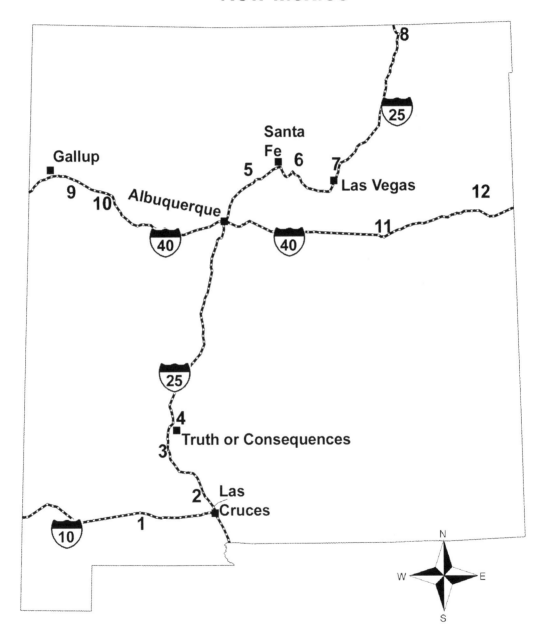

Exit 82 of I-10
Rockhound State Park [1]
Southeast of Deming
State Rate: $14-$22

(575) 546-6182

http://www.emnrd.state.nm.us/PRD/
Rockhound.htm

Camp Accommodations

29 sites, electric/water, 45 feet, dump station, sun shelters, pull throughs, reservations. Amenities include restrooms/showers, fire rings, picnic table, biking, hiking, Visitors Center, Interpretive Programs, pet friendly.

Directions

14 miles from I-10. From Exit 82 turn south on Hwy 180, which becomes Hwy 11, for 5.3 miles to Hwy 141. Turn east for 8.5 miles to the park.

Points of Interest -
The Park trails are of varying degrees of difficulty, with breathtaking views. Sunsets can be spellbinding from the SW facing camp, especially from the high elevation sites. You are allowed to take up to 15 lbs of rock for your collection (find jasper, quartz, agate, opal, thunder eggs).

Exit 144 of I-10 or Exit 19 of I-25
Leasburg Dam State Park [2]
North of Las Cruces
State Rate: $14

(575) 524-4068

http://www.emnrd.state.nm.us/PRD/
leasburg.htm

Camp Accommodations

31 paved sites, mostly electric/water, 40 feet, dump station, sun shelters, pull throughs, reservations. Amenities include restrooms/showers, fire rings, picnic table, biking, hiking, fishing, swimming, firewood, Visitors Center, Interpretive Programs, pet friendly.

Directions

20 miles from I-10. From Exit 144 turn north on I-25 for 19 miles to Exit 19. Turn southwest for 0.5 miles on Hwy 157 to the Park entrance on your right.

Points of Interest -

Las Cruces, located between the Organ Mountains and the meandering Rio Grande River, blends a unique variety of attractions, culture, and historical sites such as Old Mesilla. Enjoy excellent weather, with 350 days of sunshine per year, and world-class Mexican food!

Exit 59 of I-25
Caballo Lake State Park [3]
South of Caballo
State Rate: $14-$18

(575) 743-3942

http://www.emnrd.state.nm.us/PRD/
caballo.htm

Camp Accommodations

135 sites, electric/water or full hook ups, 40 feet, dump station, sun shelters, pull throughs, reservations. Amenities include restrooms/showers, fire rings, table, biking, hiking, fishing, swimming, firewood, Visitors Center, Geology Exploration, pet friendly.

Directions

1 mile from I-25. From Exit 59 turn north on Hwy 187 for 1 mile to the Park entrance on your right.

Points of Interest -

Try a visit to Silver City. With two dozen art galleries, studios, antique stores and a tile workshop, Silver City will meet your artistic needs. Hike or bike up to Boston Hills, a reclaimed historic mining area overlooking town; or see the Gila Cliff Dwellings.

Exit 83
Elephant Butte Lake State Park [4]
North of Truth or Consequences
State Rate: $10-$14

(575) 744-5923

http://www.emnrd.state.nm.us/PRD/
elephant.htm

Camp Accommodations

132 sites, mostly electric/water, 40+ feet, dump station, sun shelters, pull throughs, reservations. Amenities include restrooms/showers, fire rings, picnic table, biking, hiking, swimming, boating, Visitors Center, watchable wildlife, pet friendly.

Directions

4 miles from I-25. From Exit 83 turn south to Hwy 195 on the east side of the Interstate. Follow Hwy 195 for 4 miles to the park on your left.

Points of Interest -

On the banks of the Rio Grande, Truth or Consequences has long been a preferred vacation site. You can bath in soothing hot springs. Then take in the cultural life, ranging from flying fingers at the New Mexico Old Time Fiddlers Contest to the solemnity of The Geronimo Springs Museum.

Exit 259
Cochiti Lake Campground [5]
West of Santa Fe
COE Rate: $8-$14
America/Beautiful Rate: $4-$7

(505) 465-0307

www.recreation.gov/

Camp Accommodations

75 paved sites, mostly electric/water, 45+ feet, dump station, sun shelters, pull throughs. Amenities include ADA restrooms, showers, potable water, picnic table, biking, hiking, swimming, boating, Interpretive Trail, watchable wildlife, pet friendly.

Directions

13 miles from I-25. From Exit 259 go north for 13 miles, through Pena Blanca, on Hwy 22 (Cochiti Hwy) to the campground.

Points of Interest -

The Park has many opportunities for both wildlife viewing and recreation. Santa Fe, one of the top travel destinations in the US, is within a hour drive. You can see details about this fascinating city at -

http://www.santafe.org/

Exit 307
Field Tract Campground [6]
North of Pecos
Santa Fe NF Rate: $8
America/Beautiful Rate: $4

(505) 438-7840

http://www.fs.fed.us/r3/sfe/recreation/
districts/pecos/index.html#camping

Camp Accommodations

15 shaded, paved sites, dry camping, 45 feet, 10 pull throughs. Amenities include restrooms, potable water, picnic table, biking, hiking, watchable wildlife, pet friendly. No Utilities.

Directions

15 miles from I-25. From Exit 307 go north for 15 miles, through Pecos, on Hwy 63 to the campground.

Points of Interest -

Visit Pecos, located between Santa Fe and Las Vegas, New Mexico, at the site of a mountain pass used by travelers for centuries. Pecos is a place to hike, fish, and horseback ride. Relax, wander main street, shop, and enjoy a meal at one of the family owned restaurants.

Exit 343 of I-25
Storrie Lake State Park [7]
North of Las Vegas, NM
State Rate: $14

(505) 425-7278

http://www.emnrd.state.nm.us/PRD/
StorrieLake.htm

Camp Accommodations

45 shaded sites, 21 electric/water, 40 feet, sun shelters, dump station, pull throughs, reservations. Amenities include restrooms/showers, fire rings, table, biking, hiking, sailing, Visitors Center, watchable wildlife, pet friendly.

Directions

5 miles from I-25. From Exit 343 turn north on Hwy 518 and go 5 miles to the park on your left.

Points of Interest -

With the arrival of the Santa Fe Railway in 1879, the Las Vegas area became a hangout for some historic Old West characters, including Doc Holliday, Billy the Kid & Wyatt Earp. Enjoy the many culturally rich opportunities Las Vegas has to offer, from summer Fiestas to art galleries.

Exit 452 of I-25
Sugarite Canyon State Park [8]
Northeast of Raton
State Rate: $10-$14

(575) 445-5607

http://www.emnrd.state.nm.us/PRD/
Sugarite.htm

Camp Accommodations

40 shaded sites, 12 electric/water, some ADA, 40 feet, dump station, sun shelters, pull throughs, reservations. Amenities include restrooms/showers, fire rings, table, biking, hiking, fishing, swimming, firewood, Visitors Center, watchable wildlife, pet friendly.

Directions

6 miles from I-25 From Exit 452 follow Hwy 72 east for 3.7 miles. Turn north on Hwy 526 for 2 miles to the Visitor Center.

Points of Interest -

The Park's Coal Camp Interpretive Trail winds through the ruins of the Sugarite coal camp. Coal mining in the area provided an important economic boost to the region and state. Other area geologic features include the iridium layer, Raton Basin and Capulin National Volcano.

Exit 33 of I-40
McGaffey Campground [9]
Southeast of Gallup
Cibola NF Rate: $10-$15
America/Beautiful Rate: $5-$8

(505) 346-3900

http://www.forestcamping.com/dow/
southwst/cibcmp.htm#quaking%
20aspen

Camp Accommodations

21 wooded RV sites, 6 electric, 40+ feet, pull throughs. Amenities include restrooms, fire pits, table, biking, hiking, watchable wildlife, pet friendly. NO water/sewer.

Directions

10.5 miles from I-40. From Exit 33 go south on Hwy 400 for 10 miles to the campground sign. Turn right at sign onto a gravel road and go 0.4 miles to campground entrance.

Points of Interest -

Go to El Morro National Monument, located on an ancient east-west trail in western New Mexico. Close by you'll find the Ice Cave and Bandera Volcano, situated on the Continental Divide, where volcanic craters and lava tubes compare with the lunar landscape.

Exit 63
Bluewater Lake State Park [10]
Southeast of Thoreau
State Rate: $10-$14

(505) 876-2391

http://www.emnrd.state.nm.us/PRD/
Bluewater.htm

Camp Accommodations

149 sites, some water/electric, 45 feet, dump station, sun shelters, pull throughs, reservations. Amenities include restrooms/showers, fire rings, table, fishing, biking, hiking, boating, Visitors Center, watchable wildlife, Geology Exploration, pet friendly.

Directions

6 miles from I-40. From Exit 63 turn south for 6 miles on Hwy 412. This road will dead end at the Park.

Points of Interest -

The area is very interesting with many photography opportunities. Things to see include Mt. Taylor, the Zuni Mountains and Zuni Pueblo, El Malpais National Monument, and Indian ruins. Be sure to visit the Northwest New Mexico Visitor Center in Grants.

Exit 275
Santa Rosa Lake State Park [11]
North of Santa Rosa
State Rate: $10-$14

(575) 472-3110

http://www.emnrd.state.nm.us/PRD/
santarosa.htm

Camp Accommodations

76 sites, some water/electric, 40 feet, dump station, sun shelters, pull throughs, reservations. Amenities include restrooms/showers, fire rings, table, fishing, biking, hiking, boating, Visitors Center, watchable wildlife, pet friendly.

Directions

10 miles from I-40. From Exit 275 turn west on Hwy 54/84 for 1 mile to 2nd. St. (Hwy 91). Turn right and follow Hwy 91 for 9 miles to the Park.

Points of Interest -

Near Santa Rosa visit Puerto de Luna (PDL), an ancient adobe village in a beautiful landscape. PDL was once the most thriving village in the area. Tour Nuestro Señora del Refugio Church. Try PDL's famous "PDL Chile" a unique strain of chile . . . look for local restaurant specials.

Exit 356
Ute Lake State Park [12]
West of Logan
State Rate: $10-$14

(575) 487-2284

http://www.emnrd.state.nm.us/PRD/
UteLake.htm

Camp Accommodations

142 sites, many water/electric, 40 feet, dump station, sun shelters, pull throughs, reservations. Amenities include restrooms/showers, fire rings, table, fishing, biking, hiking, boating, Visitors Center, watchable wildlife, pet friendly.

Directions

24 miles from I-40. From Exit 356 go north for 19.5 miles on Hwy 469 to Hwy 54. Turn north for 2 miles into Logan. Turn west at Martinez St. (Hwy 540). Follow Hwy 540 for 2.5 miles to the Park.

Points of Interest -

Tucumcari, the Heart of the Mother Road and Gateway City of Murals is on historic Route 66. Visit their world-class Dinosaur Museum and Historical Museum. National, State and Historic Scenic Byways make for great photo opportunities, as do the beautiful vistas.

NEW YORK

The New York State Office of Parks, Recreation and Historic Preservation oversees the 178 State Parks, 68 of which have campgrounds. You will find their website at -

http://nysparks.state.ny.us/parks/

Pets must be kept on a leash at all times and the leash can be no longer than 6ft. Don't leave pets unattended and always pick up after them. A Rabies certificate is required. A new regulation is now in effect that prohibits the import of firewood into New York unless it has been kiln-dried.

Reservations can be made from 1 day to 9 months in advance by calling

(800) 456-CAMP or online at -

newyorkstateparks.reserveamerica.com

The fee structure is -

Basic Site Fee -	$12-$15
AMENITY ADD-ONS	
Weekend/Holiday (Fri/Sat/Sun) -	$4
Electric (15/20/30 amps) -	$6
Electric (50 amps) -	$8
Prime -	$4
Prime (Waterfront) -	$6
Prime (Oceanfront) -	$12
Full Hookup (water/electric/prime) -	$12
Reservation Fee -	$9

[1] **Greenwood Park**
N42 17.280 W76 05.177

[2] **Fillmore Glen State Park**
N42 42.010 W76 25.223

[3] **Green Lakes State Park**
N43 03.351 W76 00.289

[4] **Southwick Beach State Park**
N43 45.878 W76 11.764

[5] **Grass Point State Park**
N44 16.737 W75 59.723

[6] **Wellesley Island State Park**
N44 18.958 W76 01.168

[7] **Allegany State Park - Quaker Area**
N42 02.237 W78 50.759

[8] **Robert H. Treman State Park**
N42 23.893 W76 32.765

[9] **Newtown Battlefield State Park**
N42 02.629 W76 44.056

[10] **Hickories County Park**
N42 05.482 W76 13.556

[11] **Beaver Pond Campgrounds - Harriman State Park**
N41 13.750 W74 04.218

[12] **Margaret Lewis Norrie State Park**
N41 50.421 W73 55.901

[13] **Thompson's Lake State Park**
N42 39.198 W74 02.735

[14] **Moreau Lake State Park**
N43 13.624 W73 42.405

[15] **Cumberland Bay State Park**
N44 43.474 W73 25.586

[16] **Chenango Valley State Park**
N42 12.929 W75 49.066

[17] **Gilbert Lake State Park**
N42 34.362 W75 07.700

[18] **Lake Erie State Park**
N42 25.258 W79 25.715

[19] **Darien Lakes State Park**
N42 54.130 W78 25.986

[20] **Cayuga Lake State Park**
N42 53.762 W76 45.199

[21] **Stony Brook State Park**
N42 31.584 W77 41.791

NOTES:

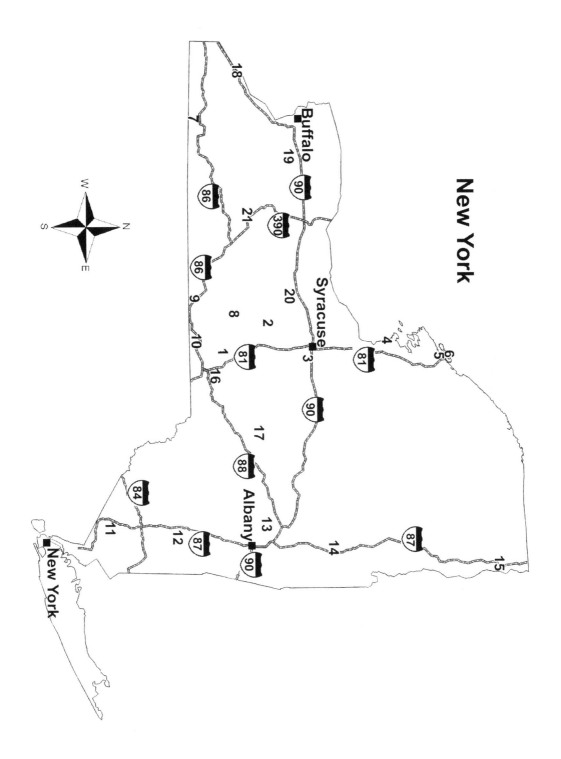

Exit 8
Greenwood Park [1]
West of Whitney Point
County Rate: $15-$18

(607) 778-2193

http://www.gobroomecounty.com/
parks/greenwood

Directions

10 miles from I-81. From Exit 8; if northbound, turn northeast on Hwy 26 for 0.6 miles too Hwy 11/79, then turn left; if southbound, exit directly onto Hwy 11/79. Follow Hwy 79 northwest for 5 miles to Cty Rd. 21 (Caldwell Hill Road). Turn south for 4 miles, then turn right onto Greenwood Road for 1 mile to the Park.

Camp Accommodations

50 sites, electricity, up to 40 feet, dump station, reservations available. Amenities include restrooms/showers, potable water, grill, picnic table, hiking, biking, fishing, swimming, boating, store, pet friendly.

Points of Interest -

In Binghamton visit farmers' markets, stroll through art galleries or antique shops. Take a spin on a restored, antique carousel. Enjoy pop, rock, jazz, blues, and salsa performances. Step into another dimension . . . visit the creator of "The Twilight Zone" Rod Serling's old stomping grounds!

Exit 12
Fillmore Glen State Park [2]
Northwest of Cortland
State Rate: $15 + amenities fee

(315) 497-0130

http://nysparks.state.ny.us/parks/157/
details.aspx

Directions

16 miles from I-81. From Exit 12 go west to Hwy 281. Turn north (right) for 0.4 miles to Hwy 90 (Cayuga St). Turn west on Hwy 90 for 13 miles to Hwy 38. Go 3 miles north to the Park on your right.

Camp Accommodations

60 shaded sites, some riverfront, some electricity, 50 feet, dump station, reservations available. Amenities include ADA restrooms/showers, potable water, grill, picnic table, hiking, biking, swimming, beach, Interpretive Programs, pet friendly.

Points of Interest -

The Park is an oasis of cool, dense woods crowding into a long, narrow gorge. Its hiking trails offer spectacular views, unique geological formations, including five waterfalls, and a botanically rich glen. Check to see if there is a special event when you plan to camp.

Either Exits from I-81 to I-481
Green Lakes State Park [3]
East of Syracuse
State Rate: $15 + amenities fee

(315) 637-6111

http://nysparks.state.ny.us/parks/172/
details.aspx

Directions

4 miles from I-481. From the northbound or southbound exits of I-81 onto I-481, proceed on I-481 to Exit 5. Follow Kirkville Rd. east for 1.3 miles to Fremont Rd. Turn south for 1.2 miles to Hwy 290. Turn east, follow signs for 1.4 miles to park.

Camp Accommodations

131 shaded sites, 4 ADA, some electric, 50 feet, dump station, reservations available. Amenities include ADA restrooms/showers, potable water, grill, picnic table, hiking, biking, swimming, beach, Interpretive Programs, pet friendly.

Points of Interest -

Explore the many neighborhoods of Syracuse. There are numerous locations to see along the Erie Canal, as well as Revolutionary War destinations. Many orchards, specialty shops, galleries and restaurants are to be found. Go here for ideas - *www.visitsyracuse.org/explore/*

Exit 40
Southwick Beach State Park [4]
West of Adams
State Rate: $15 + amenities fee

(315) 846-5338

http://nysparks.state.ny.us/parks/36/
details.aspx

Directions
7.5 miles from I-81. From Exit 40 go west
for 7.5 miles on Hwy 193 to the Park.

Camp Accommodations
100 shaded sites, 3 ADA, some electric, some water, 50 feet, dump station, reservations available. Amenities
include ADA restrooms/showers, potable water, grill, picnic table, hiking,
biking, swimming, beach, pet friendly.

Points of Interest -
The Park is adjacent to the Lakeview Wildlife Management Area, home to the envi-
ronmentally-sensitive coastal sand dunes.
Park nature and hiking trails adjoin the
wildlife management area and its trail system, which visitors are encouraged to use.

Exit 50
Grass Point State Park [5]
South of Alexandria Bay
State Rate: $15 + amenities fee

(315) 686-4472

http://nysparks.state.ny.us/parks/139/
details.aspx

Directions
1.5 miles from I-81. From Exit 50 go southwest for 1.5 miles on Hwy 12 to the Park.

Camp Accommodations
73 shaded sites, 2 ADA, some electric, some water, 40 feet, dump station, reservations available. Amenities
include ADA restrooms/showers, potable water, grill, picnic table, hiking,
biking, beach, pet friendly.

Points of Interest -
This Park puts you in the midst of the
beautiful 1000 Islands. Visit the Antique
Boat Museum and stroll among a priceless
collection of 100 antique boats; or tour the
Handweaving Museum and Arts Center.
Stop at the Thousand Islands Winery for
world class wines and local hospitality.

Exit 51
Wellesley Island State Park [6]
On Wellesley Island
State Rate: $15 + amenities fee

(315) 482-2722

http://nysparks.state.ny.us/parks/52/
details.aspx

Directions
2.5 miles from I-81. From Exit 51 go southeast for 0.5 miles on Cty Rd. 191 to Thousand Island Park Rd. Turn right for 0.5
miles to Cross Island Rd. Turn right for 1.6
miles to the Park.

Camp Accommodations
338 shaded sites, 2 ADA, from basic
to full hook ups, 40 feet, dump station, reservations available. Amenities
include ADA restrooms/showers, potable water, grill, picnic table, hiking,
biking, swimming, beach, pet friendly.

Points of Interest -
The Park's sandy beach offers swimming,
sunbathing & a golf course. A main attractions is the Minna Anthony Common Nature Center, which includes a museum and
varied habitats - wooded wetlands, miles
of shoreline, open granite outcrops, miles
of trails for hiking, & nature education.

Exit 18
Allegany State Park - Quaker Area [7]
South of Salamanca
State Rate: $15 + amenities fee

(716) 354-2182

http://nysparks.state.ny.us/parks/1/
details.aspx

Camp Accommodations

189 shaded sites, some ADA, some electric, 45+ feet, dump station, reservations available. Amenities include ADA restrooms/showers, potable water, grill, picnic table, hiking, biking, swimming, beach, Interpretive Programs, pet friendly.

Directions

7 miles from I-86. From Exit 18 go south for 4.5 miles on Hwy 280 (Quaker Run Rd) to ASP Route. Bear left for 2 miles to Quaker Run, turn left then right on Cain Hollow Rd to the campground.

Points of Interest -

Salamanca, nestled in the scenic foothills of the Allegheny River, is filled with country charm. It is the only city in the U. S. that lies almost completely on an Indian Reservation. Stop at the Seneca Iroquois National Museum and the Salamanca Rail Museum, or enjoy the gaming facilities.

Exit 54
Robert H. Treman State Park [8]
South of Ithaca
State Rate: $15 + amenities fee

(607) 273-3440

http://nysparks.state.ny.us/parks/135/
details.aspx

Camp Accommodations

58 shaded sites, 4 ADA, some electric, 45+ feet, dump station, reservations available. Amenities include ADA restrooms/showers, potable water, grill, picnic table, hiking, biking, swimming, beach, pet friendly.

Directions

24 miles from I-86. From Exit 54 go north for 24 miles on Hwy 13 to the Park on your left.

Points of Interest -

This is an area of exceptional beauty, with the rugged Enfield Glen Gorge as its scenic highlight. Winding trails follow the gorge past 12 waterfalls, including the 115-foot Lucifer Falls, where you can see a mile-and-a-half down the wooded gorge. Don't forget Ithaca, a great town to visit!

Near Exit 58
Newtown Battlefield State Park [9]
South of Elmira
State Rate: $15 + amenities fee

(607) 732-6067

http://nysparks.state.ny.us/parks/107/
details.aspx

Camp Accommodations

18 sites, 2 ADA, 2 electric, most dry, 40 feet, dump station, reservations available. Amenities include ADA restrooms/showers, potable water, grill, picnic table, hiking, biking, pet friendly.

Directions

2 miles from I-86 (Hwy 17). 1.5 miles north of Exit 58 turn northeast on Oneida Rd. for 1 mile to Newtown Reservation Rd. Turn right, go 1 mile to the campground.

Points of Interest -

Relax and enjoy the park's vistas. The Park and its monument mark the site of the battle of Newtown, which occurred in August of 1779 and was the decisive clash in one of the largest offensive campaigns of the American Revolution. Just north of the Park you can stroll through Elmira.

Exit 65 of I-86
Hickories County Park [10]
East of Owego
County Rate: $17-$19

(607) 687-1199

http://www.townofowego.com/
hickories.htm

Camp Accommodations

80 shaded, riverfront sites, some paved, electric/water, 40 feet, dump station. Amenities include restrooms/ showers, grill, picnic table, hiking, biking, swimming, fishing, pet friendly.

Directions

1 mile from I-86. From Exit 65 go northeast for 0.5 mile on the Hwy 17 Access Rd. to the Hickory Park Rd. Turn right into the campground.

Points of Interest -

Historic Owego is a charming village along the Susquehanna River in the southeast corner of the Finger Lakes Region. Enjoy over 80 gift and antique shops, local artisans & restaurants. It was named "Coolest Small Town in America" in 2009 by Budget Travel Magazine readers.

Exit 16 of I-87
Beaver Pond Campgrounds - Harriman State Park [11]
East of Harriman
State Rate: $15 + amenities fee

(845) 947-2792

http://nysparks.state.ny.us/parks/116/
details.aspx

Camp Accommodations

82 shaded sites, dry camping, 38 feet, dump station, reservations available. Amenities include ADA restrooms/ showers, laundry, potable water, grill, picnic table, hiking, biking, swimming, beach, pet friendly.

Directions

15 miles from I-87. From Exit 16 you immediately take the Averill Ave (Hwy 17) exit and turn left on to Averill. Then turn left again on to Hwy 6 going east. Follow Hwy 6 for 5.5 miles to the Rotary. Take Palisades Interstate Pky. south for 6 miles to Gate Hill Rd. Turn west (right) for 2 miles to the Park.

Points of Interest -

The campground adjoins the Lake Welch Recreation Area. A beach and plenty of outdoor activities make this a great destination not far from New York City. Stony Point Battlefield State Historic Site is near by. The campground is located 25 miles north of the George Washington Bridge.

Exit 19 of I-87
Margaret Lewis Norrie State Park [12]
East of Kingston
State Rate: $15 + amenities fee

(845) 889-4646

http://nysparks.state.ny.us/parks/171/
details.aspx

Camp Accommodations

45 shaded sites, dry camping, 40 feet, dump station, reservations available. Amenities include restrooms/showers, potable water, grill, picnic table, hiking, biking, fishing, Interpretive Programs, bird watching, pet friendly.

Directions

19 miles from I-87. From Exit 19 turn west on Hwy 28 and then north on Hwy 209, which changes into Hwy 199, for 8.5 miles in all to Hwy 9G. Turn south on 9G for 1.5 miles to Hwy 9. Turn south (right) on Hwy 9 for 9 miles to the Park.

Points of Interest -

The Park, bounded on the west by the Hudson River has bluffs overlooking the Hudson. Visit the Vanderbilt Mansion National Historic Site of 600 acres, known for its grand scale, classical ornament, and look of permanence. The majestic home is also famous for its landscaping.

Exit 23
Thompson's Lake State Park [13]
Southwest of Albany
State Rate: $15 + amenities fee

(518) 872-1674

http://nysparks.state.ny.us/parks/99/
details.aspx

Camp Accommodations

139 wooded sites, 3 ADA, dry camping, 40 feet, dump station, reservations available. Amenities include ADA restrooms/showers, potable water, grill, table, hiking, biking, swimming, beach, fishing, Interpretive Programs, Visitors Center, pet friendly.

Directions

20 miles from I-87. From Exit 23 turn south on Hwy 9W (Southern Blvd.) for 1.3 miles to Hwy 32. Go west (right) for 3 miles to Elm Ave (Cty Rd. 52). Turn right and go north for 1.7 miles to Hwy 85. Turn left on Hwy 85, go 7 miles to Hwy 157. Turn right and follow Hwy 157 for 7 miles to the Park on your right.

Points of Interest -

A good first stop to exploring Albany is at the Albany Heritage Area Visitors Center (at the intersection of Broadway and Clinton). Tour four centuries of architecture, from the newly renovated Million Dollar Staircase in the State Capital to the inspiring 'Egg' at Empire State Plaza.

Exit 17
Moreau Lake State Park [14]
North of Saratoga Springs
State Rate: $15 + amenities fee

(518) 793-0511

http://nysparks.state.ny.us/parks/150/
details.aspx

Camp Accommodations

147 wooded sites, 2 ADA, dry camping, 40 feet, dump station, reservations available. Amenities include ADA restrooms/showers, potable water, grill, picnic table, hiking, fishing, biking, swimming, beach, pet friendly.

Directions

0.8 miles from I-87. From Exit 17 turn southwest on Hwy 9 and immediately turn right on to Old Saratoga Rd. for 0.8 miles in all to the Park.

Points of Interest -

Saratoga Spa State Park is home to some of Saratoga's most popular attractions. The mineral springs have been a popular destination for wealthy vacationers since the mid 1800s. The many galleries, boutiques, restaurants, and sights downtown Saratoga Springs will keep you busy.

Near Exit 39
Cumberland Bay State Park [15]
North of Plattsburgh
State Rate: $15 + amenities fee

(518) 563-5240

http://nysparks.state.ny.us/parks/34/
details.aspx

Camp Accommodations

133 sites, 4 ADA, many electric, 50 feet, dump station, reservations available. Amenities include ADA restrooms/showers, potable water, grill, picnic table, hiking, biking, fishing, swimming, beach, food pavilions, pet friendly.

Directions

1 mile from I-87. From Exit 39 turn southeast for 1 mile on Hwy 314 (Cumberland Head Rd.) to the Park.

Points of Interest -

The Park, on Lake Champlain, is popular because of its sand beach. Visit Ausable Chasm, the oldest natural attraction in the USA (est. 1870)! Walk along towering cliff walks in the midst of a primeval forest that peers into the chasm from many scenic overlooks and vistas.

Exit 3 of I-88
Chenango Valley State Park [16]
North of Binghamton
State Rate: $15 + amenities fee

(607) 648-5251

http://nysparks.state.ny.us/parks/41/
details.aspx

Camp Accommodations

146 shaded sites, 4 ADA, many electric, 50 feet, dump station, reservations available. Amenities include ADA restrooms/showers, potable water, grill, table, hiking, biking, swimming, beach, fishing, Interpretive Programs, golf course, pet friendly.

Directions

4 miles from I-88. From Exit 3 turn north on Hwy 369 for 4 miles to Cove State Park Rd. and the Park, on the left.

Points of Interest -

The Park is an ice age wonder. Its two kettle lakes were created when the last glacier retreated and left behind huge chunks of buried ice which melted to form the lakes and bog. Birdwatchers and fishermen will especially enjoy this park. Binghamton is close by for town outings.

Exit 13 of I-88
Gilbert Lake State Park [17]
North of Oneonta
State Rate: $15 + amenities fee

(607) 432-2114

http://nysparks.state.ny.us/parks/19/
details.aspx

Camp Accommodations

229 wooded sites, 3 ADA, many electric, 50 feet, dump station, reservations available. Amenities include ADA restrooms/showers, potable water, grill, table, hiking, biking, swimming, beach, fishing, disk golf, pet friendly.

Directions

11 miles from I-88. From Exit 13 turn northwest on Hwy 205 for 6.7 miles to Laurens. Turn left at Cty Rd. 11A (Waters then south on Main through town) for 0.7 miles to Cty Rd. 12 (Gilbert Lake Rd). Turn north for 3.7 miles to the Park.

Points of Interest -

The Park's lake and three ponds lie in wooded, hilly terrain in the foothills of the Catskills. Visit Cooperstown and the Corvette Americana Hall of Fame, Fenimore House and Art Museum, Farmers Museum and of course the National Baseball Hall of Fame and Museum.

Exit 59 of I-90
Lake Erie State Park [18]
West of Dunkirk
State Rate: $15 + amenities fee

(716) 792-9214

http://nysparks.state.ny.us/parks/129/
details.aspx

Camp Accommodations

99 shaded sites, many electric, 50 feet, 2 ADA, dump station, reservations available. Amenities include restrooms/showers, potable water, grill, picnic table, hiking, biking, fishing, pet friendly.

Directions

10 miles from I-90. From Exit 59 turn north toward Dunkirk for 2 miles on Hwy 60. Turn east (left) on Hwy 5 for 7.8 miles to the Park.

Points of Interest -

The high bluffs overlooking Lake Erie provide breathtaking views. Enjoy a shoreline, which covers over three quarters of a mile. Visit Dunkirk, check out the 'Wreck & Roll Festival Series' and the 'Music on the Pier Concert Series,' or take in the Chautauqua Lake Erie Art Trail art sale and display.

Exit 48A of I-90
Darien Lakes State Park [19]
East of Buffalo
State Rate: $15 + amenities fee

(585) 547-9242

http://nysparks.state.ny.us/parks/144/
details.aspx

Camp Accommodations

129 shaded and roomy sites, 9 ADA, electricity, 40 feet, dump station, reservations available. Amenities include ADA restrooms/showers, potable water, grill, table, hiking, biking, swimming, beach, fishing, pet friendly.

Directions

10 miles from I-90. From Exit 48A turn south on Hwy 77 (Allegany Road) for 7.7 miles to Hwy 20. Turn west on Hwy 20 for 2.3 miles to Harlow and the Park entrance.

Points of Interest -

In Buffalo, see one of the world's great collections of modern art. Tour Frank Lloyd Wright's grandest Prairie Style house. Stroll one of America's great neighborhoods. Explore a South American rainforest or discover the birthplace of the American Arts and Crafts Movement.

Exit 41 of I-90
Cayuga Lake State Park [20]
On the Shores of Cayuga Lake
State Rate: $15 + amenities fee

(315) 568-5163

http://nysparks.state.ny.us/parks/123/
details.aspx

Camp Accommodations

267 shaded sites, 4 ADA, many electric, 40 feet, dump station, reservations available. Amenities include ADA restrooms/showers, potable water, grill, picnic table, fishing, biking, swimming, beach, pet friendly.

Directions

8 miles from I-90. From Exit 41 turn south on Hwy 414 then immediately turn left on Hwy 318 and go 4.4 miles in all to the intersection with Hwys 20 and 89. Take Hwy 89 southeast for 3.9 miles to the Park.

Points of Interest -

Explore Seneca Falls, the gateway to the Finger Lakes and widely believed to be the inspiration for Frank Capra's holiday classic, "It's A Wonderful Life." Visit the National Women's Hall of Fame, or Museum of Waterways and Industry. Try one of the many 'Wine Trails.'

Exit 4 of I-390
Stony Brook State Park [21]
South of Dansville
State Rate: $15 + amenities fee

(585) 335-8111

http://nysparks.state.ny.us/parks/118/
details.aspx

Camp Accommodations

119 shaded sites, 3 ADA, dry camping, 30 feet, dump station, reservations available. Amenities include ADA restrooms/showers, potable water, grill, picnic table, hiking, biking, swimming, beach, pet friendly.

Directions

2 miles from I-390. From Exit 4 turn south on Hwy 36 for 2 miles to the Park.

Points of Interest -

The Park's terrain comprises hilly woodlands; a deep gorge with rugged cliffs overlooking three waterfalls; and fascinating rock formations. Campsites are scattered in the woodlands above the gorge. Visit Letchworth - 'The Grand Canyon of the East.'

NORTH CAROLINA

North Carolina is blessed with beautiful beaches, majestic mountains and countless rivers and streams. The North Carolina Division of Parks and Recreation oversees the State Park System. Their website is located at -

http://www.ncparks.gov/Visit/main.php

Reservations can be made up to 11 months in advance at -

http://www.nc.reserveworld.com/default.aspx

Another easy way to make reserva-

tions is by calling toll-free 877-7-CAMPNC (877-722-6762). There is a $3 surcharge per reservation/per night's stay to support the reservations system.

Only three parks (Falls Lake, Jordan Lake and Kerr Lake) have entrance gate fees. Anyone who is 62 years of age or older is eligible for a senior discount on entrance fees and camping. This discount may change, contact the park office for further information. Pets are permitted so long as they are on a leash no longer than 6 feet and under the constant control of the owner.

[1] **Lake Powhatan Recreation Area**
N35 29.126 W82 37.781
[2] **Curtis Creek**
N35 41.420 W82 11.792
[3] **Hagan-Stone County Park**
N35 56.931 W79 44.179
[4] **Rolling View-Falls Lake State Park**
N36 00.271 W78 43.633
[5] **Cliffs of the Neuse State Park**
N35 14.038 W77 53.942
[6] **Carolina Beach State Park**
N34 02.718 W77 54.246
[7] **Morrow Mountain State Park**
N35 22.255 W80 06.276

[8] **Pilot Mountain State Park**
N36 20.623 W80 27.958
[9] **McDowell Nature Center & Preserve**
N35 06.038 W81 01.350
[10] **Stone Mountain State Park**
N36 22.626 W81 01.128
[11] **Dan Nicholas Park**
N35 37.926 W80 21.256
[12] **Bullocksville Campground Kerr Lake State Recreation Area**
N36 27.526 W78 21.885
[13] **Jones Lake State Park**
N34 41.911 W78 36.248

NOTES:

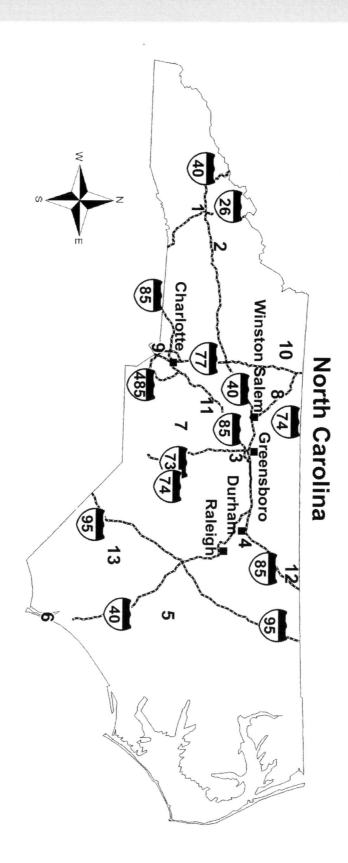

Exit 33 of I-26
Lake Powhatan Recreation Area [1]
South of Asheville
Pisgah NF Rate: $20-$29
America/Beautiful Rate: $10-$19

(828) 670-5627

http://www.recreation.gov

Camp Accommodations

54 wooded sites, some paved, electric, some full hook ups, 45+ feet, dump station, 7 pull throughs, reservations available. Amenities include ADA restroom/showers, grill, table, potable water, hiking, biking, swimming, Interpretive Programs, pet friendly.

Directions

5 miles from I-26. From Exit 33 go south west for 2 miles on Hwy 191 (Bevard Rd.) to Bent Creek Ranch Rd. Turn right for 0.3 miles, then left on Wesley Branch Rd. for 2.4 miles to the camp.

Points of Interest -

Asheville has many festivals and events. Lovers of art, crafts, and live music will enjoy the city. The Park is near the North Carolina Arboretum, Biltmore Estate and the Blue Ridge Parkway Folk Art Center and Destination Center, hot springs, and mountain lookouts.

Exit 73 of I-40
Curtis Creek [2]
North of Old Fort
Pisgah NF Rate: $5
America/Beautiful Rate: $3

(828) 652-2144

http://www.forestcamping.com/dow/southern/pisgcmp.htm#curtis%20creek

Camp Accommodations

8 paved or grassy sites, dry camping, 40 feet. Amenities include ADA restroom, grill, table, potable water, biking, fishing, pet friendly. No Utilities.

Directions

7 miles from I-40. From Exit 73 go north on Catawba for 0.4 miles to Hwy. 70. Turn east (right) for 2 miles to State Rt. 1227 (Curtis Creek Rd). Turn left and go 4.7 miles to campground.

Points of Interest -

Visit Little Switzerland, named because of its deep valleys and distant ranges resembling the foothills of the Swiss Alps. Explore Emerald Village or the many apple orchards, museums, and historic mines you will find in this part of the High Country!

Exit 38 of I-40/I-85
Hagan-Stone County Park [3]
South of Greensboro
County Rate: $18

(336) 674-0472

http://www.greensboro-nc.gov/Departments/Parks/facilities/reservations/hagan.htm

Camp Accommodations

70 wooded or grassy sites, water/electric, 45 feet, dump station, seniors discount, reservations available. Amenities include restroom/shower, grill, table, biking, hiking, swimming pool, fishing, pet friendly.

Directions

9 miles from I-40/I-85. From Exit 38 go south on Hwy 421 for 6.7 miles to Hagan-Stone Park Rd. Turn south for 2.3 miles to the Park.

Points of Interest -

With much to offer in Greensboro it is hard to choose. Examples include Castle McCulloch (Crystal Gardens and Gem Panning), Blandwood Mansion, and Carolina Model Railroaders. Or visit some of the many art galleries, museums, performing arts, venues and theater.

Exit 283
Rolling View-Falls Lake State Park [4]
North of Raleigh
State Rate: $23

(919) 676-1027

http://www.ncparks.gov/Visit/parks/
fala/main.php

Camp Accommodations

117 shaded sites, water/electric, 45 feet, dump station, seniors discount, reservations available. Amenities include restroom/shower, grill, table, biking, hiking, swimming, fishing, pet friendly.

Directions

24 miles from I-40. From Exit 283 go east on I-540 for 9 miles to exit 9 (Hwy 50, Creedmoor Rd). Turn north for 5 miles to Hwy 98 (Durham Rd). Turn west for 5.6 miles to Baptist Rd. Turn northeast for 4 miles to the Park.

Points of Interest -

With so much to offer in the Raleigh-Durham area, a good way to start planning a local tour to the region would be the following two websites:

- http://www.visitraleigh.com/

- http://www.durham-nc.com/

Exit 355
Cliffs of the Neuse State Park [5]
South of Goldsboro
State Rate: $18

(919) 778-6234

http://www.ncparks.gov/Visit/parks/
clne/main.php

Camp Accommodations

35 shaded sites, dry camping, 45 feet, dump station, seniors discount, reservations available. Amenities include restroom/shower, potable water, grill, table, biking, hiking, boating, swimming, fishing, Museum, Interpretive Programs, pet friendly.

Directions

23 miles from I-40. From Exit 355 go northeast on Hwy 1783 (joined by Hwy 117) for 10 miles to Hwy 55. Turn right, go 10.7 miles to Hwy 111. Turn left, go 2.4 miles, turn right on Cliff Park Rd. to the Park.

Points of Interest -

Turn of the century visitors to the area drank mineral water from local springs to cure their ills and take riverboat excursions to the cliffs. Visit the CCS Neuse, one of 22 ironclads commissioned by the Confederate navy. Other glimpses of the Civil War can be found in Kinston.

Exit 420
Carolina Beach State Park [6]
South side of Wilmington
State Rate: $10-$15

(910) 458-8206

http://www.ncparks.gov/Visit/parks/
cabe/main.php

Camp Accommodations

83 wooded sites, some pull through, dry camping, 35 feet, dump station, seniors discount, reservations available. Amenities include restroom/shower, potable water, grill, table, fishing, biking, hiking, Visitors Center, pet friendly.

Directions

16 miles from I-40. Beyond Exit 420 proceed on Hwy 117 for 5 miles. Go straight for 10.4 miles on Hwy 132 (which is joined by Hwy 421). After Snow's Cut Bridge turn right on to Spencer Farlow Dr. then left on Old Dow Rd., 0.7 miles to the Park.

Points of Interest -

Steeped in history & natural diversity, the Park includes a Visitor's Center with exhibits of its environment. Tour the Wilmington historic district, with historic houses, plantations and the Airlie Gardens. There are also many museums including the WWII battleship North Carolina.

Exit Hwy 24/27 Briscoe of I-73/74
Morrow Mountain State Park [7]
East of Albemarie
State Rate: $18

(704) 982-4402

http://www.ncparks.gov/Visit/parks/momo/main.php

Camp Accommodations

106 shaded sites, 6 ADA, dry camping, 45 feet, dump station, seniors discount, reservations available. Amenities include ADA restroom/shower, grill, table, biking, hiking, swimming, potable water, fishing, pet friendly. No Utilities.

Directions

27 miles from I-73/74. From Hwy 24/27 Briscoe Exit go west on Hwy 24 for 23 miles. Turn north (right) on Valley Drive for 3.3 miles to Morrow Mountain Rd. Turn right to the Park.

Points of Interest -

Your are in the Albemarie Region, which is rich in Civil War and military history, unique shops, wineries and vineyards. Go to this website to discover your options -

http://www.albemarle-nc.com/attractions/

Exit South of Pilot Mountain off I-74
Pilot Mountain State Park [8]
South of Pilot Mountain
State Rate: $15

(336) 325-2355

http://www.ncparks.gov/Visit/parks/pimo/main.php

Camp Accommodations

49 shaded sites, dry camping, 35 feet, seniors discount, reservations available. Amenities include restroom/shower, grill, table, biking, hiking, potable water, fishing, pet friendly. No Utilities.

Directions

Along I-74. Exit south of Pilot Mountain on to Pilot Mountain Park Rd. Turn west into the Park.

Points of Interest -

From any direction you see Pilot Mountain rising over 1,400 feet above the countryside of the upper Piedmont plateau. Visit Horne Creek Farm, a historical farm near Pinnacle. The farm is a North Carolina State Historic Site depicting farm life in the northwest Piedmont area, circa 1900.

Exit 1 of I-77
McDowell Nature Center & Preserve [9]
Southwest of Charlotte
County Rate: $21-$26

(704) 588-5224

http://charmeck.org/Departments/Park+and+Rec/Inside+The+Department/Divisions/Stewardship+Services/Nature+Preserves/McDowell.htm

Camp Accommodations

15 shaded, paved RV sites, 2 ADA, some pull through, water/electric, 40 feet, dump station, reservations available. Amenities include restroom/shower, grill, table, biking, hiking, fishing, pet friendly.

Directions

8 miles from I-77. From Exit 1 of I-77 go northwest on I-485 for 1 mile to exit 1 of I-485. Go southwest on Hwy 49 (S Tryon St., then York Rd) for 7 miles to McDowell Park Dr. Turn north in to the Park.

Points of Interest -

In Charlotte walk along the bustling streets of Center City. Step aboard the Historic Charlotte Trolley in South End, or stroll along the tree-lined streets of Dilworth to experience the warmth and Southern hospitality of the Queen City.

Exits 83 or 85 of I-77
Stone Mountain State Park [10]
Southwest of Mt. Airy
State Rate: $23

(336) 957-8185

http://www.ncparks.gov/Visit/parks/
stmo/main.php

Camp Accommodations

90 shaded, paved sites, electric/
water, 45 feet, dump station, seniors
discount, reservations available.
Amenities include restroom/shower,
grill, table, laundry tubs, biking, hiking, swimming, fishing, pet friendly.

Directions

18 mi. from I-77. Northbound, Exit 83 on to
Hwy 21. Southbound, Exit 85, turn west on
CC Camp Rd for 1 mi. to Hwy 21 & turn
right. All follow Hwy 21 for 10 mi. to
Traphill Rd. Turn west 4.3 mi. to John P.
Frank Pkwy. Turn right 2.5 mi. to the Park.

Points of Interest -

Visit Mount Airy, where actor Andy Griffith
grew up. A stroll down Main Street in the
"Friendly City" will remind you of Mayberry
on the popular '60s hit TV series. Show
fans can visit Floyd's City Barber Shop,
the Old Mayberry Jail, Snappy Lunch,
even Andy's childhood home.

Exit 76 of I-85
Dan Nicholas Park [11]
South of Salisbury
County Rate: $19-$24

(866) 767-2757

http://www.dannicholas.net/

Camp Accommodations

70 shaded, spacious sites, some lakefront, some pull through, water/
electric, 40 feet, dump station, reservations available. Amenities include
restroom/shower, grill, table, store,
biking, hiking, fishing, pet friendly.

Directions

8 miles from I-85. From Exit 76 go south
0.4 miles on Hwy 52 to Newsome Rd.
Turn left, go 1.0 mile to Bringle Ferry Rd.
Turn right for 6 miles to the Park on your
left.

Points of Interest -

The Park is an adventure in itself.
"Haden's Carousel" was given to Dan
Nicholas Park in memory of Haden
Holmes Hurley. Ride the narrow gauge
train at Hurley Train Station. The New
Aquarium, in a simulated habitat, includes
a Nature Center.

Exit 178 of I-85
Rolling View-Falls Lake State Park [4]
North of Raleigh
State Rate: $23

(919) 676-1027

http://www.ncparks.gov/Visit/parks/
fala/main.php

Camp Accommodations

117 shaded sites, water/electric, 45
feet, dump station, seniors discount,
reservations available. Amenities include restroom/shower, grill, table,
biking, hiking, swimming, fishing, pet
friendly.

Directions

10 miles from I-85. From Exit 178 go south
on Hwy 70 for 1.4 miles to the Holloway
exit. Turn east, go 4.8 miles (road become
the Wake Forest Hwy) to Baptist Rd. Turn
northeast for 4 miles to the Park.

Points of Interest -

With so much to offer in the Raleigh-
Durham area, a good way to start planning
a local tour to the region would be the following two websites:

- http://www.visitraleigh.com/
- http://www.durham-nc.com/

Exit 223 of I-85
Bullocksville Campground, Kerr Lake
State Recreation Area [12]
North of Henderson
State Rate: $12-$18

(252) 438-7791

http://www.ncparks.gov/Visit/parks/
kela/main.php

Camp Accommodations

60 shaded sites, many electric/water, 45 feet, dump station, seniors discount, reservations available. Amenities include restroom/shower, grill, table, biking, hiking, swimming, potable water, fishing, pet friendly.

Directions

6 miles from I-85. From Exit 223 go 2 miles northwest on Manson Rd to Drewry Crossroads. Go straight through the crossroads onto Bullocksville Park Rd. Proceed 3.6 miles west to the camp.

Points of Interest -

Kerr Lake is big. With over 850 miles of shoreline, it is one of the largest lakes in the Southeast. It's also one of the most beautiful, from wooded shores to secluded coves to tranquil picnic areas. Classic cars are a reoccurring theme for the region, with many events to choose from.

Exit 20 of I-95
Jones Lake State Park [13]
Southeast of Fayetteville
State Rate: $13-$18

(910) 588-4550

http://www.ncparks.gov/Visit/parks/
jone/main.php

Camp Accommodations

20 shaded RV sites, dry camping, 45 feet, seniors discount, reservations available. Amenities include restroom/shower, grill, table, biking, hiking, swimming, potable water, Visitors Center, fishing, pet friendly. No Utilities.

Directions

30 miles from I-95. From Exit 20 go southeast on Hwy 211 for 1.3 miles to Hwy 41. Turn east (left), go 23 miles on Hwy 41. Just north of Elizabethtown, turn north on Hwy 242. Proceed 5.4 miles to the park entrance.

Points of Interest -

Fayetteville knows what it means to be ready at a moment's notice and golf is no exception. With 20 courses by the likes of Davis Love III, Willard Byrd and Stuart Gooden, 360 holes and 19 miles of beautiful fairways, enjoy the fastest tee times, and best deals.

NORTH DAKOTA

The North Dakota Parks and Recreation Department manages 15 state parks. The website for information is -

http://www.parkrec.nd.gov/parks/index.html

Pets are welcome, provided they are restrained either by a 6 ft. leash or portable enclosure. Animals are not allowed on any designated swimming areas, playgrounds, in buildings, or other posted areas in a state park, except for animals used to assist the disabled. You are advised to leave out-of-state firewood at home. Firewood may be purchased through the park.

All motor vehicles entering a state park are required by statute to display a valid daily vehicle entrance permit or annual vehicle permit year-round. The daily fee is $5 per vehicle. A motorhome is considered a camping unit. Therefore, you need to purchase just one entrance permit, which goes on your vehicle. This applies only for motorhomes towing a second vehicle.

About half of all state park campsites are on the reservation system. There is a $3 online reservation fee, $6 Call Center fee. The remaining sites are first come, first serve. You are advised to make a reservation on holiday weekends and at selected parks on special event weekends.

Campsite reservations may be made online. Campsite reservations have a 90-day advance window. The reservation website is -

https://secure.apps.state.nd.us/pnr/sp/services/public/main.htm

Campsite reservations may also be made by phoning (800) 807-4723.

The camping fees structure is:

Electrical site -	$20
Electrical site with sewer hookup	
(Ft. Stevenson only) -	$25
Site without electricity -	$12
Little Missouri electricity -	$12
Cross Ranch electrical site -	$15
Little Missouri/Sully Creek-	
site without electricity -	$10

100% of North Dakota State Parks' visitor fees are used to maintain and operate the park system.

---

[1] Lindenwood Campground
N46 51.260 W96 47.257

[2] Turtle River State Park
N47 55.968 W97 29.006

[3] Icelandic State Park
N48 46.364 W97 44.373

[4] Cottonwood Campground
N46 56.904 W103 31.682

[5] Fort Lincoln State Park
N46 44.870 W100 50.360

[6] Eggerts Landing Campground
N47 05.736 W98 00.514

NOTES:

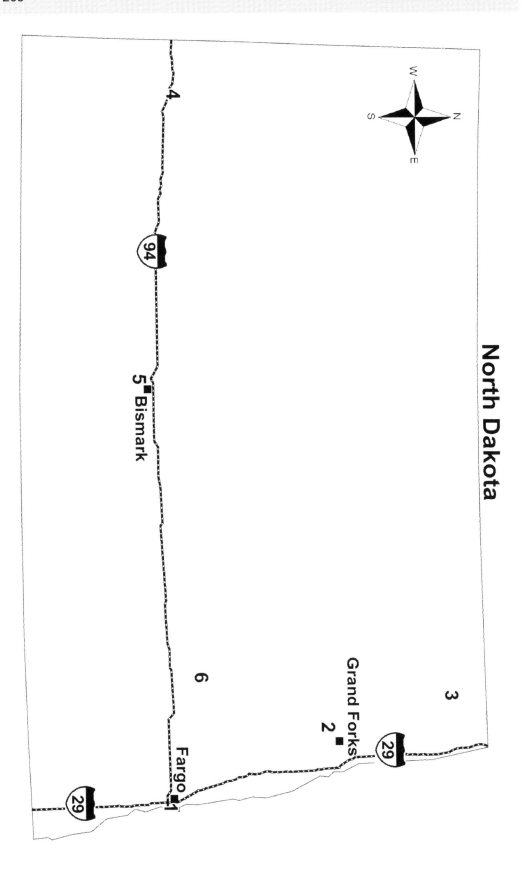

Exit 63 of I-29 or Exit 351 of I-94
Lindenwood Campground [1]
South side of Fargo
County Rate: $26

(701) 232-3987

http://www.fargoparks.com/
facility_camp.html

Camp Accommodations

46 shaded, paved, riverfront sites, electric/water, 40 feet, dump station, reservations available. Amenities include restrooms/showers, grill, picnic table, biking, Information Center, firewood, pet friendly. Near the Red River, call about flood conditions.

Directions

3 miles from I-29. From Exit 63 of I-29 go east for 2 miles on I-94 to Exit 351. Go north on University Dr. for 0.4 miles to 17th Ave. S. Turn east for 0.5 miles to the Park.

Points of Interest -

There are a number of 'should see' destinations in Fargo - The Fargo Air Museum, the Celebrity Walk Of Fame with more than 100 signatures, the 1926 restored Fargo Theatre vintage movie palace, Bonanzaville with 15 acres of historic buildings, and the Plains Art Museum.

Exit 141
Turtle River State Park [2]
West of Grand Forks
State Rate: $12-$20

(701) 594-4445

http://www.parkrec.nd.gov/parks/
trsp.htm

Camp Accommodations

125 shaded sites, electric/water, 45 feet, many pull through, dump station, reservations available. Amenities include restrooms/showers, grill, picnic table, biking, fishing, pet friendly.

Directions

18 miles from I-29. From Exit 141 go west for 18 miles on Hwy 2. The Park entrance is just after Cty. Rd. 2 (30th St. NE).

Points of Interest -

In Grand Forks visit Heritage Village, with it's steam engine threshing machines, museum displays, and demonstrations. Go downtown East Grand Forks to the Cabela's store. Enjoy the North Dakota Museum of Art, "a cultural jewel on the prairie."

Exit 203
Icelandic State Park [3]
West of Joliette
State Rate: $12-$20

(701) 265-4561

http://www.parkrec.nd.gov/parks/
isp.htm

Camp Accommodations

159 shaded sites, electric/water, 45 feet, all pull through, dump station, reservations available. Amenities include restrooms/showers, grill, picnic table, Visitors Center, biking, fishing, pet friendly.

Directions

24 miles from I-29. From Exit 203 go west for 24 miles on Hwy 5. The Park entrance is a mile after Cty. Rd 12.

Points of Interest -

Nearby attractions include Pembina County Museum, the Pioneer Machinery Site, Pembina State Museum, Gingras State Historic Site, Kittson Trading Post State Historic Site, Jay Wessel Wildlife Management Area, Frost Fire Mountain, and Pembina Gorge.

Exit 24
Cottonwood Campground [4]
Theodore Roosevelt National Park
NP Rate: $10
America/Beautiful Rate: $5

(701) 623-4730 ext. 3417

http://www.nps.gov/thro/planyourvisit/camping.htm

Camp Accommodations

76 shaded sites, dry camping, 45 feet, many pull through. Amenities include restrooms, potable water, grill, picnic table, biking, fishing, pet friendly. No Utilities.

Directions

7 miles from I-94. From Exit 24 go 1.5 miles south on Pacific Ave. to East River Rd. Turn north, follow East River Rd. for 5.6 miles to the Campground.

Points of Interest -

Buffalo are know to wander through the campground. A major feature of the South Unit is the paved, 36 mile Scenic Loop Drive with pullouts and interpretive signs. The Painted Canyon Visitors Center provides unparalleled panoramic views of the North Dakota badlands.

Exit 152
Fort Lincoln State Park [5]
South of Mandan
State Rate: $12-$20

(701) 667-6340

http://www.parkrec.nd.gov/parks/flsp.htm

Camp Accommodations

95 shaded sites, 1 ADA, electric/water, 45 feet, many pull through, dump station, reservations available. Amenities include restrooms/showers, grill, picnic table, biking, hiking, fishing, pet friendly.

Directions

9 miles from I-94. From Exit 152 go south for 1.3 miles on Hwy 6 to Main St. Turn east (left), go 0.9 miles to Hwy 1806, turn south and go 3 miles to Pleasant Valley Rd. Bare right for 4 miles to the Park entrance on the left.

Points of Interest -

Rich in military & Native American history, the Fort was an important infantry & cavalry post. From here George Armstrong Custer and the Seventh Cavalry rode out on their ill-fated expedition against the Sioux at the Little Big Horn. Portions of the military post have been reconstructed.

Exit 292
Eggerts Landing Campground [6]
North of Valley City
COE Rate: $18
America/Beautiful Rate: $9

(701) 845-2970

http://www.recreation.gov/

Camp Accommodations

41 large wooded sites, some lakefront, electric, 45 feet, dump station, reservations available. Amenities include restrooms/showers, potable water, grill, picnic table, biking, fishing, swimming/beach, pet friendly.

Directions

14 miles from I-94. From Exit 292 follow the Cty Rd. 21 signs through Valley City 0.8 miles north on 8th Ave., then east for 0.5 miles on Main to 5th Ave., then turn north, still on Cty 21 for 12.3 miles to 22nd St. Turn west for 0.5 miles to the camp.

Points of Interest -

Stop at the Valley City Visitor Center, which houses "Rosebud," an 1881 Northern Pacific Superintendent's Railcar. The 100 year old Hi Line Bridge is a great photo op. The Sheyenne Valley has abundant shops - for antiques, local artist wares, quilting supplies and unique dining.

OHIO

The Division of Parks, a unit of the Ohio Department of Natural Resources, is responsible for the System of 74 State Parks. Spread across the Parks are nine resort lodges, three dining lodges, six golf courses, more than 9,000 campsites in 57 family campgrounds, 36 visitor/nature centers, 80 swimming beaches and 19 swimming pools, 188 boat ramps and 7,583 boat docks, and 1,167 miles of trails. Most Ohio State Park campgrounds are open year-round. You can find information at -

http://www.dnr.state.oh.us/parks/resources/aboutus/tabid/90/Default.aspx

Campsites with accessible features that may include extra wide paved pads on level grades, berms, modified picnic tables, fire rings and/or grills, or water fountains, and may be close to restroom buildings with entrance ramps, accessible fixtures, grab bars and wide stalls are offered at : Barkcamp, Cowan Lake, Deer Creek, Delaware, Mosquito Lake, Paint Creek, Pymatuning, Salt Fork, and West Branch. All state park campgrounds allow pets, and many have designated areas for pets. Pets must be on a leash not exceeding 6 feet in length and must be under control at all times. Proof of rabies shots and a physical description of the animals is required upon request. You should not bring your own firewood.

Ohio remains one of the few states in the country that does not charge a general admission or parking fee at its 74 state parks. Camping reservations are encouraged, but not required. You can make your reservation up to 6 months in advance of arrival. Most campgrounds offer dump stations free of charge to registered campers. Ice and firewood are available at most campgrounds. You can make reservations (there is a $8.25 fee) at -

http://www.ohio.reserveworld.com/SearchAmenity.aspx?reg=0
You can also contact the Call Center at (866) 644-6727.

Ohio has six national parks. Cuyahoga Valley National offers camping and a variety of outdoor recreational activities. Perry's Victory and International Peace Memorial is located at Put-in-Bay on South Bass Island. The James A. Garfield National Historic Site is in Mentor. The Hopewell Culture National Historic Park is located near Chillicothe. The Dayton Aviation Heritage National Historic Park includes three landmarks around town. The William Howard Taft National Historic Site is located in Cincinnati.

[1] **Hueston Woods State Park**
N39 35.678 W84 45.896
[2] **Buck Creek State Park**
N39 56.759 W83 43.768
[3] **Dillon State Park**
N40 01.744 W82 06.181
[4] **Barkcamp State Park**
N40 02.810 W81 01.867
[5] **Caesar Creek State Park**
N39 32.318 W83 58.440
[6] **Deer Creek State Park**
N39 39.137 W83 14.733
[7] **Alum Creek State Park**
N40 14.217 W82 59.235
[8] **Mt. Gilead State Park**
N40 32.746 W82 48.533
[9] **Mohican State Park**
N40 36.578 W82 15.446
[10] **Findley State Park**
N41 08.028 W82 13.144
[11] **Lake Loramie State Park**
N40 21.455 W84 21.437
[12] **Indian Lake State Park**
N40 31.119 W83 54.027
[13] **Maumee Bay State Park**
N41 40.482 W83 22.260
[14] **Mill Creek Campground**
N41 00.623 W80 59.174
[15] **Wolf Run State Park**
N39 47.387 W81 32.411
[16] **Salt Fork State Park**
N40 04.930 W81 27.583
[17] **Harrison Lake State Park**
N41 38.232 W84 21.737
[18] **East Harbor State Park**
N41 32.495 W82 49.218
[19] **Geneva State Park**
N41 50.748 W80 57.565
[20] **Miami Whitewater Forest Camp**
N39 15.252 W84 45.734
[21] **Stonelick State Park**
N39 12.811 W84 04.926

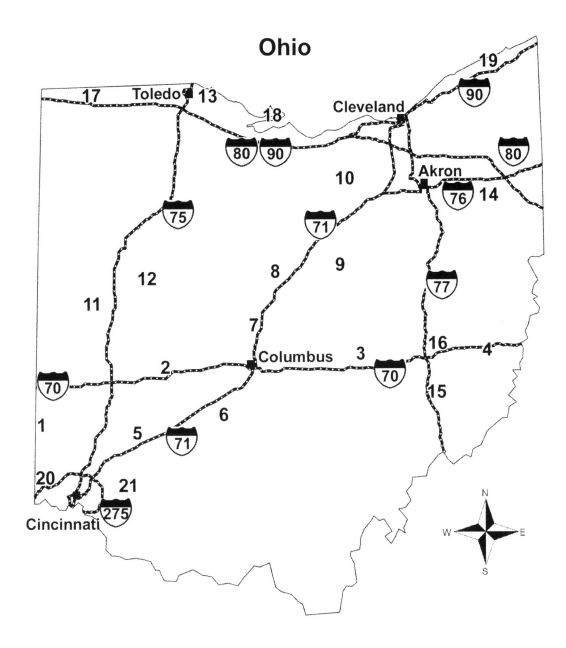

Exit 10
Hueston Woods State Park [1]
South of Eaton
State Rate: $21-$25

(513) 523-1060

http://www.dnr.state.oh.us/parks/
parks/huestonw/tabid/745/
Default.aspx

Camp Accommodations

488 shaded, paved sites, 252 electric, 45 feet, many pull through, dump station, reservations available. Amenities include restrooms/showers, grill, table, potable water, laundry, Wi-Fi, biking, fishing, swimming, pet friendly.

Directions

24 mi. from I-70. From Exit 10 go south for 14.7 miles (through Eaton) to Camden. In Camden turn west on W Central (Hwy 725), go 6 mi. to Hwy 177. Turn south for 1.8 miles, then west on Camden-College Corner Rd. for 1.5 miles to the Park.

Points of Interest -

Enjoy a meal at the Lodge, situated on a bluff overlooking Acton Lake. At the Nature Center, attend bird and flower walks, slide talks, and fossil hunts. Birders can enjoy watching for some of the park's 150 species. Lake access for dogs offers a place for your pets to frolic and swim.

Exit 62
Buck Creek State Park [2]
Northeast side of Springfield
State Rate: $23-$27

(937) 322-5284

http://www.dnr.state.oh.us/parks/
parks/buckck/tabid/716/Default.aspx

Camp Accommodations

111 paved sites, 22 electric, 35 feet, dump station, reservations available. Amenities include restrooms/showers, grill, table, potable water, biking, fishing, swimming, pet friendly.

Directions

4 miles from I-70. From Exit 62 go west for 2.4 miles on Hwy 40 (National Rd.) to N. Bird Rd. Turn north (right), go 1.7 miles to the Park entrance.

Points of Interest -

Springfield offers amenities such as awesome antiquing, the Clark State Performing Arts Center, the Springfield Museum of Art and Frank Lloyd Wright's Westcott House. The city's architectural heritage is on full display around every corner.

Exit 153 (State St.)
Dillon State Park [3]
Northeast of Zanesville
State Rate: $21-$25

(740) 452-1083

http://www.dnr.state.oh.us/parks/
parks/dillon/tabid/730/Default.aspx

Camp Accommodations

195 paved, mostly shaded sites, 183 electric, 45 feet, dump station, reservations available. Amenities include restrooms/showers, laundry, camp store, grill, table, potable water, biking, fishing, swimming, pet friendly.

Directions

8 mi. from I-70. From Exit 153: **westbound**, at State St. turn right 0.3 mi. to Hwy 146, then turn left; **eastbound**, from the off ramp immediately turn right on Jackson St, go 2 blocks and turn right on Old Newark Rd., go 0.5 mi. to Hwy 146, turn left. All travelers, go 7.3 mi. on Hwy 146 to Clay Littick Dr, turn left into the Park.

Points of Interest -

The artist colony in Zanesville is an exceptional collection of talent. With a long history of ceramic and other art forms, downtown Zanesville is becoming one of the premiere artist communities in Ohio. Visit Dresden, birthplace of the Longaberger Basket.

Exit 208 of I-70
Barkcamp State Park [4]
Southeast of Morristown
State Rate: $18-$22

(740) 484-4064

http://www.dnr.state.oh.us/parks/
parks/barkcamp/tabid/713/
Default.aspx

Camp Accommodations

123 shaded, paved sites, 2 ADA, electric, 35 feet, dump station, reservations available. Amenities include restrooms/showers, grill, picnic table, potable water, antique barn store, biking, fishing, swimming, pet friendly.

Directions

1.6 mi. from I-70. From Exit 208 go south for 0.7 miles on Hwy 149. Turn east on Hwy 92 (Barkcamp Park Rd) for 0.9 miles to the Park.

Points of Interest -

The Belmont County Museum, an impressive Romanesque-style mansion, built in 1888 with 26 rooms, houses a quilt collection, antique farm implements and interesting relics of the "Gay 90's" period. The nearby Quaker Friends Meeting House, a large restored building was built in 1914.

Exit 45 of I-71
Caesar Creek State Park [5]
Northeast of Lebanon
State Rate: $24-$28

(513) 897-3055

http://www.dnr.state.oh.us/parks/
parks/caesarck/tabid/720/Default.aspx

Camp Accommodations

283 sizable, paved sites, electric, 40 feet, dump station, reservations available. Amenities include restrooms/showers, grill, picnic table, potable water, Nature Center, biking, fishing, swimming, pet friendly.

Directions

4.7 mi. from I-71. From Exit 45 go a short distance east and just past Denny Rd. turn left on Hwy 380. Go 3 miles to Center Rd. Turn left, go 1.6 miles to the Park.

Points of Interest -

Explore the Caesar Creek Gorge nature preserve, featuring a 180 foot deep gorge displaying unique geologic formations. The Little Miami Scenic River offers canoeing and spectacular scenery. USA Today called Lebanon one of the "Ten Great Places to Browse for Antiques."

Exit 84 of I-71
Deer Creek State Park [6]
Southwest of Columbus
State Rate: $24-$28

(740) 869-3124

http://www.dnr.state.oh.us/parks/
parks/deercrk/tabid/725/Default.aspx

Camp Accommodations

227 paved sites, many shaded, electric, 45 feet, dump station, reservations available. Amenities include restrooms/showers, grill, picnic table, potable water, store, Nature Center, biking, fishing, swimming, pet friendly.

Directions

9 miles from I-71. From Exit 84 go 3.3 miles south on Hwy 56 into Mt. Sterling. Turn right on Hwy 207 (Columbus St.) and go 0.3 miles, then bare left on Hwy 207 for 3.9 miles to Crooks-Yankeetown Rd. Turn left, go 1.4 miles to the Park entrance.

Points of Interest -

The Park is central Ohio's vacation showplace. A collage of meadows and woodlands surround a scenic reservoir. This resort state park features a modern lodge, cottages, campground, golf course, swimming beach and boating for outdoor enthusiasts.

Exit 131
Alum Creek State Park [7]
North of Columbus
State Rate: $25-$29

(740) 548-4631

http://www.dnr.state.oh.us/parks/
parks/alum/tabid/711/Default.aspx

Camp Accommodations

286 shaded or sunny, paved, well spaced sites, some lake view, electric, 45 feet, dump station, reservations available. Amenities include restrooms/showers, grill, table, potable water, Wi-Fi, biking, fishing, hiking, swimming, pet friendly.

Directions

6 miles from I-71. From Exit 131 go 3 miles west on Hwy 36/37 to Lacky Old State Rd. 10. Turn south for 3 miles to the Park Welcome Center on the left.

Points of Interest -

Tour the Olentangy Indian Caverns, learn the techniques of historical gem mining. Visit the Delaware County Fairgrounds, renowned for the Little Brown Jug harness race. Shop Easton Town Center, wander the Short North Arts District, buy your fresh food items at North Market.

Exit 151
Mt. Gilead State Park [8]
East side of Mt. Gilead
State Rate: $18-$22

(740) 548-4631

http://www.dnr.state.oh.us/parks/
parks/mtgilead/tabid/772/Default.aspx

Camp Accommodations

59 paved sites, electric, 45 feet, dump station, reservations available. Amenities include restrooms/showers, grill, table, potable water, biking, fishing, Nature Programs, camp store, pet friendly.

Directions

6 miles from I-71. From Exit 151 go west for 6 miles on Hwy 95 to the Park entrance on the right, which you will find just before entering Mt. Gilead.

Points of Interest -

Places to visit include the Fostoria Glass Museum Seneca Caverns, Sorrowful Mother Shrine, the home of William G. Harding, and the Tiffin Glass Museum. You will also find many antiquing opportunities, fairs, festivals, farm days, and lots of home cooking!

Exit 165
Mohican State Park [9]
Southeast of Mansfield
State Rate: $29

(419) 994-5125

http://www.dnr.state.oh.us/parks/
parks/mohican/tabid/769/Default.aspx

Camp Accommodations

186 wooded, paved sites, many full hook ups, many pull through, 45 feet, dump station, reservations available. Amenities include restrooms/showers, grill, table, potable water, biking, fishing, pool, Nature Programs, camp store, pet friendly.

Directions

19 miles from I-71. From Exit 165 go east for 18.6 miles on Hwy 97, passing through Bellville and Butler. Turn left at Hwy 3, go 0.3 miles to the Park entrance on your left.

Points of Interest -

Enjoy a meal at the Park lodge. The Pine Run Grist Mill, in the Park, features an overshot waterwheel that powers two millstones where grain was ground into flour. Visit Malabar Farm State Park, home of noted conservationist Louis Bromfield. Take a wagon tour of the farm.

Exit 186 of I-71
Findley State Park [10]
Southwest of Cleveland
State Rate: $25-$27

(440) 647-5749

http://www.dnr.state.oh.us/parks/
parks/findley/tabid/734/Default.aspx

Camp Accommodations

271 shaded sites, many electric, 45 feet, dump station, reservations available. Amenities include restrooms/showers, grill, picnic table, potable water, laundry, biking, fishing, swimming/beach, store, Nature Programs, pet friendly.

Directions

23 mi. from I-71. From Exit 186 go west on Hwy 250 for 1.4 miles to Hwy 42. Go north on Hwy 42 for 1 mile to the Hwy 250 Bypass. Take the Bypass west for 1.5 miles and exit on to Hwy 58 north. Follow Hwy 58 for 18.7 miles north to the Park.

Points of Interest -

Findley State Park, once a state forest, is heavily wooded with stately pines and various hardwoods. The scenic hiking trails allow nature lovers to view spectacular wildflowers and observe wildlife. The fields, forests and quiet waters offer a peaceful refuge for visitors.

Exit 99 of I-75
Lake Loramie State Park [11]
Northwest of Sidney
State Rate: $23-$25

(937) 295-2011

http://www.dnr.state.oh.us/parks/
parks/lakeloramie/tabid/758/
Default.aspx

Camp Accommodations

160 paved sites, some waterfront, electric, 45 feet, pull throughs, dump station, reservations. Amenities include restrooms/showers, grill, table, potable water, Nature Center, store, biking, fishing, swimming, pet friendly.

Directions

14 miles from I-75. From Exit 99 go west on Hwy 119 for 10.8 miles to Paris St. on the east edge of Minster. Turn south for 0.5 miles to Hwy 362. Turn left, go 2.5 miles to the Park entrance on your left.

Points of Interest -

Named in honor of Neil Armstrong, first man to set foot on the moon, the museum in Wapakoneta chronicles Ohio's contributions to space flight. Among the items on display are the F5D Sky Lancer, the Gemini VIII spacecraft, Apollo 11 artifacts and a moon rock. **Also see [12].**

Exit 110 of I-75
Indian Lake State Park [12]
East of Wapakoneta
State Rate: $24-$26

(937) 843-2717

http://www.dnr.state.oh.us/parks/
parks/indianlk/tabid/746/Default.aspx

Camp Accommodations

405 paved sites, many shaded, electric, some full hook up, 45 feet, dump station, reservations available. Amenities include restrooms/showers, grill, laundry, table, potable water, store, Nature Center, hiking, biking, fishing, swimming, pet friendly/beach.

Directions

16 miles from I-75. From Exit 110 go east and south for 14 miles on Hwy 33. Continue to follow Hwy 33 when it turns south in New Hampshire. Turn east on Hwy 366, continue straight on Hwy 235, when 366 turns south, for 1.8 miles in all to the Park.

Points of Interest -

Tour the Piatt Castles. These 19th century homes of Brigadier General Abram Sanders Piatt, and his brother, Colonel Donn Piatt, opened in the 1910s. The castles contain collections of Native American tools, books, military artifacts & family furnishings from 2 centuries. **Also see [11].**

Exit 208 of I-75
Maumee Bay State Park [13]
East of Toledo
State Rate: $26-$28

(419) 836-7758

http://www.dnr.state.oh.us/parks/
parks/maumeebay/tabid/764/
Default.aspx

Camp Accommodations

252 semi-shaded, spacious, paved sites, electric, 45 feet, dump station, reservations available. Amenities include restrooms/showers, grill, table, potable water, laundry, biking, fishing, hiking, swimming, pet friendly.

Directions

12.5 miles from I-75. From Exit 208 go 3.5 miles south on I-280 to Exit 7. Turn east on Hwy 2 (Navarre Ave.) and go 6.3 miles to N Curtice Rd. Turn north for 2.5 miles to the Park entrance.

Points of Interest -

Enjoy a meal at Quilter Lodge, which overlooks the Maumee Bay of Lake Erie. Trautman Nature Center is equipped with inter-active displays, a programming auditorium, research laboratory and viewing windows. Toledo is close by and has many sites and destinations.

Exit 54 of I-76
Mill Creek Campground [14]
East of Toledo
COE Rate: $14-$24
America/Beautiful Rate: $7-$12

(330) 547-3781

http://www.recreation.gov/

Camp Accommodations

348 shaded sites, some waterfront, many electric, 2 ADA, 45 feet, dump station, reservations available. Amenities include restrooms/showers, grill, table, potable water, biking, fishing, hiking, swimming, pet friendly.

Directions

8.5 miles from I-76. From Exit 54 go 5.4 miles south on Hwy 534 (Pricetown Rd.) to Hwy 224. Turn west, go 2.1 miles to Bedell Rd. Turn south for 1 mile. Turn west to Mill Creek Campground.

Points of Interest -

Berlin Lake is renowned for its excellent walleye fishing. It is one of the few area lakes where natural reproduction of the species occurs. Berlin Lake also has nesting ospreys, beaver, and occasional sightings of bald eagles. Also visit Noah's Lost Ark Animal Sanctuary.

Exit 28 of I-77
Wolf Run State Park [15]
South of Cambridge
State Rate: $18-$24

(740) 732-5035

http://www.dnr.state.oh.us/parks/
parks/wolfrun/tabid/796/Default.aspx

Camp Accommodations

138 shaded or sunny, paved sites, many electric, 45 feet, dump station, reservations available. Amenities include restrooms/showers, grill, table, potable water, laundry, biking, fishing, swimming/beach, pet friendly.

Directions

1 mile from I-77. From Exit 28 go south but immediately turn left on Main St. Proceed straight on to and follow Cty Rd 126 (Wolf Run Rd), 1 mile in all to the Park entrance on your left.

Points of Interest -

Cambridge is the birthplace of John Glenn, U.S. Senator & American Astronaut & William "Hopalong Cassidy" Boyd - both have historic sites. Glass is a major attraction, including the National Museum of Cambridge Glass & Degenhart Paperweight & Glass Museum. **Also see [16].**

Exit 47 of I-77
Salt Fork State Park [16]
Northeast of Cambridge
State Rate: $25-$36

(740) 439-3521

http://www.dnr.state.oh.us/parks/
parks/saltfork/tabid/785/Default.aspx

Camp Accommodations

212 shaded, spacious, paved sites, some full hook ups, 18 ADA, 45 feet, dump station, reservations available. Amenities include restrooms/showers, grill, picnic table, potable water, biking, fishing, hiking, swimming/beach, store, Nature Programs, pet friendly.

Directions

6 mi. from I-77. From Exit 47 go east for 6 miles on Hwy 22 (Cadiz Rd) to Hwy 1. Turn north in to the Park.

Points of Interest -

Salt Fork Lodge features a dining room, coffee shop, & gift shop. A miniature golf course is at the beach, near the park's nature center. History buffs will enjoy Roscoe Village in Coshocton, a restored early 1800s canal town featuring historic buildings and special activities. **Also see [15]**.

Exit 25 of I-80/90
Harrison Lake State Park [17]
Northeast of West Unity
State Rate: $19-$25

(419) 237-2593

http://www.dnr.state.oh.us/parks/
parks/harrison/tabid/740/Default.aspx

Camp Accommodations

173 paved sites, electric, 45 feet, dump station, reservations. Amenities include restrooms/showers, grill, table, potable water, laundry, Nature Programs, store, biking, fishing, swimming/beach, pet friendly.

Directions

5.5 miles from I-80/90. From Exit 25 go north on Hwy 66 for 3.5 miles to Cty Rd M. Turn west, go 2 miles to the Park Check-in Station on your right.

Points of Interest -

Visit the Sauder Museum, Farm and Craft Village. The large complex includes an 1860s home, barnyard, the Craft Village (where artisans display their skills), a museum displaying antique tools and farm implements, and a restored barn housing a restaurant with country-style cooking.

Exit 91 of I-80/90
East Harbor State Park [18]
East of Port Clinton
State Rate: $21-$36

(419) 734-4424

http://www.dnr.state.oh.us/parks/
parks/eastharbor/tabid/733/
Default.aspx

Camp Accommodations

548 paved, shaded & sun sites, most electric, some full hook up, pull through, 45 feet, dump station, reservations available. Amenities include restrooms/showers, grill, picnic table, potable water, Wi-Fi, store, Nature Center, hiking, biking, fishing, swimming/beach, pet friendly.

Directions

21 miles from I-80/90. From Exit 91 go northeast for 10 miles on Hwy 53 (W Freemont Rd). Turn east on Hwy 2 for 7.1 miles to Hwy 269. Follow Hwy 269 for 3.8 miles to the Park entrance.

Points of Interest -

Tour Marblehead Lighthouse, in the village of Marblehead, the oldest lighthouse in continuous operation on the Great Lakes. Other activities include Stonehenge Estate, riding the ferry, or relaxing at Crystal Cave and Heineman's Winery, or Mon Ami Winery.

Exit 218 of I-90
Geneva State Park [19]
North of Geneva
State Rate: $27-$34

(440) 466-8400

http://www.dnr.state.oh.us/parks/
parks/geneva/tabid/736/Default.aspx

Camp Accommodations

100 sun or shaded, paved sites, electric, a few full hook up, 45 feet, dump station, reservations available. Amenities include restrooms/showers, grill, picnic table, potable water, laundry, biking, fishing, hiking, swimming, pet friendly.

Directions

5.5 miles from I-90. From Exit 218 go 5.5 miles north on Hwy 534, through Geneva, to the Park entrance.

Points of Interest -

The Lodge and Conference Center at Geneva-on-the-Lake provides beautiful views of Lake Erie. Enjoy a meal at the full-service restaurant. You are in Ashtabula County, home to 16 covered bridges, 15 award-winning wineries, nineteen museums, and two wild and scenic rivers.

Exit 25 of I-275 to Exit 3 of I-74
Miami Whitewater Forest Camp [20]
Northwest of Cincinnati
Hamilton County Rate: $25
Seniors Discount

(513) 367-9632

http://www.hamiltoncountyparks.org/
rec_camping/mwfcamp.htm

Camp Accommodations

46 shaded, electric, 40 feet, dump station, reservations available. Amenities include ADA restrooms/showers, potable water, grill, picnic table, biking, pet friendly.

Directions

4 miles from intersection of I-275 & I-74. From Exit 25 of I-275 go northwest on I-74 for 2 miles to Exit 3. Take Dry Fork Rd north for 1 mile. Turn right on West Rd, then turn left into the Park. Follow signs to the harbor, check-in at the boathouse.

Points of Interest -

The many attractions of Cincinnati include the Cincinnati Art Museum, Cincinnati Museum Center at Union Station, the Contemporary Arts Center, National Underground Railroad Freedom Center, Behringer-Crawford Museum, and Cincinnati Observatory. **Also see [21]**

Exit 257 of I-275
Stonelick State Park [21]
East of Cincinnati
State Rate: $18-$22

(866) 644-6727

http://www.dnr.state.oh.us/parks/
parks/stonelck/tabid/789/Default.aspx

Camp Accommodations

114 shaded, paved sites, electric, 45 feet, dump station, reservations available. Amenities include restrooms/showers, grill, table, potable water, laundry, biking, fishing, swimming/beach, store, pet friendly.

Directions

14 miles from I-275. From Exit 28 go east for 10.3 miles on Hwy 28. Turn south at Edenton-Pleasant Plain Rd. After 1.1 miles turn right, then left on Newtonsville Rd. and go 1.5 miles, joining Hwy 727. Go 1 more mile to the Park.

Points of Interest -

In Cincinnati you will find nostalgic rides at Cincinnati Railway's Lebanon Station, explore the Creation Museum. Also visit the famous Findlay Farmer's Market, Pyramid Hill Sculpture Park and Museum, Taft Museum of Art and the GOLD Cincinnati Museum Center. **Also see [20]**

215

OKLAHOMA

The Oklahoma Tourism & Recreation Department oversees the State Park Website. There are fifty-six State Parks, 47 of which have campgrounds. You will find details at -

http://www.travelok.com/state_parks

There is no state reservation system. The Parks generally allow pets on a leash.

There are a number of County and Federal Lands which enrich the mix of RV campgrounds.

[1] **Lake Murray State Park**
N34 08.151 W97 06.533
[2] **Chandler City Park**
N34 59.165 W97 22.590
[3] **Arcadia Park**
N35 39.158 W97 22.721
[4] **Lake Carl Blackwell - Pine Grove**
N36 07.476 W97 12.607
[5] **Osage Cove, Kaw Lake**
N36 42.809 W96 53.272
[6] **Foss State Park**
N35 31.805 W99 11.460

[7] **Red Rock Canyon State Park**
N35 27.381 W98 21.556
[8] **Lake Thunderbird State Park**
N35 13.940 W97 14.853
[9] **Lake Eufaula State Park**
N35 23.972 W95 36.313
[10] **Kiowa 1 Campground**
N34 15.654 W98 05.208
[11] **Heyburn Park Campground**
N35 56.689 W96 18.449
[12] **Hawthorn Bluff Campground**
N36 25.920 W95 40.863

NOTES:

216

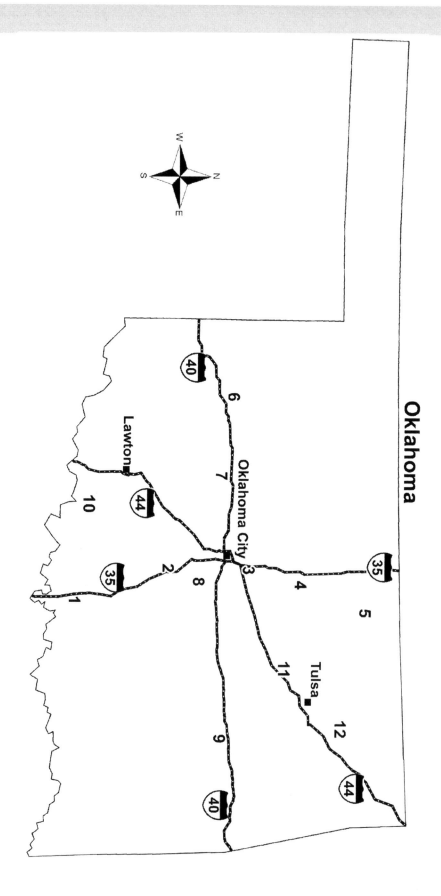

Exit 29
Lake Murray State Park [1]
Southeast of Ardmore
State Rate: $21-$25
Senior Discount

(580) 223-4044

http://www.travelok.com/listings/
view.profile/id.4358

Camp Accommodations

300 shaded sites in 9 camps, paved, full hookups, 40+ feet, dump station, pull throughs. Amenities include ADA restroom/showers, grill, table, hiking, biking, swimming/beach, golf, lodge/restaurant, Nature Center, pet friendly.

Directions

2.6 miles from I-35. From Exit 29 go east for 2.6 miles on Hwy 70 to Hwy 77S. Turn right in to the Park.

Points of Interest -

WPA and CCC laborers built this 12,000 acre park and lake. You have access to Murray Lodge, miniature golf, horseback riding, tennis courts and a pool. Tucker Tower, much like a lighthouse, built out of rock and sitting at the top of a cliff out on a point, watches over the lake.

Exit 91
Chandler City Park [2]
In Chandler
City Rate: $20

(405) 527-5114

http://chandlerok.com/recreation/
parks

Camp Accommodations

40 shaded sites, paved, electricity/water, 40+ feet, dump station nearby, pull throughs. Amenities include restrooms, grill, table, laundry, biking, city pool and golf course, pet friendly.

Directions

1 mile from I-35. From Exit 91 go northeast on Hwy 74 for 0.3 miles to Chandler Rd. Turn west (left), go 0.5 miles to Park Rd. on your right.

Points of Interest -

In Norman visit Campus Corner. From unique boutiques to worldwide cuisine, the 627,000 square feet of Campus Corner can cater to all your wants and desires. With 47 boutiques & shops and 23 restaurants and nightclubs Campus Corner is a great destination in Norman. **Also see [8].**

Exit 141
Arcadia Lake Park [3]
East of Edmond
City Rate: $15-$25
Senior Discount

(405) 216-7470

http://www.shopoklahoma.com/
arcadia_park.htm

Camp Accommodations

Multiple camps, 100+ shaded sites, paved, full hookups or electricity/water, 40+ feet, dump station, pull throughs. Amenities include restrooms/showers, grill, table, hiking, biking, swimming, disc golf, pet friendly.

Directions

2.5 miles from I-35. From Exit 141 go east on Hwy 66 for 2.2 miles to the Park on your right.

Points of Interest -

Between Oklahoma City and Edmond, there is much to see and do. A few examples are the National Cowboy Hall of Fame, Express Ranches Clydesdale Center, The Rodeo Opry, Overholser Mansion, Oklahoma Indian Art Gallery, and the American Banjo Museum.

Exit 174 of I-35
Lake Carl Blackwell - Pine Grove [4]
West of Stillwater
Oklahoma State University Rate: $20

(405) 372-5157

http://lcb.okstate.edu/PineGrove.htm

Directions

9 miles from I-35. From Exit 174 go east on Hwy 51 for 7.8 miles to Hwy 51C. Turn north, go 1.4 miles to the Park.

Camp Accommodations

140 shaded waterfront sites, paved, electricity/water, 40+ feet, pull throughs. Amenities include restrooms/showers, grill, table, biking, fishing, swimming, pet friendly.

Points of Interest -

If you like Red Dirt Music, Stillwater is the home to Red Dirt Music and top musical talent such as Garth Brooks. Wrestling fans will want to stop at the National Wrestling Hall of Fame & Museum. The Sheerar Museum houses outstanding exhibits of Stillwater and A&M/OSU history.

Exit 214 of I-35
Osage Cove, Kaw Lake [5]
East of Ponca City
COE Rate: $18
America/Beautiful Rate: $9

(580) 762-5611

http://www.recreation.gov/

Directions

27 miles from I-35. From Exit 214 go east on Hwy 60 for 25 miles (through Ponca City) to Kaw Dam Rd. Turn north 0.4 miles to Osage Cove Rd. Turn right, go 1.7 miles to Osage Park Rd on your left.

Camp Accommodations

97+ shaded sites, many waterfront, electric, 45 feet, dump station. Amenities include ADA restrooms/showers, potable water, grill, table, hiking, biking, pet friendly.

Points of Interest -

Ponca City got its name from the Ponca Native American people. You can explore the Native American culture through pow-wows, social and ceremonial dances. A short day tour might include Cann Memorial Garden, Marland Mansion and Grounds, & the Pioneer Women Museum.

Exit 53 of I-40
Foss State Park [6]
West of Clinton
State Rate: $21-$25
Senior Discount

(580) 592-4433

http://www.travelok.com/listings/
view.profile/id.2848

Camp Accommodations

110 shaded sites, paved, some waterfront, full hookups, 45 feet, dump station, pull throughs. Amenities include ADA restroom/showers, grill, table, hiking, biking, swimming/beach, boating, Visitors Center, pet friendly.

Directions

7 miles from I-40. From Exit 53 go 6.3 miles north on Hwy 44, which is joined by Hwy 73. Follow Hwy 73 when it turns west, go 0.2 to Marina Rd and the Park entrance.

Points of Interest -

In Clinton visit the Oklahoma Route 66 Museum. Take the audio tour, which will guide you through Route 66 history. Visit the Washita Battlefield, where George A. Custer led the 7th U.S. Cavalry on a surprise attack against the Southern Cheyenne village of Peace Chief Black Kettle.

Exit 101
Red Rock Canyon State Park [7]
West of Oklahoma City
State Rate: $21-$25
Senior Discount

(405) 542-6344

http://www.travelok.com/listings/
view.profile/id.6275

Camp Accommodations

56 shaded, paved sites, full hookups, 40+ feet, dump station, pull throughs. Amenities include ADA restroom/showers, grill, picnic table, hiking, biking, swimming pool, concessions, gift shop, pet friendly.

Directions

6 miles from I-40. From Exit 101 go south for 6 miles on Hwy 8/281 (through Hinton) to the Park entrance on your left.

Points of Interest -

The park and campsites are located down in a canyon (short steep entry road) among red rock canyon walls. The canyon walls are a favorite for rappelling and exploration. Visit the Chisholm Trail Museum and Governor Seay Mansion, and the American Indian Hall of Fame.

Exit 166
Lake Thunderbird State Park [8]
East of Norman
State Rate: $21-$25
Senior Discount

(405) 360-3572

http://www.travelok.com/listings/
view.profile/id.4386

Camp Accommodations

200+ shaded, paved sites, some waterfront, some full hookup, electric/water, 40+ feet, dump station. Amenities include ADA restroom/showers, grill, table, hiking, biking, swimming/beach, restaurant, pet friendly.

Directions

12 miles from I-40. From Exit 166 go south for 11 miles on 120th Ave. (Choctaw Rd). Turn east for 1 mile to the Park.

Points of Interest -

See ancient artifacts of the Five Civilized Tribes at the Jacobson House in Norman. Visit the ecological woodlands at the Oliver Nature Preserve. Tour the Crucible Foundry, Gallery & Sculpture Garden, with bronze sculptures from around the country in their sculpture garden. **Also see [2].**

Exit 259
Lake Eufaula State Park [9]
South of Checotah
State Rate: $21-$25
Senior Discount

(918) 689-5311

http://www.travelok.com/listings/
view.profile/id.4336

Camp Accommodations

94 shaded, paved sites, some waterfront, some full hookup, electric/water, 45 feet, dump station. Amenities include ADA restroom/showers, grill, table, hiking, biking, swimming/beach, golf course, pet friendly.

Directions

5.5 miles from I-40. From Exit 259 go south for 5.5 miles on Hwy 150 to the Visitors Center on your left.

Points of Interest -

Checotah is home to a number of antique malls, the Honey Springs Civil War battle site & a downtown historic district. It claims to be Steerwrestling Capital of the World. It is the hometown of 2005 American Idol winner & Country Star Carrie Underwood, & country music singer Mel McDaniel.

Exit 5
Kiowa 1 Campground [10]
Southeast of Lawton
COE Rate: $14-$18
America/Beautiful Rate: $7-$9

(580) 963-9031

http://www.recreation.gov/

Camp Accommodations
180 shaded, paved sites, 1 ADA, many waterfront, electric/water, 45 feet, 49 pull through, dump station. Amenities include ADA restrooms/showers, potable water, grill, table, hiking, biking, swimming, pet friendly.

Directions
31 miles from I-44. From Exit 5 go east on Hwy 70/277 for 24 miles. Turn north at N2750 Rd. for 7 miles to E1900 Rd. Turn right in to the Park.

Points of Interest -
Lawton is the third largest city in Oklahoma. Local attractions include Fort Sill National Historic Landmark; the Comanche National Museum & Cultural Center; Historic Mattie Beal Home; the Holy City of the Wichitas; Museum of the Great Plains & Wichita Mountains Wildlife Refuge.

Exit 196
Heyburn Park Campground [11]
Southwest of Tulsa
COE Rate: $14-$16
America/Beautiful Rate: $7-$8

(918) 247-6601

http://www.recreation.gov/

Camp Accommodations
45 shaded sites, 1 ADA, electric/water, 45 feet, pull through, dump station. Amenities include ADA restrooms/showers, potable water, grill, table, hiking, biking, swimming, pet friendly.

Directions
11 miles from I-44. From Exit 196 go north on Hwy 48/66 for 2.5 miles and bare right on Hwy 66. Go 5.7 miles on Hwy 66 to Hwy 273 Rd. Turn north for 2.3 miles to Lake Heyburn Rd. Turn west for 0.6 miles to the Park entrance.

Points of Interest -
Tulsa's cultural scene shines with ballet and symphony, sharing the downtown spotlight with cultural events, activities, architecture, and art including 18 of Frederic Remington's 22 bronzes. Visit the world's most comprehensive collection of art and artifacts of the American West.

Exit 255
Hawthorn Bluff Campground [12]
Northeast of Tulsa
COE Rate: $16-$20
America/Beautiful Rate: $8-$10

(918) 443-2319

http://www.recreation.gov/

Camp Accommodations
56 shaded sites, 2 ADA, electric, 45 feet, 2 pull through, dump station. Amenities include ADA restrooms/showers, potable water, grill, table, hiking, biking, swimming, pet friendly.

Directions
13 miles from I-44. From Exit 255 follow Hwy 20 west in to Claremore. Hwy 88 joins Hwy 20 after 1.5 miles. Now follow Hwy 88 north for 11.5 miles to the Park on your right.

Points of Interest -
Claremore is the home of Oklahoma's favorite son, Will Rogers. Visit the Will Rogers Memorial and Birthplace Ranch. Other sights include the J.M. Davis Arms & Historical Museum and The Belvidere Mansion. See the world's largest totem pole in Foyil. Stop at local vineyards too.

OREGON

The Oregon Parks and Recreation Department oversees the State Park System. Their website is -

www.oregon.gov/OPRD/PARKS/index.shtml

There are more than 50 parks with year-round and seasonal campgrounds in the Oregon State Park system. Half of Oregon's state park campgrounds accept campsite reservations; the other half are first-come, first serve. For information about a park or campground (including seasonal opening and closing dates) visit the park web page.

Most Oregon State Parks can accommodate RVs up to 50 feet in length, but site lengths vary greatly, even within the same park. You must be able to fit your tow/towed vehicle onto the campsite. The Parks along the Columbia River are generally near railroad tracks, however Parks were selected with moderate (by most standards) sound levels. Pets are allowed in the parks but must be confined by the owner, or on a leash not more than six (6) feet long, and kept under physical control at all times.

Reservations are accepted year-round for campgrounds throughout the state. You can make reservations as far in advance as 9 months, or as few as 2 days before your stay. When you make a reservation, you must pay the entire amount due for the length of your stay plus a non-refundable $8 reservation fee. Reservations may be made online with a credit card, or by calling (800) 452-5687. Online reservations are handled by ReserveAmerica, at -

www.reserveamerica.com.

No other website is authorized to handle Oregon state park reservations.

There are primarily two types of campsites of interest to RVers:

- Full hookup sites – sewer, electricity and water; paved parking area adjacent to site.
- Electrical sites – electricity and water; paved parking adjacent to site.

Oregon also has a notably fine collection of County Parks.

[1] **Emigrant Lake - Point Park**
   N42 09.208 W122 37.596
[2] **Valley of the Rogue State Park**
   N42 24.616 W123 07.798
[3] **Pine Meadows Campground**
   N43 42.021 W123 03.376
[4] **Gills Landing RV Park**
   N44 32.258 W122 53.525
[5] **Champoeg State Heritage Area**
   N45 14.896 W122 53.651
[6] **Umatilla Marina and RV Park**
   N45 55.392 W119 19.850

[7] **Ainsworth State Park**
   N45 35.745 W122 03.180
[8] **Deschutes River Recreation Area**
   N45 38.075 W120 54.502
[9] **Boardman Marina Park**
   N45 50.592 W119 42.486
[10] **Emigrant Springs State Heritage Area**
   N45 32.411 W118 27.631
[11] **Farewell Bend State Recreation Area**
   N44 18.212 W117 13.658

NOTES:

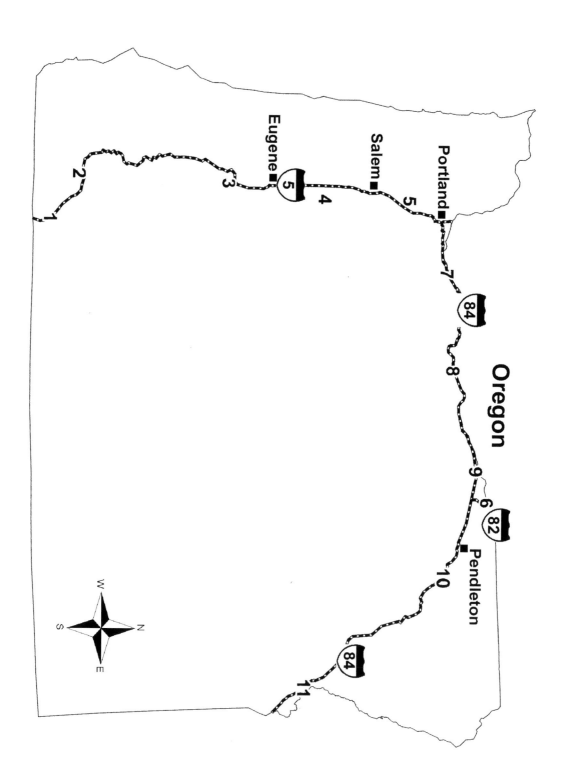

Exit 14
Emigrant Lake - Point Park [1]
Southeast of Ashland
County Rate: $26

(541) 774-8183

http://www.jacksoncountyparks.com/
emigrant_lake.htm

Camp Accommodations

32 sites, moderate shade, paved, 1 ADA, full hookups, 45 feet, dump station, 2 pull through, reservations available. Amenities include ADA restroom/showers, grill, table, hiking, biking, swimming, pet friendly.

Directions

3 miles from I-5. From Exit 14 go southeast for 3 miles on Hwy 66 to Emigrant Lake Rd. Turn left and follow Emigrant Lake Rd. to the campground.

Points of Interest -

Ashland is home of the Oregon Shakespeare Festival & other visual & vocal artistry. Talented chefs prepare locally grown cuisine to pair with award winning local wines. The Crater Rock Museum in Central Point features exhibits of minerals, gemstones, fossils & petrified wood.

Exit 45b
Valley of the Rogue State Park [2]
East of Grants Pass
State Rate: $16-$24

(541) 774-8183

http://www.jacksoncountyparks.com/
emigrant_lake.htm

Camp Accommodations

147 shaded sites, paved, full hookups or electric/water, 40+ feet, dump station, reservations available. Amenities include ADA restroom/showers, grill, table, hiking, biking, swimming, pet friendly.

Directions

Along I-5. From Exit 45b: **southbound** RVs turn right at the end on the off ramp to the registration area; **northbound** RVs proceed to Rogue River Rd, turn right and proceed to the registration area.

Points of Interest -

Camp along the river made famous by novelist and avid fisherman Zane Grey. Take day trips to Crater Lake National Park, the Oregon Caves National Monument, historic Jacksonville, Ashland's Shakespeare Festival, the Britt Music Festival, and the historic Wolf Creek Inn

Exits 172 and 174
Pine Meadows Campground [3]
South of Eugene
COE Rate: $10-$16
America/Beautiful Rate: $5-$8

(541) 942-8657

http://www.recreation.gov/

Camp Accommodations

97 shaded sites, 4 ADA, dry camping, many pull through, 45+ feet, dump station, reservations available. Amenities include ADA restroom/showers, grill, table, hiking, biking, swimming, pet friendly. No Utilities.

Directions

6-8 mi. from I-5. **Northbound**, use Exit 174, turn southbound 2 mi. to Exit 172. All travelers, now southbound, take exit 172, go 3.5 miles south on 6th St. (London Rd). Take a left on Cottage Grove Reservoir Rd. Campground is 2.6 miles on the right.

Points of Interest -

For shopping, browse among one-of-a-kind mini-boutiques at our legendary Saturday Market. Take in a live performance at a local community theater, or the Hult Center for the Performing Arts. Visit the Jordan Schnitzer Museum of Art on the University of Oregon campus.

Exit 228 of I-5
Gills Landing RV Park [4]
East of Corvallis, in Lebanon
County Rate: $23

(541) 258-4917

http://www.ci.lebanon.or.us/
index.aspx?page=125

Camp Accommodations

20 shaded sites, paved, full hookups, 45 feet, reservations available. Amenities include ADA restroom/showers, Wi-Fi, grill, table, hiking, biking, fishing, swimming/beach, pet friendly.

Directions

9 miles from I-5. From Exit 228 go east for 7.7 miles on Hwy 34 (Corvallis-Lebanon Hwy) into Lebanon to Hwy 20. Turn south on Main St. for 0.5 miles to Grant St. Follow Grant east 0.7 miles to the Park.

Points of Interest -

With 38 arts and culture options or 21 culinary and wineries possibilities, you're sure to find plenty to do in Corvallis. Shoppers will be happy too. There are also walking tours - the Historic Homes Trolley Tour, Historical Walking Tours, or do a Corvallis GPS Waymarking Hunt.

Exit 278 of I-5
Champoeg State Heritage Area [5]
South of Portland
State Rate: $16

(503) 678-1251

http://www.oregonstateparks.org/
park_113.php

Camp Accommodations

79 shaded sites, paved, 4 ADA, 12 full hookups or 67 electric/water, 40+ feet, dump station, 6 pull through, reservations available. Amenities include ADA restroom/showers, grill, table, hiking, biking, swimming, pet friendly.

Directions

6 miles from I-5. From Exit 278 go 3.5 miles west on Ehlen (then Yergen Rd) to Case Rd. Turn north for 1.3 miles to Champoeg Rd, then west for 0.9 miles to the Park.

Points of Interest -

Champoeg features a unique combination of history, nature, and recreation. This is the site where Oregon's first provisional government was formed in 1843. Tour the park's Visitor Center, Newell House, and Pioneer Mothers Log Cabin museums to discover pioneer life at Champoeg.

Exit 1 of I-82
Umatilla Marina and RV Park [6]
On the Columbia River at Umatilla
County Rate: $23

(541) 922-3939

http://www.umatillarvpark.com/

Camp Accommodations

26 shaded sites, full hookups, 40+ feet, 12 pull through, dump station, reservations available. Amenities include ADA restroom/showers, grill, table, hiking, biking, fishing, pet friendly.

Directions

1 mile from I-82. From Exit 1 turn west on Hwy 730 and immediately turn right on Brownell Blvd. Go 0.4 miles north to 3rd. Turn left, go 0.3 miles to Quincy St. Turn right to the Park.

Points of Interest -

Visit Columbia Crest Winery, Fort Henrietta or Pendleton Woolen Mills. Enjoy the Hermiston's Farm City Pro Rodeo or Pendleton Roundup. McNary Dam has a number of sights, including an Interpretive Center. Take your walk at the McNary Wildlife Nature Area.

Exit 35
Ainsworth State Park [7]
West of Hood River
State Rate: $12-$20

(503) 695-2301

http://www.oregonstateparks.org/
park_146.php

Camp Accommodations

43 shaded sites, paved, full hookups, 45 feet, dump station, some pull through. Amenities include ADA restroom/showers, grill, table, hiking, biking, Interpretive Programs, pet friendly.

Directions

1 mile from I-84. From Exit 35 go southwest on the historic Columbia River Hwy for 1 mile to the Park.

Points of Interest -

Enjoy breathtaking views of the Columbia River Gorge from the Historic Columbia River Highway State Trail. The Mosier Twin Tunnels stretch is a paved five-mile route between two trailheads. There is gorge scenery from the Bridge of the Gods at Cascade Locks.

Exit 97
Deschutes River Recreation Area [8]
East of The Dalles
State Rate: $12-$20

(541) 739-2322

http://www.oregonstateparks.org/
park_37.php

Camp Accommodations

34 shaded sites, paved, electric/water, 40+ feet, dump station (at Maryhill SP), reservations available. Amenities include restrooms, grill (no grill use July 1-Sept. 30), table, hiking, biking, Interpretive Programs, pet friendly.

Directions

3 miles from I-84. From Exit 97 go east on Hwy 206, just across the Deschutes River to the Park entrance.

Points of Interest -

Enjoy a bike ride, following the 'Old Railbed Trail,' up the canyon. The trail is an easy, flat grade but mountain bikes are recommended. Be prepared with a patch kit. Visit The Dalles, where pioneers once loaded their wagons onto rafts or barges and floated down the Columbia.

Exit 164
Boardman Marina Park [9]
North side of Boardman
County Rate: $24

(541) 481-7217

http://www.boardmanmarinapark.com/

Camp Accommodations

63 shaded, paved, waterfront sites, full hookups, 40+ feet, some pull through, dump station, reservations available. Amenities include ADA restroom/showers, laundry, grill, picnic table, Wi-Fi, hiking, biking, fishing, pet friendly.

Directions

1 mile from I-84. From Exit 164 turn north for 0.4 miles on Main St. Turn west for 0.3 miles on Marine Dr. to the Park on your right.

Points of Interest -

Visit Columbia Crest Winery, Fort Henrietta or Pendleton Woolen Mills. Enjoy the Hermiston's Farm City Pro Rodeo or Pendleton Roundup. McNary Dam has a number of sights, including an Interpretive Center. Take your walk at the McNary Wildlife Nature Area.

Exit 234
Emigrant Springs State Heritage Area [10]
Southeast of Pendleton
State Rate: $16

(541) 983-2277

http://www.oregonstateparks.org/park_23.php

Camp Accommodations

50 shaded sites, 18 full hookups, 32 dry, 40 feet, dump station (at Deadman's Pass Rest Area), reservations available. Amenities include ADA restroom/showers, grill, picnic table, hiking, potable water, biking, pet

Directions

1 mile from I-84. **Eastbound**, from Exit 234 go 0.6 miles south on the Frontage Rd to the Park. **Westbound**, from Exit 234 go 0.6 miles northwest on the Frontage Rd to the Park.

Points of Interest -

The Park preserves a site near the summit of the Blue Mountains where Oregon Trail travelers once replenished their water supplies. At the Oregon Trail Interpretive Park experience the Oregon Trail as the pioneers did - some of the best-preserved traces of the Old Emigrant Road await.

Exit 353
Farewell Bend State Recreation Area [11]
North of Ontario
State Rate: $22

(541) 869-2365

http://www.oregonstateparks.org/park_7.php

Camp Accommodations

101 shaded, paved sites, electric/water, 40+ feet, dump station, reservations available. Amenities include ADA restroom/showers, grill, picnic table, hiking, biking, watchable wildlife, pet friendly.

Directions

1 mile from I-84. From Exit 353 turn north for 1 mile on Huntington Hwy 30 to the Park entrance.

Points of Interest -

The Park offers a beautiful desert experience on the banks of the Snake River's Brownlee Reservoir. Pioneers took a final rest here before traveling to Oregon City. Oregon Trail wagon ruts are still visible. Historic markers provide information on Farewell Bend's significance.

PENNSYLVANIA

Pennsylvania's state parks competed with the best systems in the country and was awarded the top honor as the 2009 National Gold Medal Award for Excellence in Park and Recreation Management.

Pennsylvania State Parks allows up to two pets in designated campsites within 25 state park campgrounds. Other state parks will continue to prohibit pets in overnight areas. Pets are allowed if on a leash or in a cage or crate. If a maximum length of leash is specified by the Park, the leash may not exceed the length specified.

Make reservations or call toll-free 888-PA-PARKS, 7 a.m. to 5 p.m. Monday to Saturday, for state park information and reservations, or email us your postal address for an information packet. To reserve online go to -

http://www.pa.reserveworld.com/SearchPark.aspx

Campground fees are set park-by-park. Senior citizens and people with disabilities can get a reduced campsite price.

[1] **Laurel Hill State Park**
N40 00.547 W79 13.100

[2] **Shawnee State Park**
N40 03.040 W78 37.414

[3] **Cowans Gap State Park**
N39 59.929 W77 55.255

[4] **French Creek State Park**
N40 11.774 W75 47.802

[5] **Pymatuning State Park**
N41 29.938 W80 28.169

[6] **Shenango Recreation Area Campground**
N41 17.854 W80 25.826

[7] **Clear Creek State Park**
N41 19.345 W79 04.598

[8] **Bald Eagle State Park**
N41 02.160 W77 39.113

[9] **Hickory Run State Park**
N41 01.569 W75 41.788

[10] **Caledonia State Park**
N39 54.488 W77 28.630

[11] **Locust Lake State Park**
N40 47.097 W76 07.187

[12] **Lackawanna State Park**
N41 33.922 W75 42.475

[13] **Gifford Pinchot State Park**
N40 03.264 W76 54.626

[14] **Promised Land State Park**
N41 19.170 W75 12.584

[15] **Blue Knob State Park**
N40 17.717 W78 34.744

[16] **Black Moshannon State Park**
N40 54.911 W78 03.513

[17] **Tobyhanna State Park**
N41 12.405 W75 23.798

NOTES:

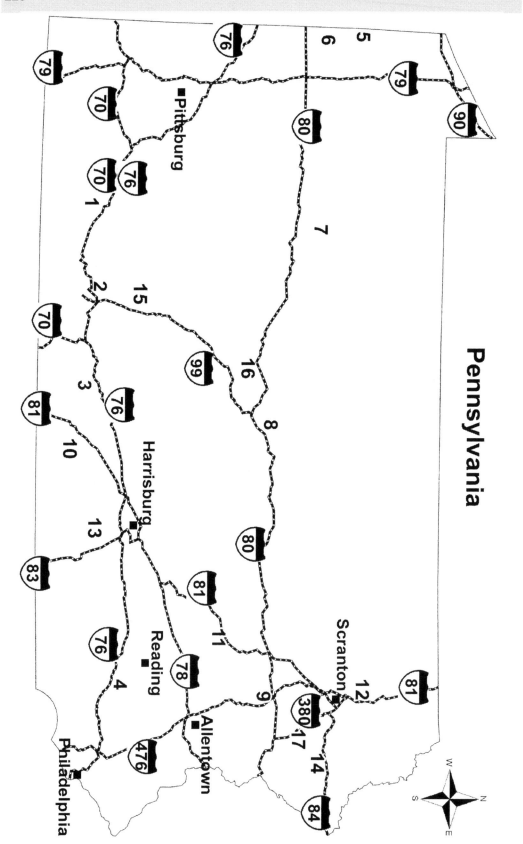

Pennsylvania

Exits 91 or 110 of I-70/76
Laurel Hill State Park [1]
West of Somerset
State Rate: $27-$29

(814) 445-7725

http://www.dcnr.state.pa.us/
stateparks/parks/laurelhill.aspx

Camp Accommodations

264 shaded sites, paved, most electric, 40 feet, dump station, reservations available. Amenities include ADA restroom/showers, potable water, grill, table, hiking, biking, fishing, swimming, pet friendly (selected sites).

Directions

11-14 miles from I-70/76. From Exit 91, go 12 miles southeast on Hwy 31 to Trent Rd. Turn right for 2 miles to the Park. From Exit 110, go south 0.5 miles on Hwy 601 to Hwy 31. Turn east, go 8 miles to Trent Rd. Turn left for 2 miles to the Park.

Points of Interest -

You are in the Pennsylvania Laurel Highlands. History buffs will want to visit French & Indian War sites including Fort Necessity and Fort Ligonier where a key strategic battle of the French & Indian War occurred. Stop by Frank Lloyd Wright's Fallingwater®.

Exit 146 of I-70/76
Shawnee State Park [2]
West of I-99 Junction
State Rate: $27-$29

(814) 733-4218

http://www.dcnr.state.pa.us/
stateparks/parks/shawnee.aspx

Camp Accommodations

293 shaded sites, 3 ADA, many electric, 40 feet, dump station, reservations available. Amenities include ADA restroom/showers, potable water, laundry, grill, table, hiking, biking, fishing, swimming, pet friendly (selected sites).

Directions

9 miles from I-70/76 & I-99 Junction. From I-70/76 & I-99, turn south on I-99 for 2 miles to Hwy 30 exit. Go west for 7 miles to the Park entrance on your left (just after Harrison Rd).

Points of Interest -

At Old Bedford Village and Fort Bedford enjoy military and civilian re-enactments, colonial crafts, exhibits and instructions, and festivals. The only fossilized coral reef cavern known to be in existence is found at Coral Caverns. For some fun, go to Gravity Hill.

Exit 180 of I-76
Cowans Gap State Park [3]
West of Hustontown
State Rate: $27-$29

(717) 485-3948

http://www.dcnr.state.pa.us/
stateparks/parks/cowansgap.aspx

Camp Accommodations

224 shaded sites, many electric, 40 feet, some pull through, dump station, reservations available. Amenities include ADA restroom/showers, potable water, grill, table, hiking, biking, fishing, swimming/beach, Visitor Center - concessions, pet friendly (selected sites).

Directions

12 miles from I-76. From I-76, turn north on Hwy 522 for 5 miles to Burnt Cabins. Bare right on to Hwy 1010 (Grist Mill Rd) for 0.8 miles. Turn south on Hwy 1005 (Allens Valley Rd). Follow Hwy 1005 for 6 miles to the Park entrance.

Points of Interest -

Tour the Historic Burnt Cabins Grist Mill. Listed in the National Register of Historic Places, this operating mill produces cornmeal, buckwheat, whole wheat and rye flour. Visit President James Buchanan's birthplace, marked by a stone pyramid monument.

Exits 298 of I-76
French Creek State Park [4]
Southeast of Reading
State Rate: $27-$29

(610) 582-9680

http://www.dcnr.state.pa.us/
stateparks/parks/frenchcreek.aspx

Camp Accommodations

201 shaded sites, many electric, 40 feet, dump station, reservations available. Amenities include ADA restroom/showers, potable water, grill, picnic table, hiking, biking, fishing, swimming, watchable wildlife, pet friendly (selected sites).

Directions

6 miles from I-76. From Exit 298 go east 0.4 miles on Reading, then right for 1 mile on Joanna Rd, then right for 0.6 miles on Elverson Rd to Hopewell. Go left on Hopewell, which becomes Park Rd, for 3.6 miles to the Park entrance.

Points of Interest -

Set amidst the picturesque farmland of southeast Pennsylvania, French Creek offers two lakes, extensive forests, and 40 miles of hiking trails. Nearby the Hopewell Furnace National Historic Site features a cold-blast furnace restored to its 1830s appearance.

Exit 147 of I-79
Pymatuning State Park [5]
West of Meadville
State Rate: $27-$29

(724) 932-3141

http://www.dcnr.state.pa.us/
stateparks/parks/pymatuning.aspx

Camp Accommodations

388 shaded sites, some electric & some full, 45 feet, some pull through, dump station, reservations available. Amenities include ADA restroom/showers, potable water, laundry, grill, table, hiking, biking, fishing, swimming/beach, store, pet friendly (selected sites).

Directions

20 miles from I-79. From Exit 147 follow Hwy 322 for 20 miles to the Park.

Points of Interest -

This is the largest state park in the Commonwealth, within Pennsylvania's Great Lakes Region. Ride in a train or be entertained at a dinner theatre. There is also a century-old amusement park, the state's largest agricultural fair and museums of all types.

Exit 4 of I-80
Shenango Recreation Area Camp [6]
North of Sharon-Hermitage
COE Rate: $17-$22
America/Beautiful Rate: $9-$11

(724) 646-1124

http://www.recreation.gov/

Camp Accommodations

322 shaded sites, 3 ADA, 110 electric, 45 feet, 4 pull through, dump station, reservations available. Amenities include ADA restroom/showers, potable water, grill, table, hiking, biking, fishing, pet friendly.

Directions

12 mi. from I-80. From Exit 4 go north on I-376 & Hwy 18 north, crossing the causeway, 9.7 mi. in all. The park is on the left of the divided highway. Continue north, exit to the right at Rutledge Dr, make the turn-around, go south on Hwy 18 for 1.7 mi. Before the causeway go right on West Lake Rd, and 0.4 mi. to the Park.

Points of Interest -

In the Sharon-Hermitage area, every Sunday and Wednesday evening in the summer, concerts are held in the Performing Arts Building at the Buhl Farm Park. Do part of the Underground Railroad Driving tour. See the following website -
www.discovermercercountypa.org/urr.asp

Exit 78
Clear Creek State Park [7]
Northeast of Clarion
State Rate: $27-$29

(814) 752-2368

http://www.dcnr.state.pa.us/
stateparks/parks/clearcreek.aspx

Camp Accommodations

53 shaded sites, most electric, 40 feet, dump station, reservations available. Amenities include ADA restroom, potable water, grill, table, hiking, biking, fishing, swimming/beach, pet friendly (selected sites).

Directions

11.5 miles from I-80. From Exit 78, go 7.5 miles north on Hwy 36 to Hwy 949. Turn right, go 4 miles to the Park.

Points of Interest -

During the summer, an environmental educator presents guided walks, hands-on activities and evening campfire programs. The Visitor Center has logging and nature exhibits. Clarion County Festivals and attractions include The Horsethief Festival, and Autumn Leaf Festival.

Exit 158
Bald Eagle State Park [8]
West of I-99 Junction
State Rate: $27-$29

(814) 625-2775

http://www.dcnr.state.pa.us/
stateparks/parks/baldeagle.aspx

Camp Accommodations

97 shaded, paved sites, 2 ADA, electric, 40 feet, dump station, reservations available. Amenities include ADA restroom/showers, potable water, grill, table, hiking, biking, fishing, swimming/beach, pet friendly (selected sites).

Directions

8.5 miles from I-80. From Exit 158, turn northeast on Hwy 150 for 8.2 miles to the Park entrance on your right.

Points of Interest -

Visit the new Nature Inn at Bald Eagle. Tour Penn's Cave by boat, one of the only all water caverns in the United States. See the PA Military Museum in Boalsburg, with 20th Century armed services exhibits. Have dinner at the Gamble Mill in Bellefonte, a once working grist mill.

Exit 274
Hickory Run State Park [9]
West of I-476
State Rate: $27-$29

(570) 443-0400

http://www.dcnr.state.pa.us/
stateparks/parks/hickoryrun.aspx

Camp Accommodations

381 shaded sites, most electric, 40 feet, dump station, reservations available. Amenities include ADA restroom/showers, potable water, grill, table, hiking, biking, fishing, swimming/beach, concessions, disc golf, pet friendly (selected sites).

Directions

6 miles from I-80. From Exit 274, turn south on Hwy 534, go 6 miles to the Park entrance.

Points of Interest -

Do the Lehigh Gorge State Park and Hickory Run State Park "Auto Tour." Tour Eckley, one of the hundreds of company mining towns or "patches" built in the anthracite region of Pennsylvania during the nineteenth century. Go on down to Pocono Raceway.

Exit 16
Caledonia State Park [10]
East of Chambersburg
State Rate: $27-$29

(717) 352-2161

http://www.dcnr.state.pa.us/
stateparks/parks/caledonia.aspx

Camp Accommodations

175 shaded sites, 2 ADA, many electric, 40 feet, some pull through, dump station, reservations available. Amenities include ADA restroom/showers, potable water, grill, picnic table, hiking, biking, fishing, swimming pool, pet friendly (selected sites).

Directions

9 miles from I-81. From Exit 16 go 8.5 miles east on Hwy 30 to Hwy 233. Turn north for 0.2 miles to the Park entrance.

Points of Interest -

A Park naturalist offers campfire programs, guided hikes and environmental education programs in the summer months. The Thaddeus Stevens Blacksmith Shop is a historical center. Be sure to visit nearby Gettysburg National Military Park/Battlefield.

Exit 131
Locust Lake State Park [11]
South of Mahanoy City
State Rate: $27-$29

(570) 467-2404

http://www.dcnr.state.pa.us/
stateparks/parks/locustlake.aspx

Camp Accommodations

282 shaded sites, some ADA, many electric, 40 feet, dump station, reservations available. Amenities include ADA restroom/showers, potable water, grill, picnic table, hiking, biking, fishing, swimming/beach, store, pet friendly (selected sites).

Directions

6 miles from I-81. At Exit 131 ramp (caution tight curves) to Mahanoy City and/or Locust SP, on the west side of I-81, turn southwest on to Hwy 1008 (Morea Rd). Go 1.1 miles to Hwy 1006 (Burma Rd). Turn left, go 1 miles to Hwy 1011 (Brockton Mtn Rd). Turn left, go 1.6 miles to Rd. 489 (Locust Lake Rd). Turn right for 1.2 miles to the Park.

Points of Interest -

This is Schuylkill County, with America's Oldest Brewery. Tour a coal mine or visit a classic car museum. Enjoy the Schuylkill County Fair, the Pottsville Car Cruise, ethnic and community festivals. Taste the offerings from five wineries.

Exit 199
Lackawanna State Park [12]
North of Scranton
State Rate: $27-$29

(570) 945-3239

http://www.dcnr.state.pa.us/
stateparks/parks/lackawanna.aspx

Camp Accommodations

61 shaded sites, some ADA, many electric, 40 feet, dump station, reservations available. Amenities include ADA restroom/showers, potable water, grill, picnic table, hiking, biking, fishing, swimming pool, pet friendly (selected sites).

Directions

3.5 miles from I-81. From Exit 199 go 3.1 miles on Hwy 524 (Kennedy Creek Rd) to Hwy 407. Turn north for 0.4 miles to Lake View Dr. Turn left in to the Park.

Points of Interest -

Lacka-wanna is Indian for "the meeting of two streams." In Scranton take a trip underground - tour a coal mine. Board a trolley at the Electric City Trolley Station and Museum for a 5 mile ride to Montage Mountain. Check out America's largest collection of steam locomotives.

Exit 32 of I-83
Gifford Pinchot State Park [13]
North of York
State Rate: $27-$29

(717) 292-4112

http://www.dcnr.state.pa.us/
stateparks/parks/giffordpinchot.aspx

Camp Accommodations

339 shaded, paved sites, most electric, some ADA, 45 feet, dump station, reservations available. Amenities include ADA restroom, potable water, grill, table, hiking, biking, fishing, swimming/beach, disc golf, pet friendly (selected sites).

Directions

10 miles from I-83. From Exit 32, go east on Hwy 382 (Lewisberry Rd) for 3.5 miles. Turn left on Hwy 177, go 6 miles to Hwy 74. Turn left for 0.7 miles to the Park entrance.

Points of Interest -

The Park is with 2 hours of Gettysburg, Hershey, Lancaster County (Amish Country) & Baltimore. Some options include the Antique Auto Museum, National Watch & Clock Museum, and The Daylily Farm. Do the UnCork York Wine Trail, with stunning views of the Susquehanna River.

Exit 26 of I-84
Promised Land State Park [14]
East of Scranton
State Rate: $25

(570) 676-3428

http://www.dcnr.state.pa.us/
stateparks/parks/promisedland.aspx

Camp Accommodations

447 shaded, sites, some ADA, electric, some pull through, 45 feet, dump station, reservations available. Amenities include ADA restroom/showers, potable water, grill, table, hiking, biking, fishing, swimming/beach, pet friendly (selected sites).

Directions

3 miles from I-84. From Exit 26, go south on Hwy 390 for 3 miles to the Park.

Points of Interest -

The Delaware Water Gap National Recreation Area is near by and has much to offer in outdoor hikes and sights. Streams tumble off the Pocono plateau and rush through dark hemlock groves to the river. Watch the watershed in action at Dingmans Falls, Raymondskill, or Childs Park.

Exit 23 of I-99
Blue Knob State Park [15]
South of Altoona
State Rate: $27-$29

(814) 276-3576

http://www.dcnr.state.pa.us/
stateparks/parks/blueknob.aspx

Camp Accommodations

48 sun or shaded sites, 25 electric, 40 feet, dump station, reservations available. Amenities include ADA restroom/showers, potable water, grill, table, hiking, biking, fishing, swimming pool, environmental education, watchable wildlife, pet friendly (selected sites).

Directions

12.5 miles from I-99. From Exit 23, turn east to the first intersection, then south and east on Hwy 164, for 8 miles to Hwy 3003/4035 (Blue Knob Rd). Turn south for 4.5 miles and in to the Park.

Points of Interest -

The Park is named for the majestic dome-shaped mountain. Overlooking the scenic Ridge and Valley Province to the east, Blue Knob has spectacular views. Unique photographic opportunities are available during low humidity weather and with changes of season.

Exits 61 or 62 of I-99
Black Moshannon State Park [16]
Northwest of State College
State Rate: $24-$26

(814) 342-5960

www.dcnr.state.pa.us/stateparks/
parks/blackmoshannon.aspx

Camp Accommodations

80 shaded sites, some ADA, many electric, 40 feet, dump station, reservations available. Amenities include ADA restroom/showers, potable water, laundry, grill, picnic table, hiking, biking, fishing, swimming/beach, pet friendly (some sites).

Directions

20 miles from I-99. From Exits 61/62 go northwest for 11.5 miles on Hwy 322 to Hwy 504, near north Phillipsburg. Turn east for 8.5 miles to the Park.

Points of Interest -

College Station has many cultural, entertainment, shopping, and dining opportunities. The presence of Penn State University opens up possibilities for campus programs open to the public plus an attractive place to walk and sightsee.

Exit 8 of I-380
Tobyhanna State Park [17]
Northeast of Tobyhanna
State Rate: $27-$29

(570) 894-8336

http://www.dcnr.state.pa.us/
stateparks/parks/tobyhanna.aspx

Camp Accommodations

140 shaded sites, some ADA, many electric, 45 feet, dump station, reservations available. Amenities include ADA restroom/showers, potable water, grill, picnic table, hiking, biking, fishing, swimming/beach, pet friendly (selected sites).

Directions

3 miles from I-380. At Exit 8 proceed to and turn east on Hwy 423, go 2.5 miles to the Park.

Points of Interest -

The list if things to do in the Poconos is too long to mention. Theaters, concerts, museums, shopping, dining . . its all there.

Go to -

http://www.800poconos.com/things-to-do/

SOUTH CAROLINA

From the Blue Ridge Mountains to the sand dunes of the Atlantic, South Carolina State Parks have much to offer. Discover forested mountains and towering water-falls, blackwater rivers and scenic inland lakes, white sand beaches and ancient island shores, American historic sites and cultural treasures. Find out specific information at -

http://www.southcarolinaparks.com/maps.aspx

RVers who are at least 65 years of age, legally blind or disabled, qualify for certain rate reductions at selected Parks.

Pets must be on a leash up to 6 feet or other physical restraint at all times.

Depending on services, the basic camping fee (before extra fees, if any) will be $7-$28.

Reservations at state parks may be made up to 11 months in advance. There are three ways to make reservations at South Carolina State Parks:

- Call toll free 1-866-345-7275;
- Online at SouthCarolinaParks.com;
- At the park of your choice, by calling the park directly.

[1] **Aiken State Natural Area**
N33 33.024 W81 29.365
[2] **Sesquicentennial State Park**
N34 06.148 W80 54.641
[3] **Lee State Natural Area**
N34 12.263 W80 10.487
[4] **Croft State Natural Area**
N34 53.495 W81 52.282
[5] **Givhans Ferry State Park**
N33 01.638 W80 23.112
[6] **James Island County Park**
N32 44.157 W79 58.949
[7] **Lake Wateree State Recreation Area**
N34 25.849 W80 52.229

[8] **Chester State Park**
N34 41.010 W81 14.932
[9] **Lake Hartwell State Recreation Area**
N34 29.585 W83 01.673
[10] **Coneross Campground**
N34 35.559 W82 53.547
[11] **Paris Mountain State Park**
N34 55.512 W82 21.919
[12] **Colleton State Park**
N33 03.657 W80 36.955
[13] **Little Pee Dee State Park**
N34 19.764 W79 17.035

NOTES:

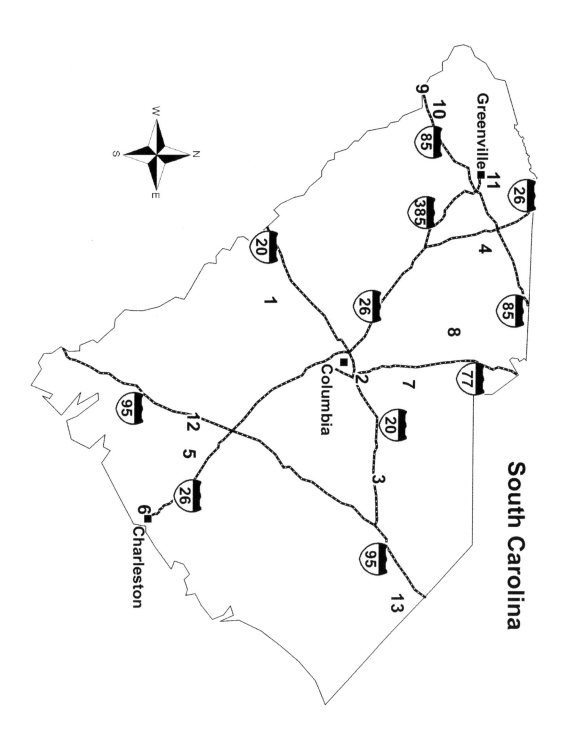

Exit 22
Aiken State Natural Area [1]
Northeast of Augusta, GA
State Rate: $12-$14

(803) 649-2857

http://www.southcarolinaparks.com/
park-finder/state-park/1831.aspx

Camp Accommodations

25 shaded sites, all electric/water, 45 feet, 2 pull through, dump station, reservations available. Amenities include restroom/showers, grill, picnic table, hiking, biking, fishing, watchable wildlife, pet friendly.

Directions

26 miles from I-20. From Exit 22, go south for 8 miles on Hwy 1 to Aiken. Turn east (left) on Hwy 78 for 13 miles to State Park Rd. turn north (left), go 5 miles to the Park.

Points of Interest -

Spring is a wonderful time to see the beautiful South Fork of the Edisto River. From its broad parkways to rambling "cottages," Aiken is one of the most picturesque communities in the southeast. Augusta, GA is also close, with many sites and events to enjoy.

Exit 74
Sesquicentennial State Park [2]
Northeast of Columbia
State Rate: $16-$18

(803) 788-2706

http://www.southcarolinaparks.com/
park-finder/state-park/469.aspx

Camp Accommodations

84 shaded sites, all electric/water, 40 feet, 14 pull through, dump station, reservations available. Amenities include ADA restroom/showers, grill, picnic table, hiking, biking, fishing, watchable wildlife, pet friendly.

Directions

3 miles from I-20. From Exit 74 turn northeast (left) for 3 miles on Hwy 1 (Two Notch Rd.) The Park will be on the right.

Points of Interest -

There is 2-acre dog park, fenced-in, for dogs to run off-leash. The Columbia area offers a variety of year-round attractions. You'll find historical & cultural attractions, festivals, parks & sporting events. Browse over 80 Columbia attractions at www.columbiacvb.com/attractions/

Exit 123
Lee State Natural Area [3]
West of Florence
State Rate: $12-$13

(803) 428-5307

http://www.southcarolinaparks.com/
park-finder/state-park/891.aspx

Camp Accommodations

25 shaded sites, all electric/water, 40 feet, dump station, reservations available. Amenities include ADA restroom/showers, grill, picnic table, hiking, biking, fishing, watchable wildlife, pet friendly.

Directions

1 mile from I-20. From Exit 123 turn north for 1 mile on Cty Rd 22 (Lee State Park Rd) to Loop Rd and the Park on the left.

Points of Interest -

If engines and speed are your thing then Florence and the Pee Dee Region is for you, with Darlington Raceway, Florence Motor Speedway and the annual Pee Dee Air Show. Bargain hunters will enjoy the Pee Dee State Farmers' Market and the Florence Flea Market for deals galore.

Exit 22
Croft State Natural Area [4]
Southeast of Spartanburg
State Rate: $14

(864) 585-1283

http://www.southcarolinaparks.com/
park-finder/state-park/1443.aspx

Camp Accommodations

45 shaded sites, all electric/water, 45 feet, 6 pull through, dump station, reservations available. Amenities include restroom/showers, grill, picnic table, hiking, biking, fishing, watchable wildlife, pet friendly.

Directions

9 miles from I-26. From Exit 22, go 1 mile east on Hwy 296 (Reidville Rd) to Hwy 295 (Southport Rd). Turn right and follow Southport for 6 miles to Hwy 56 (Cedar Springs Rd). Turn right, go 2 miles to Dairy Ridge Rd. Turn left in to the Park.

Points of Interest -

In the foothills of the Blue Ridge Mountains, Spartanburg has top museums, a thriving art community, unique boutique & antique shopping. Start at the Spartanburg Regional History Museum, then drive the Historic Hampton Heights Neighborhood & visit the Hub City Train Museum.

Exit 187
Givhans Ferry State Park [5]
West of Summerville
State Rate: $14

(843) 873-0692

http://www.southcarolinaparks.com/
park-finder/state-park/1219.aspx

Camp Accommodations

22 shaded sites, all electric/water, 45 feet, dump station, reservations available. Amenities include restroom/showers, grill, picnic table, hiking, biking, fishing, watchable wildlife, pet friendly.

Directions

13 miles from I-26. From Exit 187, go 1 mile south on Hwy 27 to Hwy 78. Turn left, go 0.4 miles, then turn right on Hwy 27. Follow Hwy 27 for 8 miles to Hwy 61. Turn right, go 3.1 miles to Givhans Ferry Road. Turn right to the Park entrance.

Points of Interest -

From June through December, Charleston hosts a variety of public festivals and events. Experience destinations like Ft. Sumter or The Battery. For ideas & details go to - ww.charlestoncvb.com/visitors/.

Also see [6].

Exit 220
James Island County Park [6]
Southwest side of Charleston
County Rate: $48

(843) 795-7275

http://www.ccprc.com/index.aspx?
nid=68

Camp Accommodations

124 shaded, paved ADA sites, full hook-ups, 45 feet, pull through, dump station, reservations available. Amenities include restroom/showers, grill, picnic table, hiking, biking, fishing, store, laundry, Wi-Fi, pet friendly with off-leash area.

Directions

7 miles from I-26. From Exit 220, take Hwy 17S, 1.5 miles to the Lockwood Blvd. exit. Turn left, then bare right to take the Scarborough Bridge and join Hwy 30W for 2.7 miles to Hwy 171 (Folly Rd). Turn left for 1.1 miles to Camp Rd. Turn right, go 0.8 miles to Riverland Dr. Turn right, go 0.2 miles to the Park entrance.

Points of Interest -

Charleston is probably the top travel destination on the east coast. Walk the French Quarter and Battery. Bring your camera! Go to the Mount Pleasant Farmers Market. Visit Boone Hall. Enjoy sea food and wine.

Also see [5].

Exit 41
Lake Wateree State Recreation Area [7]
North of Columbia
State Rate: $16-$19

(803) 482-6401

http://www.southcarolinaparks.com/
park-finder/state-park/936.aspx

Camp Accommodations

72 shaded, paved sites, all electric/
water, 40+ feet, 5 pull through, some
waterfront, dump station, reservations
available. Amenities include restroom/
showers, grill, picnic table, hiking, biking, fishing, watchable wildlife, pet
friendly.

Directions

10 miles from I-77. From Exit 41 turn east
for 2.4 miles on Old River Rd to Hwy 21.
Turn north (left) and go 2.1 miles to Hwy
101 (River Rd). Turn east (right), go 5.1
miles to State Park Rd. Turn left to the
Park.

Points of Interest -

Camden & Kershaw County are places
where tradition mingles with the fast-paced
world of steeplechase racing & other recreational offerings. Whether it's historic
sightseeing, antique shopping, fine dining
or joining the crowds at the Catfish Stomp
Festival, this area is first rate.

Exit 65
Chester State Park [8]
Southwest of Chester
State Rate: $14

(803) 385-2680

http://www.southcarolinaparks.com/
park-finder/state-park/1564.aspx

Camp Accommodations

20 shaded sites, all electric/water, 35
feet, 5 pull through, dump station,
reservations available. Amenities include ADA restroom/showers, grill,
picnic table, hiking, biking, fishing,
watchable wildlife, pet friendly.

Directions

14 miles from I-77. From Exit 65 go west
for 9.5 miles on Hwy 9 to the Chester Hwy
9/72/121 Bypass. Go southwest for 3
miles to Hwy 72/121. Turn southwest for
1.4 miles to State Park Rd.

Points of Interest -

Discover the charm of the true South in
South Carolina's 'Olde English District.'
Visit antique stores, artists studios, and
numerous historic sites. A few 'must sees'
are the Hill Plantation State Historic Site &
Gist Mansion, Historic Brattonsville, and
the South Carolina Railroad Museum.

Exit 1
Lake Hartwell State Recreation Area [9]
West of Anderson
State Rate: $16-$19

(864) 972-3352

http://www.southcarolinaparks.com/
park-finder/state-park/927.aspx

Camp Accommodations

115 shaded, paved, waterfront sites, 4 ADA, all electric/water, 40 feet, 8 pull through, dump station, reservations available. Amenities include ADA restroom/showers, grill, picnic table, hiking, biking, fishing, Visitors Center, store, pet friendly.

Directions

0.4 miles from I-85. From Exit 1, go northwest for 0.4 miles to the Park entrance on the left.

Points of Interest -

The Parks main attraction is fishing, with a reputation for excellent angling. The lakefront park's information center displays a wide variety of vintage fishing equipment. This location is a gateway to South Carolina's mountain country on the Cherokee Foothills National Scenic Highway.

Exit 11
Coneross Campground [10]
Northwest of Anderson
COE Rate: $14-$22
America/Beautiful Rate: $7-$11

(888) 893-0678

http://www.recreation.gov/

Camp Accommodations

106 shaded sites, many waterfront, 1 ADA, most electric/water, 45 feet, 36 pull through, dump station, reservations available. Amenities include restroom/showers, grill, picnic table, potable water, hiking, biking, fishing, swimming, pet friendly.

Directions

8 miles from I-85. From Exit 11, go 6 miles north on Hwy 24, through Townville, to Hwy 37/184. Turn right, go 0.6 miles to Coneross Creek Rd. turn right, go 1 mile to the camp.

Points of Interest -

Pendleton boasts an entire district on the National Register of Historic Places. The charming community offers the opportunity to dine, shop and step back in time with guided tours of the nearby antebellum plantations such as Woodburn and Ashtabula.

Exit 51
Paris Mountain State Park [11]
North of Greenville
State Rate: $14-$15

(864) 244-5565

http://www.southcarolinaparks.com/
park-finder/state-park/722.aspx

Camp Accommodations

39 shaded, paved sites, all electric/water, 40 feet, 4 pull through, dump station, reservations available. Amenities include ADA restroom/showers, grill, picnic table, hiking, biking, fishing, swimming, watchable wildlife, pet friendly.

Directions

10 miles from I-85. From Exit 51, go 3.5 miles north on I-385 to exit 40. Exit north on Hwy 291 (N. Pleasantburg Rd), go 2.5 miles to Piney Mountain Rd. Turn right, go 1.3 miles to Hwy 253 (Paris Mountain Rd). Turn right, go 1.2 miles to Cty Rd 344. Bare left for 0.8 miles to the Park.

Points of Interest -

In the Greenville area, experience breathtaking views and Southern charm, from the Liberty Bridge, a 355 foot pedestrian walkway overlooking the historic waterfalls in the heart of downtown, to panoramic views from the mountains. Visit museums, shop, enjoy fine eateries.

Exit 68
Colleton State Park [12]
North of Walterboro
State Rate: $14

(843) 538-8206

http://www.southcarolinaparks.com/
park-finder/state-park/1876.aspx

Camp Accommodations

25 shaded, sites, all electric/water, 40 feet, 3 pull through, dump station, reservations available. Amenities include ADA restroom/showers, grill, picnic table, hiking, biking, fishing, pet friendly.

Directions

3 miles from I-95. From Exit 68, go southeast for 2.8 miles on Hwy 61 to Hwy 15 (Jefferies Hwy). Take Hwy 15 north (left) for 0.4 miles to the Park.

Points of Interest -

Walterboro is a town of summer tree-lined streets where quaint homes with broad porches are surrounded by centuries-old azaleas, camellias, and beautiful churches that date to the 18th century. Wander streets of antiques shops and restaurants. There's a farmers' market too.

Exit 193
Little Pee Dee State Park [13]
South of Dillon
State Rate: $12-$13

(843) 774-8872

http://www.southcarolinaparks.com/
park-finder/state-park/881.aspx

Camp Accommodations

32 shaded sites, all electric/water, 40+ feet, 4 pull through, dump station, reservations available. Amenities include restroom/showers, grill, picnic table, hiking, biking, fishing, watchable wildlife, pet friendly.

Directions

13 miles from I-95. From Exit 193 go southeast on Hwy 57/9 (through Dillon). Stay with Hwy 57 for 11 miles in all to Cty Rd 22 (State Park Rd). Go left for 2 miles to the Park on your right.

Points of Interest -

Dillon County is home to one of the most famous traveler stops on I-95. . . South of the Border, the unique Mexican-motif mini-resort. Take in the Dillon Motor Speedway, a 4/10 mile asphalt racetrack. Originally a dirt track, it was completely refurbished and reopened for the 2007 racing season.

SOUTH DAKOTA

Following the Lewis and Clark Trail? Do you enjoy old cabins, military forts, and prehistoric sites? The South Dakota state parks are the largest outdoor museums in the state. The State Park system is overseen by the South Dakota Game, Fish and Parks. You can find much information about the Parks statewide at -

http://www.sdgfp.info/Parks/index.htm

Your pet is allowed in parks. Pets should be kept on a leash no longer than 10 feet and you should not leave your pet alone.

There are two options for park entrance - an annual entrance license ($28, valid May to May) or daily licenses (available @ $4 per person or $6 per vehicle; not available at Custer).

Camping fees vary based on the facilities available at the individual park. Entrance fees are in addition to camping fees. Call the reservation line at (800) 710-CAMP (2267) or make reservations online at www.campSD.com. Reservations for accessible campsites, are available at the same number. There is a $7.70 per site non-refundable reservation fee (not applicable to South Dakota residents).

[1] **Union Grove (aka Union County) State Park**
N42 55.245 W96 47.134
[2] **Oakwood Lakes State Park**
N44 26.977 W96 59.305
[3] **Pelican Lake Recreation Area**
N44 50.846 W97 12.530
[4] **Roy Lake State Park**
N45 42.200 W97 25.178

[5] **Spearfish Campground**
N44 28.849 W103 51.573
[6] **Pactola Campground**
N44 03.558 W103 29.854
[7] **Cedar Pass Campground**
N43 44.787 W101 56.909
[8] **Lake Mitchell Campground**
N43 44.081 W98 01.560
[9] **Big Sioux Recreation Area**
N43 34.358 W96 35.665

NOTES:

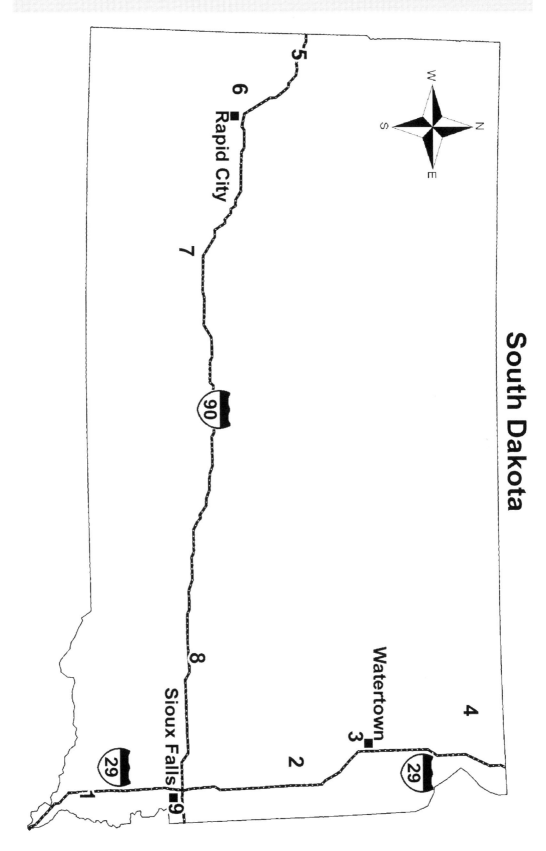

South Dakota

Exits 31 or 38
Union Grove (aka Union County)
State Park [1]
South of Beresford
State Rate: $10-$14

(605) 987-2263

http://www.sdgfp.info/Parks/Regions/
Heartland/UnionGrove.htm

Camp Accommodations

25 shaded sites, 17 electric, 45 feet, dump station (at exit 29 rest area), reservations available. Amenities include restrooms/showers, potable water, grill, table, biking, pet friendly.

Directions

3 or 5 miles from I-29. **Northbound**, from Exit 31, go east 0.4 miles to Cty Rd 1. Turn north 4.4 miles to the Park. **Southbound**, from Exit 38, go east 0.4 miles to Cty Rd 1. Turn south 2.2 miles to the Park.

Points of Interest -

Climb Sprit Mound (Paha Wakan), where Lewis and Clark had heard of legends of little spirits. Tour W. H. Over Museum, which features exhibits of life in the upper Midwest. Visit the Austin-Whittemore House. Admission is free to this 1883 Italian villa filled with Victorian furnishings.

Exit 140
Oakwood Lakes State Park [2]
Northwest of Brookings
State Rate: $12-$16

(605) 627-5441

http://www.sdgfp.info/Parks/Regions/
GlacialLakes/OakwoodLakes.htm

Camp Accommodations

135 shaded sites, 2 ADA, all electric, 45 feet, dump station, reservations available. Amenities include restrooms/showers, potable water, grill, table, hiking, fishing, biking, swimming, disc golf, game equipment checkout, pet friendly.

Directions

13 miles from I-29. From Exit 140, go west for 11 miles on Hwy 30 (204th St, becomes Cty Rd 6) to Oakwood Shoreline Dr. Turn north for 2 miles to the Park.

Points of Interest -

Brookings boasts a downtown with beautiful historic buildings, great shops and restaurants. Join costumed guides to discover Laura Ingalls Wilder with a visit to "The Little Town on the Prairie", in De Smet; including The Loftus Store, and the store from the Wilder's Book, The Long Winter.

Exit 177
Pelican Lake Recreation Area [3]
West of Watertown
State Rate: $16

(605) 882-5200

http://www.sdgfp.info/Parks/Regions/
GlacialLakes/PelicanLake.htm

Camp Accommodations

76 shaded, sites, many waterfront, 1 ADA, all electric, 45 feet, dump station, reservations available. Amenities include restrooms/showers, potable water, grill, table, hiking, fishing, biking, archery, swimming/beach, game equipment checkout, pet friendly.

Directions

12 miles from I-29. From Exit 177, go west for 8.3 miles on Hwy 212 (9th Ave) to 449th Ave (Thompson Point). Turn south for 3 miles to 175th St. Turn east 1 mile to 450th Ave, then turn north in to the Park.

Points of Interest -

Naturalists will enjoy the migrating birds and vast numbers of prairie grasses and wildflowers at the Park. Visit the Terry Redlin Art Center. Mr. Redlin is one of the country's most widely collected painters of wildlife and Americana. Tour the Mellette House, home of the state's first governor.

Exit 232 of I-29
Roy Lake State Park [4]
South of Lake City
State Rate: $12-$16

(605) 448-5701

http://www.sdgfp.info/Parks/Regions/
GlacialLakes/RoyLake.htm

Camp Accommodations

102 shaded sites, 1 ADA, most electric, 45 feet, 1 pull through, dump station, reservations available. Amenities include restrooms/showers, potable water, grill, table, hiking, fishing, biking, swimming, disc golf, game equipment checkout, pet friendly.

Directions

24 miles from I-29. From Exit 232 go west for 22.4 miles on Hwy 10 (119th St, Walnut St) to where Hwy 25 turns south. Go south on Hwy 25 for 1 mile to Northside Dr. (Roy Lake Rd). Turn west to Park Number 2 (East Campground).

Points of Interest -

East Roy is smaller and more secluded than West Roy. Roy Lake is known for its excellent walleye, bass, panfish, and pike fishing. The earliest know inhabitants of Roy Lake were members of the Woodland Culture. Artifacts dating between 900 and 1300 A.D. have been found near the park.

Exit 12 of I-90
Spearfish Campground [5]
South side of Spearfish
City Rate: $18-$33

(605) 642-1340

http://www.spearfishparksandrec.com/
campground/index.html

Camp Accommodations

212 shaded sites, 61 full hook ups, some riverfront, 40+ feet, dump station, reservations available. Amenities include restrooms/showers, potable water, grill, table, walking, biking, cable and Wi-Fi, pet friendly.

Directions

1.5 miles from I-90. From Exit 12 go west 0.7 miles on Jackson Blvd. to Canyon St. Turn left and go 0.7 miles south, past the Spearfish City Park and across the bridge to the Campground.

Points of Interest -

Downtown Spearfish is within walking distance of the campground. You'll find public laundry facilities, grocery and hardware stores, the D.C. Booth Historic Fish Hatchery and the Matthews Opera House. This is a great base camp for touring the Black Hills and Mt. Rushmore.

Exit 55 of I-90
Pactola Reservoir Campground [6]
West of Rapid City
Black Hills NF Rate: $16-$21
America/Beautiful Rate: $8-$11

(605) 574-4402

http://www.recreation.gov/

Camp Accommodations

57 shaded sites, dry camping, 38 feet, 7 pull through, reservations available. Amenities include ADA restrooms, potable water, grill, table, hiking, swimming/beach, biking, pet friendly. No Utilities.

Directions

24 miles from I-90. From Exit 55 go south for 2.3 miles on Highway 445 (Deadwood Ave) to Hwy 44 (Mountain View Rd). Go south, then west on Hwy 44 for 17 miles. Turn south for 2.8 miles on Hwy 385 to Custer Gulch Rd and go 1.4 miles to campground sign (Forest Rt. 545). Turn right, go 0.5 miles to the campground.

Points of Interest -

From the camp the following are within a day trip distance - Jewel Cave National Monument, Badlands National Park, Mt. Rushmore National Monument, Custer State Park, Crazy Horse Monument and Wind Cave National Park. The attractions and restaurants of Rapid City also beckon.

Exit 131
Cedar Pass Campground [7]
South of Cactus Flat
Badlands NP Rate: $8-14
America/Beautiful Rate: $4-$7

(605) 433-5233

http://www.badlands.national-park.com/camping.htm

Camp Accommodations

100 shaded pull over sites, dry camping, 40+, dump station. Amenities include ADA restrooms, potable water, table, hiking, biking, pet friendly. No Utilities.

Directions

8.5 miles from I-90. From Exit 131 go south for 8.5 miles on Hwy 240 to the Campground, which is located just past the Ben Reifel Visitor Center at the Hwy 377 turn.

Points of Interest -

Drive the Hwy 240 Loop Road. Take a trip down Sage Creek Rim Road to Robert's Prairie Dog Town, see wildlife and experience spectacular views of the park. Attend the Night Sky Program. Visit the new tipi village located between the Ben Reifel Visitor Center & the Cedar Pass Lodge.

Exit 330
Lake Mitchell Campground [8]
North side of Mitchell
City Rate: $15-$21

(605) 995-8457

http://www.cityofmitchell.org/park_rec/campground/index.htm

Camp Accommodations

70 shaded sites, from basic to full hook ups, 40+ feet, pull throughs, reservations available. Amenities include restrooms/showers, potable water, laundry, grill, table, biking, fishing, swimming, cable, pet friendly.

Directions

3.5 miles from I-90. From Exit 330 go 3.5 miles north on the Hwy 37 Bypass to Hwy 37, then north to the Park entrance.

Points of Interest -

The Mitchell Corn Palace was established in 1892. Early settlers displayed the fruits of their harvest on the building exterior in order to prove the fertility of South Dakota soil. The exterior decorations are completely stripped down and new murals are created each year.

Exit 406
Big Sioux Recreation Area [9]
East of Sioux Falls
State Rate: $12-$16

(605) 582-7243

http://www.sdgfp.info/Parks/Regions/Heartland/BigSioux.htm

Camp Accommodations

43 shaded sites, 1 ADA, most electric, 45 feet, dump station, reservations available. Amenities include restrooms/showers, potable water, grill, table, biking, fishing, archery range, disc golf, pet friendly.

Directions

3.5 miles from I-90. From Exit 406 go 2.9 miles south on Hwy 11 to Sioux Blvd. Turn right, go 0.3 miles to Park St. Turn left, go 0.3 miles to the Park entrance.

Points of Interest -

Sioux Falls is the largest city in South Dakota. Two Information Centers, located at Falls Park and at The Empire Mall, have information you need for your visit, including attraction and event information, maps, and brochures. Also visit -

http://www.siouxfallscvb.com/visitorInfo.cfm

TENNESSEE

The Tennessee State Parks were selected best in nation for 2007. The system is managed by the Department of Environment & Conservation. Their website, which has an excellent FAQ list, is -

http://tn.gov/environment/parks/

There are 33 RV friendly parks but only two take telephone reservations (Meeman Shelby and Rock Island). Reservations for campsites at selected parks can be made up to 11 months prior to check-in.

RV campsites are available for vehicles ranging in length from 20 to 76 feet. Most campsites maintain a soft gravel pad and each is equipped with water and electricity. Most parks have a centrally located dump station. Some parks offer drive through and waterfront locations.

Camping rates in Tennessee State Parks are standardized according to the facilities available. The standardized rates range from $8 (4 people) per night for primitive sites up to $25 (4 people) for premium sites. Typical campsites with water & electric are $20 per night for 4 people with additional people $1 each. There is no access fee charged for any state park.

Tennessee State Parks provides a year-round discount to all active duty U.S. military regardless of their branch of service or where they are stationed. Year-round camping discounts are available to residents and non-residents of Tennessee who are disabled. From April 1 through October 31 disabled campers will receive a discount of approximately 20% off base rates and from November 1 through March 31 the disability discount will be approximately 50% off base rates.

Dogs, cats and other pets are prohibited unless they are crated, caged or on a leash, or otherwise under physical restrictive control at all times.

There are also 14 sites that are classified either as National Cemeteries, Battlefields, Scenic Trails, Rivers, Areas or Parks in Tennessee.

[1] **Poole Knobs, J Percy Priest Dam**
N36 03.155 W86 30.741
[2] **Old Stone Fort State Park**
N35 29.668 W86 06.146
[3] **T.O. Fuller State Park**
N35 03.826 W90 07.081
[4] **Natchez Trace State Park**
N35 47.636 W88 15.947
[5] **Cedars of Lebanon State Park**
N36 05.637 W86 20.138
[6] **Floating Mill Campground**
N36 02.969 W85 45.137
[7] **Cumberland Mountain State Park**
N35 53.859 W84 59.576
[8] **Henry Horton State Park**
N35 35.379 W86 41.711
[9] **Harrison Bay State Park**
N35 10.072 W85 06.694
[10] **Cove Lake State Park**
N36 18.522 W84 12.669
[11] **Indian Mountain State Park**
N36 35.465 W84 08.541
[12] **Warriors' Path State Park**
N36 29.937 W82 29.237

NOTES:

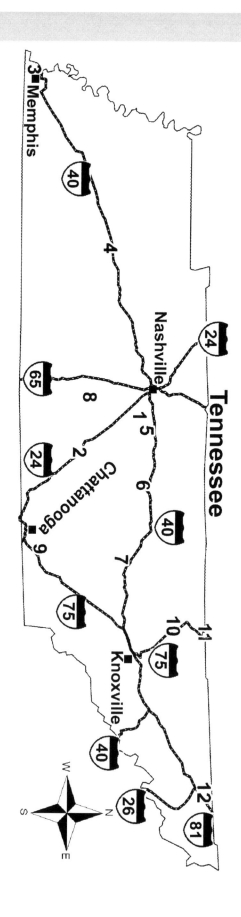

Exit 66 of I-24
Poole Knobs, J Percy Priest Dam [1]
Southeast of Nashville
COE Rate: $14-$24
America/Beautiful Rate: $7-$12

(615) 459-6948

http://www.recreation.gov/

Camp Accommodations

81 shaded sites, waterfront, 4 ADA, electric, 45 feet, 56 pull through, dump station, reservations available. Amenities include restroom/showers, potable water, grill, table, laundry, hiking, biking, fishing, pet friendly.

Directions

9 miles from I-24. From Exit 66, go 2.6 mi. northeast on Hwy 266 (Sam Ridley Pkwy). Exit north on to Hwy 41N (Murfreesboro Rd), go 1.3 mi. to Fergus Rd. Go right 1 mi. to Jones Mill Rd. Go right 4 mi. to Poole Knobs Camp on the left.

Points of Interest -

Nashville, 'Music City,' has much to see and many great venues, attractions, events, tours, shopping, restaurants and live entertainment. Visit this website for lots of ideas -

http://www.visitmusiccity.com/visitors/index

Exit 110 of I-24
Old Stone Fort State Park [2]
Northwest of Manchester
State Rate: $20

(931) 723-5073

http://www.state.tn.us/environment/
parks/OldStoneFort/index.shtml

Camp Accommodations

51 shaded, spacious sites, all electric/water, 40 feet, dump station. Amenities include restroom/showers, grill, picnic table, hiking, biking, fishing, golf, museum, watchable wildlife, pet friendly.

Directions

1.5 miles from I-24. From Exit 110 go 0.8 miles south on Hwy 53 (Woodbury Hwy) to Hwy 2/41. Turn west (right), go 0.7 miles to the Park entrance on your left. **Note, the bridge into the campground has a 36,000 pound weight limit!**

Points of Interest -

Old Stone Fort is a 2,000 year-old American Indian ceremonial site. Local sights include Jack Daniels Distillery; Cumberland Caverns; Historic Bell Buckle (a railroad village of restored Victorian homes and churches); and Foothills Crafts (the oldest artisan's guild in Tennessee).

Exit 1e of I-40 to I-240N
T.O. Fuller State Park [3]
Southwest of Memphis
State Rate: $20

(901) 543-7581

http://www.state.tn.us/environment/parks/
TOFuller/index.shtml

Camp Accommodations

45 shaded, spacious sites, all electric/water, 45 feet, dump station. Amenities include restroom/showers, grill, picnic table, laundry, hiking, biking, Nature Center, museum, swimming, golf, pet friendly.

Directions

12 miles from I-40. From Exit 1e of I-40 go south on I-240 for 5 miles to I-55N. Take I-55N 1.5 miles to exit 7 (Hwy 61). Go south on Hwy 61 (S 3rd. St) for 1.8 miles to Mitchell Rd. Turn west (right) and follow Mitchell Rd. for 3.6 miles in to the Park.

Points of Interest -

Within the Park you can visit the Chucalissa Indian Museum and/or play the 18-hole golf course. Memphis offers Graceland, the Home of Elvis Presley, including tours. Street corners are alive with music performances or go to downtown Memphis blues clubs. Don't forget to try the ribs!

Exit 116
Natchez Trace State Park [4]
Northeast of Lexington
State Rate: $25

(731) 968-3742

http://www.state.tn.us/environment/
parks/NatchezTrace/index.shtml

Camp Accommodations

77 shaded, spacious sites, full hook-ups, 45 feet, pull throughs, dump station. Amenities include restroom/showers, grill, picnic table, hiking, biking, fishing, store, laundry, swimming/beach, pet friendly.

Directions

0.5 miles from I-40. From Exit 116 go south on Hwy 114 (Camden Rd) for about 0.5 mile to the Park Office. The campground is a number of miles into the Park.

Points of Interest -

Of the three camping areas, the Pin Oak RV Campground is the primary location for RVs. Pin Oak Lodge is situated on the wooded shores of Pin Oak Lake. The Park Inn restaurant, regulation pistol firing range, archery range and assorted outdoor activities should keep everyone busy.

Exit 238
Cedars of Lebanon State Park [5]
South of Lebanon
State Rate: $20

(615) 443-2769

http://www.state.tn.us/environment/
parks/Cedars/#camping

Camp Accommodations

117 shaded, paved sites, electric/water, 40 feet, pull throughs, dump station. Amenities include restroom/showers, grill, table, hiking, biking, store, laundry, swimming pool, Nature Center, pet friendly.

Directions

6.3 miles from I-40. From Exit 238 go south on Hwy 10/231 (Murfreesboro Rd) for 6.3 miles to the Park.

Points of Interest -

Lebanon is nicknamed "The Antique City of the South" with over 20 antique stores in the county. Parkland Flea Market and Shopper's Alley are two flea markets that are open on weekends. Nashville Super-speedway is not far. Visit "Fiddler's Grove" and the Fessenden House.

Exit 273
Floating Mill Campground [6]
Southwest of Cookeville
COE Rate: $16-$24
America/Beautiful Rate: $8-$12

(931) 858-3125

http://www.recreation.gov/

Camp Accommodations

67 shaded sites, waterfront, some full hookups or electric, 45 feet, 4 pull through, dump station, reservations available. Amenities include ADA restroom/showers, potable water, grill, picnic table, laundry, hiking, biking, fishing, swimming, pet friendly.

Directions

4.5 miles from I-40. From Exit 273, go south on Hwy 56 (Smithville, then Cookeville Hwy) for 3.5 miles to Floating Mill Rd. Turn right, go 1 mile to the campground.

Points of Interest -

With many antique shops and bookstores, downtown Cookeville should keep you busy. You can buy contemporary and traditional crafts at the South's premier retailer of fine crafts. Stroll through history - visit the Cookeville History & Depot museums, or view beautiful historic architecture.

Exit 317 of I-40
Cumberland Mountain State Park [7]
South of Crossville
State Rate: $20-$25

(931) 484-6138

http://www.state.tn.us/environment/
parks/CumberlandMtn/index.shtml

Camp Accommodations

143 shaded, all electric/water, 14 have sewer, 40 feet, dump station. Amenities include restroom/showers, grill, picnic table, hiking, biking, fishing, store, laundry, swimming pool, pet friendly.

Directions

8.5 miles from I-40. From Exit 317 go south on Hwy 127, through Crossville, for 8.5 miles in all. Just past the Homestead Tower Center and Museum, turn right at Pigeon Ridge Rd in to the Park.

Points of Interest -

Visit the Homestead Tower Center and Museum. Shop the Cumberland General Store. Take in a play at the Cumberland County Playhouse Theatre. Golfers will want to try the Bear Trace at Cumberland Mountain. Cumberland Mountain Restaurant is noted for it's Friday catfish dinner.

Exit 46 of I-65
Henry Horton State Park [8]
East of Columbia
State Rate: $20

(931) 364-2222

http://www.state.tn.us/environment/
parks/HenryHorton/index.shtml

Camp Accommodations

56 shaded sites, all electric/water, 40 feet, pull throughs, dump station. Amenities include restroom/showers, grill, picnic table, hiking, biking, fishing, golf, swimming pool, gift shop, watchable wildlife, pet friendly.

Directions

12.5 miles from I-65. From Exit 46, travel 3.8 miles east on Hwy 99/412 to Hwy 431. Turn south and travel 0.7 miles to Hwy 99. Turn east again for 7.5 miles to where 99 dead-ends at Hwy 31A. Turn south, go 0.7 miles to the Park entrance on the left.

Points of Interest -

The Park, located on the former estate of the late Henry H. Horton, 36th governor of Tennessee, is well known for its championship 18 hole golf course, Inn, campgrounds and trap & skeet range. Henry Horton Restaurant is said to serves an outstanding southern cuisine buffet.

Exit 4 of I-75
Harrison Bay State Park [9]
West of Cleveland
State Rate: $25

(423) 344-6214

http://www.state.tn.us/environment/
parks/HarrisonBay/index.shtml

Camp Accommodations

128 shaded sites, all electric/water, 45 feet, some pull through, dump station. Amenities include restroom/showers, grill, picnic table, hiking, biking, fishing, swimming pool, golf, store, pet friendly.

Directions

13.5 miles from I-75. From Exit 4 go northwest for 4.1 miles on Hwy 153 to Hwy 58 (exit 5). Drive northeast (right) for 8.3 miles to Harrison Bay Road. Turn left, go 1 mile to the Park entrance on the left.

Points of Interest -

Try the Chattanooga River Walk (aka Tennessee Riverpark). Visit the Tennessee Aquarium, one of the top aquariums in the USA. Railroaders will want to see the 48 Victorian train cars at the Chattanooga Choo Choo complex. Lookout Mountain is minutes from downtown Chattanooga.

Exit 134 of I-75
Cove Lake State Park [10]
Northeast side of Caryville
State Rate: $20

(423) 566-9701

http://www.state.tn.us/environment/
parks/CoveLake/index.shtml

Camp Accommodations

101 shaded sites, electricity/water, 45 feet, pull throughs, dump station. Amenities include restroom/showers, grill, picnic table, hiking, biking, fishing, swimming pool, pet friendly.

Directions

0.8 miles from I-75. From Exit 134 go east and north for 0.8 miles on Hwy 9/63/25W (Veterans Memorial Hwy) to the Park entrance on the left.

Points of Interest -

Enjoy badminton, shuffleboard, horseshoes, ping-pong, tennis, and other activities including a paved walking and bicycling trail. Recreation equipment is available on a free checkout system. Hikers should try Devil's Race Track. At dinner time try Rickard Ridge BBQ in the Park

---

Exit 160 of I-75
Indian Mountain State Park [11]
West side of Jellico
State Rate: $20

(423) 784-7958

http://www.state.tn.us/environment/
parks/IndianMtn/index.shtml

Camp Accommodations

49 shaded, paved sites, 1 ADA, electric/water, 45 feet, dump station. Amenities include ADA restroom/showers, grill, table, hiking, biking, swimming pool, pedal boats, watchable wildlife, pet friendly.

Directions

2 miles from I-75 From Exit 160 go 0.9 miles northwest on Hwy 9/25W to State Hwy. 297 (S Main St). Turn left, go 0.3 miles then make a right on London, go 0.8 miles turn left on Indian Mountain State Park Circle. Proceed to the Park entrance.

Points of Interest -

Take a day trip to the Lenoir Museum Cultural Complex, which includes a Museum, an 18th Century Rice Grist Mill and Crosby Threshing Barn. The museum holds early American displays of thousands of items. Exhibits also include Appalachian artifacts & a pre-dam pictorial account of the area.

Exit 59 of I-81
Warriors' Path State Park [12]
Northwest of Colonial Heights
State Rate: $20

(423) 239-8531

http://www.state.tn.us/environment/
parks/WarriorsPath/index.shtml

Camp Accommodations

134 shaded sites, electric/water, 40 feet, dump station. Amenities include restroom/showers, grill, table, hiking, biking, fishing, horseback riding, swimming pool, disc golf, watchable wildlife, pet friendly.

Directions

3 miles from I-81 From Exit 59 go 1.2 miles northwest on Hwy 36 (Fort Henry Dr.) to Hemlock Rd. Turn right and go 1.6 miles to the Park.

Points of Interest -

The first country music recordings gave Bristol the title of 'Birthplace of Country Music.' Today you can still enjoy great live performances. The "World's Fastest Half Mile Track," Bristol Motor Speedway/Dragway are favorites for high-powered stock car and drag racing.

TEXAS

Texas State Parks are rich in natural beauty and cultural history. Texas has 11 eco-regions with a wide variety of landscapes, from lush forests to rugged canyons and mountains. Many State Parks feature spectacular lakes and rivers where you can go boating, fishing and swimming or just enjoy a relaxing float. Other parks offer wonderful trails for hiking, biking, birding and horseback riding.

Texas Parks and Wildlife Department oversee the State Park System. You will find comprehensive statewide information at their website -

http://www.tpwd.state.tx.us/spdest/

The websites for the individual Parks are extensive and should provide you with information to answer most questions.

The State Park System of Texas launched a new software system mid-year of 2010, as this book was being written. It has been reported that the online system, called TxParks, integrates customer-friendly features and is expected to improve the reservation functions for parks. A key benefit for RVers is people making online camping reservations will no longer pay the traditional extra $3 fee.

Daily entrance fees are charged in addition to the campsite fee. About half of all the Parks have Wi-Fi service. Pets are allowed at the Parks but must be on a leash no more than six feet long.

The Corps of Engineers has almost two dozen project locations in Texas and a number of those campgrounds are included in this chapter.

[1] **Hueco Tanks State Park & Historic Site** N31 55.628 W106 02.572	[15] **Potters Creek Campground** N29 54.483 W98 15.791
[2] **Balmorhea State Park** N30 56.732 W103 47.206	[16] **McKinney Falls State Park** N30 10.759 W97 43.275
[3] **Kerrville-Schreiner Park** N30 00.624 W99 07.253	[17] **Jim Hogg Park** N30 41.192 W97 44.791
[4] **Palmetto State Park** N29 35.838 W97 35.079	[18] **Union Grove - Stillhouse Hollow** N31 00.646 W97 37.244
[5] **Stephen F. Austin State Park** N29 48.723 W96 06.488	[19] **Midway Camp** N31 31.537 W97 13.602
[6] **Lake Colorado City State Park** N32 18.956 W100 56.123	[20] **Lake Whitney State Park** N31 55.815 W97 21.498
[7] **Lake Mineral Wells State Park** N32 48.874 W98 02.535	[21] **Ray Roberts Lake State Park - Isle du Bois Unit** N33 21.931 W97 00.809
[8] **Holiday Campground** N32 37.092 W97 29.823	[22] **Hickory Creek Park** N33 06.883 W97 02.346
[9] **Cedar Hill State Park** N32 37.339 W96 58.780	[23] **Padre Island National Seashore** N27 28.615 W97 16.918
[10] **Tyler State Park** N32 28.914 W95 16.832	[24] **Lake Corpus Christi State Park** N28 03.323 W97 52.081
[11] **Palo Duro Canyon State Park** N34 59.078 W101 42.096	[25] **Galveston Island State Park** N29 11.863 W94 57.440
[12] **East Fork Campground** N33 02.122 W96 30.940	[26] **Cagle Recreation Area** N30 31.611 W95 35.238
[13] **Cooper Lake (So. Sulphur) State Park** N33 17.199 W95 39.441	[27] **Fairfield Lake State Park** N31 45.920 W96 04.328
[14] **Clear Springs/Wright Patman Lake** N33 21.506 W94 11.181	[28] **Waxahachie Creek Park** N32 17.592 W96 41.476

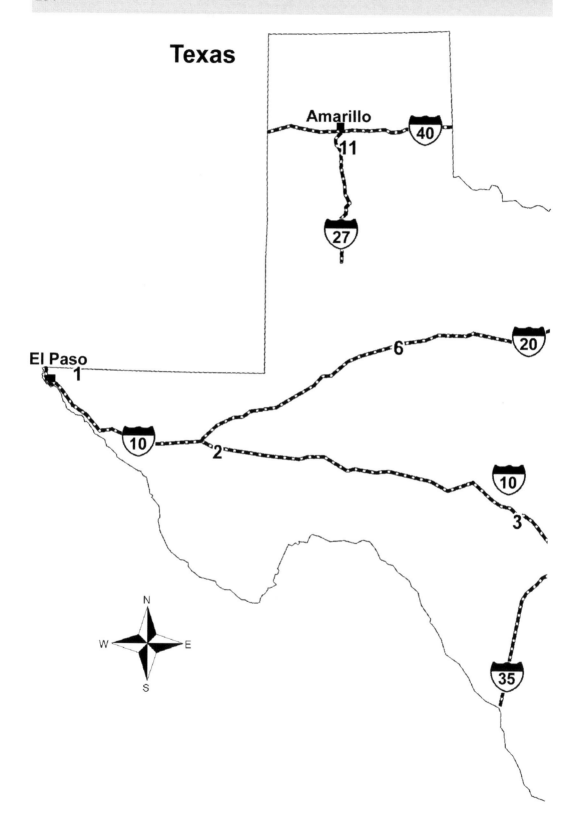

Texas

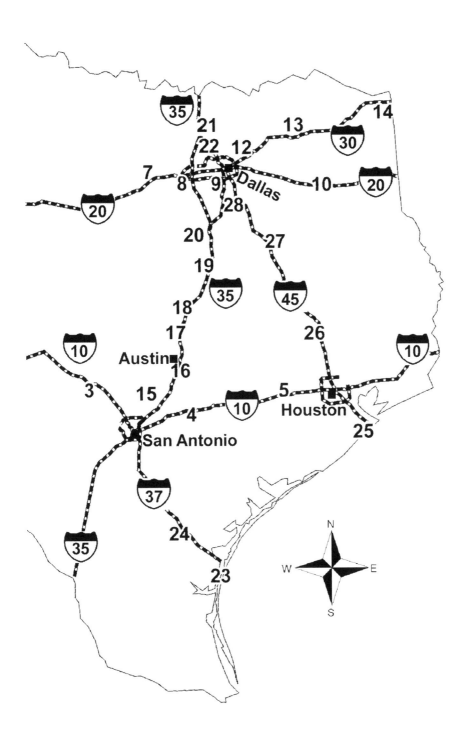

Exit 23
**Hueco Tanks State Park
& Historic Site [1]
Northeast of El Paso
State Rate: $12-$16**

(915) 857-1135

http://www.tpwd.state.tx.us/spdest/
findadest/parks/hueco_tanks/#fac

Camp Accommodations

20 shaded paved sites, Ramadas, 17 electric/water & 3 water, 40+ feet, dump station, reservations available. Amenities include restroom/showers, grill, table, hiking, biking, historic site/museum, Wi-Fi, store, pet friendly.

Directions

29 miles from I-10. From Exit 23 go north and east for 21.5 miles on Hwy 62/180 (Montana Ave) to Ranch Road 2775. Turn north for 7.5 miles to the Park entrance.

Points of Interest -

The Park's focus is a unique legacy of fantastic rock paintings. Archaic hunters & recent Native Americans have drawn strange mythological designs & figures on area rocks. For the protection of these resources, visitation is limited. Special reservations are required. Call ahead!

Exits 206 or 209
**Balmorhea State Park [2]
South of Balmorhea
State Rate: $11-$17**

(432) 375-2370

http://www.tpwd.state.tx.us/spdest/
findadest/parks/balmorhea/

Camp Accommodations

34 spacious, paved sites, 2 ADA, Ramadas, 28 electric/water & 6 water, 45 feet, 14 pull throughs, dump station, reservations available. Amenities include ADA restroom/showers, grill, table, hiking, biking, some cable, pet friendly.

Directions

6-7 miles from I-10. **Eastbound**, from Exit 206 go south 1.7 miles on Ranch Rd 2903 (I-10 Bus) to Hwy 17. Turn right, go 4.2 miles to the Park. **Westbound**, From Exit 209 go south 7 miles to the Park.

Points of Interest -

The Park's main attraction is a large artesian spring pool. Swimmers and scuba divers are welcomed. Two 'must visits' are the renowned McDonald Observatory and Fort Davis, one of the best surviving examples of an Indian Wars' frontier military post in the Southwest.

Exit 508
**Kerrville-Schreiner City Park [3]
South side of Kerrville
City Rate: $20-$26**

(830) 257-5392

http://www.kerrvilletx.gov/index.aspx?
nid=318

Camp Accommodations

62 shaded, sizable RV sites, all utility options, 45 feet, many pull throughs, dump station, reservations available. Amenities include ADA restroom/showers, grill, picnic table, laundry, hiking, biking, fishing, pet friendly.

Directions

5 miles from I-10. From Exit 508 go 0.2 miles to Hwy 534 (Memorial Pkwy). Turn left, go 4.3 miles to Hwy 173. Turn left, go 0.2 miles to the Park Headquarters and Registration, on the left

Points of Interest -

Kerrville has the Hill Country Arts Foundation, local craft shops, Museum of Western Art, Kerr Arts and Cultural Center, Kerrville Performing Arts Society and Callioux Theater. Also drive around Hill Country to Bandera, Boerne, Blanco, Fredericksburg, Ingram.

Exit 632 of I-10
Palmetto State Park [4]
Northwest of Gonzales
State Rate: $10-$18

(830) 672-3266

http://www.tpwd.state.tx.us/spdest/
findadest/parks/palmetto/

Camp Accommodations

41 shaded sites, all utility options, 45 feet, dump station, reservations available. Amenities include ADA restroom/showers, grill, table, hiking, biking, fishing, swimming, boat rental, Interpretive Programs, store, pet friendly.

Directions

4.3 miles from I-10. From Exit 632 go south for 2.5 miles on Hwy 183 (E Pierce St) to Cty Rd 261. Turn right, drive 1.8 miles to the Park entrance.

Points of Interest -

The Park is a "hot spot" for birding opportunities. In Gonzales tour the Old Jail Museum, the Pioneer Village Living History Center, and the Gonzales Memorial Museum. Luling offers a year-round Farmers' market, antique and collectible shopping, and dining (including a famous barbecue).

Exit 723 of I-10
Stephen F. Austin State Park [5]
West of Houston
State Rate: $15-$20

(979) 885-3613

http://www.tpwd.state.tx.us/spdest/
findadest/parks/
stephen_f_austin_and_san_felipe/

Camp Accommodations

78 shaded sites, 40 full hook-up, 38 water, 45 feet, many pull through, dump station, reservations available. Amenities include restroom/showers, grill, table, hiking, biking, fishing, golf course, pet friendly.

Directions

3 miles from I-10. From Exit 723 turn north for 2 miles on FM 1458. Go left on Park Road 38 for 1 mile to the Park Headquarters.

Points of Interest -

Walk the old town site of San Felipe, the fabled Cradle of Texas Liberty. Houston is close, with numerous attractions, such as Hermann Park Zoo, the Museum of Natural Science, & NASA. You could also visit the San Jacinto Battleground and Monument as well as the Battleship TEXAS.

Exit 210 of I-20
Lake Colorado City State Park [6]
South of Colorado City
State Rate: $12-$20

(325) 728-3931

http://www.tpwd.state.tx.us/spdest/
findadest/parks/lake_colorado_city/

Camp Accommodations

112 spacious paved sites, 78 electric/water, 34 water, 45 feet, 9 pull through, dump station, reservations available. Amenities include restroom/showers, grill, picnic table, hiking, biking, fishing, pet friendly.

Directions

5.7 miles from I-20. From Exit 210 go 5.7 miles south on FM 2836 (Lake Rd) to the Park entrance.

Points of Interest -

Colorado City is in the 'Heart of Texas.' Area attractions include Heart of West Texas Museum (where the prehistoric bison roamed), Heritage House, Ruddick Park, and numerous antique stores. Check out the Branding Wall. Walk the historic downtown.

Exit 386
Lake Mineral Wells State Park [7]
East of Mineral Wells
State Rate: $12-$25

(940) 328-1171

http://www.tpwd.state.tx.us/spdest/
findadest/parks/lake_mineral_wells/

Camp Accommodations

88 shaded sites, 77 electric/water & 11 water, 5 ADA, 40+ feet, dump station, reservations available. Amenities include ADA restroom/showers, grill, picnic table, hiking, biking, swimming, fishing, boat rental, Interpretive Programs, store, pet friendly.

Directions

19.5 miles from I-20. From Exit 386 turn north for 15 miles on Hwy 281 to Hwy 180 in Mineral Wells. Turn east for 4 miles to Park Rd 71. Turn north for 0. 5 miles in to the Park.

Points of Interest -

Go fossil collecting at the Mineral Wells Fossil Park. Visit the 35 acre Clark Botanical Gardens. Walk through the sandstone Old Jail Museum, built in 1882 and displaying dated artifacts of Palo Pinto County. Downtown, look for local flavor at one of the many antique shops.

Exit 429
Holiday Campground [8]
Southwest of Fort Worth
COE Rate: $20
America/Beautiful Rate: $10

(817) 292-2400

http://www.recreation.gov/

Camp Accommodations

103 shaded sites, 51 ADA, 79 electric/water, 45 feet, 40 pull through, dump station, reservations available. Amenities include ADA restroom/ showers, potable water, grill, table, hiking, biking, fishing, pet friendly.

Directions

7.5 miles from I-20. From Exit 429 go 5.7 miles south on Hwy 377 (Benbrook Dr) to S Lakeview Dr. Turn left, go 1.7 miles to the Park.

Points of Interest -

Fort Worth, the "City of Cowboys and Culture" offers an array of things to do from museums and galleries to great shopping and historic sites. To discover all you can and want to see, go to -
http://www.fortworth.com/visitors/
Also see [9]

Exit 457
Cedar Hill State Park [9]
South of Arlington & Grand Prairie
State Rate: $20

(972) 291-3900

http://www.tpwd.state.tx.us/spdest/
findadest/parks/cedar_hill/

Camp Accommodations

355 wooded sites, all electric/water, 40+ feet, dump station, reservations available. Amenities include ADA restroom/showers, grill, picnic table, hiking, biking, swimming, fishing, boat rental, bird watching, store, pet friendly.

Directions

4 miles from I-20. From Exit 457 go south for 3.7 miles on FM Rd 1382 (Belt Line Rd) to W Spine Rd. Turn right for 0.3 miles in to the Park.

Points of Interest -

A few area attractions include Dallas Museum of Art, Dallas Symphony, Dallas Opera, Billy Bob's Texas, horse racing at Lone Star Park, NASCAR racing at Texas Motor Speedway, Traders Village flea market, Farmers Market, and the JFK Memorial. **Also see [8]**

Exit 562 of I-20
Tyler State Park [10]
North of Tyler
State Rate: $17-$20

(903) 597-5338

http://www.tpwd.state.tx.us/spdest/
findadest/parks/tyler/

Camp Accommodations

77 shaded sites, 57 full hook up, 20 electric/water, 40+ feet, many pull through, dump station, reservations available. Amenities include ADA restroom/showers, grill, table, hiking, biking, fishing, swimming, boat rental, store, pet friendly.

Directions

2 miles from I-20. From Exit 562 go north for 2 miles on State Park Hwy to Park Rd 16. Turn left to the Park entrance.

Points of Interest -

Tyler's brick streets lead visitors to an array of attractions, quaint antique shops and unique specialty stores. Noted for its roses and festivals, Tyler also has Broadway and ballet performances, symphony concerts, world-class art museums and cuisine sure to please all.

Exit 106 of I-27
Palo Duro Canyon State Park [11]
South of Amarillo
State Rate: $22-$25

(806) 488-2227

http://www.tpwd.state.tx.us/spdest/
findadest/parks/palo_duro/

Camp Accommodations

79 shaded sites, electric/water, some Ramadas, 45 feet, many pull through, dump station, reservations available. Amenities include restroom/showers, grill, picnic table, hiking, biking, bird watching, Visitors Center, pet friendly.

Directions

10 miles from I-27. From Exit 106 turn east for 10 miles on Hwy 217 to the Park Headquarters.

Points of Interest -

In Amarillo visit the American Quarter Horse Hall of Fame, the Alibates Flint Quarries National Monument, or the Amarillo Botanical Gardens with acres of seasonal themed plantings surrounding the Mary E. Bivins Tropical Conservatory. For a fun dinner go to River Breaks Ranch.

Exit 68
East Fork Campground [12]
East of Plano
COE Rate: $18
America/Beautiful Rate: $9

(972) 442-3141

http://www.recreation.gov/

Camp Accommodations

50 lakefront sites, all electric/water, 45 feet, dump station, reservations available. Amenities include ADA restroom/showers, potable water, grill, table, hiking, biking, fishing, pet friendly.

Directions

13 miles from I-30. From Exit 68 go north on Hwy 205 (S Goliad St) for 8.1 miles to Hwy 78. Turn west, go 3.7 miles to Eubanks Lane. Turn north 0.4 miles, then bare right on Forrest Ross. Continue 0.5 miles north in to the campground.

Points of Interest -

Historic downtown Plano offers unique and one-of-a-kind stores and boutiques along its brick street. Stroll through Fairview Farms and Farmer's Market, experience the great taste of their fresh produce. Go to the Interurban Railway Museum, once a part of the Texas Electric Railway.

Exit 122
Cooper Lake (South Sulphur) State Park [13]
North of Sulphur Springs
State Rate: $14

(903) 945-5256

http://www.tpwd.state.tx.us/spdest/findadest/parks/cooper_lake/

Camp Accommodations

87 shaded, paved sites, all electric/water, 6 ADA, 40+ feet, pull throughs, dump station, reservations available. Amenities include ADA restroom/showers, grill, table, hiking, biking, swimming, fishing, birding, pet friendly.

Directions

17 miles from I-30. From Exit 122 travel north 11.5 miles on Hwy 19. Turn west for 4.2 miles on FM 71 to FM 3505. Go north for 1.5 miles to the park entrance.

Points of Interest -

In Sulphur Springs, shop for antiques on the Town Square, or find the item you desire in one of many factory direct stores. Festivals are a frequent occurrence. You'll want to look for local treasures at the frequent Farmer's Market and Flea Market on the Square.

Exit 220
Clear Springs/Wright Patman Lake [14]
Southwest of Texarkana
COE Rate: $10-$24
America/Beautiful Rate: $5-$12

(903) 838-8781

http://www.recreation.gov/

Camp Accommodations

114 shaded, paved sites, 87 electric, 5 ADA, 45 feet, dump station, reservations available. Amenities include ADA restroom/showers, potable water, grill, table, biking, fishing, swimming/beach, pet friendly.

Directions

11 miles from I-30. From Exit 220 go south on Hwy 59, staying with Hwy 59 as it bares right at S Lake St, for 8.1 miles in all to FM 2148. Turn right, go 1.4 miles to Clear Springs Rd. Turn left, go 1.5 miles to Clear Springs Park.

Points of Interest -

In Texarkana visit the Ace of Clubs house built in the shape of a playing card. Tour Historic Washington State Park. Music buff's will seek the mural of favorite son Scott Joplin. Check out the Perot Theater (an Italian Renaissance Theater built in 1924), & find Photographer's Island.

Exit 191
Potters Creek Campground [15]
North of New Braunfels
COE Rate: $18
America/Beautiful Rate: $9

(830) 964-3341

http://www.recreation.gov/

Camp Accommodations

114 paved sites, 50 ADA, many lake-front, all electric/water, 45 feet, dump station, reservations available. Amenities include ADA restroom/showers, potable water, grill, table, hiking, biking, fishing, swimming, birding, pet friendly.

Directions

23 miles from I-35. From Exit 191 go north on FM 306 for 20.5 miles to Potters Creek Rd. Turn south for 2.5 miles to the Campground.

Points of Interest -

You will enjoy this location, with numerous attractions like the San Antonio River Walk, the Alamo, Natural Bridge Caverns, Wonder World Cavern and Aquamarina Springs in San Marcos, or the Historic town of Gruene - 'gently resisting change since 1872.'

Exit 230
McKinney Falls State Park [16]
South of Austin
State Rate: $16-$20

(512) 243-1643

http://www.tpwd.state.tx.us/spdest/findadest/parks/mckinney_falls/

Camp Accommodations

81 shaded sites, all electric/water, 40+ feet, pull throughs, dump station, reservations available. Amenities include ADA restroom/showers, grill, picnic table, hiking, biking, fishing, Wi-Fi, pet friendly.

Directions

6 miles from I-35. From Exit 230 go east on Hwy 71/290 (Ben White Blvd) for 2.2 miles to Montopolis. Turn south (right) 0.5 miles to Burleson Rd. Turn left for 1.5 miles to McKinney Fall Pkwy. Turn right, go 1.8 miles to the Park entrance.

Points of Interest -

Enjoy Austin, the Live Music Capital of the World, a creative community filled with designers, painters, sculptors, dancers, filmmakers, musicians and artists of all kinds. The Botanical Gardens is 30 acres of themed gardens. Don't forget the best barbeque - ribs and a side of potato salad!

Exit 261
Jim Hogg Park [17]
North of Austin
COE Rate: $18
America/Beautiful Rate: $9

(512) 930-5253

http://www.recreation.gov/

Camp Accommodations

133 paved & shaded sites, many lake-front, all electric/water, 45 feet, dump station, reservations available. Amenities include ADA restroom/showers, potable water, grill, table, hiking, biking, fishing, pet friendly.

Directions

8 miles from I-35. From Exit 261 go north-west on FM 2338 (Williams Dr) for 5.6 miles to Jim Hogg Rd. Turn south for 1.7 miles to the park entrance. Cedar Breaks Park is another close by COE camp option.

Points of Interest -

Enjoy Austin, the Live Music Capital of the World, a creative community filled with designers, painters, sculptors, dancers, filmmakers, musicians and artists of all kinds. The Botanical Gardens is 30 acres of themed gardens. Don't forget the best barbeque - ribs and a side of potato salad!

Exit 286
Union Grove - Stillhouse Hollow [18]
Southwest of Belton
COE Rate: $16
America/Beautiful Rate: $8

(254) 947-0072

http://www.recreation.gov/

Camp Accommodations

30 paved sites, many lakefront, all electric/water, 45 feet, 4 pull through, dump station, reservations available. Amenities include ADA restroom/ showers, potable water, grill, picnic table, hiking, biking, fishing, swimming/beach, pet friendly.

Directions

8 miles from I-35. From Exit 286 go west for 6.5 miles on FM 2484 to Union Grove Park Road. Turn right, go 1 mile to the Park.

Points of Interest -

Visit Salado, the 'Best Art Town in Texas.' Main Street is a marketplace with over 60 shops and artists galleries. Find fine art, antiques, pottery, crafts, collectibles, Americana, southwest or south-of-the-border decor, handcrafted furniture, gourmet foods and wines.

Exit 330
Midway Camp [19]
Southwest side of Waco
COE Rate: $20
America/Beautiful Rate: $10

(254) 756-5359

http://www.recreation.gov/

Camp Accommodations

33 paved sites, many lakefront, 5 ADA, 11 full hook-ups, 22 electric/ water, 45 feet, 6 pull through, dump station, reservations available. Amenities include ADA restroom/ showers, potable water, grill, table, fishing, swimming, pet friendly.

Directions

6 miles from I-35. From Exit 330 go 5 miles west on Hwy 6 (TX Loop 340). Exit right at Midway Park exit on to Old Fish Pond Rd. Circle under the bridge and go 0.5 miles south, following the service road, to the Park.

Points of Interest -

Waco's 18 museums and attractions offer a unique, relaxing getaway. Enjoy the revitalized downtown and restored warehouse district with restaurants, clubs, and specialty shops, as well as the scenic River Walk along the Brazos River. See www.wacocvb.com/visitor.asp

Exit 368
Lake Whitney State Park [20]
Southwest of Hillsboro
State Rate: $12-$16

(254) 694-3793

http://www.tpwd.state.tx.us/spdest/ findadest/parks/lake_whitney/

Camp Accommodations

71 shaded sites, all water & 66 electric, 40+ feet, many pull throughs, dump station, reservations available. Amenities include ADA restroom/ showers, grill, table, hiking, biking, swimming, fishing, pet friendly. A small airstrip is not a noise problem.

Directions

18 mi. from I-35. From Exit 368 take Hwy 22/171 (Corsicana Hwy) west for 14 mi. to the east side of Whitney. Go straight at TX 180 Spur (W Jefferson Ave) for 0.6 mi. to S Colorado. Turn south for 0.4 mi. to W Lee Ave. Turn west, W Lee becomes FM 1224, go 2.4 mi. to the Park.

Points of Interest -

In Hillsboro, the campus of Hill College allows you to delve into history at the Texas Heritage Museum or to embrace the arts with the Performing Arts Series. From music to theater to jazz, Hill College offers free performances to arts enthusiasts.

Exit 479 of I-35
Ray Roberts Lake State Park - Isle du Bois Unit [21]
North of Denton
State Rate: $25

(940) 686-2148

http://www.tpwd.state.tx.us/spdest/
findadest/parks/ray_roberts_lake/

Camp Accommodations

115 paved, shaded sites, all electric/
water, 40+ feet, pull throughs, dump
station, reservations available.
Amenities include ADA restroom/
showers, grill, table, hiking, biking,
fishing, swimming, Wi-Fi, pet friendly.

Directions

11 miles from I-35. From Exit 479 go east
on FM 455 (Chapman Dr) for 10.5 miles.
Turn north on Parkway 4137 for 0.4 mile to
the Park.

Points of Interest -

Walk Denton's Courthouse Square. Enjoy
its music and innovative arts, history and
heritage - symptomatic if the energy of
college-town living mixed with family-
friendly festivals. Denton's restaurants,
concerts, shopping and tours will keep you
busy.

Exit 457 of I-35E
Hickory Creek Park [22]
North of Lewisville
COE Rate: $16-$18
America/Beautiful Rate: $8-$9

(469) 645-9100

http://www.recreation.gov/

Camp Accommodations

122 paved sites, some lakefront, 33
ADA, 1 full hook-up, 116 electric/
water, 45 feet, 10 pull through, dump
station, reservations available.
Amenities include ADA restroom/
showers, laundry, grill, table, fishing,
swimming, golf, pet friendly.

Directions

1 mi. from I-35E. **Northbound**, from Exit 457
go on frontage road, to N Denton Dr, take the
overpass and turn south on Stemmons to the
first right, Tuberville Rd. **Southbound**, from
Exit 457, go on to Stemmons to the second
right, Tuberville Rd. All travelers go 0.2 mi. to
Point Vista Rd, turn left, go 0.5 mi. to the Park.

Points of Interest -

Lewisville strikes a good balance between
small-town USA and urban. It's old-town
charm is still there when you see and visit
the antique shops, specialty stores, and
restaurants of Old Town Lewisville. Factor
in excellent shopping, fine dining and attractions and you have a nice day trip.

Exit 1c of I-37
Padre Island National Seashore [23]
Southeast of Corpus Christi
NPS Rate: $8
America/Beautiful Rate: $4

(361) 949-8068

http://www.nps.gov/pais/planyourvisit/
index.htm

Camp Accommodations

42 Gulf view sites, no hook-ups, water
filling station, 40+ feet, dump station.
Amenities include restroom/showers,
shade structures, picnic table, grills,
fishing, birding, biking, pet friendly. No
Utilities.

Directions

31 mi. from I-37. From Exit 1c go 4.7 mi.
south on Hwy 286 (Crosstown Expy) to
Hwy 358. Turn southeast, go 26 mi., follow
Hwy 358 (after crossing the JFK Causeway onto Padre Island, Hwy 358 changes
to Park Rd 22) to the Visitors Center.

Points of Interest -

Bring your beachcombing bucket, currents
that flow through the Gulf of Mexico bring
endless curiosities onto the beach. Bicycling is a popular activity in the park. With
more bird species that any other city in the
U.S., Corpus Christi has won the competi-
tion for being the Birdiest City in America.

Exit 34 of I-37
Lake Corpus Christi State Park [24]
Northwest of Corpus Christi
State Rate: $10-$20

(361) 547-2635

http://www.tpwd.state.tx.us/spdest/
findadest/parks/lake_corpus_christi/

Camp Accommodations

108 paved, shaded sites, 25 full hook-ups, 23 electric/water, 60 water, 40+ feet, pull throughs, dump station, reservations available. Amenities include ADA restroom/showers, grill, table, walking, biking, fishing, swimming, bird watching, pet friendly.

Directions

6 miles from I-37. From Exit 34 go southwest on Hwy 359 for 4.6 miles to Park Rd 25. Turn north for 1.2 miles to the campground.

Points of Interest -

In Corpus Christi, tour the USS Lexington, learn about "The Blue Ghost", check the Ship's store for some fine memorabilia and gift items. Walk Heritage Park and Cultural Center of historic Victorian homes. Try the Harbor Playhouse community theatre with a history of quality productions.

Exit 1 of I-45
Galveston Island State Park [25]
Southwest of Galveston
State Rate: $15-$25

(409) 737-1222

http://www.tpwd.state.tx.us/spdest/
findadest/parks/galveston/

Camp Accommodations

66 sites, shade shelters, 56 electric/water, 10 water, 40+ feet, dump station, reservations available. Amenities include ADA restroom/showers, grill, table, hiking, biking, fishing, swimming, bird watching, pet friendly.

Directions

11 miles from I-45. From Exit 1 turn south for 1.5 miles on 61st St to Seawall Boulevard (FM 3005). Turn west (right), go 9.5 miles, the road name changes to Termini-San Luis Pass Rd, to the park entrance at Park Rd 66.

Points of Interest -

Attractions in Galveston include numerous historical homes; the Railroad Museum; the Strand Historical District, where the Tall Ship Elissa (an 1877 sailing vessel) is moored; the Seaport Museum; and the Galveston County Museum. Space Center Houston is also nearby.

Exit 102 of I-45
Cagle Recreation Area [26]
South of Huntsville
Sam Houston NF Rate: $20
America/Beautiful Rate: $10

(361) 949-8068

http://www.nps.gov/pais/planyourvisit/
index.htm

Camp Accommodations

47 spacious, wooded, paved sites, 5 ADA, full hook-ups, 45 feet, dump station. Amenities include ADA restroom/showers, picnic table, grills, fishing, bird watching, biking, pet friendly.

Directions

6 mi. from I-45. From Exit 102 go west for 5.5 miles on FM 1375 to Kagle Rd. Turn south (left) 0.2 mile to the Recreation Area.

Points of Interest -

Visit Huntsville, Sam Houston's home town. Huntsville offers an array of places to explore - historic locations, prominent state institutions, antiques, all mixed with hometown hospitality. The small-town, historic flair of Huntsville brings new meaning to 'Texas Charm.'

Exits 197 or 198
Fairfield Lake State Park [27]
Northeast of Fairfield
State Rate: $12-$22

(903) 389-4514

http://www.tpwd.state.tx.us/spdest/
findadest/parks/fairfield_lake/

Camp Accommodations

135 spacious, shaded, lakefront sites, 96 electric/water, 35 water, 40+ feet, pull throughs, dump station, reservations available. Amenities include ADA restroom/showers, grill, picnic table, hiking, biking, fishing, swimming, bird watching, pet friendly.

Directions

8 miles from I-45. From either Exit 197 or 198 go 1.5 miles in to Fairfield, onto Commerce St, then proceed to Main St. Turn left on Main St (Ranch Rd 488), go 1.8 miles to Ranch Rd 2570/FM1124. Bare right, go 1.3 miles to Ranch Rd 3285, Bare right again, go 3.3 miles to Park Rd 64. Turn left in to the Park.

Points of Interest -

Visit the 'Texas State Railroad' which offers train excursions. Tour Old Fort Parker, a reconstructed fort that pays tribute to the Parker family & other pioneers who paid a high price to settle Texas. See Confederate Reunion Grounds State Historic Site, a gathering place for living history events.

Exit 247
Waxahachie Creek Park [28]
South of Ennis
COE Rate: $14-$18
America/Beautiful Rate: $7-$9

(972) 875-5711

http://www.recreation.gov/

Camp Accommodations

71 shaded sites, all electric/water, 45 feet, 14 pull through, dump station, reservations available. Amenities include ADA restroom/showers, grill, hiking, biking, boating, picnic table, pet friendly.

Directions

9 miles from I-45. From Exit 247 go 4.3 miles on Hwy 287 to the Bardwell Lake exit (Hwy 34). Turn west (left) onto Hwy 34 and travel 2.8 miles southwest to Bozek Rd. Turn right and travel 1.6 miles to the Waxahachie Creek Park entrance.

Points of Interest -

Ennis was established in 1872 and named after Cornelius Ennis, Director of the Houston & Texas Central Railroad. You will find Railroad Memorabilia, Crystal Exhibits, Rail Line China Exhibit, the Czech Heritage Exhibit, the National Polka Festival, and Bluebonnet flowers galore!

UTAH

Utah State Parks and Recreation manages 43 state parks. Their website, with all detailed information, is -

http://stateparks.utah.gov/about

Statewide, park restrooms and parking areas are accessible to those with physical challenges and limitations. Many of the parks have accessible ramps, camping, and showers.

Pets are allowed at most Utah State Parks. Pets are not allowed in buildings, on beaches, or in the lakes or reservoirs. Pets must always be on a maximum six-foot leash and never left unattended.

RV camping fees range from $10-$28 per night per site, which includes one RV, one vehicle and up to 8 people.

Individual campsite reservations are accepted up to 16 weeks in advance from park departure date. If campsites are available, reservations can be made a minimum of two days in advance of arrival date. An $8 non-refundable reservation fee is charged for each site reserved. Camping reservations can be made through the Reservations webpage (a contract with ReserveAmerica) or by calling (801) 322-3770 or toll-free at (800) 322-3770. To make online reservations go to -

http://utahstateparks.reserveamerica.com/

[1] **Snow Canyon State Park**
N37 12.169 W113 38.493
[2] **Cedar Canyon**
N37 35.476 W112 54.305
[3] **Little Cottonwood**
N38 15.304 W112 32.426
[4] **Yuba State Park (Oasis Camp)**
N39 22.618 W112 01.694
[5] **Utah Lake**
N40 14.230 W111 44.020

[6] **Anderson Cove**
N41 14.978 W111 47.192
[7] **Castle Rock**
N38 33.489 W112 21.304
[8] **Green River State Park**
N38 59.410 W110 09.289
[9] **Rockport State Park**
N40 45.170 W111 22.558

NOTES:

Utah

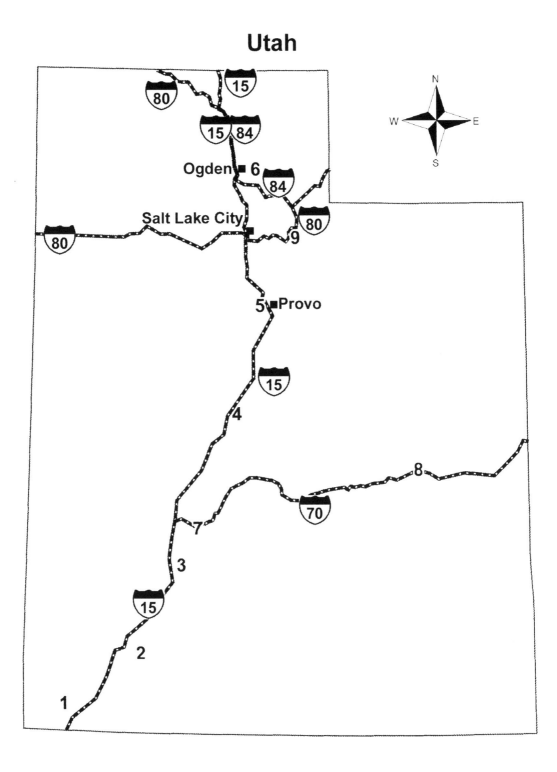

Exit 6
Snow Canyon State Park [1]
North of St. George
State Rate: $16-$20

(435) 628-2255

http://stateparks.utah.gov/parks/snow-canyon

Camp Accommodations

24 sites, electric/water or dry, 40 feet, 14 pull throughs, covered patios, dump station , reservations available. Amenities include ADA restrooms, showers, potable water, grill, table, hiking, biking, rock climbing, wildlife viewing, Visitors Center, pet friendly.

Directions

10 miles from I-15. From Exit 6 go north for 3.6 miles on Hwy 18 (Bluff Street). Turn west on Snow Canyon Parkway for 4 miles to Hwy 8 (Snow Canyon Drive). Take a right, go 2.6 miles to the south entrance of the park.

Points of Interest -

St. George is known as "Utah's Dixie" because of its temperate climate. You can golf year-round. Take an Historic Downtown Tour, enjoy a concert, see a play, visit an art museum or wildlife museum. See "real" dinosaur tracks. Stop by the Visitor's Center at the St. George Temple.

Exit 59
Cedar Canyon [2]
East of Cedar City
Dixie NF Rate: $12
America/Beautiful Rate: $6

(435) 865-3200

http://www.recreation.gov

Camp Accommodations

19 shaded, paved sites, dry camping, 40 feet, reservations available. Amenities include restrooms, potable water, grill, table, hiking, mountain biking, wildlife viewing, pet friendly. No Utilities.

Directions

14 miles from I-15. From Exit 59 go east for 0.9 miles on Hwy 56 (W 200 N St) to Hwy 130 (N Main St). Turn south, go 0.3 miles to Hwy 14 (E Center St). Go east 12.2 miles. Turn in to the left, just below the S curve.

Points of Interest -

The Camp is close to Cedar City, Cedar Breaks National Monument, Ashdown Gorge Wilderness and the Virgin River Rim Trail. Other attractions include Bryce Canyon National Park and Zion National Park. Rainbow Trout fishing is available for children at Kid's Pond at Woods Ranch.

Exits 109 or 112
Little Cottonwood [3]
East of Beaver
Dixie NF Rate: $14
America/Beautiful Rate: $7
(435) 438-2436

http://www.forestcamping.com/dow/intermtn/fishcmp.htm#little%20cottonwood

Camp Accommodations

13 shaded, paved sites, dry camping, 40+ feet, 1 pull through. Amenities include ADA restrooms, potable water, grill, table, fly fishing, pet friendly. No Utilities.

Directions

7.5 miles from I-15. From either Exit 109 or 112 turn east, go 1.7 miles on Hwy 160 in to Beaver. Turn east on Hwy 153 for 6.7 miles to the campground on the right.

Points of Interest -

Beaver County claims to have the most beautiful and varied scenery in the West. Notable sites to visit are the ghost towns of Frisco and Newhouse or the historic railroading and mining town of Milford. Walk around Beaver, the birthplace of Butch Cassidy.

Exit 202 of I-15
Yuba State Park (Oasis Camp) [4]
South of Nephi
State Rate: $10-$16

(435) 758-2611

http://stateparks.utah.gov/parks/yuba

Directions

4 miles from I-15. From Exit 202 go south for 4 miles on Hwy 78 to the campground on your left.

Camp Accommodations

28 sites, 1 ADA, electric/water or dry, 45 feet, 14 pull throughs, dump station, reservations available. Amenities include ADA restrooms/showers, potable water, grill, table, fishing, hiking, biking, swimming, watchable wildlife, pet friendly.

Points of Interest -

The warm waters and sandy beaches make this campground a great place to relax. When you walk along the reservoir you may find evidence of the ancient Native Americans that once lived in the area. Rock art, pieces of pottery, and stone tools are among items that have been found.

Exit 265 of I-15
Utah Lake [5]
West of Provo
State Rate: $20

(801) 375-0731

http://stateparks.utah.gov/parks/utah-lake

Directions

2.5 miles from I-15. From Exit 265 go west on Hwy 114 (W Center St) for 2.5 miles to the Park.

Camp Accommodations

47 paved sites, 2 ADA, 6 full hook up, 41 electric/water, 45 feet, 23 pull throughs, dump station, reservations available. Amenities include ADA restrooms/showers, grill, covered table, fishing, hiking, biking, swimming, watchable wildlife, pet friendly.

Points of Interest -

Take a drive to Robert Redford's rustic Sundance Resort. Explore Timpanogos Cave National Monument, with its colorful deposits, beautiful formations, and clear underground pools. Time out for some shopping at Cabela's is always interesting and fun.

Exit 344 of I-15/84
Anderson Cove [6]
East of Ogden
Cache NF Rate: $20
America/Beautiful Rate: $10

(801) 745-3215

http://www.recreation.gov

Directions

13 miles from I-15/84. From Exit 344 go 13 miles east on Hwy 39 (Ogden Canyon) to the campground on the left side of highway.

Camp Accommodations

45 partially shaded, paved sites, dry camping, 37 ADA, 40+ feet, reservations available. Amenities include ADA restrooms, potable water, fire ring, picnic table, fishing, swimming, store, pet friendly. No Utilities.

Points of Interest -

Visit Fort Buenaventura, the first permanent settlement by people of European descent in the Great Basin on Utah. Tour Hill Aerospace Museum on Hill Air Force Base. The Museum exhibits more than 90 military aircraft, missiles, and aerospace vehicles.

Exit 17 of I-70
Castle Rock [7]
Southwest of Richfield
Fishlake NF Rate: $13
America/Beautiful Rate: $7

(800) 322-3770

http://www.forestcamping.com/dow/
intermtn/fishcmp.htm#castle%20rock

Camp Accommodations

30 shaded sites, dry camping, 45 feet, 9 pull throughs, reservations available. Amenities include ADA restrooms, potable water, fire ring, picnic table, pet friendly. No Utilities.

Directions

1.3 miles from I-70. From Exit 17 go east and on to Forest Rt. 478 (gravel) and go 1.3 miles into the campground.

Points of Interest -

Fremont Indian State Park has a museum, excellent collection of rock art, and access to archaeological sites. Bullion Canyon (Canyon of Gold Driving Tour) will give RVers a chance to glimpse the life and times of the canyon's mines and miners.

Exits 160 or 164 of I-70
Green River State Park [8]
At Green River
State Rate: $16

(435) 564-3633

http://stateparks.utah.gov/parks/
green-river

Camp Accommodations

29 shaded paved sites, dry camping, 40+ feet, 6 pull throughs, dump station, reservations. Amenities include ADA restrooms, showers, potable water, grill, table, biking, golf, bird watching, pet friendly. No Utilities.

Directions

2-3 miles from I-70. **Eastbound**, from Exit 160 take I-70 Bus 1.7 miles in to Green River to Green River Blvd. **Westbound**, from Exit 164 take I-70 Bus 2.6 miles in to Green River to Green River Blvd. All travelers turn south for 0.4 miles to the Park.

Points of Interest -

Take day trips to Arches, Canyonlands, and Capitol Reef National Parks; or Dead Horse Point and Goblin Valley state parks and Horseshoe Canyon. Green River is situated near great scenery, world-class rafting, dinosaur fossils, and Native American rock art panels.

Exit 155 of I-80
Rockport State Park (5 camps) [9]
South of Wanship
State Rate: $10

(435) 336-2241

http://stateparks.utah.gov/parks/
rockport

Camp Accommodations

75 shaded sites, 6 ADA, some hook ups, 45 feet, 8 pull throughs, dump station, reservations available. Amenities include ADA restrooms, showers, potable water, grill, table, biking, fishing, swimming, bird watching, pet friendly.

Directions

5 miles from I-80. From Exit 155 go south for 5 miles on Hwy 32 to the Park.

Points of Interest -

Take the 'Echo Canyon' driving tour, near Coalville, with over 2 dozen notable sites to stop and see. Download the detailed brochure and read about the tour at -

http://www.summitcounty.org/history/
summit/driving_cities.pdf

VERMONT

The Vermont State Parks are managed by the Department of Forests, Parks, and Recreation. You can start you exploration of the state parks at -
http://www.vtstateparks.com/

Vermont State Parks are said to be natural in character and different than most public campgrounds or RV parks. The State says sites tend to be more private, though not specifically designed for pull-throughs, are charming and accessible. Sites will accommodate RV's from smaller trailers to rigs as large as 40 feet.

Vermont is a dry camping state. At this time there are no water, sewer or electric hookups in Vermont State Parks. Campgrounds within the parks are usually laid out in loops with water spigots located every few campsites, with centrally located restrooms, most with hot and cold running water and coin operated showers. There are dump stations and parks do allow some limited generator use. In Vermont terminology, tent and RV sites are the same thing. Each site has a fire ring or fireplace with grill for cooking and a picnic table. Most parks sell wood and ice and many have nature programs, performances and other events. Besides the fireplace or fire ring and picnic bench, sites are said to be roomy and level. Some sites are wooded and some open. Most campgrounds permit pets (10 foot leash) but some have specific pet loops.

Campsite fees typically run $18-$20. There is a pet fee of $1 per night per pet. Reservations can be made up to 11 months in advance, and the inventory for the entire month opens the first business day of the month. Reservations for dates 15 days or more in advance may be made online or through the Reservation Call Center at (888) 409-7579. The online reservation site is -

https://securevtstateparks.com/cgi-bin/parkCGI.py?postpage=startResv

During the parks operating season, reservations for dates 14 days or less in advance are made by calling the park directly. There is a $6 reservation fee. Most parks have first come, first serve sites.

[1] **Quechee State Park**
N43 38.229 W72 24.070
[2] **Little River State Park**
N44 23.382 W72 46.051
[3] **Grand Isle State Park**
N44 41.257 W73 17.689
[4] **Fort Dummer State Park**
N42 49.459 W72 34.000
[5] **Mt. Ascutney State Park**
N43 26.270 W72 24.344
[6] **Ricker Pond State Park**
N44 14.733 W72 15.227

NOTES:

Vermont

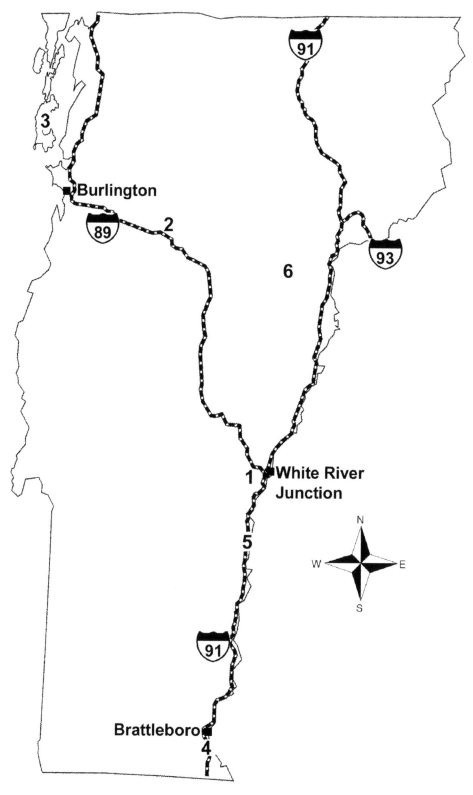

Exit 1
Quechee State Park [1]
West of White River Junction
State Rate: $18-$20

(802) 295-2990

http://www.vtstateparks.com/htm/
quechee.htm

Camp Accommodations

45 semi-shaded sites, 3 ADA, dry camping, 40 feet, dump station, reservations available. Amenities include restroom/showers, potable water, grill, table, hiking, biking, pet friendly. No Utilities.

Directions

2.5 miles from I-89. From Exit 1 go 2.2 miles southwest on Hwy 4 (Woodstock Rd) to the Park.

Points of Interest -

The Parks focal point is Vermont's deepest gorge. Visit Woodstock, a quaint village, called "the prettiest small town in America". Walk the village green, with a covered bridge in the middle of town, and stately homes. Browse unique shops, galleries, artisan studios, and country stores.

Exit 10
Little River State Park [2]
North of Waterbury
State Rate: $18-$20

(802) 244-7103

http://www.vtstateparks.com/htm/
littleriver.htm

Camp Accommodations

81 shaded sites, 2 ADA, dry camping, 40 feet, dump station, reservations available. Amenities include restroom/showers, potable water, grill, table, hiking, biking, fishing, swimming/beach, Interpretive Programs, museum, pet friendly. No Utilities.

Directions

5 miles from I-89. From Exit 10 go southwest on Hwy 100 for 0.2 miles to Hwy 2 (Main St). Turn right, go 1.3 miles to Little River Rd. Turn north for 3.4 miles to the Park.

Points of Interest -

Wander the Waterbury Flea Market. Don't miss Ben and Jerry's Ice Cream Factory and the Cold Hollow Cider Mill. In Barre visit granite quarries & museums. Tour the Vermont State House in Montpelier. Drive up to Moss Glen Falls and to the Trapp Family Lodge in Stowe.

Exit 17
Grand Isle State Park [3]
On South Hero Island
State Rate: $18-$20

(802) 372-4300

http://www.vtstateparks.com/htm/
grandisle.htm

Camp Accommodations

117 shaded sites, 3 ADA, dry camping, 40 feet, dump station, reservations available. Amenities include restroom/showers, potable water, grill, table, hiking, biking, swimming, fishing, pet friendly. No Utilities.

Directions

13 miles from I-89. From Exit 17 go west for 12 miles, following Hwy 2 over Lake Champlain on to South Hero Island. The park entrance road is just past Pearl St. Turn right on State Park Rd, go 1 mile to the Park.

Points of Interest -

The Park is the most visited camp in the state system. With 4,150 feet of shoreline, it is popular with many destination RVers, who spend their entire vacation here. Some local sights include Chazy Reef, Hyde Log Cabin, St. Anne's Shrine, and Hacketts' Orchard.

Exit 1
Fort Dummer State Park [4]
South of Brattleboro
State Rate: $18

(802) 254-2610

http://www.vtstateparks.com/htm/
fortdummer.htm

Camp Accommodations

50 shaded sites, dry camping, 40 feet, dump station, reservations available. Amenities include restroom/showers, potable water, grill, table, hiking, biking, pet friendly. No Utilities.

Directions

2 miles from I-91. From Exit 1 go 0.2 miles north on Hwy 5 (Canal St). Turn right on Fairground Rd, go 0.6 miles to S Main Street. Turn south (right) on S Main, which becomes Old Guilford Rd, go 1.1 miles to the Park.

Points of Interest -

In Brattleboro, walk the historic downtown, go shopping and enjoy a meal. Visit the Brattleboro Museum and Art Center, and Estey Organ Museum. Take a scenic drive to Wilmington, stock-up at roadside farmstands, explore downtown Wilmington.

Exit 8
Mt. Ascutney State Park [5]
South of Windsor
State Rate: $18

(802) 674-2060

http://www.vtstateparks.com/htm/
ascutney.htm

Camp Accommodations

39 wooded sites, dry camping, 30 feet, dump station, reservations available. Amenities include restroom/showers, potable water, grill, table, hiking, biking, pet friendly. No Utilities.

Directions

3 miles from I-91. From Exit 8 go east on Hwy 131 for 0.4 miles to Hwy 5. Turn north (left) for 1.1 miles, then bear left on Hwy 44A for 1.1 miles to the Park.

Points of Interest -

Drive the Park summit road to the top for excellent views. Hikers can try the 12 plus miles of trails to sites of former quarries and homesteads, relics of past logging operations and other remains of a bygone era. Each trail boasts spectacular viewpoints. **Also see [1]**.

Exit 17
Ricker Pond State Park [6]
South of Windsor
State Rate: $18-$20

(802) 584-3821

http://www.vtstateparks.com/htm/
ricker.htm

Camp Accommodations

27 wooded sites, 1 ADA, dry camping, 40 feet, dump station, reservations available. Amenities include restroom/showers, potable water, grill, table, hiking, biking, fishing, swimming/beach, pet friendly. No Utilities.

Directions

11 miles from I-91. From Exit 17 go northwest on Hwy 302 for 8.5 miles to Hwy 232. Turn north for 2.5 miles to the Park on the right.

Points of Interest -

In St. Johnsbury visit the Maple Grove Museum, the Fairbanks Museum & Planetarium or the St. Johnsbury Athenaeum & Art Gallery. In Barre visit granite quarries & museums and the Vermont Historical Society Library. Tour the Vermont State House in Montpelier.

VIRGINIA

The 35 Virginia State Parks offer thousands of campsites, more than 500 miles of trails and convenient access to Virginia's major waterways. Also you have access to beaches, picnic shelters, family lodges, festivals, concerts, nature programs, and cultural happenings. You can start with the Park Systems main website at -

http://www.dcr.virginia.gov/state_parks/

Twenty-four of the state parks have campgrounds. Site sizes and configurations vary. Some parks provide sites with electric and water hook-ups, which tend to be larger to accommodate RVs. Developed campsites have picnic tables, grills and access to bathhouses. All campgrounds, except False Cape, provide a grill or fire ring that can be used for charcoal or wood.

Virginia State Parks strive to make each park as barrier-free as possible for the convenience of those with limited mobility. Facilities continue to be upgraded for everyone's enjoyment. Each park page has information on the availability of facilities for people with disabilities.

Pets are allowed at all overnight camping facilities, however, there is a $5/pet per night fee. To avoid potential inconvenience, we ask that you bring proof of current rabies vaccination. Your pet must be confined or kept on a leash no longer than six feet and under constant supervision while in the park.

Park fees for standards sites range from $16-$20, electric/water are $22-$30, and full hook ups are $28-$35.

Reservations should be made as early as possible. Unreserved campsites are available on a first-come, first-served basis, but reservations are strongly recommended. Reservations can be made up to 11 months in advance. The system does not generally accept same-day reservations.

Reservations for camping can be made by calling the Reservation Center at (800) 933-7275. Reservations can also be made online, through ReserveAmerica. Each park's web page has a "Reserve Now" button on the right side of the page. Clicking it takes you to the Web reservation page for that park.

Virginia also has a number of excellent County and City Parks that provide good camping options, particularly near the metropolitan areas.

[1] **Lake A. Willis Robertson Park**
     N37 47.861 W79 36.599
[2] **First Landing State Park**
     N36 55.088 W76 03.097
[3] **Bull Run Regional Park**
     N38 48.240 W77 28.613
[4] **Stony Fork Campground**
     N37 00.619 W81 10.874
[5] **Sugar Hollow Park**
     N36 38.758 W82 06.631
[6] **Hungry Mother State Park**
     N36 52.238 W81 31.479
[7] **Claytor Lake State Park**
     N37 03.701 W80 37.428
[8] **Natural Chimneys Park**
     N38 21.122 W79 05.272
[9] **North Bend Campground**
     N36 35.689 W78 18.664
[10] **Pocahontas State Park**
     N37 21.947 W77 34.344
[11] **Pohick Bay Regional Park**
     N38 40.246 W77 10.493

NOTES:

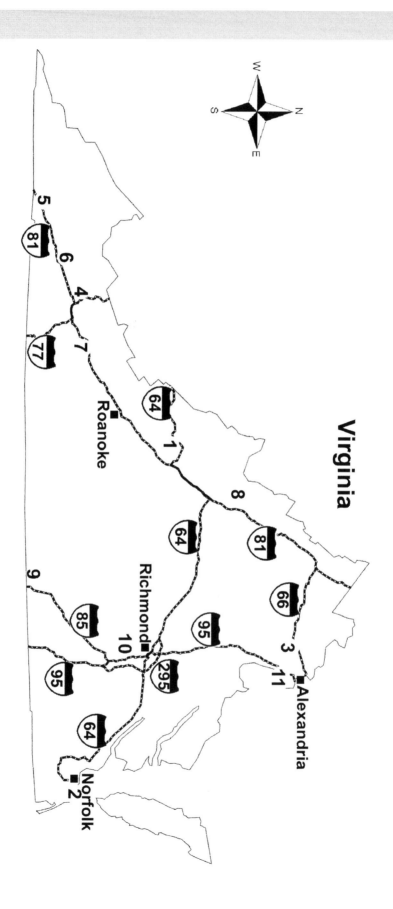

Exit 55 of I-64
Lake A. Willis Robertson Park [1]
West of Lexington
County Rate: $28
America/Beautiful Discount

(540) 463-4164

http://www.co.rockbridge.va.us/
departments/Recreation/
lake_robertson.htm

Camp Accommodations

53 shaded sites, electric/water, 40 feet, pull throughs, dump station, reservations. Amenities are restroom/showers, grill, table, hiking, fishing, swimming, store, laundry, pet friendly.

Directions

15 miles from I-64. From Exit 55 take Hwy 11 southwest for 2.8 mi. to Hwy 251. Continue straight onto Hwy 251. Follow Hwy 251 for 10.3 mi. to Collierstown, where 251 merges into Cty 770 (Turnpike Rd). Follow Turnpike Rd for 1.6 mi. to the Park.

Points of Interest -

Nearby are Natural Bridge, Goshen Pass, and the birthplaces of Sam Houston and Woodrow Wilson. The area also has the home of the first McCormick reaper, the tombs of Robert E. Lee and Stonewall Jackson, as well as many other historical attractions.

Exit 282 of I-64
First Landing State Park [2]
East of Norfolk
State Rate: $24-$30

(757) 412-2300

http://www.dcr.virginia.gov/
state_parks/fir.shtml

Camp Accommodations

230 shaded sites, electric/water, 45 feet, pull throughs, dump station, reservations available. Amenities are restroom/showers, grill, table, hiking, fishing, swimming, store, laundry, pet friendly.

Directions

9 miles from I-64. From Exit 282 take Hwy 13 (Northampton Blvd) for 4.1 miles to the Shore Drive/Hwy 60 exit (the last exit before the Chesapeake Bay Bridge Tunnel). Go right on to Shore Drive for 4.5 miles to Hwy 343. Turn left at the park entrance.

Points of Interest -

The Park, Virginia's most visited, is located by Chesapeake Bay, with shoreline and dunes to walk. In Virginia Beach try a seaside restaurant after a stroll along the 3-mile boardwalk. Special sights include Cape Henry Light Houses, the Naval Aviation Monument, and King Neptune Statue.

Exit 52 of I-66
Bull Run Regional Park [3]
Southwest of Centerville
County Rate: $22-$40

(703) 631-0550

http://www.nvrpa.org/park/bull_run

Camp Accommodations

150 shaded sites, electric/water or full hook ups, 40 feet, 100+ pull throughs, dump station, reservations. Amenities are restroom/showers, grill, table, hiking, biking, swimming pool, shooting center, store, disc golf, pet friendly.

Directions

4.5 miles from I-66. From Exit 52 go west for 2 miles on Hwy 29. Turn south on Bull Run Post Office Rd for 2.5 miles to the park.

Points of Interest -

The Park is not far from Washington & Northern Virginia attractions. You are 15 miles from the Vienna Metro Station. Convenient destinations include the Dulles area's Steven F. Udvar-Hazy Center of the National Air & Space Museum & Manassas National Battlefield Park.

Exit 47 of I-77
Stony Fork Campground   [4]
North of Wytheville
Jefferson NF Rate: $12
America/Beautiful Rate: $6

(276) 783-5196

http://www.recreation.gov/

Directions

4 miles from I-77. From Exit 47 go west on Hwy 717 (Krenning Rd) for 4 miles to the campground on your left.

Camp Accommodations

50 shaded, paved sites, 3 ADA, electric/water or electric, 45 feet, 1 pull through, dump station, reservations. Amenities are ADA restroom/showers, potable water, grill, table, hiking, biking, fishing, host, pet friendly.

Points of Interest -

Shoppers should visit the Wytheville Snoopers Antique Mall & the downtown shops. Take a drive up Big Walker Mountain and stop at the Country Store there. For Arts & History try the Wytheville Heritage Museum, or Haller-Gibboney Rock House and the Thomas J. Boyd Museum.

Exit 7 of I-81
Sugar Hollow Park [5]
East of Bristol
City Rate: $10-$12

(276) 645-7275

http://www.bristolva.org/parklist.html

Directions

1.5 miles from I-81. From Exit 7 turn north to Hwy 11 (Lee Hwy). Turn east, drive 0.6 miles to Sugar Hollow Rd. Turn north, follow the road for 0.8 miles to the campground.

Camp Accommodations

75 shaded sites, dry or electric, 35 feet, potable water, dump station. Amenities are restroom/showers, grill, table, hiking, pet friendly (leash free dog area).

Points of Interest -

Visit Natural Tunnel, called the Eighth Wonder of the World by William Jennings Bryan. Try a concert or ballet at the Paramount Center for the Arts. Peddle the Virginia Creeper Trail, Virginia's premiere mountain biking trail. Take in the music at the Carter Family Memorial Music Center.

Exit 47 of I-81
Hungry Mother State Park [6]
North of Marion
State Rate: $20-$28

(276) 781-7400

http://www.dcr.virginia.gov/
state_parks/hun.shtml

Directions

4 miles from I-81. From Exit 47 travel southwest for 1.1 mile on Route. Turn right on Route 16 north and go 3 miles to the park.

Camp Accommodations

52 shaded sites, standard to full hook-ups, 35 feet, pull throughs, dump station, reservations available. Amenities are restroom/showers, grill, table, hiking, fishing, store, swimming, store, lodge, pet friendly.

Points of Interest -

Marion, in the Blue Ridge Highlands region of Virginia is home of the Lincoln Theater, one of three existing Art Deco Maya Revival-style theaters in America. Built in 1929, this historic landmark hosted legends like Roy Rogers, Ralph Stanley and Roy Acuff.

Exit 101 of I-81
Claytor Lake State Park [7]
East of Pulaski
State Rate: $20-$25

(540) 643-2500

http://www.dcr.virginia.gov/
state_parks/cla.shtml

Camp Accommodations

110 shaded sites, dry or electric/
water, 35 feet, pull throughs, dump
station, reservations available.
Amenities are ADA restroom/showers,
grill, table, hiking, fishing, swimming,
Visitor Center/Store, pet friendly.

Directions

2.5 miles from I-81. From Exit 101 go
south 2.2 miles on State Park Road (State
Route 660) in to the park.

Points of Interest -

Visit Glencoe Museum and explore the
rich heritage of Radford and the New River
Valley. Hike the Cascades National Recreation Trail, which ascends a gorge for
two miles to the picturesque 66-foot Cascades Waterfall - it is a four-mile round
trip. Take the Dixie Caverns Tour.

Exit 240 of I-81
Natural Chimneys Park [8]
Southwest of Harrisonburg
County Rate: $22-$31

(540) 350-2510

http://www.co.augusta.va.us/
Index.aspx?page=616

Camp Accommodations

145 shaded, spacious sites, electric/
water or full hook up, 40 feet, some
pull throughs, dump station, reservations. Amenities are restroom/
showers, grill, table, hiking, biking,
fishing, swimming, pet friendly.

Directions

11 mi. from I-81. From Exit 240 follow Hwy 257
northwest for 3.3 mi. to Hwy 42. Turn left, go
3.6 mi. When Hwy 42 turns south at Hwy 747
(Iron Works Rd, which becomes Mossy Creek)
continue straight, following Hwy 747 for 3.4 mi.
to Mt. Solon. Turn right on Natural Chimney Rd
for 0.6 mi. to Natural Chimney Lane & the Park.

Points of Interest -

The Park's rock chimneys are a special sight.
From music & arts to bikes & bakeries, Harri-
sonburg is a great destination. Stroll downtown
or take a tour. Harrisonburg and Rockingham
County played a significant role during the Civil
War, with 23 Civil War Sites, complete with
Trails markers. Of the many museums, visit the
Virginia Quilt Museum.

Exit 12 of I-85
North Bend Campground [9]
Southwest of South Hill
COE Rate: $15-$20
America/Beautiful Rate: $8-$10

(434) 738-0059

http://www.recreation.gov/

Camp Accommodations

238 shaded, spacious sites, 2 ADA,
dry or electric/water, 45 feet, 7 pull
throughs, dump station, reservations.
Amenities are ADA restroom/showers,
grill, table, Visitor Center, hiking, biking, swimming, fishing, pet friendly.

Directions

17 mi. from I-85. From Exit 12 go west and
follow Hwy 58 for 10.8 miles to Hwy 4
(Buggs Island Rd). Turn south, go 5.9
miles to Hwy 678 (Mays Chapel Rd). Go
right for 0.5 miles in to the Campground
area. There are multiple camping areas.

Points of Interest -

South Hill's museums are free. The To-
bacco Farm Life Museum presents the
region's rich farming heritage & its ties to
the "golden leaf." The Model Railroad Museum has a unique & panoramic display of
model trains & authentic model scenery.
Tour the Virginia S. Evans Doll Museum.

Exit 62
Pocahontas State Park [10]
South of Richmond
State Rate: $25

(804) 796-4255

http://www.dcr.virginia.gov/
state_parks/poc.shtml

Camp Accommodations

114 shaded sites, electric/water, 45 feet, some pull throughs, dump station, reservations available. Amenities are ADA restroom/showers, grill, table, hiking, fishing, swimming, laundry, Nature Center, store, pet friendly.

Directions

12 miles from I-95. From Exit 62 go west on Hwy 288 for 6 miles to Hwy 10. Exit south on Hwy 10 for 1.8 miles to Hwy 655 (Beach Rd). Turn right and drive 4.1 miles to State Park Rd and Park the entrance on your right.

Points of Interest -

The Richmond Region, provides four centuries of history and modern day culture - a unique heritage. Enjoy magnificent architecture, monument-lined cobblestone streets, world-class museums, and steeplechase racing. Go here for details -

http://www.richmondva.org/

Exit 163
Pohick Bay Regional Park [11]
Southwest of Alexandria
County Rate: $25-$42

(703) 339-6104

http://www.nvrpa.org/park/pohick_bay

Camp Accommodations

100 shaded sites, electric/water or full hook ups, 40 feet, all pull throughs, dump station, reservations. Amenities are restroom/showers, grill, table, hiking, biking, pool, store, laundry, guided canoe/kayak tours, pet friendly.

Directions

5 mi. from I-95. From Exit 163 go 0.2 mi. east on Lorton Rd. Turn right on Lorton Market St. Go 1.1 mi. (Rd changes to Gunston Rd) to Hwy 1. Go straight through light on Gunston Rd (Hwy 242) for 3.3 mi. to Pohick Bay Dr & Park entrance on left.

Points of Interest -

The Park is not far from Washington & Northern Virginia attractions. You are 11 miles from the Springfield Metro Station. Convenient destinations include Mount Vernon, & Gunston Hall Plantation (home of George Mason). Trails leads walkers to the waterfront, mini golf and outdoor pool.

WASHINGTON

The Washington State Parks and Recreation Commission oversees the parks. Their website is - http://www.parks.wa.gov/

Basic camping fees (2010) are:

Standard campsite $19 - $24*. A designated campsite served by nearby domestic water, sink waste, garbage disposal and flush comfort station.

Utility campsite $25 - $33*. A standard campsite with the addition of electricity. May have domestic water and/or sewer.

Primitive campsite $12 - $14. Campsite does not include a nearby flush comfort station. Primitive campsites may not have any amenities of a standard campsite. Sites are accessible by motorized/non-motorized vehicles and water trail camping.

(*Higher prices include an additional fee for popular destination parks and select premium campsites.)

Central Reservation System (non-refundable reservation fee):

- $6.50 for reservations made online at - https://secure.camis.com/WA/
- $8.50 for reservations made by calling (888) 226-7688.

Due to limited staff within each state park, the ranger on duty is typically in the park rather than in the park office, so reaching park staff by phone is often very difficult, so a park phone list is not published on the website. Visitors can call State Parks at (360) 902-8844 to request a phone number for a state park. A different number listed in this chapter for a specific park should be that park's number.

Senior citizens 62 years of age and older may apply for a Senior Citizen Limited Income Pass. The pass is free of charge and offers a 50 percent discount on night camping.

Pets are allowed in most state parks, but must be under physical control at all times on a leash no more than eight feet long.

As you might expect the state is rich in campgrounds sponsored by the COE, National Forest Service, National Park Service, and counties.

[1] **Battle Ground Lake State Park**
N45 48.177 W122 29.199
[2] **Seaquest State Park**
N46 17.742 W122 49.055
[3] **Millersylvania State Park**
N46 54.576 W122 54.356
[4] **Flowing Lake (Leckies Beach) Park**
N47 57.139 W121 59.439
[5] **Bay View State Park**
N48 29.254 W122 28.813
[6] **Kachess Campground**
N47 21.366 W121 14.797

[7] **Ginkgo Petrified Forest State Park**
N46 54.025 W119 59.571
[8] **Riverside State Park**
N47 41.791 W117 29.769
[9] **Big Pines**
N46 47.701 W120 27.491
[10] **Plymouth Campground (John Day Lock and Dam)**
N45 56.023 W119 21.449

NOTES:

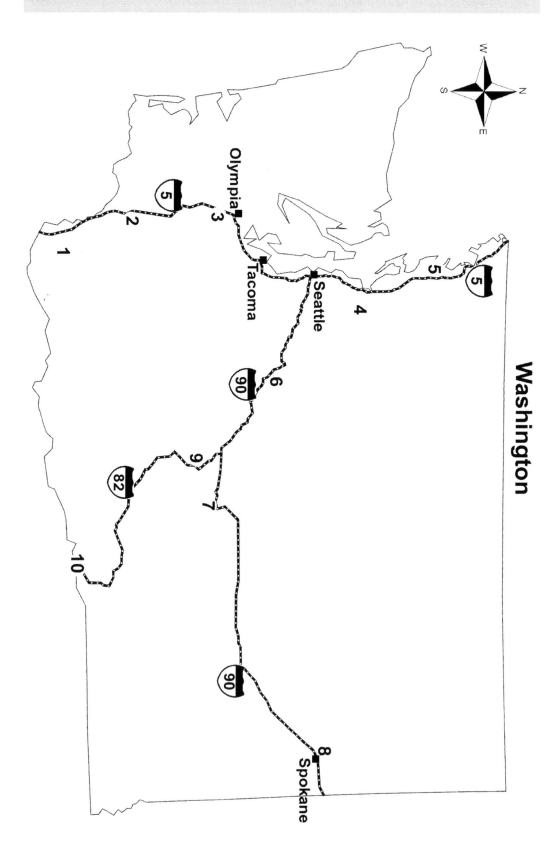

Washington

Exit 11
Battle Ground Lake State Park [1]
Northeast of Vancouver
State Rate: $21-$28

(360) 687-4621

http://www.parks.wa.gov/parks/?
selectedpark=Battle%20Ground%
20Lake

Camp Accommodations

31 shaded sites, 6 electric/water, 35 feet, some pull throughs, dump station, reservations available. Amenities are restroom/showers, potable water, grill, table, hiking, fishing, swimming, store, pet friendly.

Directions

11 mi. from I-5. From Exit 11, go east 6 mi. on Hwy 502 to Hwy 503. Turn left, go 1.3 mi. to 244th. Turn right, go 0.5 mi. to 132nd. Turn left, go 0.2 mi. to 249th. Turn right, go 1 mi. to 152nd. Turn right, go 0.2 mi. to 244th, then left, 1.5 mi. to the Park.

Points of Interest -

Visit Vancouver, it's downtown area has quaint eateries, art galleries, boutiques and antiques. The area also offers numerous year-round attractions and events to keep you busy and entertained. Learn more at the Visitor Center at Fort Vancouver National Site.

Exit 49
Seaquest State Park [2]
North of Longview
State Rate: $21-$28

(360) 274-8633

http://www.parks.wa.gov/parks/?
selectedpark=Seaquest

Camp Accommodations

33 shaded sites, some electric/water, 35 feet, some pull throughs, dump station, reservations available. Amenities are ADA restroom/showers, potable water, grill, table, hiking, watchable wildlife, pet friendly.

Directions

5.5 miles from I-5. From Exit 49 go east on Hwy 504 (Spirit Lake Hwy) for 5.4 miles to the Park entrance on the left.

Points of Interest -

The Park is near Mount St. Helens (Visitor Center at the park), an excellent day trip. The forested park has over a mile of Silver Lake shoreline. Try the one mile wetland trail and six miles of woodland trails for hiking and bicycling. You may also see some spectacular views of wildlife.

Exit 95
Millersylvania State Park [3]
South of Olympia
State Rate: $21-$28

(888) 226-7688

http://www.parks.wa.gov/parks/?
selectedpark=Millersylvania

Camp Accommodations

48 shaded or sunny, paved sites, electric/water, 45 feet, some pull throughs, dump station, reservations available. Amenities are ADA restroom/showers, potable water, grill, table, hiking, fishing, swimming, bird watching, pet friendly.

Directions

3 miles from I-5. From Exit 95 go east on Hwy 121 for 3 miles to the Park entrance on the left.

Points of Interest -

Tour Olympia by trolley car or carriage. Sites to see could include the State Capital; Schmidt House, built in 1904 for the owner of the Olympia Brewing Company; Percival Landing (1860) including the "Sandman" Tug Boat; and the End of the Oregon Trail.

Exit 194
Flowing Lake (Leckies Beach) Park [4]
East of Everett
County Rate: $20-$28

(360) 568-2274

http://www1.co.snohomish.wa.us/
Departments/Parks/Park_Information/
Park_Directory/Regional_Parks/
Flowing_Lake.htm

Camp Accommodations

30 shaded sites, most electric/water, 40 feet, some pull throughs, reservations. Amenities are restroom/showers, potable water, grill, table, hiking, fishing, swimming, pet friendly.

Directions

15 mi. from I-5. From Exit 194 go east on Hwy 2 for 9.7 miles to Westwick Rd. Turn east & follow Westwick, it will turn north and become 171st Ave SE (Iverson Knutsen Rd), going 5 miles in all to 48 St SE. Turn east 0.5 miles to the Park.

Points of Interest -

Everett is home to the largest building in the world (Boeing), where aerospace and aviation based tours are offered, including tours of the Boeing facility. The Everett waterfront is home to the largest marina on the West Coast, with an authentic 1890s marina marketplace.

Exit 230
Bay View State Park [5]
West of Burlington
State Rate: $21-$28

(360) 757-0227

http://www.parks.wa.gov/parks/?
selectedpark=Bay%20View

Camp Accommodations

29 shaded sites, electric/water, 45 feet, dump station (may be closed), reservations available. Amenities are restroom/showers, potable water, grill, table, hiking, fishing, swimming, pet friendly.

Directions

10 miles from I-5. From Exit 230 take Hwy 20 for 6.3 miles west to Whitney-Bayview Rd. Turn north (becomes Bay View-Edison Rd) for 3.6 miles to the park.

Points of Interest -

The park is on the coast and offers views of the San Juan Islands, one of 28 existing national marine estuaries. On clear days, you can see the Olympic Mountains and Mt. Rainier. Plan a day trip down Whidbey Island (book the Clinton Ferry). Stop south of Deception Pass (photo above).

Exit 62
Kachess Campground [6]
East of Snoqualmie Pass
Okanogan-Wenatchee NF Rate: $18
America/Beautiful Rate: $9

(509) 656-0366

http://www.recreation.gov

Camp Accommodations

129 shaded sites, 2 ADA, some paved, dry camping, 45 feet, 18 pull throughs, reservations available. Amenities are ADA restrooms, potable water, grill, table, hiking, fishing, swimming, berry/mushroom picking, bird watching, pet friendly. No Utilities.

Directions

5 mi. from I-90. From Exit 62 go east for 5 miles on Road 49 to the campground.

Points of Interest -

The camp, located at the north end of the beautiful Kachess Lake is a pleasant drive from I-90. Surrounded by high mountains, the camp is considered one of the most beautiful in the Cle Elum Ranger District. Fish for Kokanee salmon and trout. Enjoy the sandy swimming beach.

Exit 136
Ginkgo Petrified Forest State Park [7]
East of Ellensburg
State Rate: $28

(509) 856-2700

http://www.parks.wa.gov/parks/?selected-park=Ginkgo+Petrified+Forest%2FWanapum+Recreational+Area

Camp Accommodations

50 shaded sites, full hookups, 45 feet, some pull throughs, reservations. Amenities are restroom/showers, grill, table, fishing, hiking, swimming, watchable wildlife, pet friendly.

Directions

3 miles from I-90. From Exit 136 turn south on Huntzinger Rd for 2.8 miles to the camping area.

Points of Interest -

Ginkgo Petrified Forest is a registered national natural landmark, & is regarded as one of the most unusual fossil forests in the world. Events to look for in Ellensburg are 'The First Friday Artwalk,' Ellensburg Film Festival, Ellensburg Rodeo, Jazz in The Valley, or the Kittitas County Fair.

Exit 280
Riverside State Park [8]
West side of Spokane
State Rate: $21-28

(509) 465-5064

http://www.parks.wa.gov/parks/?selectedpark=Riverside

Camp Accommodations

32 shaded sites, many electric/water, 45 feet, dump station, reservations. Amenities are restroom/showers, grill, table, fishing, hiking, swimming, boating, Interpretive Programs, watchable wildlife, store, pet friendly.

Directions

6 mi. from I-90. From Exit 280 go to Walnut St. Turn north on Walnut, which become Maple, go 1.3 mi. to Maxwell Ave. Turn left, go 4.7 mi. in all. Maxwell becomes (curve right) Pettit Dr, then W Downriver Park Dr (stay along the river), then (bear left) N. Aubrey L. White Pkwy (Riverside State Park Dr) to the park entrance.

Points of Interest -

Take a self-guided tour of downtown Spokane. For fun try your luck at a local casino or do some driving at an indoor speedway. The Spokane Region is "wine country" with some of the country's finest winemakers in the area. Flower lovers will want to go to Manito Park.

Exit 3 or 26
Big Pines [9]
North of Yakima
BLM Rate: $15
America/Beautiful Rate: $8

(509) 665-2100

http://www.blm.gov/or/resources/
recreation/site_info.php?siteid=247

Camp Accommodations

41 shaded, paved sites, dry camping, 45 feet, pull throughs. Amenities are restrooms, potable water, grill, table, hiking, fishing, swimming, boating, pet friendly. No Utilities.

Directions

10 or 15 miles from I-82. **Eastbound**, from Exit 3 go west for 0.5 miles on Thrall Rd. Turn south on Hwy 821 (Canyon Rd) for 15 miles to the campground. **Westbound**, from Exit 26 go west and north for 9.6 miles to the campground.

Points of Interest -

Big Pines is in the very scenic Yakima River Canyon, which cuts through massive basalt cliffs and rolling desert hills. There are 4 recreation areas in all - the daily fee gives access to all locations. Fees cover garbage collection, cleaning, law enforcement, site staff, & site improvements.

Exit 131
Plymouth Campground
(John Day Lock and Dam) [10]
Plymouth, on the Stateline
COE Rate: $18
America/Beautiful Rate: $9

(541) 506-7819

http://www.recreation.gov

Camp Accommodations

32 shaded, paved sites, 16 full hook-up, 16 electric/water, 45 feet, 29 pull throughs, dump station, reservations available. Amenities are restrooms/showers, grill, table, laundry, swimming, fishing, boating, pet friendly.

Directions

2 miles from I-82. From Exit 131 go west on Hwy 14 for 0.7 miles to Plymouth Rd. Turn south for 0.7 miles to Christy Rd. Turn west for 0.3 miles to the Park on your left.

Points of Interest -

Visit Columbia Crest Winery, Fort Henrietta or Pendleton Woolen Mills. Enjoy the Hermiston's Farm City Pro Rodeo or Pendleton Roundup. McNary Dam has a number of sights, including an Interpretive Center. Take your walk at the McNary Wildlife Nature Area.

WEST VIRGINIA

The West Virginia Division of Natural Resources (DNR) mission is . . . "to promote conservation by preserving and protecting natural areas of unique or exceptional scenic, scientific, cultural, archaeological, or historical significance and to provide outdoor recreational opportunities for the citizens of this state and its visitors." The Division website is -

http://www.wvstateparks.com/

West Virginia's state parks and forests offer camping experiences from primitive tent sites to full-hook up service. The DNR defines RV relevant sites as follows -

Deluxe. Grill, tent pad, pull-off for trailers, picnic table, electric hookups, some with water and sewer hookups, dumping station, bathhouses with hot showers, flush toilets and laundry facilities.

Standard. Same as deluxe, but generally no hookups are available. Some sites at some areas may have electric hookups.

Rustic. Improved sites with limited facilities, well water and pit toilets.

Dogs and cats are the only pets permitted in state parks, state forests, and state wildlife management area, and they must be restrained on a leash not to exceed ten feet in length.

You must check with the park of your choice for rates associated with individual campsites. Campsite reservations may be made in writing or by calling toll free 1-800-CALL-WVA. Reservations may be made up to two days in advance. A minimum of two nights, (up to a maximum of 14 nights) is required when making a reservation. The majority of campsites are rented on a first come first serve basis. West Virginia State Parks only offer online reservations for parks with lodges and cabins.

---

[1] Beech Fork State Park
N38 18.482 W82 20.683
[2] Coopers Rock State Park
N39 38.503 W79 47.644
[3] Camp Creek State Park (Mash Fork)
N37 30.289 W81 08.068

[4] Gerald Freeman Camp
N38 40.676 W80 32.807
[5] Stonewall Resort State Park
N38 56.529 W80 29.866
[6] Tygart Lake State Park
N39 18.452 W79 59.668

NOTES:

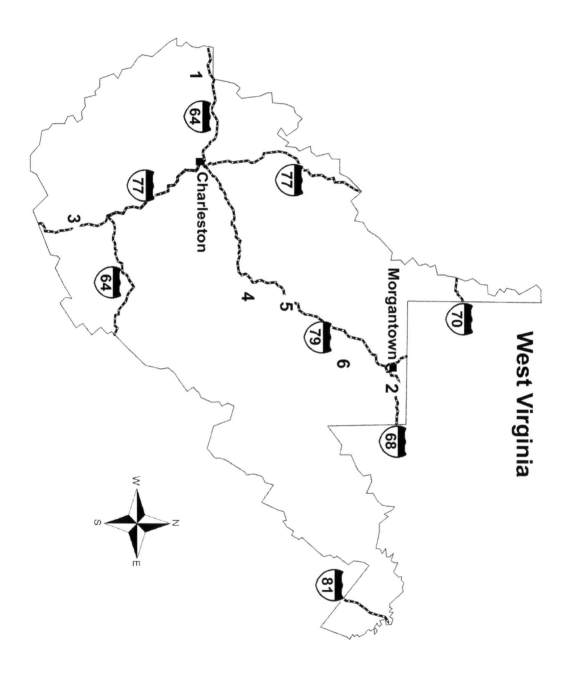

Exit 11 of I-64
Beech Fork State Park [1]
South of Huntington
State Rate: $22-$28
Seniors (60+): 10% discount

(304) 528-5794

http://www.beechforksp.com/

Camp Accommodations

275 shaded sites, 80 lakefront, 49 full hook-ups, electric/water, standard/ electric, 40 feet, some pull throughs, dump station, reservations. Amenities are ADA restroom/showers, grill, table, hiking, fishing, swimming, watchable wildlife, pet friendly.

Directions

10 mi. from I-64. There are a few tight curves the last few miles. From Exit 11 take Hwy 10 (Hal Greer Blvd) for 6 miles to Cty Rd 43 (Hughes Branch Rd). Turn south (right) for 3.7 miles to the Park.

Points of Interest -

Visit the Blenko Glass Company and observe artisans creating unique handmade glassware that is famous throughout the world. At the Heritage Farm Museum & Village, experience life as it was in an Appalachian pioneer community. Also see the Jenkins Plantation.

Exit 15 of I-68
Coopers Rock State Park [2]
East of Morgantown
State Rate: $23
Seniors (60+): 10% discount

(304) 594-1561

http://
www.coopersrockstateforest.com/

Camp Accommodations

25 shaded sites, 2 ADA, electric, 40 feet, 7 pull throughs, dump station, reservations available. Amenities are restroom/showers, potable water, grill, table, hiking, fishing, swimming, watchable wildlife, store, pet friendly.

Directions

2 mi. from I-68. From Exit 15 go south for 0.5 miles on Cty Rd 73/12. Continue straight as 73/12 becomes 73/16 for 1.2 miles to the campground.

Points of Interest -

Hike to Coopers Rock Overlook. Walk to rockcliffs, lining the Cheat River Gorge, which provide numerous overlooks. Find Henry Clay Iron Furnace Trail, located in a grassy glade in an otherwise undisturbed forest, a huge stone structure used for producing iron in the 1800's.

Exit 20 of I-77
Camp Creek State Park (Mash Fork) [3]
North of Princeton
State Rate: $26
Seniors (60+): 10% discount

(304) 425-9481

http://www.campcreekstatepark.com/

Camp Accommodations

26 shaded sites, 19 electric, 7 electric/water, 3 pull through, 40 feet, dump station, reservations available. Amenities are ADA restroom/showers, laundry, potable water, grill, table, hiking, fishing, game courts, store, pet friendly.

Directions

2.5 miles from I-77. From Exit 20 turn south 0.1 mile on Hwy 19. Go right 2.3 miles on Camp Creek Rd to the campgrounds.

Points of Interest -

Tour Beckley Exhibition Coal Mine, the largest and most popular coal heritage destination in the region. The Bramwell Town Historic District reflects large fortunes amassed by local coal barons & is renowned for having over 14 well preserved Victorian & Tudor style mansions.

Exit 67
Gerald Freeman Camp [4]
Southeast of Flatwoods
COE Rate: $16-$18
America/Beautiful Rate: $8-$9

(304) 765-7756

http://www.recreation.gov

Camp Accommodations

159 shaded, paved sites, 1 ADA, 2 full, 77 electric, 11 electric/water, 30 water, 45 feet, 1 pull through, dump station, reservations. Amenities are ADA restroom/showers, laundry, grill, table, hiking, fishing, swimming, watchable wildlife, pet friendly.

Directions

13 miles from I-79. From Exit 67 turn south then turn right, go 1.1 mile on Hwy 4 to Hwy 15. Turn left, go 11.5 miles to Government Access Rd, on your right. This will lead you to the campground.

Points of Interest -

Just north is Lewis County, with antique shops, glass artists, wineries, and good old-fashioned home cooking. There are many fairs and festivals. Take a tour of the Trans-Allegheny Lunatic Asylum. Finally, board an old steam engine train and ride through the wonderful mountains.

Exit 91
Stonewall Resort State Park [5]
South of Weston
State Rate: $38-$40
Seniors (62+): 10% discount

(888) 278-8150

http://www.stonewallresort.com/

Camp Accommodations

40 paved, waterfront sites, full hook-ups, 40 feet, dump station, reservations available. Amenities are restroom/showers, potable water, grill, table, hiking, fishing, swimming, watchable wildlife, lodge (shuttle service), pet friendly.

Directions

3.2 miles from I-79. From Exit 91 go 2.7 miles south on Hwy 19 to State Park Rd. Turn north for 0.4 miles to the camping area.

Points of Interest -

An optional resort fee of $14 daily can be purchased for a Resort Activities Pass for use of resort facilities. In Weston, try the Mountaineer Military Museum or Jackson's Mill Farmstead? See **[4] above** for other local activities. Did we mention the resort's Arnold Palmer Signature golf course?

Exit 124
Tygart Lake State Park [6]
East of Clarksburg
State Rate: $20-$23
Seniors (62+): 10% discount

(304) 265-6144

http://www.tygartlake.com/

Camp Accommodations

40 shaded sites, 14 electric, 40 feet, dump station, reservations available. Amenities are restroom/showers, potable water, grill, table, hiking, fishing, swimming, lodge/restaurant, store, pet friendly.

Directions

19.5 mi. from I-79. From Exit 124 go southeast on Hwy 279 for 2.5 mi. to Hwy 50. Turn east for 13 mi. to Hwy 119 at Grafton/Blueville. Turn south (right) on Hwy 119, go 1 mi. to Bridge St. Turn left, cross the river, 0.1 mi. to Barrett St. Turn left, follow Barrett (becomes Knottsville) for 2.9 mi. to Bath House Rd (Scab Hollow). Turn right to the Park.

Points of Interest -

Visit historic Grafton, the "Birthplace of Mother's Day." Visit the International Mother's Day Shrine and Museum. Tour the Historic B&O Depot museum ("West Virginia's Finest B&O Depot"). Take a drive to Fairmont, explore historic sites there, indulge in shopping and dining.

WISCONSIN

The Wisconsin State Park System provides places for outdoor recreation and for learning about nature and conservation. State parks, forests, trails, and recreation areas report about 14 million visits a year. Spend a night with nature in one of more than 4,600 campsites. The system website is -

http://dnr.wi.gov/ORG/land/parks/

A typical RV campsite is in a natural setting with road access, a fire ring, and a picnic table. Some sites are accessible for people with disabilities. Responsible pet owners and their pets are welcome in Wisconsin State Parks. Pets are **not** allowed in buildings, picnic areas and picnic shelters, beaches, except designated "dogs allowed" beaches, or playgrounds.

Camping fees are:

Site - $12-$17

Electricity - $5

Water View - $3

Reservations - $10

Certain disabled veterans and former prisoners of war are eligible to receive waivers of vehicle admission and trail pass fees.

A vehicle doing the towing or carrying must have an annual or daily admission sticker. Any vehicle that is towed or carried into a vehicle admission area is provided free admission.

The reservations Website has campground maps and details about each site. You can zoom in on the maps and click on a campsite symbol, or click "All the Sites in this Campground" on the menu below a park map and then click the site number. You can also call (888) 947-2757 to make a reservation. The toll-free TTY number for reservations is (800) 274-7275. The system does not accept written campsite reservation requests.

The online registration system is managed by ReserveAmerica. You begin the reservation process at -

http://wisconsinstateparks.reserveamerica.com/

[1] **Roche-A-Cri State Park**
N44 00.061 W89 48.737
[2] **DuBay Park**
N44 40.655 W89 41.823
[3] **Council Grounds State Park**
N45 11.075 W89 44.074
[4] **Kohler-Andrae State Park**
N43 40.360 W87 43.079
[5] **Point Beach State Forest**
N44 12.701 W87 30.904
[6] **Veterans' Memorial Park**
N43 53.943 W91 06.878

[7] **Rocky Arbor State Park**
N43 38.463 W89 48.101
[8] **Mirror Lake State Park**
N43 33.681 W89 48.488
[9] **Lake Kegonsa State Park**
N42 58.564 W89 13.816
[10] **Highland Ridge Campground**
N44 52.746 W92 14.231
[11] **Castle Mound,
Black River State Forest**
N44 17.099 W90 49.804
[12] **Cliffside Park**
N42 49.088 W87 49.531

NOTES:

Wisconsin

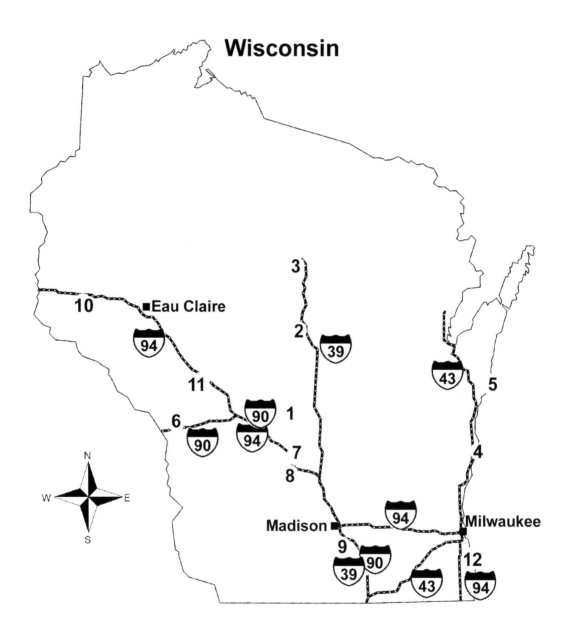

Exit 124
Roche-A-Cri State Park [1]
West of Coloma
State Rate: $12-$14

(608) 339-6881

http://dnr.wi.gov/org/land/parks/
specific/roche-a-cri/

Camp Accommodations

41 shaded sites, 1 ADA with electric, 40 dry camping, 40 feet, dump station, reservations available. Amenities are restrooms, potable water, grill, table, hiking, fishing, host, pet friendly. No Utilities.

Directions

16 miles from I-39. From Exit 124 go west for 14.4 miles on Hwy 21 to Hwy 13. Turn south for 1.7 miles to the Park entrance on your right.

Points of Interest -

Hike to the top of the Park's 300 foot high rock. The accessible ramp and observation deck allow all visitors to view the petroglyphs and pictographs. Tour the Petenwell Hydroelectric Plant. Bike the Elroy-Sparta or "400" bike trails. Go to Volk Field and watch military aircraft training.

Exit 175
DuBay Park [2]
South of Mosinee
County Rate: $13-$18

(715) 346-1433

http://www.co.portage.wi.us/parks/

Camp Accommodations

31 shaded sites, 2 ADA, electricity, 35 feet, dump station, reservations available. Amenities are restrooms, potable water, grill, table, hiking, fishing, swimming/beach, host, pet friendly.

Directions

6.5 miles from I-39. From Exit 175 go southwest on Hwy 34 for 5 miles to Cty Rd E. Turn left, go 1.5 miles to the Park.

Points of Interest -

Walk the historic Main St. of Stevens Point, a member of the National Register of Historic Places. See more than 60 buildings of different architectural styles. You will also see murals depicting the area's history. Stop at the Q Gallery Artist's Cooperative and Sculpture Park.

Exit 208
Council Grounds State Park [3]
West side of Merrill
State Rate: $10-$17

(715) 536-8773

http://dnr.wi.gov/org/land/parks/
specific/councilgrounds/

Camp Accommodations

46 shaded sites, 1 ADA, 19 electric, 27 dry camping, 45 feet, dump station, reservations available. Amenities are restrooms/showers, potable water, grill, table, hiking, fishing, swimming/beach, ranger, pet friendly.

Directions

5.5 miles from I-39. From Exit 208 go west for 3 miles on Hwy 64. Turn right at Hwy 107 (Grand Ave), go 1.8 miles to Council Grounds Rd. Turn left, go 0.5 miles in to the Park.

Points of Interest -

Stroll around Merrill, the 'City of Parks.' Visit the T.B Scott Mansion. Began in 1884, the original owner, said his house was fit for a lumber king and he doubted it had an equal anywhere in Wisconsin. Scott died before the house was finished and the "curse" began . . .

Interstates 43 and 90

Exit 120 of I-43
Kohler-Andrae State Park [4]
South of Sheboygan
State Rate: $12-$17

(920) 451-4080

http://dnr.wi.gov/org/land/parks/
specific/ka/

Camp Accommodations

122 shaded sites, some paved, 1 ADA, 56 electric, 66 dry, 45 feet, 12 pull throughs, dump station, reservations available. Amenities are restrooms/showers, potable water, grill, table, hiking, swimming/beach, laundry, ranger, pet friendly.

Directions

2.5 miles from I-43. From Exit 120 go 2.2 miles east on Cty Rd V. Where Cty Rd V turns north, continue straight on Beach Park Lane in to the Park.

Points of Interest -

The Park is home to majestic sand dunes & golden beaches. In Sheboygan, South Pier & Riverfront Boardwalk offer fish shanties full of unique gifts, art & food treats. Harbor Centre Downtown offers eclectic shopping, dining, & entertainment in beautifully restored historic buildings.

Exit 154 of I-43
Point Beach State Forest [5]
North of Two Rivers
State Rate: $12-$17

(920) 794-7480

http://dnr.wi.gov/org/land/parks/
specific/pointbeach/

Camp Accommodations

127 shaded sites, 1 ADA, 70 electric, 57 dry, 45 feet, 2 pull throughs, dump station, reservations available. Amenities are restrooms/showers, potable water, grill, table, hiking, swimming/beach, store, Nature Center, ranger, pet friendly.

Directions

14 mi, from I-43. From Exit 154 go 8.7 mi. east on Hwy 310 into Two Rivers to Hwy 42. Turn left on Hwy 42. After 0.8 miles, when Hwy 42 turns north, go straight on 22nd St, which becomes Sandy Bay Rd and Cty Rd O. Go 4.8 mi. to Park Rd.

Points of Interest -

Jutting seven miles into the lake, the point provides a six-mile beach, dunes and occasional pieces of 19th century sunken ships. The sandy shore is a great place to walk, explore the lighthouse area, and have a good time beachcombing. Sunrises will please photographers.

Exit 12 of I-90
Veterans' Memorial Park [6]
Northeast of La Crosse
County Rate: $25

(888) 540-8434

http://www.lacrosseriverstatetrail.org/
vets.htm

Camp Accommodations

100 shaded sites, electricity, 40 feet, some pull through, dump station. Amenities are restrooms/showers, potable water, grill, table, hiking, fishing, store, host, pet friendly.

Directions

3 miles from I-90. From Exit 12 turn south and then go right for 1.4 miles on Cty Rd C (Buol Rd) to Cty Rd M. Turn north for 0.8 miles to Hwy 16. Turn west 0.7 miles to the Park on your left.

Points of Interest -

Step aboard the La Crosse Queen, a modern day replica of the grand riverboats, & one of the few "true" paddlewheelers still in operation, which plied the Mississippi in the early 1900s. Go to the La Crosse Fairgrounds Speedway for NASCAR Racing on Saturdays, April-September.

Exit 85 of I-90/94
Rocky Arbor State Park [7]
At the Wisconsin Dells
State Rate: $12-$14

(608) 254-8001

http://dnr.wi.gov/org/land/parks/
specific/rockyarbor/

Camp Accommodations

89 shaded sites, 2 ADA, 16 electric, 73 dry camping, 45 feet, dump station, reservations available. Amenities are restrooms, potable water, grill, table, hiking, fishing, pet friendly.

Directions

1 mile from I-90/94. From Exit 85 go east for 0.8 miles on Hwy 12/16 to the park entrance, on your right.

Points of Interest -

'The Dells' has enhanced its appeal with boutique shopping and additional dining options. The Ducks still provide a great river tour and water lovers will have much to choose from, including the classic Tommy Bartlett Show. Nearby, go to Ringling Bros. Circus World. **Also see [8].**

Exit 92 of I-90/94
Mirror Lake State Park [8]
At Delton
State Rate: $10-$17

(608) 254-2333

http://dnr.wi.gov/org/land/parks/
specific/mirrorlake/

Camp Accommodations

151 shaded sites, 2 ADA, 47 electric, 104 dry camping, 45 feet, dump station, reservations available. Amenities are restrooms, potable water, grill, table, Visitors Center, hiking, swimming, fishing, pet friendly.

Directions

2 miles from I-90/94. From Exit 92 go south for 0.4 miles on Hwy 12 to Fern Dell Rd. Turn west for 1.5 miles to the Park entrance on your right.

Points of Interest -

Visit the Seth Peterson Cottage at the Park. It is the only Frank Lloyd Wright-designed house in the world available for rental occupancy. Designed in 1958, it was one of Wright's last commissions. Go here for Dells activities - http://wisdells.com/   **Also see [7].**

Exit 147 of I-90/39
Lake Kegonsa State Park [9]
Southeast of Madison
State Rate: $12-$28

(608) 873-9695

http://dnr.wi.gov/org/land/parks/
specific/lakekegonsa/

Camp Accommodations

80 shaded sites, 2 ADA, 25 electric, 55 dry, 45 feet, 3 pull throughs, dump station, reservations available. Amenities are restroom/showers, potable water, grill, table, hiking, fishing, swimming/beach, ranger, pet friendly, pet swim area.

Directions

3.5 miles from I-90/39. From Exit 147 take Hwy N south for 0.6 miles to Koshkonong Rd. Turn west (right), go 1.7 miles to Door Creek Rd. Turn south for 1.1 miles to the end of Door Creek Rd, on the right hand side.

Points of Interest -

From the historic University of Wisconsin - Madison campus to the beauty of Olbrich Botanical Gardens there is something for everyone, Don't miss the Farmers' Market (150+ vendors) on the Capital Square, one of the best in the country. Take a day trip to the 'House on the Rock' or Taliesin.

Exit 24
Highland Ridge Campground [10]
West of Menomonie
COE Rate: $18-$20
America/Beautiful Rate: $9-$10

(715) 778-5562

http://www.recreation.gov

Camp Accommodations

38 shaded sites, 1 ADA, 35 electric, 3 dry, 45 feet, dump station, reservations available. Amenities are restrooms/showers, potable water, grill, table, hiking, swimming, host, pet friendly.

Directions

6 miles from I-94. From Exit 24 go south for 2.0 miles on Cty Rd B to Cty Rd N. Turn east for 2 miles to Cty Rd NN. Go south 1.8 miles to the entrance sign, turn right.

Points of Interest -

Take a day trip drive south to the St. Croix River and Lake Pepin. Drive along Hwy 35 through Maiden Rock, Stockholm, and Pepin. Any of these towns are great lunch stops. In Pepin visit Laura Ingalls Wilder Park and other Wilder landmarks. Go to a Friday fish fry dinner.

Exit 116
Castle Mound, Black River State Forest [11]
Southeast of Black River Falls
State Rate: $10-$14

(715) 284-4103

http://dnr.wi.gov/forestry/stateforests/SF-BlackRiver/

Camp Accommodations

35 shaded sites, 1 ADA, 6 electric, 30 dry, 45 feet, 17 pull through, dump station, reservations available. Amenities are restrooms/showers, potable water, grill, table, hiking, ranger, pet friendly.

Directions

2.5 miles from I-94. From Exit 116 go west for 1 mile on Hwy 54 to Hwy 12/27. Turn south, go 0.5 miles to where Hwy 12 goes east. Turn and drive 0.6 miles to the campground.

Points of Interest -

Go scuba diving at Wazee Lake, Wisconsin's deepest lake and a year-round diving destination. Take a country drive - explore the area's many unique shops and antique dealers, or sample brews from one of the fine microbreweries. Learn about the area's tradition of cranberry growing.

Exit 322
Cliffside Park [12]
North of Racine
County Rate: $23

(262) 884-6400

http://publicworks.racineco.com/Parks/Index.aspx

Camp Accommodations

92 shaded sites, some electric and water, 45 feet, dump station, reservations available. Amenities are restrooms/showers, potable water, grill, table, hiking, host, pet friendly.

Directions

9 miles from I-94. From Exit 322 go east for 3.8 miles on Hwy 100 to Hwy 32. Turn south for 4.2 miles to 6 Mile Rd. Turn east 0.4 miles to Michna Rd. Turn north for 0.3 miles to the park.

Points of Interest -

Celebrated art, dramatic architecture, scenic gardens - go to the Milwaukee Art Museum. Visit the 1892 Flemish Renaissance Revival Mansion of Captain Frederick Pabst, world famous beer baron and accomplished sea captain. Tour Miller Brewing Company.

WYOMING

The Wyoming State Parks are managed by the Division of State Parks, Historic Sites & Trails. The Division manages 12 State Parks and 21 Historic Sites. Camping is available at 7 Parks and one Historic Site. Visit their site for details at -

http://wyoparks.state.wy.us/

The non-resident overnight camping fee currently, for a single night (which includes the daily use fee) is $17.

All pets must be in a vehicle or on a leash no longer than ten (10) feet in length and physically controlled at all times. Pets are prohibited in public eating places and food stores, public buildings, and on designated beach areas.

Reservations can be made no more than 90 days in advance. You can make reservations online or by calling the Reservation Center at (877) 996-7275. For online reservations go to -

http://travel.wyo-park.com/find-state-results-list/Campgrounds-and-RV-Parks/All/Wyoming/All/

The National Forests also have a number of good campground locations.

[1] Guernsey State Park
N42 16.902 W104 46.128
[2] Glendo State Park
N42 29.097 W105 00.653
[3] South Fork Campground
N44 16.698 W106 57.029
[4] Buckboard Crossing
N41 14.944 W109 35.817
[5] Curt Gowdy State Park
N41 11.458 W105 15.274
[6] Keyhole State Park
N44 21.374 W104 45.005

NOTES:

298

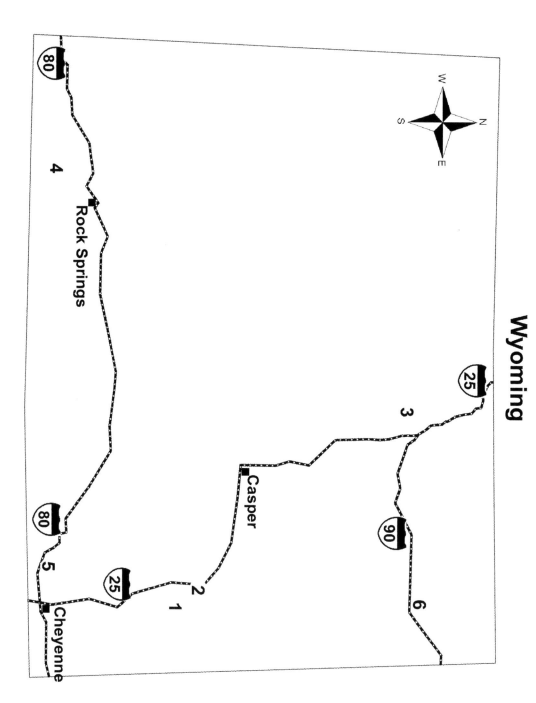

Exit 92
Guernsey State Park [1]
Northeast of Wheatland
State Rate: $17

(307) 777-6323

http://travel.wyo-park.com/
Campgrounds-and-RV-Parks/All/
Guernsey-State-Park/Overview

Camp Accommodations

142 shaded sites (7 camps), dry camping, some pull through, 45 feet, dump station, reservations available. Amenities are restrooms, potable water, grill, table, swimming/beach, hiking, fishing, host, pet friendly.

Directions

15 miles from I-25. From Exit 92 go 14 miles west on Hwy 26 to Hwy 317. Turn north for 1 mile to the Park.

Points of Interest -

This Park is notable for the exceptional building construction done by the Civilian Conservation Corps (CCC) and for artifacts and landmarks from the days of the Oregon Trail. Sites to visit could include Brimmer Point, the Castle, and the Guernsey Museum. Also visit Register Cliff.

Exit 111
Glendo State Park [2]
Northeast of Glendo
State Rate: $17

(307) 735-4433

http://travel.wyo-park.com/
Campgrounds-and-RV-Parks/All/
Glendo-State-Park/Overview

Camp Accommodations

435 sites (11 camps), many shaded, dry camping, pull throughs, 45 feet, dump station, reservations available. Amenities are restrooms, potable water, grill, table, swimming, hiking, fishing, birding, host, store, pet friendly.

Directions

2 miles from I-25. From Exit 111 go east into Glendo, 0.2 miles to Hwy 319 (Yellowstone Hwy). Turn south for 2 blocks to C St. turn left 1 block to Lincoln Ave. Turn south (Lincoln becomes Glendo Park Rd) for 1.5 miles to the Park.

Points of Interest -

Diggings in the area shows good evidence for the historic presence of a number of Indian tribes. Near Sandy Beach you'll find, rising out of the reservoir's east side, a series of sand dunes. While boating is a big draw, fishing, hiking and biking can be equally enjoyed.

Exit 229
South Fork Campground [3]
West of Buffalo
Bighorn NF Rate: $14
America/Beautiful Rate: $7

(406) 587-9054

http://www.recreation.gov

Camp Accommodations

6 shaded sites, dry camping, 40 feet, reservations available. Amenities are ADA restrooms, potable water, grill, table, fishing, pet friendly. No Utilities.

Directions

17 miles from I-25. From Exit 229 go 16.6 miles west on Scenic Hwy 16 to FS Rd 337 (Clear Creek Campground Rd). Turn left to the campground.

Points of Interest -

Hwy 16 is a scenic byway. The campground is along the South Fork of Clear Creek, where trout fishing is popular. Sightseeing & photo opportunities are excellent. You can walk to the South Fork Mountain Lodge for a meal &/or check out the Bighorn Mountain adventure options.

Exit 91 of I-80
Buckboard Crossing [4]
South of Green River
Ashley NF Rate: $16-$20
America/Beautiful Rate: $9

(435) 784-3445

http://www.recreation.gov

Camp Accommodations

46 shaded sites, 8 electric, 38 dry camping, 45 feet, dump station, 3 pull throughs, reservations available. Amenities are ADA restrooms/showers, potable water, cabana, grill, table, fishing, store, marina, pet friendly.

Directions

25.5 miles from I-80. From Exit 91 go southwest to Hwy 530 (Uinta Dr). Follow Hwy 530 for 24 miles, south from Green River, to Buckboard Rd. Turn left, go 1.5 miles to the Campground.

Points of Interest -

The camp is in the Flaming Gorge National Recreation Area and is famous for trophy lake trout. A number of 30+ pound fish are caught each year. Petroglyphs & artifacts suggest Fremont Indians hunted game here for many centuries. The high elevation keeps temperatures moderate.

Exit 323 of I-80
Curt Gowdy State Park [5]
Between Laramie and Cheyenne
State Rate: $17

(307) 632-7946

http://wyoparks.state.wy.us/Site/SiteInfo.asp?siteID=4

Camp Accommodations

40 sites (2 camps), water or dry camping, many pull throughs, 45 feet, dump station, reservations available. Amenities are restrooms, potable water, grill, table, hiking, fishing, archery range, bird watching, host, Lodge, pet friendly.

Directions

13.5 miles from I-80. From Exit 323 turn east on Hwy 210, go 13.3 miles to the Park.

Points of Interest -

Both Cheyenne & Laramie are less than an hours drive, each is the best of the Old West - the reality won't disappoint. In Laramie you'll also find unique galleries, shops, boutiques & antiques in its Historic Downtown. In Cheyenne check out the Big Boy Steam Engine, find the 8 'Big Boots.'

Exit 165 of I-90
Keyhole State Park [6]
North of Moorcroft
State Rate: $17

(307) 756-3596

http://wyoparks.state.wy.us/Site/SiteInfo.asp?siteID=10

Camp Accommodations

120 sites (4 camps), 8 ADA, sun or shade, dry camping, some pull throughs, 45 feet, dump station, reservations available. Amenities are restrooms, potable water, grill, table, hiking, fishing, bird watching, host, store, pet friendly.

Directions

6 miles from I-90. From Exit 165 go north on the Keyhole Access Rd (Cty Rd 160, then 205) for 5.6 miles to the Park.

Points of Interest -

The Park is on the western edge of the Black Hills and is a mecca for resident and migrating birds of all species. Devils Tower is a short distance north and is an excellent day trip. Visit Sundance and walk the main street, where the 'Kid' got this name.

55475127R00168

Made in the USA
Middletown, DE
10 December 2017